START BUILDING YOUR JAZZ LIBRARY WITH ESSENTIAL CDs FROM THESE GIANTS OF JAZZ ...

*Louis Armstrong *Bix Beiderbeck
*Duke Ellington *Fats Waller
*Benny Goodman *Count Basie
*Ella Fitzgerald
*Charlie Parker *Bud Powell
*Thelonious Monk *Miles Davis
*Chet Baker *Art Pepper *Dizzie Gillespie
*Sonny Rollins *Art Blakey and the Jazz Messengers
*Sarah Vaughan *Charles Mingus
*John Coltrane *Stan Getz
*Bill Evans *Ornette Coleman
*Wynton Marsalis *Herbie Hancock
*Chick Corea *Cassandra Wilson
*Pat Metheny
and more

NEIL TESSER is a noted jazz critic. He is *Playboy*'s jazz columnist, and his *Jazz Forum* programs are heard regularly over WBEZ-FM in Chicago. In 1985 he received a Grammy nomination for his liner notes to the Stan Getz reissue *The Girl from Ipanema*.

THE **PLAYBOY**
GUIDE TO
JAZZ

NEIL TESSER

A PLUME BOOK

PLUME
Published by the Penguin Group
Penguin Putnam Inc., 375 Hudson Street,
New York, New York 10014, U.S.A.
Penguin Books Ltd, 27 Wrights Lane,
London W8 5TZ, England
Penguin Books Australia Ltd, Ringwood,
Victoria, Australia
Penguin Books Canada Ltd, 10 Alcorn Avenue,
Toronto, Ontario, Canada M4V 3B2
Penguin Books (N.Z.) Ltd, 182–190 Wairau Road,
Auckland 10, New Zealand

Penguin Books Ltd, Registered Offices:
Harmondsworth, Middlesex, England

First published by Plume, an imprint of Dutton NAL,
a member of Penguin Putnam Inc.

First Printing, August, 1998
10 9 8 7 6 5 4 3 2 1

Copyright © Playboy Enterprises, Inc., 1998
All rights reserved.

Playboy is a trademark of Playboy Enterprises, Inc., and is used with permission.

 REGISTERED TRADEMARK—MARCA REGISTRADA

Library of Congress Cataloging-in-Publication Data:

Tesser, Neil.
    The Playboy guide to jazz / Neil Tesser.
        p.   cm.
    Discography: limited to compact discs.
    ISBN 0-452-27648-9
    1. Jazz—Discography.   I. Playboy (Chicago, Ill.)   II. Title.
ML156.4.J3T47   1998
781.65'0266—dc21   98-14753
                                                                          CIP
                                                                          MN

Printed in the United States of America
Set in Palatino
Designed by Leonard Telesca

Without limiting the rights under copyright reserved above, no part of this publication
may be reproduced, stored in or introduced into a retrieval system, or transmitted, in any
form, or by any means (electronic, mechanical, photocopying, recording, or otherwise),
without the prior written permission of both the copyright owner and the above
publisher of this book.

BOOKS ARE AVAILABLE AT QUANTITY DISCOUNTS WHEN USED TO PROMOTE
PRODUCTS OR SERVICES. FOR INFORMATION PLEASE WRITE TO PREMIUM
MARKETING DIVISION, PENGUIN PUTNAM INC., 375 HUDSON STREET, NEW
YORK, NEW YORK 10014.

Acknowledgments

No matter whose name appears under the title, no book of any substance belongs to the author(s) alone.

My editor, Arnold Dolin, has exhibited Job-like patience regarding the completion of this project, and has my everlasting gratitude; so does Jonathan Black, managing editor of *Playboy* magazine, who conceived the *Guide*, spurred its production, and managed to withstand my work pace without incurring serious illness. Also, thanks to *Playboy* music editor Barbara Nellis for moral support, and to copy editor Lee Froelich, who submitted an invaluable preliminary draft of chapter 9, without which this book would very likely not exist.

Among those who served as sounding boards and discussion mates throughout my work on this volume, Michael Friedman of Premonition Records deserves special notice for his critical eye, his knowledge of history, and his opinionated cheerleading. Jazz critic Art Lange and educator Dr. Richard Wang took the time to read and vet key chapters, thus compounding their expertise with equal generosity. Jim DeJong of Tower Records proved essential in helping me establish the availability of many CDs mentioned within. Gary Burton and Bill Kirchner, both musicians and educators of a very high order, made small but important contributions.

A handful of books provided factual information and validation, including *Jazz (A History)* by Frank Tirro; *West Coast Jazz* by Ted Gioia; *The Jazz Tradition* by Martin Williams; and two books by my friend and colleague John Litweiler, *The Freedom Principle* and *Ornette Coleman: A Harmolodic Life*.

Finally, without the network of family and friends, I never

could have persevered on this project. You know who you are, but let me mention Frank Anello, Holly Birnbaum, Judy Cole, Kurt and Jennifer Elling, Kahil El'Zabar, Louise Huneault, Amy Jeppsen, Ron Litke, Matt Mirapaul, Mark Sherman, and Kiki Stathakis. And of course, thanks to my always supportive parents, Ira and Judith; my sister, Nancy Hiller, and her family; and Dewey, for helping me maintain perspective on what really matters in the long run.

—Neil Tesser
February 1998

Contents

Introduction ix

1 Calling Doctor Jazz 1
1917–1932
JAZZ IN TRANSITION—HOW 2 SWING LARGE 21

2 Let's Dance 26
1935–1945
JAZZ IN TRANSITION—SWING 2 BEBOP: EVOLUTION IN THE REVOLUTION 51

3 Everybody's Boppin' 57
1941–1955

4 Cool Blues (Hot Blues) 81
1953–1965
JAZZ IN TRANSITION—BORN 2 BE FREE: INTIMATIONS OF LIBERATION 131

5 Freedom Now 137
1959–?
JAZZ IN TRANSITION—FREE 2 ROAM: ECHOES OF LIBERATION 166

6 Plug Me In 176
1967–1984

JAZZ IN TRANSITION—FROM THERE 2 HERE: A SHORT LOOK AT THE LONG
HISTORY OF FOREIGN INFLUENCE 202

7 Letter from Home 208
1973–1998

8 Hesitation 230
1982–1998

9 Open on All Sides 256
1990–?

10 An Essential Jazz Collection 284

Index 287

Introduction

Another guide to jazz CDs?

Yes—and no. As I write this, I can glance up from the keyboard at no fewer than five books that have the words *jazz* and *guide* in their titles, and I can lay my hands on a half dozen more within the half hour. But this book aspires to something quite different from the rest of them, and in that sense it is anything but "just another . . ."

The key lies in that ubiquitous word *guide*, which this book takes quite literally. I have designed *The Playboy Guide to Jazz* not to cover the map but to point the way—to note the milestones and markers in the history of recorded jazz and thus serve as an inspiration for further exploration.

Other books attempt to assess the entire jazz CD discography— which comprises thousands and thousands of currently available recordings—but the *Playboy Guide* takes another tack entirely. This book *selectively* navigates the oceans of jazz on CD. It provides a discriminating examination of the jazz catalog and recommends the best and most important of these recordings for the new listener. For those willing to take a few more risks and spend a little more money, I have included second- and third-tier recordings in each chapter. These are not discs of lesser quality or value, but rather of less importance in providing a basic appreciation of an artist's work or a historical style.

(Please keep in mind that this book serves as a guide to *compact discs*; if an album has never been transferred to digital, or if the company has removed it from distribution, you won't find it mentioned here. This should not suggest that the only good music exists on CD, and I encourage the investigation of valuable music on LP; but this book's premise recognizes that we live in a primarily digital environment. A similar concession has led me to avoid, for the most part, those CDs available only as imports, because of both their expense and the inconsistency of their distribution. In a few cases, however, the absolute best example of an artist's work exists only on a Japanese or European pressing; I have included these in case you want to make the search and spend the cash.)

At the end of the book, you will find a chapter that culls all these recommendations down to fifty essentials. Buy one a week, and at the end of a year you will have an impeccable basic jazz collection—one that will also serve as the foundation for continued growth and enjoyment as we head into jazz's second century.

Beyond that, by placing these albums in their proper historical context, the *Playboy Guide* can act as a "hands-on" history of the music itself. I have grouped the selected CDs into chapters that roughly correspond to the nine decades of recorded jazz, with each chapter devoted to a significant movement (or movements). Each features a brief introductory essay to give a fuller understanding of the context for the albums under discussion, while the index allows you to pinpoint a particular artist and his work without having to know his stylistic heading or historical period. In addition, you will find a few "transition" sections, which concentrate on albums and anthologies that link disparate styles but truly belong to neither of them. These transition periods often escape the notice of books that survey jazz history, but they remind us that the maturing of jazz—like that of any art form—is not a cut-and-dried, by-the-textbook affair.

On the subject of textbooks, a small flash from the past. For this book, I have resurrected a valuable analytical tool taught to me by a college English prof: the Useful Lie. The Useful Lie refers to a particular form of generalization. You probably know that all generalizations are false (including, of course, the generalization that "all generalizations are false"). But the Useful Lie functions as a big, blunt arrow in the right direction. It contains just enough truth and packages it in a sufficiently easy-to-remember way to prove extremely helpful. The trick lies in remembering the important *exceptions* to the Useful Lie. The generalizations let you head in the right direction; the exceptions let you fill in the map.

Here's an example. For years, popular retellings of jazz history began with the Useful Lie that the music "was born in New Orleans" and then "traveled up the Mississippi River" to Chicago. More recent evidence has shown that while the music we call jazz did indeed sprout in New Orleans, the elements necessary for the development of jazz did not so conveniently confine themselves to that city: ragtime and blues, both vital ingredients in the musical stew that became jazz, actually originated elsewhere. And while many jazz musicians did relocate from New Orleans to Chicago, making the Illinois metropolis the next great jazz center, many other jazzmen headed directly to New York and Washington, D.C., to Kansas City, and to parts of Texas. The Useful Lie traces a broad outline, but the devil is in the details.

The detail work proved indeed devilish when it came to putting this book together. It involved studying the realm of jazz CDs in the store, in the catalogs—hell, just on my own shelves, which bulge with more than twelve thousand—and deciding on the essentials. For instance, I know of more than 160 Duke Ellington CDs; in this book, I have recommended seven. Almost every one of the excluded discs contains some degree of spectacular music by a man who stands among the great twentieth-century composers—music that I return to regularly. The longer you listen to jazz, the more likely the chance that you will eventually discover many of these same albums. But for the purposes of understanding Ellington, and of understanding jazz, the ones I have mentioned are the ones that you need.

An Ellington scholar could quibble about the albums not mentioned, and any astute jazz fan could easily list a dozen important and immensely listenable musicians whose names appear nowhere in this book. But if you follow where the *Playboy Guide* leads, you'll eventually locate them all. For example, if you were to buy one of the Miles Davis albums listed in Chapter Four and one of those listed in Chapter Five, the combined list of sidemen would include Cannonball Adderley, John Coltrane, Herbie Hancock, Wayne Shorter, and Tony Williams. If you were to then buy an album by one of those musicians and again peruse the sidemen—let's take Hancock, for example, and his album *Takin' Off*—you'd find yourself exposed to the young trumpeter Freddie Hubbard and the saxophone giant of a previous generation, Dexter Gordon. Buy an album by either of them and repeat the process, again and again, and you can see how you would eventually create your own "family tree" of distantly related musicians, spreading out over a far wider area than you might have imagined.

In choosing which albums to recommend, I could easily have cheated; let me explain.

The CD revolution has given rise to the "completist" mentality. For most major jazz artists, you can now find huge collections—many of them running to eight, twelve, even eighteen discs—that assemble everything a given musician recorded for a particular label. Counting a massive production like these as a single "album" would certainly make selection a lot simpler. But despite their high-concept production values and the interest they hold for scholars and experts, most such boxed sets contain far more music—and far costlier price tags—than new jazz listeners really want. They make great gifts, and I have mentioned some of the more impressive of these anthologies at the end of each chapter. But in recommending the best purchases, I have set as a limit the three-CD box and chosen these only when they clearly outclassed everything else.

You will notice that I have tended to recommend these two- and three-CD anthologies in the earlier chapters, while relying on single, self-contained albums in the later chapters. This decision rests on a strong respect for the aesthetic and historical importance of the CD's predecessor, the individual long-playing album (LP).

Before the development of the LP in the 1950s, jazz musicians didn't go into a recording studio with the intent of creating a forty- to sixty-minute documentation of their artistry. Instead, they thought in terms of single tunes, each referred to as a "side" (since each song occupied one *side* of a shellac platter). They usually recorded four at each session, then released two "sides" at a time (on one record), without a great deal of concern for how these might fit together or contrast with each other.

In a sense, the CD anthology hearkens back to the spirit of these 78 RPM platters. By assembling the music from dozens of these records in a random-access format—susceptible to the re-

mote control, which lets us program the music to our liking—
such anthologies allow us to re-create the experience of a listener in the 1930s or 1940s. Such a listener might spend an
afternoon with his or her painstakingly assembled collection of
Louis Armstrong or Charlie Parker sides, listening to them in
whatever order one might choose, mixing and matching the
songs to catch the moment. Since these songs were never in-
tended to fit together or complement each other in any particular order, they welcome the libertarian playback possibilities of
the CD.*

The invention of the LP changed all this by giving musicians
the chance to expand their scope, and to work within a theme.
One could now create, for example, a discrete collection of love
songs or marches, or of works by an individual composer, of
the repertoire for a given instrument or of tunes that all had *blue*
or *spring* in their titles. And by the mid-fifties, such musicians
as Ella Fitzgerald, Charles Mingus, Stan Getz, and Miles Davis
(working with Gil Evans) had begun to brilliantly exploit the
possibilities of this new format. From that point on, the jazz
album—not the individual tune—became the working unit of
creation, discussion, and appreciation. A good example is John
Coltrane's 1965 album, *A Love Supreme*. Even though two of its
four movements have gained individual fame through later
recordings by other artists, Coltrane conceived the work as an
album-length suite, and the music on it remains known as such.

For this reason, when recommending music from the 1950s
to the present, I have tried to stick with the original albums, as
opposed to the multidisc sets that contain all the music from a
given period. Many of the original albums have a dramatic arc,
a pacing and texture, that go beyond the individual tracks, pre-
saging and then mirroring the concept albums that proliferated
in rock music in the sixties and seventies. Once you have lis-
tened a few times to Charles Mingus's *Mingus Moves* or Weather

---

*In those days, many such devoted fans kept their discs in hardbound books that
resembled photograph albums—except that instead of pages, they contained record
sleeves. If you devoted one such book to storing, say, a dozen of your Sinatra or
Goodman sides, you then had a Sinatra or Goodman "album." When the record in-
dustry developed the LP, this new technology made it possible to pack those same
dozen Sinatra tunes into a single disc; it thus made sense to simply borrow the
word *album* for this new format. And that's why the term can apply to compact
discs as well as LPs: it really refers to a *collection* of many musical pieces, rather than
to the vinyl *disc* that supplanted those earliest "albums."

Report's *Mysterious Traveler*, for example, and started to appreciate the ways in which the songs interact, it becomes difficult to listen to just one track from the album and not the others. On these original LP (now CD) albums, such musicians expanded not only their own scope but ours as well.

In writing this book, I have clung to the hope that it too will expand the scope of not only new jazz listeners but also perennial fans. If you have enjoyed the music for years, you may nonetheless have missed out on a long-unavailable album; or you may have had no reason to keep up with the excellent compilations that bring together several recordings you've enjoyed separately over the years; or you may simply not know that your well-worn fave LP—the one you danced to or romanced to—has finally come out on CD. If you fall into any of these categories, I think that the *Playboy Guide* will prove useful as a reference book.

But of course, it's *not* just a reference book. A dictionary or encyclopedia doesn't even try to communicate the magic of the music, the colors of the instruments, the complex and essential pulse of the rhythm. Such books don't deal with the network of emotions tapped by a steaming bebop set or the limpid, lyrical poetry of the Bill Evans trio; they don't try to paint the brash brilliance of Louis Armstrong's horn in the twenties or the multilayered voice (amplified by his saxophone) of Sonny Rollins in the nineties. They don't attempt to share with you the miracle of improvisation, the immediacy of spontaneous composition, or the situational drama that faces every jazz soloist when he steps beyond the written notes to create something brand-new and excitingly memorable in the blink of an eye.

This books attempts exactly that, however. You'll know soon enough if it succeeds.

Calling Doctor Jazz*
1917–1932

To hear the story as told by Ferdinand Joseph Lamothe—better known as Jelly Roll Morton (or, as one of his songs portrayed him, "Mr. Jelly Lord")—he himself invented jazz, in 1902, in his hometown of New Orleans. Among the Useful Lies scattered throughout the *Playboy Guide*, this one would seem to be useful mostly to Jelly Roll Morton.

But his contention does convey a few facts worth knowing. However jazz got "invented," New Orleans did indeed serve as the laboratory. The date cited by Morton indicates that the raw materials of jazz had gathered in New Orleans early in the twentieth century—by which time the fifteen-year-old Morton had begun supporting himself as a whorehouse piano player in that city's thriving (and legal) red-light district. In addition, his declaration of proprietorship, while preposterous on its face, suggests that Morton believed he had *something* important to do with the music's early growth. And he had. Even though his jazz prowess was rivaled by his colorful boasting—and despite that he worked not only as a pianist and bandleader but also as a successful pool hustler, an occasional chef and bartender, and almost certainly a pimp—Morton did indeed play a vital role in the development of jazz.†

---

*"Calling Doctor Jazz" was composed by Joe "King" Oliver and made famous in a 1927 record by Jelly Roll Morton. Its careless and exuberant lyrics recall the time when this new music represented freedom, excitement, and the dawning of "the American century."

†The word itself has a somewhat cloudy history, but it most likely comes from Southern African-American slang for sexual intercourse. In 1931, *Scribner's Magazine* wrote that the word "has meant first sex, then dancing, then music. It is associated

Morton's recordings of the mid-1920s treated the infant art form with care and discipline, as he creatively organized the innovations of the earliest jazz musicians (including his own). He did this primarily via the classic songs he wrote and arranged for his Red Hot Peppers, which earned him the mantle of jazz's first important composer. And organization was indeed called for, because the first jazz—like the city and culture from which it sprang—involved a sprawling array of influences.

A major port city, a destination point for the slave trade, and a gateway to both the Atlantic and the Caribbean, New Orleans had long brimmed with foreign cultures. The French settled it first, then ceded it to the Spanish, who returned it to the French—all before the fledgling United States obtained it through the Louisiana Purchase, in 1803. By then, the Crescent City had a large population of Creoles—the American-born offspring of French or Spanish settlers. Their neighbors included many free people of color (Africans who had arrived or been born as slaves, but who had gained their freedom under Spanish rule); a sizable number of black immigrants who had arrived as freemen from the West Indies; and "Creoles of color"—the children of mixed marriages.

Carrying both European and African genes, the Creoles of color offered living testament to the near equality of whites and blacks in early-1800s New Orleans. But as the century unfolded, each group settled into its own social stratum. The Creoles of color held a spot just below the whites; successful, educated professional men, they lived in desirable downtown neighborhoods, spoke French as well as English, and often owned slaves themselves. They had their own opera house where the musicians, trained in European techniques of harmony and melodic variation, played with precision and grace. Creole-of-color musicians also served as teachers for their less privileged cousins who lived in the Uptown district—poorly educated former slaves who had been freed after the Civil War. But these people had *their* own music too, a much rougher style derived from African rhythms and folk forms and filled with

with a state of nervous stimulation." A corollary theory suggests that the word originated in the Gold Coast of Africa, where it meant "hurry up"; that African slaves imported to the New World applied it to the escalating passions of intercourse; and that their descendants used it to describe the "speeded-up" tempos and rhythms of New Orleans music in the early twentieth century.

simple improvisation. Today, we would recognize it as an early form of blues.

Other elements soon slid into place in New Orleans, a high-times town bursting with live performance. Brass bands, descended from military tradition, had emerged as a vital part of the social landscape, performing at everything from outdoor dances to political rallies. An influx of Mexican immigrants provided a south-of-the-border flair. (Jelly Roll Morton, himself a Creole of color, would later opine that one really couldn't have jazz without this "Spanish tinge.") Meanwhile, the popular Midwest-based idiom called ragtime—in which the compositions combined European harmony and melody with "ragged" rhythms inspired by African-American music—provided a middle ground for the city's diverse musical traditions.

The United States traditionally represents itself as a melting pot of immigrants, a land in which the various parts create a synergistically greater whole. In the same way, early jazz drew its strength, in fact its very existence, from the competing combination of cultures. While the various components of jazz may have originated elsewhere, there existed no other city quite like New Orleans, where so many of these elements could smash together with enough force to synthesize an entirely new musical form.

The catalyst was inadvertently provided by the city's white politicians, in the form of two legislative actions. In 1894, New Orleans rebuked its own early history of racial tolerance by enacting a Jim Crow code, a strict set of segregationist laws. These defined the Creoles of color as black and dictated that they move to the Uptown neighborhoods. Suddenly, the city's two black musical traditions were forced into closer proximity than ever before. A natural cross-pollination took place as each influenced the other, and jazz—essentially a hybrid of European and African musical techniques—began to evolve.

Then, in 1897, the New Orleans City Council provided a hothouse in which this new hybrid could root and grow. In an effort to "clean up" the neighborhoods, the legislators zoned a forty-block area for legalized prostitution. This district, called Storyville, came alive with hundreds of salons and sporting houses, and they all needed "parlor music." Upper-class whites wouldn't debase their craft in such settings, so the city's African-American musicians, whether Creole or freed slave, found plenty of steady work.

The city's brass bands also spurred the development of jazz. By the early twentieth century, many such bands had affiliated themselves with New Orleans social clubs, which provided funeral benefits to their members. Featuring trumpet, trombone, clarinet, tuba, drums, and cymbals, these bands were a common sight as they marched through the city to the cemetery, accompanying the cortege with somber hymns. But the trip back, memorialized in paintings and literature, was another matter. Now en route to a rollicking wake, the musicians changed their repertoire to bright and lively tunes, letting their hair down and improvising the arrangements. Their performances took the form of *polyphony* (literally, "many voices"); in other words, each musician played an independent part, while keeping an ear on the whole group to make it all fit together.

This use of polyphony resulted in ensemble improvisation, in which each instrument contributes equally to the swirl of sound, and it distinguishes the first recorded jazz bands. (Later generations called the music Dixieland, but most musicians and longtime listeners avoid that term in favor of "early jazz," "trad[itional] jazz," or "New Orleans style.") From this environment came the first great jazz players, such as the "cornet kings" Freddie Keppard and Buddy Bolden (who never recorded); trumpeter Bunk Johnson; the virtuoso clarinetists Sidney Bechet and Jimmy Noone; the "tailgate" trombonist Kid Ory, known for his boisterous tonal effects; and the Dodds brothers, clarinetist Johnny and drummer Baby. Their music— loud, emotional, and dynamic—poured out tremendous energy, thanks to its syncopated rhythms and the abstract interplay of its polyphony. (*Syncopation* refers to the practice of displacing the normal rhythmic flow by placing the accent on unexpected beats. It's the "rag" in ragtime, and much of the "hot" in hot jazz.)

The ensemble improvisations did not highlight any one soloist; instead, the entire *group* seemed to solo, and the various melody lines wove new patterns unlike anything heard before. Improvisation, found to some degree in most African music, had also played an important role in European music of the eighteenth and mid-nineteenth centuries. But it had never enjoyed the definitive role that it did in jazz.

This music had a buzz, and it was exactly what the United States needed after the debilitations and exhilarations of World

War I, which ended in 1918. The previous year, the nation had heard the debut jazz recording, "Livery Stable Blues," by a group of white musicians, originally from New Orleans, who had moved to New York by way of Chicago. Calling themselves the Original Dixieland Jazz Band, they offered only a pale imitation of the black jazz players down South; but even in this form, the new sound captured the nation's fancy.

By the early 1920s, the phenomenon had become synonymous with a decade devoted to the giddy pleasures of peace, prosperity, and a newfound importance on the world stage: the Jazz Age. This development coincided with a shift in operations as Chicago, the nation's burly and bustling Second City, became the preeminent jazz hub. Hence the Useful Lie that the music came "up the river from New Orleans to Chicago," a fanciful image enhanced by the fact that riverboats featuring jazz really did ply the Mississippi River from New Orleans north. As it turns out, any map will confirm that the Mississippi gets no closer to Chicago than the Iowa border, more than 125 miles away. As it also turns out, musicians traveled not only to Chicago but to other areas that became smaller, regional jazz centers, such as Los Angeles and Kansas City, Houston and Indianapolis, Washington, D.C., and Boston.

By the early twenties, though, jazz was ensconced in Chicago and also poised for the next leap in its rapid development. For this, we can partly thank Joe "King" Oliver. The last of the New Orleans "cornet kings," King Oliver had earned fame as a solid musician and disciplined bandleader. But it was his keen ear for talent that secured Oliver's reputation; it led him to hire Louis Armstrong.

A few years earlier, like many other musicians, Oliver had left New Orleans for Chicago. A Useful Lie ties this migration to the demise of Storyville: in 1917 the U.S. Navy, concerned about the prevalence of venereal disease among sailors stationed in New Orleans, had forced the closure of the district, supposedly putting the city's musicians out of work. Actually, this did affect the solo pianists who provided entertainment at the brothels—virtually the only musicians who depended on Storyville for their living. But almost everyone else appears to have left simply in hopes of reaching a larger audience and improving their economic condition. The most important of these musicians headed for Chicago, home to hundreds of thousands of transplanted Southern blacks. There, at the Lincoln Gardens on the city's South Side, Oliver established his Creole Jazz Band, acclaimed as the best of its time. They made their first record in 1923, which featured a powerful two-cornet sound, since by then Oliver had sent for Armstrong, a younger musician whom he had briefly employed in New Orleans.

But the bumptious teenager Oliver had known five years earlier had grown into a musically mature virtuoso, and the strictures of traditional jazz could barely contain him. Armstrong had outstripped his mentor with a style unbeholden to past masters. The classic New Orleans sound still steamed along, somewhat stiffly, to a rather rigid if syncopated beat; but Armstrong learned to roll his rhythms *between* the beats, in a relaxed and natural way, and introduced the music world to the concept of "swing" (see chapter 2). He also displayed an unprecedented virtuosity and an uncanny command of spontaneous composition, which allowed him to construct brilliantly conceived solos: complete musical statements, rather than snippets of improvisation.

These qualities led him to move jazz in a new direction. With Louis Armstrong, small-group jazz evolved from a music dependent on collective improvisation to a soloist's art, one that placed the contributions of individual improvisers in the spotlight. He accomplished all this via a sound that others marveled at and tried to imitate. (Armstrong himself attributed it to his large and pliable lips. Satchelmouth, they called him, and this was shortened into the most famous of his several nicknames, Satchmo.)

In Oliver's band, Armstrong found a high-profile showcase for his burgeoning abilities—not only among the African-American dancers who crowded the Lincoln Gardens, but also among the city's more adventurous white musicians. These included a number of young men just finishing their educations at Austin High School—most prominently, the cornetist Jimmy McPartland, clarinetist Frank Teschemacher, and saxist Bud Freeman—who were later joined by other teenagers, such as a clarinetist from the city's north side named Benny Goodman. This "Austin High Gang" began by copying the New Orleans style, but with an edgy excitement that distinguished them; they then adopted the example of Armstrong to emphasize solos over ensemble improvisation. Their efforts resulted in a distinctive variation on the New Orleans sound, which earned the label "Chicago style." It served as a "second wave" of early jazz, and it would exert an important influence on the nation's jazz musicians for the next decade.

Still, it was a satellite member of the Austin High Gang—a native not of Chicago but of Davenport, Iowa—who had the most impact of them all. The cornetist Leon "Bix" Beiderbecke became the first white musician to command the full respect of the New Orleans musicians. He played solos as elegantly constructed as Armstrong's, but they arrived on the angel wings of his translucent, understated tone. In an era dominated by the gargantuan emotionalism of the New Orleans musicians, Bix offered a marked contrast with his comparatively restrained, even introspective style. This sensibility lies at the base of an increasingly important jazz lineage. Along with the limpid sax work of his frequent bandmate Frankie Trumbauer, Bix's style cut a romantic swath across the late 1920s; it would find further development in the music of Lester Young in the thirties and forties, and by the fifties, it had evolved into the "cool jazz" ethos extolled by Miles Davis.

Beiderbecke's death in 1931, before he had even turned thirty, only enhanced his image as a romantic figure in jazz. By that time, however, most of his Midwestern colleagues had relocated to New York, led by Armstrong himself. Having taken its baby steps out of New Orleans and having enjoyed its adolescence in Chicago, the still-maturing music would now make the nation's entertainment capital its permanent home base.

The Discs

In general, I have shied away in this book from the "sampler" anthologies that survey a variety of artists, each represented by one or two tracks. But I also make exceptions. Of the generally excellent "Masters of Jazz" series from Rhino Records, the first volume, *Traditional Jazz Classics*, scores especially high marks, with Louis Armstrong featured in several contexts and some early classics by Sidney Bechet, Duke Ellington, Jelly Roll Morton, and a nineteen-year-old Benny Goodman. (It also includes a track by the New Orleans Rhythm Kings, a group of white musicians who moved to Chicago and made some of the earliest jazz records in the early 1920s.) Many of these tunes appear on the other collections recommended below, but this still makes an excellent introduction to the era.

Louis Armstrong deserves his exalted place in jazz history by virtue of his groundbreaking accomplishments. The first indisputable genius among jazz improvisers, he elevated the role of the soloist and thus changed jazz forever. His mastery of the New Orleans style, and his subsequent extension of its precepts—which accompanied his move "up the Mississippi"—carried jazz beyond its birth and helped point the way toward the Swing Era, in which he again starred. And his popularization of scat vocalizing, or wordless improvisation, provided an accessible public voice (and face) for jazz up until his death in 1971. Even into the 1950s, much of Armstrong's music continued to gleam with the stamp of originality, justifying Miles Davis's statement, "You can't play anything on the horn that Louis hasn't played . . . even modern."

The Hot Fives Volume I (Columbia/Legacy) collects the earliest mature recordings by Armstrong, heading up the quintet that would affect jazz—and the whole of American music—for decades to come. The Hot Five wasn't a regular gigging band, but rather a studio group, which allowed Satchmo to document his prolific innovations while continuing to record and perform in a variety of other groups. The first sides, from late 1925, belong to the tradition of New Orleans jazz; they feature the important New Orleans players Johnny Dodds and Kid Ory in a format that emphasizes ensemble improvisation. But the later tracks, recorded through the middle of 1926, reveal the sea change that Armstrong introduced, transforming the "no-star" ensemble to one that featured a leader/soloist with talented accompaniment. (Such songs as the exhilarating "Cornet Chop Suey" document this evolution.) For all intents and purposes, this represents the birth of jazz as we now know it.

Armstrong had upped the ante in 1927–28, when the tracks on *Volume IV, Louis Armstrong and Earl Hines* (Columbia/Legacy) were recorded. His combo now contained up to seven pieces, including drums, which earlier recording techniques could not adequately capture. Armstrong himself had switched from the sweet-toned cornet to the heavier, brassier trumpet. More important, he had replaced his sidemen with younger and in most cases better-trained improvisers, men who could create balanced and attention-grabbing statements—further confirmation that jazz had become a soloist's idiom. The best of these, pianist Earl Hines, was perhaps the only other musician on a par with Armstrong in terms of virtuosity and vision, and he and the trumpeter experienced the musical equivalent of love at first sight. You can hear this on their still amazing duet "Weather Bird," in which they goad each other to previously undreamed-of heights. Another track in this collection, "West End Blues," features an introductory trumpet cadenza that remains one of the purest and most satisfying improvisations in jazz history. As it floats free of rhythmic constraints and across the century, this clarion call reminds you that there has never existed a more "avant-garde" sound than Armstrong's trumpet in its prime.

(For those with access to import recordings, your best bet is *The 25 Greatest Hot Fives & Hot Sevens*, a single disc comprising the most important of these sides, from the British label ASV Living Era.)

Volume VI: St. Louis Blues (Columbia/Legacy) continues the story, with Armstrong having relocated from Chicago to New York and expanding his group still further: by the end of 1929, he had lent his name and star power to a ten-piece band led by the pianist Luis Russell. With this relatively small "orchestra," Armstrong helped plant the seeds of the Swing Era by virtue of the band's primitive big-band arrangements and his own increasingly smoother melodies and more relaxed phrasing. On such tunes as "St. Louis Blues," the frenzied version of the famous "Tiger Rag," and the mock-mournful "Rockin' Chair," you can also hear the sound that spurred the imagination of the next decade's trumpet sensation, Roy Eldridge—who would later make his own definitive recordings of some of these same tunes.

Pops: The 1940s Small-Band Sides (Bluebird). After leading big bands for more than fifteen years, Armstrong returned to the small groups of his early days, and this remained his favored setting for the rest of his career. (He found a ready audience too, because in the mid-1940s a trad-jazz revival had sprung up in reaction to bebop, the prevailing idiom of that time. See chapter 3.) Most of the songs heard on this CD starred the trombonist and vocalist Jack Teagarden, an Armstrong contemporary and—although a white man—one of the finest blues singers in history. The other sidemen include some of the most accomplished jazzmen of the previous three decades—the trombonist Kid Ory and the legendary drummers Zutty Singleton and Big Sid Catlett among them—and they played with a relaxed ease that indicated the already classic stature of their music. These recordings also give a marvelous indication of Armstrong's importance and vitality, and of the rapid development of jazz itself. Although his own idiom had been supplanted by two subsequent styles of jazz (swing and bebop), Armstrong had not yet turned fifty, and these dates brim with all the strength and artistry of his earlier recordings.

Louis Armstrong, *Louis Armstrong and King Oliver* (Milestone). Here you'll find Armstrong's very first recordings, made in 1923 as a member of King Oliver's Creole Jazz Band. Rejoining his former boss in the bustling metropolis of Chicago, the young Armstrong—still playing cornet, the same instrument as Oliver—quickly began to eclipse the older musician. (The following year, he would move briefly to New York and make the first records under his own name.) On these sides you can hear the essence of the first New Orleans jazz, with its innovative reliance on ensemble improvising interrupted by the occasional short solo. The stiff rhythms convey energy, but not the subtle and complex swing that Armstrong would soon introduce. Nonetheless, you might detect the music's imminent evolution in the young cornetist's occasional burst of free melody. This CD also includes seven tunes that Armstrong recorded in 1924 with a group called the Red Onion Jazz Babies, some of which feature the cornetist's friendly rival, Sidney Bechet. All of this music has a "prehistoric" nature, in that it came before Armstrong's reinvention of jazz as a soloist's art, and because it has so little connection with modern music—and such low-fidelity sound—it makes for a poor introduction. Check out the other recommended Armstrong discs before turning to this one.

Sidney Bechet, *The Legendary Sidney Bechet, 1932–1941* (Bluebird). Besides Armstrong, only two other early jazzmen played with a comparable level of virtuosic genius and focused vision: pianist Earl Hines and the New Orleans clarinetist Sidney Bechet, who early in his career switched his main instrument to the soprano saxophone. Bechet actually attracted the earliest recognition. Fourteen years older than Armstrong, he began to receive rave reviews while touring Europe in 1919—nearly three years before Armstrong had even arrived in Chicago. Bechet was a true jazz pioneer in a number of ways. His use of the soprano saxophone established the role of that instrument for the next four decades; his emotionally charged sound soon came to define the bluesy intersection of African influence and Creole artistry; and he became, after Armstrong, the prevailing ambassador of New Orleans jazz until his death in 1959. This excellent overview illustrates all these points in twenty-two tracks. They cover the period of Bechet's greatest musical power, during which time he played with reckless creativity and stood alone in terms of sheer flamboyance.

Bix Beiderbecke, *Vol I: Singin' the Blues* (Columbia/Legacy). One famous story about the sweet-toned cornetist tells how, while staying with a friend, he would pick up his horn and play for his own pleasure at any hour of the day or night. When the neighbors mentioned to the apartment's owner that they had been awakened before dawn by the music they heard, they would caution him not to say anything to Bix, explaining, "We would hate for him to stop." Taking a step back from the ferocious extroversion of Armstrong's music, Beiderbecke created solos of simplicity and grace that established an alternate school of improvising, which would substantially affect the future of jazz. And he did this in a recording career of less than a decade. (Bix died at the age of twenty-eight, from illnesses associated with alcoholism.) This excellent collection contains many of the sides that gave rise to the Beiderbecke legend, including "Singin' the Blues," "Riverboat Shuffle," and the piano composition "In a Mist." On this last tune, Bix became the first jazz musician to successfully incorporate ideas of the French impressionist composers Ravel and Debussy (whose theories would have more impact on jazz musicians twenty years later). Most of the tracks also feature the saxist Frankie Trumbauer—whose similarly reflective style left its influence on younger saxophonists looking for a subtler and more romantic approach to "hot jazz"—and one of the first jazz guitarists, Eddie Lang.

Bix Beiderbecke and the Chicago Cornets (Milestone). Beiderbecke made his first recordings with the Chicago-based band the Wolverines. All of them appear on this collection of 1924 recordings, which also includes a handful of tracks recorded by Bix with two other groups. His bandmates played with the earnest clunk of other jazz bands copying the strict New Orleans style: they hadn't yet learned to imitate Armstrong's example. But Beiderbecke didn't have to imitate anyone to escape these musical constraints. The melodic power of his improvisations, along with the way he shaped and linked the phrases of his solos, gave a unique rhythmic impetus to his playing. He didn't swing like Armstrong, but he certainly did swing, in a light and almost detached manner, and in syncopated contrast to his accompaniment. The famous "Davenport Blues," the last recording on this disc, is a certified masterpiece. The melody hints at advanced hidden harmonies, the phrasing carries a subtle rhythmic freedom, and Bix's solo achieves a bittersweet rapture that soon became his musical calling card.

Duke Ellington and His Orchestra, *The Okeh Ellington* (Columbia/Legacy). Although Ellington's greatest achievements came in later decades, he still belongs in the top ranks of traditional jazz, thanks to many of the compositions found on this album. (You can also find them elsewhere. During these years, Ellington recorded for several different labels and often revised his best pieces in later recordings.) Like Jelly Roll Morton, Ellington helped give shape to the still young music. But he didn't write music like Morton's or anyone else's. Instead, he used the music of his predecessors and contemporaries to spur his imagination, adapting the New Orleans–Chicago style to create totally original sounds and textures. On such tunes as "The Mooche," "East St. Louis Toodle-Oo," and the haunting "Black and Tan Fantasy" (all heard on this collection), he began personalizing such idioms as the blues, dance music, and "hot jazz." This set of two discs, comprising fifty tracks originally recorded for the Okeh label, lays out the principles in the Ellington canon: his ability to expand the jazz orchestra's spectrum of sounds; his attraction to exotic rhythms; and his reliance on the unique musical personalities of his bandsmen. Several of these tunes were co-composed by Ellington and his groundbreaking trumpeter of the early years, Bubber Miley, whose "growl" trumpet sound and uninhibited blues sensibility provided the first of many valuable resources that Ellington would incorporate into his musical repertoire. (He would soon put such sounds to colorful use with his "Jungle Band"; it catapulted him into the national spotlight during a four-year engagement at the Cotton Club in Harlem, which entertained white audiences with black music.)

Earl "Fatha" Hines's technique was a tightly packed spore containing the seeds of a half dozen piano styles. Some pianists built an entire musical personality on the lacy filigrees of his more relaxed tempos. Most heard his "trumpet-style" attack—in which he brought a new lyricism to the piano by emphasizing melodies in the right hand and applying the phrasing used by horn players—and made at least some use of this technique. Art Tatum (see chapter 2) used Hines's frantic ambidexterity and rhythmically daring "stop-time" breaks to fashion a much more impressionistic body of music. Still others adapted the bouncy rhythms and clean melodies of Hines's compositions in their own writing and playing. And they could continue doing so for decades, since Hines performed to critical acclaim well into his seventies.

A Monday Date (Fantasy/OJC) brings together eight piano solos recorded in 1928 and a handful of tunes on which Hines accompanied the singer Lois Deppe, recorded in 1923—the earliest documentation of his work. The CD opens with the breathtaking title track, which instantly reveals most of the stylistic flourishes mentioned above. In fact, it serves as a primer on jazz piano, while sweeping the listener along in its inventive improvisation and irresistible rhythms. Hines shows off the piano's tonal possibilities on "Chimes in Blues," mimicking the sound of glockenspiel; the introduction to "Panther Rag" has an impressive orchestral flourish; and the simple but inventive "Blues in Thirds" became one of his best-known compositions. Even accompanying Deppe, a bluesy but rather stagy singer, Hines displays a commanding presence. With this collection, you can make a case for Hines being the most important piano player in jazz history. The expansive and often explosive virtuosity heard here (and on his recordings with Armstrong) would exert an active influence on two generations of pianists. And after that, the modernist pianists of the 1940s and 1950s designed their own techniques in part to *escape* the prevailing model established by Hines.

Like Armstrong, Hines made an enormous impact at a young age. Consequently, he could remain an active, vibrant performer long after newer jazz styles had supplanted his own. In the 1960s, he reemerged as a major stylist, expanding upon his many technical innovations to create fantasialike improvisations that his earlier recordings had only hinted at. *Reunion in Brussels* (Red Baron), a 1965 concert recording, presents this aspect of Hines's music better than any other single-disc recording. It includes several of the extended medleys that became a trademark of his later years (one of them, almost eleven minutes long, is made up of three of his own delightful compositions); and his performance of "Tea for Two" has enough sheer invention to make even this old chestnut seem fresh off the tree. Altogether, the album brims with keyboard magic and shows that even in his sixties, Hines's fingers could still dance circles around pianists half his age.

James P. Johnson, *Snowy Morning Blues* (Decca Jazz). The early jazz pianists based their playing on the principles of ragtime, the first uniquely American piano music. Ragtime featured syncopated right-hand rhythms placed against the bass patterns of the left hand—which would "stride" between the lowest and middle portions of the keyboard, thus mimicking the "oom-pah" patterns of nineteenth-century band music. But the tradition of *stride piano*—of which James P. Johnson and Willie "the Lion" Smith became the greatest practitioners—went way beyond ragtime. Developed primarily in Harlem, it incorporated a rich amalgam of other influences, from blues to classical music and all the popular songwriting that lay in between. It also demanded a level of virtuosic improvisation that earned the top stride men an obeisance usually directed at minor deities. Johnson embodied all of this, not only in his brilliant and exciting performances, but also in his writing, which included dozens of songs, larger orchestral works, and several hit Broadway shows (one of which featured the famous dance tune "The Charleston"). More than any other pianist, Johnson established the stride piano style as the dominant one for the 1920s and 1930s. His numerous innovations pulled the jazz piano away from the stiff rudiments of ragtime and created a model for such younger players as Earl Hines and Duke Ellington. This collection starts with four piano solos from 1930, then jumps ahead to several trio sessions from 1944, with a remake of Johnson's best-known piano piece, "Carolina Shout."

Jelly Roll Morton, *Birth of the Hot* (Bluebird). If later listeners really did place credence in Morton's claim to have invented jazz, you can blame these 1926–27 recordings—nearly twenty sides that have enough authority, imagination, and vitality to make you believe their creator capable of just such a feat. Employing a number of the New Orleans musicians who had moved to Chicago—including Kid Ory and the Dodds brothers— Morton's pieces ingeniously displayed the hallmarks of the New Orleans style by balancing passages of ebullient polyphony with short sections that emphasized the sound and style of each instrumentalist. This gave his recordings a textural variety not often heard in early jazz, almost as if Morton were leading a chamber orchestra instead of his seven-piece band, the Red Hot Peppers. This technique also showed that compositional structure could coexist with—and even enhance—the spontaneity at the heart of jazz. Such Morton songs as "Black Bottom Stomp," "Grandpa's Spells" (both heard here), and "King Porter Stomp" became classics. But in his arrangements, even others' works—such as "Doctor Jazz" and "The Chant"— proved just as pliant to his sculptor's touch. The commanding control and professional precision that Morton brought to his writing extended to the way he ran his band: he insisted on frequent rehearsals and a reasonable adherence to the music as written. This differed significantly from the way the music had been performed in New Orleans. Ironically, these recordings nonetheless became famous as sterling examples of the New Orleans style.

Jelly Roll Morton 1923–24 (Milestone) contains the first sides recorded by Morton after he moved to Chicago in 1922: some twenty piano solos, a few sextet recordings, and two duets with King Oliver on cornet. Even with modern recording wizardry, these still sound somewhat scratchy and uneven, but you'll quickly ask yourself, "Who cares?" The solos—which include "King Porter Stomp," "The Pearls," "Mamanita," and several other important Morton compositions—give an unrestricted view of Morton's gracious piano style, with its vivid rhythmic impulse, its lively interpolations, and its echoes of Storyville. Morton never took piano playing to the technical heights of

Earl Hines or James P. Johnson, but he certainly played well. More to the point, his solos provide further insight into the mind of the first great jazz composer. "The piano should always be an imitation of a jazz band," Morton once said, and his solos oblige: they sound like miniature arrangements. It's worth comparing his sextet sides with recordings made that same year by King Oliver and Louis Armstrong to see how Morton stood head and shoulders above his contemporaries in organizing what such jazz bands could accomplish.

Joe Venuti, *Violin Jazz 1927–1934* (Yazoo). As the first musician to play real jazz on the violin, Venuti stands as a pioneer of both jazz *and* the violin. Combining a roughened tone with effortless technique, he proved that a master jazzman could play as "hot" a violin as a trumpet or clarinet. Venuti imbued his playing with the same robust humor he employed offstage. In fact, the legendary wit and folly of Venuti (an inveterate prankster) often threatens to obscure his musical contribution, which extends beyond his capacities as a violinist. For instance, he was among the first musicians on any instrument to learn Louis Armstrong's lessons about rhythm, and throughout his life he could summon up the forward propulsion of a locomotive. Because of the instrument he played, Venuti opened a window on jazz to early listeners attuned to more violin-friendly idioms such as classical music and folk dancing—particularly when he toured with the Paul Whiteman Orchestra, which sought to "translate" jazz for the larger (white) audience. And Venuti's first recordings, which he co-led with guitarist Eddie Lang in the mid-twenties, became a model for small-group jazz and virtuosic interplay—this *before* Louis Armstrong hooked up with Earl Hines. The Venuti–Lang sides heard on this collection occurred a bit later, and the improvement in recording techniques provides a better sense of the fluid intensity of their partnership.

Fats Waller, *Piano Solos: Turn on the Heat* (Bluebird). Before he became one of the consummate entertainers of the Swing Era (see chapter 2), pianist Thomas "Fats" Waller had perfected what classicists would call a "portmanteau" style, in which he really summed up all the previous developments on his instrument: ragtime, the stride tradition of Harlem, the blues piano sound of the South, early boogie-woogie, and the sophisticated innovations of Earl Hines. But it wasn't until 1991 that you could find all of the solo-piano sides he recorded for the RCA Victor label—over a fifteen-year period starting in 1927—in one place. The program includes terrific Waller arrangements of the era's pop tunes, but also his original works, the mere titles of which—"Handful of Keys," "Numb Fumblin'," "Smashing Thirds"—suggest their place as uniquely pianistic jazz compositions. With their rough-hewn elegance, these pieces serve as early jazz's answer to the piano miniatures of Chopin and Schumann, and this set remains an important favorite among listeners of all persuasions.

Still Hungry?

The more music you hear by Louis Armstrong, the more you may want. Once you get past its old-time surface, you begin to realize the true timelessness of his art. One more of his early small-band collections, *The Hot Fives & Hot Sevens, Volume III* (Columbia/Legacy), contains a half dozen more gems from these pivotal groups. The four-CD set entitled *Portrait of the Artist as a Young Man 1923–1934* (Columbia/Legacy) provides a great introduction. It contains eighty-one tracks and a Grammy-winning liner booklet (with an excellent and up-to-date critical biography). It duplicates many of the important tracks found on the Columbia and ASV discs listed above, so if you splurge on this one, you won't need the others. Another multidisc set worth noting is *The Complete RCA Victor Recordings* (BMG), four CDs that concentrate on Armstrong's recordings of the early thirties—when he emerged as a major force in popular music—and the forties (including all the tracks found on *Pops*, one of the albums recommended above).

Several recordings document the working combo that Armstrong led in his later years, the best being the studio date *Louis Armstrong Plays W. C. Handy* (Columbia/Legacy) and the concert recording *Mack the Knife* (Pablo). For another route, you might try the double-disc *Highlights from His Decca Years* (Decca/GRP), which covers small groups and big bands between 1924 and 1958 and includes vocal collaborations with Billie Holiday and Bing Crosby, among others. Finally, Armstrong made a number of late-fifties records for the Verve label, three of which paired him with Ella Fitzgerald. You can survey these on the double CD *Let's Do It* or go directly to the source with *Ella and Louis*.

Among the fledgling big-band discs worth considering, *Bix Lives!* (Bluebird), under Bix Beiderbecke's name, provides a glimpse of what jazz meant to most Americans at the time: good-timey music in pallid arrangements, featuring violins and diluted rhythms, performed by the large and societally acceptable "orchestra" of Paul Whiteman. Out of this dance-music swamp, Bix's cornet solos rise like Excalibur from the depths. And if you don't mind hunting for imports, the British label JSP Records offers some marvelous tracks from 1927–28 on *Bix Beiderbecke and Frankie Trumbauer*, with Bix heard throughout and Trumbauer featured on two-thirds of the tunes. (The sound and the pressing are both pristine.)

The recordings of Beiderbecke's compatriots—the Austin High Gang and its honorary members—have all but disappeared from the shelves. Two albums reproducing sessions led by guitarist Eddie Condon will have to suffice. The best buy, *Chicago Style* (ASV Living Era), features a host of excellent players (including Gene Krupa, Pee Wee Russell, and Muggsy Spanier), but not cornetist Jimmy McPartland, the putative leader of the Gang and the leading disciple of Beiderbecke. To hear McPartland, as well as the influential early tenor saxist Bud Freeman, go for Condon's *Windy City Jazz* (Pearl), a somewhat pricey import. Both CDs contain material recorded between the late twenties and the early forties.

The music Duke Ellington wrote for his engagement at the Cotton Club—replete with growling trumpets and trombones, serpentine saxes, and other "exotic" effects—is best heard on *Jungle Nights in Harlem* (Bluebird), featuring sides recorded mostly between 1929 and 1931. The album opens with a studio re-creation of the actual stage show at the Cotton Club.

Earl Hines recorded often during his last twenty years, when latter-day audiences began to pay new attention to the legend in their midst. Most often, he recorded unaccompanied, the better to display his still active imagination and unfailing technique. The best such albums are probably the 1965 *Blues in Thirds* (Black Lion) and *Earl Hines Plays Duke Ellington* (New World), a project undertaken in the mid-seventies. *Grand Reunion* (Verve), a "live" double CD recorded just three days prior to *Reunion in Brussels* (above), contains perhaps Hines's best trio work on disc. However, roughly half the program features trumpeter Roy Eldridge and saxist Coleman Hawkins (see next chapter), neither one of them in exceptional form and both taking performance time from Hines, making this a slightly less satisfying document. *Another Monday Date* (Prestige) contains more than seventy minutes of music divided between unaccompanied solos and a Hines-led quartet.

More piano: The stride master James P. Johnson's *Running Wild* (Tradition) contains some of his earliest recordings (1921–26). The other best-regarded stride men were Willie "the Lion" Smith—who left a considerable impact on the young Duke Ellington—and Luckey Roberts. You can hear them together on the album *Piano Solos* (Good Time Jazz) or go straight to Smith on *Echoes of Spring* (Milan), the title track of which remains Smith's most famous composition. In addition, the music of pianist and composer Eubie Blake offers an appealing mixture of stride and its predecessor, ragtime piano, of which Blake was one of the greatest practitioners. You can hear how he sounded *before* the development of modern recording techniques on *Memories of You* (Biograph), which features early player-piano rolls, recorded by Blake starting in 1915 and later transferred to disc. *The Greatest Ragtime of the Century* (Biograph) assembles such piano-roll recordings from Blake, Johnson, Jelly Roll Morton, Fats Waller, and even Scott Joplin.

More Morton: In 1938, Morton undertook a recording marathon for the Library of Congress in Washington, D.C. These sessions form a musical autobiography featuring Morton's piano, his vocals, and recountings of his life and times. You can hear music and memoirs on *The Library of Congress Recordings, Volume One* (Solo Art). Or you can hear the music only on a three-volume series on Rounder Records, of which *Kansas City Stomp* provides the greatest variety. Meanwhile, *Jelly Roll Morton: The Piano Roll* (Nonesuch) presents re-creations of Morton's early solos taken from the piano rolls that he made circa 1924.

The bandleader Fletcher Henderson did as much as anyone to create the dominant sound of the Swing Era in the 1930s, but his best work fits into the transition section following this chapter. Nonetheless, he led perhaps the top jazz orchestra of the 1920s, thanks in large part to the early arrangements of Don Redman. The French label Classics has an extensive series, *Fletcher Henderson & His Orchestra*; the albums subtitled *1924/1927* and *1925–26* won't let you down.

Upon moving to Chicago, the clarinetist Jimmie Noone assembled a marvelous working band that starred his own precision-drilled clarinet and Earl Hines's piano. They captivated fellow veterans of the New Orleans scene—as well as the teenaged Benny Goodman, and the other young Chicagoans who would form the Austin High Gang—with an especially sleek and excitingly virtuosic brand of traditional jazz. *Apex Blues* (Decca/GRP) is the ticket here.

In the digital era, Joe Venuti has become an almost forgotten man: only a handful of albums exist on CD (with a few others on cassette or LP). But certainly consider two that he made when he was in his mid-seventies and still playing with undiluted energy and humor: *Alone at the Palace* (a duo date with the tradition-minded pianist Dave McKenna) and *Joe Venuti and Zoot Sims* (a quintet date featuring the great sax stylist named in the title), both on Chiaroscuro Records.

Finally, one more "sampler" album will fill in a number of gaps. *Volume 1, 1917–1929* (RCA) comes from the *RCA Victor 80th Anniversary* series, an ambitious program started in 1997. The series as a whole is limited by its inclusion of only recordings in the Victor vaults, but in its early days the company had a spectacular catalog. The twenty-five tracks here star Ellington and Morton, Hines and Venuti and Waller, as well as several lesser-known but still important bands and musicians. Here too you'll find the Original Dixieland "Jass" Band's "Livery Stable Blues," the first jazz record ever released.

How 2 Swing Large

Modern listeners might have trouble fully appreciating the evolution from traditional-style New Orleans jazz (and its Chicago offshoot) to the big bands of the 1930s. After all, both styles involved many of the same musicians, playing many of the same tunes; and from the standpoint of the late twentieth century, it all sounds—well, pre–World War II (which in jazz terms is the same as saying "early American"). In addition, prototypical "big bands" had been playing jazz since the early 1920s, a nod to polite society's preference for, and ability to afford, larger ensembles for their dancing pleasure.

But the concept of rhythmic flow—the phenomenon known as *swing* (see next chapter)—did not immediately transfer from the small-group jazz of Louis Armstrong to the big bands of stage and screen fame. In fact, it took a moment for the concept to transfer to Armstrong's *own* big-band recordings. The big bands were really small orchestras, and like any orchestras, they required written scores or *arrangements* ("charts," in musicians' lingo). These arrangements insured that all the players' individual parts would coalesce into a unified performance. As discussed in greater detail in chapter 2, it took some experimentation before jazz arrangers mastered the art of getting a big band to truly swing. To do so, they had to learn to write charts that combined the power of an orchestra with the immediacy of hot, improvised jazz.

If you listen to some of the first big bands, such as Fletcher Henderson's early outfits and even (to some extent) Glen Gray's Casa Loma Orchestra, you can easily hear the difference between a few improvisers playing off one another—as in the New Orleans style—and groups of ten or more instrumentalists, their eyes glued to the music stands, reading uncomfortable and complicated arrangements while still trying to capture that elusive beast called swing. No wonder that so many of the early big bands played with a stiff, clunky beat, and little of the insouciant flow that you hear from Armstrong, Hines, and their contemporaries.

The albums described below fall somewhere between the spirited polyphony of the first jazz and the polished excitement of the Swing Era. In these recordings, you can hear the transition taking place from early orchestral jazz to the heyday of big-band swing, as arrangers figured out how to divide the band into "sections" of instruments (see chapter 2), and drummers learned to provide a powerful but less intrusive pulse for this finely tuned musical machinery.

Fletcher Henderson, *Tidal Wave* (Decca/GRP). Widely considered the true progenitor of the Swing Era, Fletcher Henderson led one of the most popular dance bands of the early twenties, and the pioneering jazz orchestra of the late twenties—even though he received little of the wealth and acclaim that accrued to the musical leaders of the thirties, who built upon his work to create the Swing Era. Much of Henderson's success stemmed from the fact that his early bands boasted such star soloists as Louis Armstrong and saxist Coleman Hawkins. Much of his reputation comes from his decision to hire the visionary Don Redman in putting together his first orchestra. Redman's arrangements soon began treating the various "sections" of the jazz orchestra—saxophones, trombones, trumpets, and rhythm—as individual units, which he would then combine and contrast. This method of writing did more than any other technique to make the big bands swing. It reduced a cumbersome mob of twelve or fifteen instruments to a more manageable group of four basic elements—which, not incidentally, mirrored the reed, brass, and drum components of the New Orleans–style combos. And within the sections, Redman most often harmonized the melody line into trumpet or saxophone chords, which became the hallmark of the Swing Era's velvety tonal palette. After Redman left the band—followed by his equally gifted successor, Benny Carter—Henderson finally began turning out his own arrangements, which gained a second life in Benny Goodman's band. As critic Doug Ramsey has succinctly observed of Henderson, "He set the format and the standards for large ensembles playing syncopated music that incorporates improvised solos." By 1931, when he recorded the first of the tunes on *Tidal Wave*, Henderson commanded a band that pointed directly to the future.

* * *

Glen Gray and the Casa Loma Orchestra (Columbia/Legacy "Best of Big Bands" series). Was this fourteen-piece outfit, headed up by saxist Glen Gray (and named for a Toronto nightclub), the first big band to actually swing? Possibly; in any case, when they began recording in 1929, no white band (and few black ones) could so accurately represent the unique feel of true jazz in the setting of a large ensemble. The Casa Loma had flashy arrangements and well-rehearsed musicians with the skill to pull them off; but more important, these arrangements had begun to pare away the excess effects and to smooth out the rough-hewn rhythms of the New Orleans style. This set contains some of their earliest available recordings, which still display the tonal palette and staccato phrasing of the band's predecessors—qualities that make the music sound a bit cartoonish. But these tracks also show the undeniable rudiments of big-band swing in their silky harmonies, the effortless interaction of instrumental sections, and the relatively relaxed beat. And the fact that a white band could achieve success playing "hot" music— during the Depression, no less—was not lost on younger white musicians who had come under the spell of Louis Armstrong, Earl Hines, and Fletcher Henderson, and who would soon dominate jazz in the Swing Era. In Gray's own words, "I think everyone knows that we were the band that made swing commercial."

McKinney's Cotton Pickers, *1929–1930* (Classics). There really was a McKinney: drummer William McKinney, who abandoned his instrument to become conductor and manager of the band in 1923. But the band that bore his name achieved its true fame as a showcase for bright young soloists and the innovative arrangements of Don Redman, who became the Cotton Pickers' musical director in 1927. By this point in his career, Redman had pretty much mastered the art of writing for sections, and his work began to showcase tricky but rewarding figures for the horns. As musical director, he also emphasized a comparatively light touch in the rhythm section. Such devices gave the band a propulsive bounce that was a direct forerunner of big-band swing. This distinguished it from most of the decade's other large ensembles, which tended to lumber rather than skip through their arrangements. In this band Redman further explored techniques that he had pioneered in arrangements for Fletcher Henderson, which would become the foundation for big-band writing in the following decade. And in their straightforward inventiveness, these arrangements also served as a model for Redman's contemporary Duke Ellington. But no band of this period—not even Ellington's—did a better job of translating the thrust of Louis Armstrong's innovations to the arena of the jazz orchestra. (Note: The Classics label, while produced in France, is often available in U.S. stores and sold through the World Wide Web site for BMG Records.)

Duke Ellington, *Jubilee Stomp* (Bluebird). While Ellington would eventually emerge as the greatest composer in jazz history, he had no secret key that might unlock the mystery of making an orchestra swing. The recordings on this disc, made between 1928 and 1934, show him edging consistently closer to the streamlined power that would distinguish the big bands in general, while developing the rich mixture of street life and regal elegance that would distinguish his bands in particular. Such earlier tunes as "Stevedore Swing" and "Jubilee Stomp" still have the jumpy quality typical of big-band "hot jazz" in the twenties. But by the later sides, the experience gained by both Ellington and his sidemen resulted in a more unified sound and modernistic concept: their fast numbers sound busy but not frantic. An interesting sidelight to this set is that it contains more tunes credited to other composers than to Ellington. It thus lifts the curtain on Ellington's working band, building a repertoire of not only the Maestro's classic compositions but also the pop hits of the day—songs like "Dinah" and "Cocktails for Two" (although always ennobled by the Duke's signature arrangements).

Bennie Moten's Kansas City Orchestra, *1930–32* (Classics). Modern jazz histories usually identify pianist and bandleader Bennie Moten as the man who gave us pianist Count Basie; and indeed, after Moten's death in 1935, Basie used the core of the band to organize his own. But Moten deserves credit for more than that. In the late twenties and thirties the jazz explosion created a number of "territory bands"—dance bands, centered in such regional capitals as Kansas City, Denver, and Dallas, that worked an outlying "territory" around the home base—and Moten led one of the best. More important, the rhythm section that he built around Basie and bassist Walter Page soon adopted a new approach to propelling the band: they addressed the beat without all the clutter heard in most other orchestras. By the end of 1932, when the band recorded such tunes as "Prince of Wales" and their signature, "Moten Swing," they had developed a way of swinging that combined precision and flow, and this formula became a model for the Swing Era. (In fact, Benny Goodman achieved his first success largely by applying this rhythmic concept to arrangements provided by Fletcher Henderson.) The Moten rhythm section—later to become Basie's—*nudged* the band forward, instead of pulling it, and allowed the music to breathe. This in turn gave the band a unique flexibility, both in interpreting their top-notch arrangements and in supporting the noteworthy soloists—such as trumpeter Hot Lips Page, saxist Eddie Barefield, and Basie—who became an increasingly important part of the Moten band's profile.

The Bluebird label from RCA has a fine single-disc anthology titled *Early Black Swing: The Birth of Big Band Jazz 1927–1934*. It includes a few tracks from everyone mentioned above (except of course the Casa Loma Orchestra), plus tracks by Jimmie Lunceford, Henry "Red" Allen, and others. It makes a great if superficial introduction.

If this period of jazz history really grabs your fancy, you should also consider popping for the three-CD boxed set *A Study in Frustration: The Fletcher Henderson Story* (Columbia/Legacy). It covers a fifteen-year period beginning in 1923, clearly evidencing the transition from the earliest big-band writing to the success enjoyed by Benny Goodman and other students of Henderson's arrangements. In addition, it features surefire soloists from Armstrong to Waller (including Benny Carter, Roy Eldridge, Coleman Hawkins, Cootie Williams, and Ben Webster) and makes a case, in the liner book, for the Henderson Orchestra being "the single most important musical force in big band history."

Other recommended albums: Louis Armstrong, *Vol. 7: You're Driving Me Crazy* (Columbia/Legacy) and Don Redman, *Doin' What I Please* (ASV Living Era).

chapter two

Let's Dance*
1935-1945

The Swing Era began on August 21, 1935, the night the Benny Goodman Orchestra opened at the Palomar Ballroom in Los Angeles.

Goodman, a twenty-six-year-old clarinetist from Chicago, had begun assembling a jazz orchestra in 1934 and at year's end had landed a spot on a new coast-to-coast radio broadcast called *Let's Dance,* originating from New York. Sponsored by the National Biscuit Company, this program—a radio precursor to television's *American Bandstand*—featured three big bands playing the prevalent dance-music styles of the day: "Latin," "sweet," and "hot," the sound exemplified by Goodman and his men. *Let's Dance* ran from December 1934 until the end of May 1935 (when National Biscuit shut down due to a strike by its workers—giving extra meaning to the phrase *no bread*). In midsummer, cut loose from their weekly radio spot, the Goodman band embarked on a long road trip, through Michigan and Wisconsin and including three-week engagements in both Denver and L.A.

The trip went badly: the Midwest audiences, especially hard-hit by the Depression, wanted to escape into dreamy tunes of the "sweet" bands and hadn't yet learned to appreciate

---

*"Let's Dance," which soon became Benny Goodman's theme song, was adapted from a 110-year-old classical-music melody: *Invitation to the Dance* by the German composer Carl Maria von Weber. Goodman first played it as part of the radio program of the same name, and even today, "Let's Dance" remains an emblem of the Swing Era, when America shagged, jitterbugged, and "cut a rug" away from the Depression.

the "hot" music that Goodman preferred to play. During their stay in Denver—where the club owner complained that their arrangements were too long, and dancers reportedly asked for ticket refunds—the band hit bottom. They trudged on to California to fulfill their contract. At the Palomar, Goodman started the set with the least adventurous tunes in his repertoire. But when even these failed to elicit much response, he followed the advice of one of his musicians: "If we're gonna die, let's die playing our own thing." Goodman switched to the music closer to his heart, and to the band's surprise, the crowd erupted: *this* was the music they'd come to hear.

Unknown to Goodman, or anyone else in New York, young Californians had fallen in love with his music by listening to the *Let's Dance* programs. The Goodman band always played last on those broadcasts, at twelve-thirty in the morning, a little too late for many listeners in the East. But on the West Coast, three time zones away, the Goodman sets began at 9:30 P.M., prime time for Saturday-night audiences. As a result, the California kids already knew (and craved) Goodman's exciting, up-tempo repertoire, and word of the band's success in L.A. began to spread. Buoyed by this unexpected vindication, the band stormed into Goodman's hometown, Chicago. Scheduled for one month at the Congress Hotel, they stayed for six, as cheering crowds of teenagers packed the room. In December, they received a full-page write-up in *Time* magazine: the first certification of the nation's new mania for hot swing.

The "birth announcement" that opens this chapter constitutes one of those Useful Lies, although this one proves even more useful than most. The style called swing actually developed from seeds planted in the twenties and nurtured throughout the early thirties; and plenty of other bands, specifically black bands, were already attracting considerable attention in their regional bases when Goodman's band reached L.A. Yet Goodman's success there remains a demarcation point. Before the summer of '35, many people enjoyed a great deal of big-band music, for both listening and dancing. But after that summer, this music went from being a merely popular musical style to a national phenomenon unprecedented in American history. The country had caught a swing-dance fever. The first popular craze to be spread by the broadcast media, it reached everyone who had either the money to buy a radio receiver or even the opportunity just to hear one.

Benny Goodman did not invent swing music; he spruced it up and packaged it for mass consumption, gaining the encomium "the King of Swing" along the way. The pianist and jazz journalist Art Hodes later explained, none too charitably, that "the white public was looking for someone who could play black jazz in a style acceptable to them, and the crown fell onto Goodman's head. He dethroned the black musicians for the white public." (But Goodman, despite his considerable ego, never flinched from crediting those who came before him. And while he may have borrowed or even stolen ideas from black musicians, he did more than anyone else in American music to break down racial barriers. Before Goodman hired pianist Teddy Wilson and vibraphonist Lionel Hampton for his bands, no one had bucked segregation by employing black and white musicians in the same band.)

It doesn't take much investigation to see that swing music had already been in the air for several years. *Swing* originally referred, and still does, to the rhythmic pulse essential to virtually every idiom of jazz throughout its history: an underlying tension, created by subtle differences in accent, that gives jazz its unique propulsion. The term may have come from Louis Armstrong, and it had already started to gain popular currency in 1932—three years before Goodman's escape to L.A.—when Duke Ellington scored a hit with his song "It Don't Mean a Thing (If It Ain't Got That Swing)." In all likelihood, the word moved easily from that declaratory song title to the style of music played by Ellington's contemporaries.

But the possibility that Armstrong coined the term carries a grand symmetry, because the swing idiom drew directly upon the accomplishments of Armstrong and his traditional-jazz colleagues. The musicians of the late twenties and thirties took the raw, dynamic rhythms of New Orleans and Chicago and smoothed them out, making them more palatable to a larger audience but maintaining much of their aggressive thrust. They also began to transfer the music from the small groups of the mid-twenties to progressively larger ensembles, which eventually grew into jazz orchestras such as Goodman's. These big bands developed for two main reasons. One was the desire to tame or even "civilize" the New Orleans sound, in this case via the jazz *orchestra*, with the word itself carrying European echoes. The other reason concerned the desire of forward-thinking composers and arrangers—men such as Ellington, Fletcher Henderson, Don Redman, and Sy Oliver (of the Jimmie Lunceford Orchestra)—to expand and explore the potential of jazz.

Whereas Armstrong had turned the solo into the defining characteristic of jazz improvisation, the swing bands offered a new wrinkle on this concept by fashioning elaborate arrangements to introduce, cushion, and frame the solos. These carefully rehearsed arrangements—the "charts" of musicians' slang—replaced the spontaneous orchestrations of the New Orleans sound. Eventually, the arrangements took on a life of their own, often eclipsing or absorbing the individual solos entirely, and the distinctive sound of the big bands—characterized by lushly harmonized melody lines, purring rhythms, and an elegant sophistication—took shape.

It also took time.

It might not seem like such a big deal to translate the basic sound and spirit of jazz from the small combos (with five or seven musicians) to the big bands (which featured two and three times as many musicians as the combos). But teaching a large ensemble to weave the loose-knit rhythmic fabric essential to jazz—in other words, to really *swing*—proved tricky. The small New Orleans bands usually used no written arrangements and allowed the rhythm to breathe organically, as three or four horn players each improvised his part while keeping an ear on the others'. If an orchestra of twelve or fifteen had tried that, it would have produced cacophony: too many melody lines crashing into each other.

The answer lay in written arrangements. But the first arrangements proved bulky and unwieldy, as arrangers had most of the instruments play the melody and the others provide mere comment and filigree (colorful though it may have been). It took a while before Fletcher Henderson and his music director, the saxist Don Redman, learned to divide the instruments into teams or *sections*—trumpets, trombones, saxes, and rhythm instruments—and to then use these sections as the basic building blocks of their arrangements. Each section worked as a cohesive unit, in the way that the individual trumpet, saxophone, etc., functioned in smaller groups.

By giving each of these sections a distinct identity, Redman and Henderson had gone a long way to solving the problem of getting a large ensemble to really swing. In addition, the basic beat of the music began to change. Earlier jazz had an "oom-pah" sound left over from the influence of military bands, with an emphasis on the first and third beats of a four-beat measure. In the bands of Henderson and a few others, this evolved into a steady, smoother pulse emphasizing all four beats. And his arrangements stood up to changing times. In 1934, squeezed by financial setbacks, Henderson sold several of his best charts to Benny Goodman, and these arrangements formed the core of Goodman's early success.

Henderson's musical discoveries had other significant reper-cussions. They influenced the bandleader Jimmie Lunceford, whose polished performances set the standard for flamboyant professionalism. They also made it possible for a radically dif-ferent style of big-band music to flourish in the territory around Kansas City, Missouri, where many jazz orchestras worked steadily throughout the Depression. These bands, led by such men as Benny Moten and Andy Kirk—and epitomized by the Count Basie Orchestra—dispensed with many of the elaborate written arrangements of Henderson and his followers. But they retained the Hendersonian concept of instrument sections, each with a loosely defined role. Using this as a matrix, these bands could generate spontaneous "arrangements," built out of short, familiar phrases, and use these to frame the solos, which remained the focal point. (The musicians had a quite specific term for these phrases—*riffs*—that today refers to most any bit of melody, whether or not there's a big-band arrangement in sight.)

For all their power, elegance, and charisma, the big bands had their limitations. Even the most successful orchestra lead-ers (Basie, Goodman, Artie Shaw, and Tommy Dorsey) estab-lished small groups, often with musicians selected out of the larger ensemble, which allowed them more freedom and flexi-bility than the tightly controlled arrangements that had made them rich. The same impulse led many pianists of the Swing Era—Art Tatum, Fats Waller, Teddy Wilson (all of whom bor-rowed freely from Earl Hines)—to establish a special domain of their own, in which the piano keyboard became a little orches-tra in itself. This was especially true in the case of Tatum, whose oceanic virtuosity equaled that of the greatest classical pianists of his day. He most often performed without accompaniment: his spellbinding piano arrangements didn't need any help.

All of these musicians played a part in the Swing Era, but one of their contemporaries soon set himself apart *from* the Swing Era—even though he had composed its anthem. After attracting national attention during his four-year residency at the famous Cotton Club in New York's Harlem, Duke Ellington led one of the most requested bands of the 1930s, toured widely, had his share of hit records, and fully competed in the pop-music phenomenon of the Swing Era. But his compositions and orchestrations quickly began to reveal other agendas and a separate genius, setting his music off from the comparatively narrow focus of the other bands. His music tapped into emotional groundwaters and the roots of African-American history with unmatched depth and imagination.

To gauge the popularity and corresponding success of swing, one really has to look ahead, to the frenzy that surrounded the British invasion led by the Beatles some three decades later. Benny Goodman and the Dorsey brothers, Artie Shaw and Glenn Miller, and even Ellington became the rock stars of their day. Soon enough, this status also applied to the singers who appeared with their orchestras, from Billie Holiday and Ella Fitzgerald to Frank Sinatra and the Andrews Sisters.

The proof of their success lies in the sales figures and record charts of the 1930s. The big bands played the music that America danced to, sang to, spooned over, and eventually went to war with. Music lovers argued over who had the best band, or the most powerful soloist, the way sports fans of today compare baseball teams and shortstops. In fact, many of the big bands had their own baseball teams, which would square off against each other in the afternoons when they found themselves playing the same city. The Swing Era remains the only period in American history when the nation's popular music and jazz were one and the same.

The Discs

No jazz orchestra featured more great soloists over as long a period as Count Basie's band, and their contributions—played out over the seamless pulse of the "all-American rhythm section" anchored by bassist Walter Page and drummer Jo Jones—made Basie's one of the most exciting bands in jazz history. By the 1950s, it had also become a welcome home to a constant stream of terrific arrangers who polished and updated the "Basie Sound," a combination of urbane sophistication and down-home soulfulness.

The Complete Decca Recordings 1937–1939 (Decca/GRP) catches the Basie band near the beginning of their decades-long run. Without the benefit of a lawyer or a manager, Basie had signed a three-year contract with the Decca label, which required him to record twenty-four songs a year for the ridiculous sum of $750—cold cash, and no royalties! But despite his financial foolishness, Basie left Decca with a spectacular down payment on his musical reputation. This two-CD set contains lots of basic Basie, with such famous standbys as "Topsy," "One O'Clock Jump," "Every Tub," and "Jive at Five," and starring the soloists who cemented the band's reputation as a haven for jamming: saxists Lester Young and Herschel Evans, trumpeters Buck Clayton and Harry "Sweets" Edison, trombonist Dickie Wells, and the blues-shouting vocalist Jimmy Rushing. You won't find a better example of the music that Basie played nightly at the Reno Club in Kansas City—music that influenced musicians as varied as Benny Goodman and the young Charlie Parker (see chapter 3).

The Essential Count Basie, Volume 1 (Columbia/Legacy). This single-disc anthology features several masterpieces from 1939— including "Taxi War Dance," with one of Lester Young's most admired performances—recorded immediately after Basie's contract with Decca had ended. In addition, it has four sides by a smaller group listed as Basie's Bad Boys—on which the Count plays pipe organ as well as piano—and one 1936 track, "Lady Be Good," which is the earliest great example on disc of Young's genius.

April in Paris (Verve), the best-known and most popular of all Basie albums, features the spectacular collection of writers and soloists that gathered around the Count in the mid-fifties. Most important was the interaction between these two elements. The arrangements of Thad Jones and of Neal Hefti—who a few years later would toss off the *Batman* TV theme—were filled with sizzling ideas that could inspire the top-drawer soloists, and they solidified the direction that Basie would follow for the next three decades. And the soloists, particularly trumpeter Joe Newman and the "two Franks, please" (saxmen Frank Foster and Frank Wess), crafted solos so compatible that they sounded as if the arrangers had written them beforehand. (They had not.) The album cover, a seemingly candid shot that shows Basie charmingly outfitted in beret and buying flowers from an elderly Parisian peddler, captures the ease with which the Count greeted his international acclaim. And the famous arrangement of the title tune, with its opening brass fanfare and the lush statement of the theme by the saxophone section, sums up the Basie Sound in just a few seconds of music. (This album can also be purchased in an audiophile pressing on the Mobile Fidelity Label.)

Nat "King" Cole, *Hit That Jive, Jack* (Capitol). When pianist Nat Cole stumbled onto the sound of his trademark trio—using bass and the innovative guitarist Oscar Moore in place of a drummer—he created a format that made him famous and inspired pianists for the next two generations. It also provided the perfect cushion for his light, reedy voice and effortless phrasing, paving the way for his eventual abandonment of the trio to earn success as one of the greatest pop vocalists. But before all that, Cole had already earned the nickname King with his sparkling piano improvisations, which took an especially airy and uncluttered approach to the lessons taught by Earl Hines. The King Cole Trio established a new standard for "chamber jazz" groups. With their urbane blend of pop and jazz, ghetto jive and down-home blues, they created a distinctly African-American music accessible to the larger white audience. This placed them in a niche that only Fats Waller completely shared. Of the many reissues drawn from his hundreds of sides for the Capitol label, this one offers the best introduction to Cole's overall importance as a jazz artist. (If you don't care about his singing, try *The Best of the Nat "King" Cole Trio: Instrumental Classics,* also on Capitol.)

Tommy Dorsey/Frank Sinatra, *All-Time Greatest Hits Volume 1* or *Volume 2* (Bluebird). The polished, rounded tone of Tommy Dorsey's trombone, surrounded by translucent reeds and the brushed-suede brass of his orchestra, defines the "sweet" band sound favored by dancers and pop-music fans of the Swing

Era. And Dorsey's music reached its zenith with the arrival of the young Sinatra, his voice still callow but intensely expressive and eager to grow. Bewitched by the phrasing of Billie Holiday (see below), Sinatra—dubbed The Voice—sought to bring a new romanticism to popular singing. Sinatra continued to show the influence of jazz on his singing throughout his career. In the 1960s, he went so far as to record separate albums with both Basie and Ellington. The greatest pop singer never quite crossed over to become a *jazz* vocalist per se. But remember—in the thirties and forties, jazz *was* pop, and these sides show Sinatra at his early best, fronting one of the finest dance bands ever. Both albums overflow with the sweet, full harmonies that Dorsey favored, which made an effective backdrop for his own ballad work. But Dorsey always managed to balance sentimentality with strong solos from hard-swinging sidemen (such as trumpet star Bunny Berigan and the young drum sensation Buddy Rich). As a result, his band earned kudos from other musicians as well as the record-buying public.

Roy Eldridge, *After You've Gone* (Decca). From Louis Armstrong to Wynton Marsalis, no trumpeter ever blew a hotter horn than Roy Eldridge (aka Little Jazz). Some experts go so far as to judge him the premier instrumentalist of the Swing Era, despite the fact that the saxophone had begun to vie with the trumpet as the preeminent jazz horn. But Eldridge found himself well prepared: as a teenager, he had patterned his style not on the model of other trumpeters, but rather on the more fluid and florid playing of the great saxophonists of early jazz— Coleman Hawkins and Benny Carter. Eldridge forms the second link in the main strand of jazz trumpet. He captured the high-note bravado and improvisational craftsmanship of Armstrong but raised both the tempo and the range of his solos another notch. In turn, Eldridge's work would soon inspire Dizzy Gillespie, who pushed the style still further in becoming the signal trumpeter of the bebop era (see chapter 3). These early-forties sides find Eldridge—a veteran of the Fletcher Henderson band—fresh off Gene Krupa's payroll, leading his own relatively short-lived orchestra. It provides a serviceable showcase for his blinding speed and stratospheric fireworks, not to mention his sunny, high-spirited vocal work.

* * *

To describe Duke Ellington, it pays to use a phrase he himself coined: "beyond category." Ellington's achievements stagger the imagination. His roughly two thousand compositions—songs, suites, sacred concerts, movie and ballet scores—place him among the century's greatest American composers, regardless of genre. Dozens of his songs became popular hits and enduring standards, even though he began to turn his attention to other formats—primarily his extended suites—as early as the 1940s. Most important, he conceived the jazz orchestra as something more than a pop-music vehicle, tailoring his writing to the individual talents of his band members, some of whom played with Ellington for twenty years (and in a few cases more than thirty). With them in mind, he designed previously unheard tonal colors and new orchestral techniques.

The Blanton-Webster Band (Bluebird). The title refers to the arrival in the Ellington band of two important stylists: Jimmy Blanton, whose expert technique made him the first modern bassist, and the dynamic Kansas City tenor saxist Ben Webster (1940–42). Their presence galvanized Ellington—who had already reached new creative heights in the late thirties—to soar even higher, writing such masterworks as "Cottontail," "Main Stem," "Jack the Bear," "Rockin' in Rhythm," and "Koko." These short bursts of sustained brilliance raised the bar for jazz composition, as Ellington seemed to top himself with each new piece. Taken together, they form a primer on jazz composition and arranging, demonstrating imaginative devices for building tension, framing solos, combining instruments, etc. This three-CD set compiles more than fifty tracks, including the original recording of Ellington's famous theme song, "Take the A Train." The song was actually composed by Ellington's collaborator and alter ego Billy Strayhorn, who joined the band in 1939 and remained until his death in 1967. This set also showcases Strayhorn's heavy-lidded sensuality in such songs as "Passion Flower" and "Lotus Blossom," both of which—like so many other Strayhorn ballads—seemed custom-fitted to the languorous alto saxophone of Johnny Hodges.

(The single-disc *Sophisticated Lady* on Victor Jazz offers eight of the classics from this set, plus a dozen more recorded from 1944 to 1946. For the extremely budget-conscious, it makes a passable alternative, but it omits a wealth of material you really want to hear.)

Piano Reflections (Capitol) presents Duke Ellington *without* his orchestra. Instead, it highlights his widely overlooked abilities as a keyboardist. Unlike many piano-playing arrangers, Ellington did not simply reduce his orchestral scores to fit the instrument. He thought of the jazz orchestra as his primary vehicle, and this allowed him to perfect a piano style—originally inspired by the East Coast stride pianists of the 1920s—that had a separate and distinct personality. And while Ellington's piano played its role in the grand scheme of his writing, it could also stand on its own in a trio setting, as this 1953 recording proves. The haunting melancholy of the ballads is especially enhanced by the more intimate format, but the entire album exhibits the salient aspects of Ellington's piano—physical strength, economy of notes, and relatively stark harmonies—which would leave their influence most noticeably on the work of Thelonious Monk (see chapter 3).

At Newport (Columbia Jazz Masterpieces). Unbelievable as it seems today, Ellington fell out of favor with jazz critics in the 1950s, and audiences had begun to take him for granted after nearly three decades of fame. But in 1956, his band's debut appearance at the Newport Jazz Festival changed all that. The Maestro had composed a special suite in honor of the festival (which was then in only its third season), but the concert audience, and record buyers for years after, were left buzzing about a piece Ellington had written some twenty years earlier, "Diminuendo and Crescendo in Blue." On this tune, simply a blues, tenor saxist Paul Gonsalves took the solo, and the leader egged him on until Gonsalves dropped into his seat, nearly exhausted, twenty-seven choruses and nearly ten minutes later. That solo lit up the festival, landed Ellington on the cover of *Time* magazine a few weeks later, and reestablished him as a major figure in jazz, providing a platform for his increasingly exploratory work of the 1960s.

In the latter part of his life, Ellington devoted more and more time to extended compositions, usually in the form of suites. Two of them—"The Controversial Suite" and the extraordinary "A Tone Parallel to Harlem"—appear on *Uptown* (Columbia/Legacy). "The Controversial Suite" is an Ellington rarity, in that the Maestro used its two short movements as music criticism. The first lampoons the Dixieland revival of the 1940s, and the second movement sends up a contemporaneous band, the somewhat portentous jazz orchestra of Stan Kenton. But the sublime "A Tone Parallel to Harlem" (also known as "Harlem") carries no such baggage. Many Ellington mavens consider this piece the single greatest example of his extended compositions: a fourteen-minute work that flows effortlessly from one episode to another, in which carefully crafted musical motifs blossom and wither, creating an urban garden of colors, shapes, textures, and even odors. Despite a couple other excellently performed tunes, "Harlem" provides virtually the entire reason for purchasing *Uptown*. If that seems like an insufficient reason, it's only because you haven't heard it.

Ella Fitzgerald, *The Early Years—Part 2* (Decca/GRP). Some excellent singers had arrived on the swing scene before Ella Fitzgerald, but she changed the rules. Her innate craftsmanship and marvelous range stamped her as not just a singer but a full-fledged jazz *musician*, "playing" her voice as the great instrumentalists played their horns. This was even more evident in her intuitive mastery of the scat-vocal style made famous by Louis Armstrong, in which the singer abandons the lyrics to join the instrumentalists as an improvising soloist. (Some people credit Armstrong with inventing scat, but Fitzgerald snatched the patent, creating melodies of dazzling, saxophonelike virtuosity.) She made her debut with the solid big band led by drummer Chick Webb when she was just seventeen; these recordings, made between 1939 and 1941, find her leading the band after Webb's death. Her voice had just begun to deepen, and you can hear a burgeoning confidence in her vocal projection and rhythmic authority—although her sound and style still have the essential girlishness that she retained into her seventies. Fitzgerald made her fair share of great swing records, with a couple of huge hits. Nonetheless, her importance reaches its full potential in the next two chapters.

Benny Goodman, *Sing, Sing, Sing* (Bluebird). From the pile of worthwhile reissues by the Benny Goodman Orchestra, this one does the best job of summing up not only the Goodman sound but also that of the "hot jazz" orchestras in general. It shapes up as "Benny's Greatest Hits," sixteen tunes recorded between 1935 and 1938, the intoxicating inaugural years of the Swing Era. Goodman was a virtuoso of the first rank who later recorded classical concertos and continued to improvise with grace and power into his seventies. Here, his superheated clarinet leads the way on performances that define big-band precision. They include several of the classic Fletcher Henderson arrangements, such as "King Porter Stomp," "Christopher Columbus," and "Down South Camp Meeting"; a guest shot by Ella Fitzgerald; one tune featuring Lester Young; and the title track, a raucous bacchanalia on which Gene Krupa essentially invented the drum solo. The Swing Era starts here.

Benny Goodman, *After You've Gone* (Bluebird). If you think of Goodman's big band as a luxury liner, you can see his small groups as sprightly pleasure craft out for a spin. They quickly became the model for "chamber jazz" bands of the next two decades. Goodman started his trio with Gene Krupa (his band's drummer) and pianist Teddy Wilson, whose lacy solos belied a rhythmic backbone made of steel. It became a quartet when Goodman invited in vibraphonist Lionel Hampton, a soloist with a strong imagination and extroverted technique. (Notice that neither the trio nor the quartet included a bass player. Years later, when Goodman reunited this group, he did add a bassist to expand to a quintet.) These units, and the other small groups they inspired, served as laboratories for the most adventurous musical ideas of the period. They also fulfilled the demand—on the part of musicians themselves and also discerning fans—for virtually unfettered improvisation. *After You've Gone* divides the spoils splendidly: ten tracks by the trio (including a flowing "Body and Soul," a blowsy "Oh Lady Be Good," and a frantic "China Boy"), and twelve more by the quartet (with Hampton aglow on "Stompin' at the Savoy" and "Runnin' Wild").

Coleman Hawkins, *A Retrospective 1929–1963* (Bluebird), introduces the enormous range of this all-time all-star. With his fat tone, his swaggering vibrato, and his harmonic ingenuity, Hawkins served as the model for jazz tenor saxophonists—especially such immediate descendants as Ben Webster and Don Byas—until Lester Young came along to provide an alternative. Hawkins established himself as the star of Fletcher Henderson's early bands before emerging as leader of small groups and the occasional big band of his own. He raised the improvised solo to new heights when, in 1939, he improvised two perfect choruses of the song "Body and Soul." This off-the-cuff masterpiece of logical (but still romantic) lyricism also elevated the tenor sax to a new level of stardom in the jazz family. Among the few older musicians revered by the beboppers of the 1940s—thanks to his mastery of complicated harmony, which would become a cornerstone of bebop—Hawkins for his part proved open to such newer developments. Along these lines, he later made a famous recording with Sonny Rollins, who had adapted Hawkins's influence to a new generation. This double-CD set features music from all these settings and several others. About half these same recordings make up the less extensive (but less expensive) single-disc *Body and Soul* (Victor Jazz).

Billie Holiday's impact on American culture reached beyond jazz and into the world of popular music for decades after. She would have iconic status if her influence had reached *only* to Frank Sinatra, who publicly credited her ability to give lyrics a naturalistic (rather than melodramatic) shading. But others, notably Carmen McRae and Sarah Vaughan, always made clear their own debt to "Lady Day," as saxist Lester Young nicknamed her. Her most famous composition, "God Bless the Child," reached new audiences in the sixties via the jazz-rock band Blood, Sweat & Tears.

The Quintessential Billie Holiday (Columbia/Legacy) is a series of nine single-CD volumes that trace the early successes of the singer, from 1933 to 1940, when her voice had a bounce and spirit that would begin to ebb a decade or so later. You won't go wrong with any of them, but *Volume Five (1937–1938)* provides the best start. On all but four tunes, the band features Lester Young, Holiday's musical soul mate. His light tone and sympatico commentary intertwine telepathically with the singer's liberated phrasing and plaintive voice. (Holiday considered Young "the president of all the saxophone players," which gave rise to his ubiquitous nickname, Pres.) Working often in bands led by pianist Teddy Wilson, the singer quickly became a favorite among jazz musicians, and although she lacked the privileged gloss of most of her white counterparts, their validation of her work soon helped her reach a wider national audience. A close runner-up is *Volume Eight (1939–1940)*, which features a number of great hornmen and a terrific song list. (Or you can splurge on *The Legacy [1933–1958]*, a three-disc set culled from the entire *Quintessential* series.)

Billie Holiday's Greatest Hits (Decca Jazz/GRP). For once, the bombast of the title fits. This set really *does* include Lady Day's best-selling songs, which stem from her years at Decca Records (1944–50). There she received the full star treatment: string-orchestra arrangements on the ballads, big-band charts for the swing tunes, glossy promotional photos, and the backing of a young and vital record label. This disc marks the zenith of Lady Day's career, with her still vital skills in balanced harmony with popular acclaim. It contains recordings of such signature tunes as "Lover Man," "Don't Explain," "Good Morning Heartache," "My Man," and "God Bless the Child."

From 1952 until her death in 1959, Holiday recorded for Verve, always backed by a star-studded aggregation of accompanists (most of them contemporaries of hers from the Swing Era). By this time, the bloom had left Holiday's voice: it now had a leathery twang, which Holiday purists tend to decry. In one respect, they're right: her voice sounds tired and embattled by comparison with earlier records, the result of hard living and plenty of hard knocks. But her interpretative skills allow her to wrench ever more emotion from even the most carefree tunes. *Billie's Best* (Verve) skims the cream off these albums and provides the final chapter of her difficult life.

Glenn Miller, *Greatest Hits* (RCA). Perhaps the most popular bandleader of the Swing Era, trombonist Glenn Miller didn't find immediate fame. It took several years before his style of arranging—which often featured clarinet and saxophone playing the melody together, backed by the luscious sound of burnished brass—began to yield the dozens of hits that made him famous. The Glenn Miller sound fell somewhere between that of "sweet" and "hot" bands. With its smooth contours, the band's music was perfect for dancing, but Miller also had a feel for the bright swing of Goodman and Artie Shaw—even though his band lacked the requisite high-powered soloists. Still, only the most rigid purists can today resist the Miller band's string of pearls, among them "In the Mood," "Tuxedo Junction," "Chattanooga Choo-Choo," and "American Patrol." These songs, more than those of any other bandleader, conjure up a nostalgic vision of America on the verge of World War II, and this collection contains all of them. Miller himself appeared in several films, along with his orchestra. His mysterious death in a presumed air crash during the war (neither the plane nor his body was ever found) elevated his status from star to legend.

Django Reinhardt and Stephane Grappelli, *Souvenirs* (London). Because of the "melting-pot" origins of jazz and its unique place in American culture, most people believed that no one outside the United States could really play jazz—that is, until the guitarist Django Reinhardt gained fame in the mid-1930s. Reinhardt, a Belgian gypsy who grew up outside Paris, cofounded the Quintette du Hot Club de France with the remarkable violin virtuoso Stephane Grappelli. Two more acoustic guitars and bass (but no drums) provided backing for the soloists. The resulting sound tapped both Reinhardt's folk roots and the string-band format of European popular music. A spectacular, rhythmically exciting accompanist, Reinhardt transferred that excitement to his deftly outlined improvisations and became an equally startling soloist—even though as a teenager, he had lost the use of two fingers on his left hand in a fire. (Some say that his unusual melodic patterns resulted in part from his disability.) Of the dozens of Reinhardt collections, this one is best at presenting the mature Quintette, with twenty sides—most of them recorded between 1938 and 1940—which include the indelible Reinhardt compositions "Nuages," "Daphne," and "Nocturne." This music—driven yet buoyant, edgy but elegant—marks the beginning of the European jazz tradition.

Artie Shaw, *Begin the Beguine* (Bluebird). The title track of this collection, which keeps picking up steam as it sways along, shows why Shaw's band gave even Goodman's a run for the money among the great "hot" swing orchestras. (In fact, you can make a strong case for the charismatic Shaw being the better swing-clarinet improviser. But you'll find no argument over who made a better matinee idol. Shaw was romantically involved with movie stars Lana Turner and Ava Gardner, and he married seven times.) Intellectually restless and unimpressed with success, Shaw had great instincts that allowed him to make his music both novel and popular. Meanwhile, the title and mood of his theme song ("Nightmare") hint at Shaw's icono-clastic sense of humor. This anthology offers as highlights the work of vocalists Billie Holiday and Helen Forrest; hit tunes such as "Frenesi" and "Moonglow"; and the ferocious drum-ming of a quite young Buddy Rich. And when Shaw ends "Beguine" with his breathtaking, now-famous, two-octave glissando (an uninterrupted slide between notes, such as you usually hear only on a trombone), you understand what the fuss was about.

Art Tatum, *Solos* (1940) (Decca/GRP). To imagine the tower-ing technique Art Tatum brought to the piano, just think of him as *two* of the greatest pianists who ever lived. Indeed, his earli-est record session, in 1933, produced a version of the famous "Tiger Rag" that suggested at least three hands at work (and sometimes four). Admired by classical virtuosos as well as the jazz world, Tatum employed his lightning fingerwork, and the extraordinary independence between his left and right hands, to create Technicolor arrangements of pop, jazz, and semiclassi-cal tunes. Filled with magical leaps, sudden rhythmic stops, dizzying harmonies, and hallucinatory melodic swirls, each performance became an odyssey of improbable proportions. For his studio sides (which number well over two hundred solo tracks), Tatum worked out the structure of his complicated arrangements in advance, restricting his actual improvising within these confines. As a result, it doesn't matter that much whether you listen to his work from the mid-thirties or the mid-fifties, when he undertook a massive series of recordings designed to permanently preserve his legacy. This collection contains several of his best-known masterpieces, such as "Get Happy," "Begin the Beguine," "St. Louis Blues," and of course "Tiger Rag." Tatum didn't write any of them, but in his hands they became gleaming new compositions nonetheless.

Fats Waller, *The Joint Is Jumpin'* (Bluebird). In the Swing Era, Waller's spectacular skills as a stride pianist (see chapter 1) took a backseat to his abilities as a bandleader, songwriter, and all-around entertainer. The composer and popularizer of such classic tunes as "Ain't Misbehavin'," "Jitterbug Waltz," and "Honeysuckle Rose," Waller led wonderfully spirited small bands throughout the 1930s and up until his death in 1943 at age thirty-nine. But those songs didn't earn him the title of "clown prince of jazz." For that, he could thank "Your Feet's Too Big" and the always appetizing "Fat and Greasy," as well as the irrepressible persona he presented onstage: the party animal, bowler hat cocked to one side, stogie jammed into one corner of his smiling mouth below his dancing, pencil-thin mustache. (As these novelty songs became bigger and bigger hits, Waller tried to distance himself from the material with verbal interpolations that verged on the sardonic; still, his public demanded more and more.) Waller's bonhomie extended to his piano playing, which rolled and bubbled and managed to both accent and draw attention from his virtuosic technique. This collection touches all the bases; for anthologies that explore Waller's art in more depth, see below.

Lester Young, the tenor saxist who rose to fame in Count Basie's band, presented a radically different style from the prevailing model of Coleman Hawkins. Young had a dry, lighter-than-air tone, and his ethereal, relaxed solos seemed to float above a song's underlying harmonies (instead of burrowing deep within them, as did the more complicated solos of Hawkins). It took a while for Young's approach to gain favor. In 1934, when he replaced Hawkins in Fletcher Henderson's band, the bandleader's wife forced him to listen to Hawkins's records while encouraging him to "try playing more like that." She might just as well have tried teaching a right-handed child to scribble with his left. Young's music would leave its mark on the beboppers—particularly Charlie Parker—while his languorous sound and dreamlike improvisations prophesied the "cool" sounds of the 1950s.

Young played his greatest early solos with Basie and behind Billie Holiday, on discs already discussed above. You can also hear many of these solos in *Lester Leaps In: His Greatest Recordings 1936–44* (ASV Living Era), a twenty-four-track compilation of his work with those artists.

You can hear more vintage Young on *Master Takes* (Savoy Jazz), which gathers the fruits of four different sessions of the 1940s. The first features Pres in a reunion with the Basie band, reprising the featured role he had in the thirties, while the next two showcase him in small groups of the type he had been leading since leaving Basie in 1940. With these, he offers a rapturous version of "These Foolish Things" (a tune he recorded often); a blues solo that masks its emotional depths beneath a jaunty exterior ("Blue Lester"); and a marvelously swinging statement on the fast blues "Jump Lester Jump" (with Basie on piano). Most of these sides were made a few months before Young was drafted into the army, a disastrous and defining event in his life. Eccentric even among the jazz crowd, Private Young might as well have come from Neptune as New Orleans (where he grew up). Because of his traumatic military experience, Young's postwar recordings are inconsistent and once earned blanket dismissal from critics—even though they still contain many great performances.

An excellent introduction to Young's work as a leader is *Lester Young Trio* (Verve), dominated by a 1946 session featuring Nat "King" Cole on piano and Buddy Rich on drums. It's an unusual grouping, in that Rich had little in common with the other musicians, but it works surprisingly well. Cole's relaxed, almost casual virtuosity at the piano makes a wonderful foil for Young's laconic magic, which fits such dreamy ballads as "I Cover the Waterfront" and "The Man I Love" the way soda suits Scotch. On the other hand, Young's propulsive solo on "I Found a New Baby" all but defines his up-tempo style. This disc also features four sides with a sextet that includes trumpeter Harry Edison and the then-young tenor man Dexter Gordon, one of Young's most accomplished stylistic inheritors.

Most of Young's later records placed him in the company of younger musicians—the beboppers who so admired his music—and thus belong to the transition section linking the Swing Era with the music that would supplant it.

Still Dancing?

You can spend some big money on the Swing Era: multidisc sets compiling the work of these musicians abound. The four-CD set titled *Nat "King" Cole* (Capitol) offers a sampling of the pianist's work for that label—*all* of which can be found in a massive eighteen-CD box from the mail-order label Mosaic. Similarly, the Glenn Miller disc recommended above represents a fraction of the music he recorded for RCA; the remaining twelve CDs' worth of material makes up *The Complete Glenn*

Miller (Bluebird). Get the picture? Because the swing musicians also qualified as pop artists, they recorded constantly, and their career output makes for some lovely (and expensive) gift packaging. In general, however, you have to ask yourself whether you're likely to listen carefully to ten or more hours of any one artist.

Another reason you can find so many recordings by the swing artists has to do with the miracle of radio. Since so many of their concerts were broadcast live and transcribed onto master discs—this before the advent of recording tape—the market bulges with small-label reissues of "air shots" and "one-night stands." Even with modern technology, you can't always guarantee the sound quality of these recordings, but once you've heard the studio versions recommended above, you may want to buy some of the "live" collections and make comparisons.

For a general feel of the Swing Era, you can also consider a few of the many anthologies that compile a track or two from a variety of artists—including many not previously listed among the recommendations for this chapter. Although the *RCA Victor 80th Anniversary* series contains only recordings owned by the label, the twenty-five tracks on *Volume 2, 1930–1939* (RCA) still boast Ellington, Goodman, Hampton, Hawkins, and Shaw—as well as Cab Calloway, Bunny Berrigan, and Charlie Barnet, all stars in their own right. Even more wide-ranging is *Big Bands of the '30s and '40s* (volume 3 of Rhino Records' "Masters of Jazz" series), with many of the same artists as well as otherwise unavailable tracks by Earl Hines's big band. The album concludes with two tunes that show the big-band format making the transition from swing to bebop.

Basic Basie would also include *The Essential Count Basie, Volume 2* (Columbia/Legacy), containing several classics from 1939 to 1940 ("Volcano," "Super Chief," and "Lester Leaps In" among them); *The Complete Atomic Basie* (Roulette/Blue Note), the signal representation of Basie's fabulous fifties bands; a companion to that album, *Basie in London* (Verve), actually recorded in Sweden(!) and featuring the same band in a live setting; and *Count Basie Swings, Joe Williams Sings* (Verve), highlighting the vital contributions of the vocalist who built his reputation during his Basie years (1954–61). *The Golden Years* (Pablo), a four-CD set of recordings from 1972 to 1981, provides a nightcap to the Basie legacy, with the pianist featured in small groups, live jam sessions, and the later editions of his big band—which by this time had become an institution, albeit a still swinging one.

For the further adventures of Duke Ellington after his "Blanton-Webster Band," turn to another three-CD package, *Black, Brown & Beige* (Bluebird), which compiles recordings from 1944 to 1946. The title piece is Ellington's first extended work, containing a number of themes that he would later develop into freestanding songs. Starting in 1943, Ellington presented a series of concerts at Carnegie Hall, at which he regularly premiered new compositions; go for *Carnegie Hall Concerts January 1946* (Prestige) or *Carnegie Hall Concerts January 1943* with the debut of "Black, Brown & Beige" (as an alternative to the first set mentioned in this paragraph). For other Ellington suites from this period, the clear choice is *Three Suites* (Columbia/Legacy), topped by the witty and inventive Ellington-Strayhorn adaptation of Tchaikovsky's "Nutcracker Suite." For an excellent view of his later band on stage, it's the two-CD *Great Paris Concert* (Atlantic), a wedding of grand musicianship and pure excitement.

Ellington's stature made younger artists eager to work with him, often in small groups. The trio recording *Money Jungle* (Blue Note) remains a classic, with Charles Mingus on bass and Max Roach on drums—the best known of the albums to focus on the pianist beneath the composer. And *Duke Ellington & John Coltrane* (Impulse) is a surprisingly compatible collaboration between two giants of opposing eras.

A few other leaders managed to rise above the proliferation of swing orchestras to carve their niche in jazz history, most notably Jimmie Lunceford. His band, as heard to best advantage on *Stomp It Off* (Decca/GRP) and *Jimmie Lunceford & His Orchestra 1939* (Classics), played complex and often fascinating arrangements and combined musical skill of the highest order with flashing showmanship. The vocalist and professional hipster Cab Calloway led the band that followed Duke Ellington's into the famous Cotton Club, where Calloway took showmanship—and jazz fashion—to new levels; *Cab Calloway—Best of the Big Bands* (Columbia/Legacy) tells the tale.

The most important of these leaders is Benny Carter, an influential saxist, sparkling trumpeter, and brilliant arranger, who made his orchestra a showcase for all his talents; check out *All of Me* (Bluebird). Carter created one of the two prevailing alto saxophone styles of the 1930s (Johnny Hodges had the other), and you can hear him at his limpid, lyrical best on *Cosmopolite* (Verve), recorded in the mid-fifties; discs that chart his reemergence as a soloist are mentioned in chapter 8. Also look for *Further Definitions* (Impulse/GRP), a 1961 masterpiece in which Carter's arrangements spark an octet that stars his contemporary and friend, Coleman Hawkins.

Benny Goodman's *Carnegie Hall Concert—Complete*, a double CD on Columbia/Legacy, documents the seminal 1938 concert— the first jazz performance ever given at the venerable New York odeum—in which Goodman led a hand-picked ensemble that included Count Basie, Lester Young, Lionel Hampton, trumpet great Harry James, and the meat of the Duke Ellington band's saxophone section (altoist Johnny Hodges and baritone saxist Harry Carney). A three-CD set called *The Birth of Swing* (Bluebird) expands the material found on *Sing, Sing, Sing* (see above). Both sets draw from the sixteen-CD treasure trove *The RCA Victor Years* (Bluebird).

Goodman continued to lead small groups during these years and even after he retired as a big-band leader. You can follow his evolution in this setting with *Small Groups* (Columbia/Legacy), featuring music of the early forties; *Slipped Disc (1941–1946)* (Columbia/Legacy); and *Together Again* (RCA Victor), a 1963 reunion of the original thirties quartet. Meanwhile, *The King of Swing* (MusicMasters) boxes up five CDs of Goodman recordings from the fifties and sixties, during which time the clarinetist played with continued zeal and barely diminished skill.

Goodman was not the only leader to escape the restrictions of a big band by forming a smaller, more casually structured group to showcase his talents. Artie Shaw led one of the most admired such combos, a "band within the band" called the Gramercy Five, which would step out from the big band for a featured spot during concerts. This band—which at first included harpsichord, as well as trumpet and guitar—recorded infrequently, permitting *The Complete Gramercy 5 Sessions* (Bluebird) to fit on one CD. Various members of Ellington's band regularly recorded with their colleagues in small-group affairs. The single-disc *The Fabulous Ellingtonians* (volume 5 of "The Essential Keynote Collection" on Mercury) showcases four such bands, and the two-CD *The Duke's Men: Small Groups Vol. 1* (Columbia/Legacy, listed under Ellington's name) has several more, led by such ducal stalwarts as Barney Bigard, Johnny Hodges, and Rex Stewart. And Lionel Hampton, the pioneering vibraphonist who left Goodman and started his own big band, made dozens of excellent small- and medium-group sessions with all-star lineups. The best of these are now available on the double CD *The Complete Lionel Hampton* (RCA Victor), while the single-disc *Tempo and Swing* (Bluebird) offers a cost-effective alternative.

Tommy Dorsey's combo, the Clambake Seven, starred distinctive soloists and recalled the New Orleans polyphonies that had inspired Dorsey in the first place, as heard on *The Clambake Seven: Best of 1936–38* (Challenge). Meanwhile, Dorsey made many more sides with Frank Sinatra than those contained on the albums mentioned above. They make up a splendiferously packaged five-CD box, *The Song Is You*, available on RCA.

Coleman Hawkins continued making excellent records almost right up to his death in 1969. The 1957 *April in Paris* (Bluebird) and the 1965 *Wrapped Tight* (Impulse/GRP) both display his mastery of the modified "concerto" format, in which his horn plays the central role in a dialogue with the backing ensemble. *Encounters* (Verve), with Ben Webster, brings together teacher and prize-student-turned-equal. For a good example of Hawkins in concert—and he could be a ferocious competitor in cutting contests with other hornmen—hear him with Roy Eldridge on *At the Opera House* (Verve).

The commentary (above) on Billie Holiday's career leaves out one important period—the war years, when she made the fleeting transition from jazz to pop star. You'll find these recordings on *The Complete Commodore Recordings* (Commodore/GRP), designed for aficionados. Although she recorded only sixteen titles for the label, a slew of alternate takes stretches these over forty-five tracks, with most heard two or three times (for those who wish to compare). By the fifties, the LP had appeared, and

Verve has reissued several of Holiday's long-playing albums under their original titles. Try the famous *Lady Sings the Blues* or the legendary *Billie Holiday at Carnegie Hall*, documenting a concert that paid tribute to Lady Day with her own music and a running autobiographical narrative (at times *very* graphic: Holiday spent her first months in New York as a $20 call girl). For the best deal, get *All or Nothing at All*, which considerately compresses three of her best Verve LPs onto two CDs.

Django Reinhardt had an exotic charisma that rivaled that of Bix Beiderbecke, and as a result, various labels have issued every scrap of his music in a bewildering array of series. The double-disc *Djangologie/USA, Vol. Two* (Disques Swing), compiled and distributed for a U.S. audience, is a fine sampler of Reinhardt's work not only with the Hot Club Quintet but also alongside such visiting Americans as trumpeter Rex Stewart and a pioneering violinist, Eddie South. The single-CD *Djangology 49* and the double-disc *Pêche à la Mouche*, both on Verve, offer good encapsulations of his later work. The latter includes recordings made just before his death in 1953 and after he had made the switch to amplified (electric) guitar.

Reinhardt's partner Stephane Grappelli, born in 1908, died in late 1997, and his long career yielded many intriguing collaborations with younger players, as well as timeless reissues of great swing improvising. For the latter, there's *Stephane Grappelli* (No. 11 in the Verve "Jazz Masters" series). For the former, try *Parisian Thoroughfare* (Black Lion) with pianist Sir Roland Hanna; *One on One* (Milestone), a duet date with pianist McCoy Tyner; and the in-concert recording *85 and Still Swinging* (Angel).

Art Tatum's *Classic Early Solos* (Decca/GRP) gives you excellent performances of the mid-thirties, and *Piano Starts Here* (Columbia) balances a 1949 in-concert recording with his first three solo sides from 1933. The solos he cut for famed producer Norman Granz in the 1950s fill eight separate CDs on the Pablo label, and you can pick any of them with safety or go for the whole megillah with *The Complete Solo Masterpieces* (seven CDs; don't ask me how). Tatum did record from time to time with others, and *The Complete Pablo Group Masterpieces* offers all these tracks on six discs. They're also available in eight individual albums with different groups, of which I'd recommend *Volume 1* (with Benny Carter and drummer Louis Bellson) and *Volume 7* (a quartet setting with clarinet great Buddy DeFranco).

Fats Waller and His Rhythm (as the group was called) did most of their work for the Victor label, and these recordings fill no fewer than fifteen CDs, issued in six separate sets. Go first for the two-CD *I'm Gonna Sit Right Down* ... (1935–36) and the three-CD *The Last Years* (1940–43), both on Bluebird.

Virtually every saxist of the Swing Era bore the stamp of Coleman Hawkins, but Ben Webster wore it best of all, using the Hawk's basic ingredients to create his own indelible mix of tenor machismo and tender sexuality. His work with Ellington's band (*The Blanton-Webster Band*, above) is only the start. Also try *Soulville* or the double-disc *The Soul of Ben Webster*, which contains music that originally filled three LPs. *See You at the Fair* offers delightful, almost puckish Ben from the mid-sixties. For some of the smoothest balladry in jazz history (backed by strings), go for the double-disc *Music for Loving* and turn down the lights. (All the Webster discs mentioned are on Verve.)

The Complete Lester Young on Keynote (Mercury), containing sessions from 1943–44, reunites Pres with some of his old Basie bandmates (including the Count himself) and recaptures the spirit of Kansas City a decade earlier. But because he recorded for a variety of labels without benefit of a long-term contract, Young has yet to receive much of the big-package treatment from any one of them. To find all of his great recordings with the Basie band of the thirties in one place (which would seem to be a natural package), you have to look east—all the way to France—for the double CD collection titled *The Quintessence* (Fremeaux & Associés).

Swing 2 Bebop: Evolution in the Revolution

In the 1940s, jazz took a sharp left turn. Younger musicians who had begun to think of themselves as artists first (rather than primarily entertainers) came to the fore, and with them came new ideas that had percolated in the late thirties, during the heyday of big-band swing. Accelerated by the uncertainties of World War II, the development of this "new music"—later to be called bebop—seemed to swoop down on the unsuspecting public. The "bebop revolution" had taken place, promoted and debated in fan magazines throughout the forties and destined to affect virtually every aspect of American music.

The next chapter in this book lays out the specific ways in which bebop did indeed represent a radical departure from the music of the Swing Era (such as heavy harmonic experimentation, a new role for rhythm, smaller ensembles). But the emergence of bop also reflected an *evolution* in jazz, in that some of these ideas grew directly out of questions first asked in swing music. While many big-band adherents looked askance at bebop, and many boppers looked down on their predecessors, the battle lines were not so cleanly drawn. Fans of the Useful Lie, take note.

It could hardly have been otherwise. To start with, most of the musicians who carried these new ideas had gained their first experience in the very groups their music would replace—the big bands, whose popularity (and sheer size!) made them the obvious training ground for young players of the thirties. What's more, the jazz world revealed the presence of several transitional figures ("double agents"): members of the old guard who got the new sounds, as well as rebels who knew enough not to disrespect *all* their elders.

The recordings listed below prove this in the most straightforward way, since in all cases they involve fraternization between supposed "enemies": swing giants such as Coleman Hawkins and Lester Young mix easily with such Young Turks as Dizzy Gillespie and Thelonious Monk. Accordingly, the music has flux, a quality of being neither completely here nor there. To complete our analogy, it takes place in a sort of musical demilitarized zone. On the one hand, you can hear the first cries of a new idiom, and on the other, the efforts of the old as it stretches toward an uncertain, if exciting, future.

Don Byas, *Savoy Jam Party* (Savoy Jazz). In addition to having a name that lent itself to clever song titles—"Byas'd Opinion," "Byas a Drink," and the pronunciation-twisting "Donby" (as in "Don't Be")—tenor saxist Don Byas carried strong swing credentials into the forties. Originally a talented disciple of Coleman Hawkins, he had played in bands led by Lionel Hampton, Don Redman, and Count Basie by the time of these 1944–46 recordings. He had Hawkins's big sound and wide vibrato, and if anything, an even greater facility with the inner machinery of jazz harmonies. This last quality made his playing compatible with bebop. Before long, Byas had also begun to exhibit some of the rhythmic characteristics of bebop, although his phrasing remained for the most part rooted in the Swing Era. As you wend your way through the twenty-five selections on this single CD, you can hear bits of bop fluttering in and out of his solos. In addition, the bands he leads become more heavily weighted toward bop as the years pass, eventually including the excellent trumpeter Benny Harris and the greatest of bebop drummers, Max Roach. Those who believed that an impassable gulf separated the exemplars of swing and the firebrands of bebop had only to listen to recordings like these—particularly songs that the boppers had annexed, such as "How High the Moon" and "Cherokee"—to learn otherwise.

Charlie Christian, *Swing to Bop* (Natasha). If Charlie Christian had not died at the tender age of twenty-five, leaving only a handful of recordings, history would likely have made a still bigger fuss over him. Even so, he has earned a twofold niche in the evolution of jazz. In the late thirties, he became one of the first jazz guitarists—and certainly the most prominent—to play an electric (amplified) guitar, which elevated his solos to the same status as those of the horns and piano. (Previously, guitarists had strummed their naturally quiet instrument into an onstage or recording-studio microphone, which didn't help much.) In addition, no figure represents the transition of swing to bop better than Christian. For his "straight" gig, he played guitar in Benny Goodman's big band and small groups, but after hours he often headed uptown, to Minton's Playhouse in Harlem (see chapter 3), where he took part in the jam sessions conducted by Dizzy Gillespie, Thelonious Monk, and Charlie Parker—musical experiments that soon produced the new music, bebop. Christian brought to these sessions his sprightly ideas on harmony and on *chromaticism*, the use of previously unexpected sharps and flats in a melody line. These ideas imparted lively new colors to his improvisations and influenced his fellow proto-boppers. The loose-knit performances on this disc feature Gillespie, Monk, and Don Byas among others; dating from 1941, they capture the very moment when bebop started taking shape. (To hear Christian in his pure swing mode, get *The Genius of the Electric Guitar* on Columbia/Legacy, comprising sides made under Goodman's direction.)

Coleman Hawkins, *Rainbow Mist* (Delmark). The great tenor man had "big ears," to use a jazz term. He was the first famous swing musician to embrace the intrinsic musical value of bebop—the idiom that would soon supplant his own—by hiring two of bebop's inventors, pianist Thelonious Monk and trumpeter Dizzy Gillespie. In this collection of 1944 sessions, Gillespie plays on six tracks (along with Max Roach). One of them, "Woody'n You," was a durable Gillespie composition that became a bop classic, and it thus represents the first official recording of the "new music." The context is a twelve-piece jazz orchestra, closer in size to the Swing Era bands in which Hawkins first starred than to the small groups that would become the norm for bop. But the rhythm section features shades of bebop in the chattering cymbals, jabbing chords, and uneven accents that appear under Gillespie's solos; this too points to the "transition" nature of the music. The album's last session shows that a few others quickly grasped what Hawkins had heard in bop. Recorded around the same time, by a big band under the direction of tenorist Georgie Auld (an alumnus of Benny Goodman's bands), it boasts two players who would soon gain bop fame—saxist Al Cohn and trumpeter Howard McGhee—and, on a piece called "Concerto for Tenor," an arrangement that stands squarely between the smooth textures of the swing bands and the jumpy verve of bop. If you have trouble finding this album, go for Hawkins's *Bean and the Boys* (Prestige), which includes the October 1944 session at which Monk made his recording debut.

Woody Herman, *The Thundering Herds 1945–1947* (Columbia/Legacy). In the nearly three years covered by this collection, the popular reedman Woody Herman transformed his big band from a true swing outfit ("The Band That Plays the Blues") to a true bebop orchestra. This represented a total metamorphosis. On one end you have the foursquare swing and classic section writing of "Apple Honey," and the Glenn Miller groove of a tune like "Goosey Gander," with its now corny brass effects and Hamptonesque vibes solo. On the other, you have the volatile accents and hip harmonies of "The Goof and I" and "Four Brothers," two of the most convincing examples of big-band bop ever recorded. And in between lay stops at Ellingtonian exotica ("Bijou") and frantic prebop ("Backtalk"). Plenty of credit belonged to the composers and arrangers—pianist Ralph Burns, saxists Al Cohn and Jimmy Giuffre, and trumpeter Neal Hefti—but it was Herman who acted to reorganize his band in 1946 to meet the new music head-on. The Herd made bebop more commercially viable than did any other band and introduced such future stars as Stan Getz (tenor sax), Shorty Rogers (trumpet), Bill Harris (trombone), and Serge Chaloff (baritone sax).

Charlie Parker with Jay McShann and His Orchestra, *Early Bird* (Stash). Recommended—with reservations. Of these twenty-three tracks, fifteen feature Charlie Parker performing with the band that launched his career, led by the irresistible pianist and blues singer Jay McShann; but the sound quality of these "live" and radio takes, recorded in 1940 and 1942, ranges from okay to scratchy-poor. Once you get past that, you have a remarkable preview of things to come. This has little to do with McShann's band itself—a fine swing orchestra, and the last great band to emerge from Kansas City—and everything to do with Parker. His solos (the earliest Parker on disc) all but leap from the saxophone section; they fit their context, but at the same time, his phrasing and conception are utterly different from anything that preceded them. This duality helps you hear the ways in which bebop evolved from swing. The last eight sides on the album come from a 1944 broadcast made by McShann after Parker had left. They reveal a mixture of the band's older swing style and the influential new sounds that Parker, Gillespie, and Monk had started to create in after-hours jam sessions in Manhattan. In a way, this album could also fit in the next chapter, since Parker's solos on "Oh! Lady Be Good" and "Cherokee" represent the first contractions before the birth of the bebop.

Don Redman, *For Europeans Only* (SteepleChase). In 1946, the Swing Era pioneer Don Redman assembled a fourteen-piece orchestra to make an extensive European tour. For jazz lovers in many of the cities they visited, their concerts represented a *true* postwar "return to normalcy": the first appearance by a U.S. big band since the defeat of the Nazis a year earlier. What's more, these concerts also gave many listeners their first taste of the new sounds emanating from New York. Redman's repertoire included one composition (the title track) by the up-and-coming bebop composer Tadd Dameron; a blues called "Oo-Ba-Ba-La-Ba," which incorporates Charlie Parker's bop anthem "Anthropology"; and several other tunes that have at least inflections of bop (such as tenor saxist Don Byas's arrangement of "How High the Moon"). The band also included a handful of musicians—pianist Billy Taylor and a trumpeter named Alan Jeffries, in addition to Byas—with obvious sympathies toward bop. Their presence among more traditional-minded swing men, all under the baton of the open-minded Redman, makes the music a fine example of the crosscurrents circulating in jazz during this period. This concert took place in Copenhagen, the band's opening date, and the crowd went wild over the excellent performance. From this low-fidelity recording, we can only guess at how much better still the band sounded several concerts into the tour.

Lester Young, *The Complete Aladdin Sessions* (Blue Note). The first twenty minutes of this set come from a 1942 trio session featuring Nat "King" Cole, and the last session reunites Young with his old Basie bandmate vocalist Helen Humes. But in between lie thirty-one tracks that find the prebop tenor giant playing with the next generation—the young beboppers who had built upon some of Young's own musical discoveries—and this music proves the prophetic nature of his style. From the beginning, Young had employed a greater degree of rhythmic imagination than any of his contemporaries, which gave his improvisations a fantasy-world phraseology. Bebop rhythm sections employed a similar degree of rhythmic flexibility, and the ones heard here—which star such fine forgotten pianists as Joe Albany and Argonne Thornton—complement Young as swing players never could. Along with his phrasing, the milky, introspective tone of Young's tenor embodied the concept of "cool" (see chapter 4), another quality admired by the boppers—and another reason these bigenerational groupings sound so compatible. Young's solos on "These Foolish Things" (from 1945), "It's Only a Paper Moon" (1946), and the blues "Easy Does It" (1947) are classics, and the presence of a fiery bop trumpeter named Shorty McConnell on the later tracks pushes them even more surely into the realm of bop. It's fortunate that this material exists on disc at all; unfortunately, it exists only as a full-priced double CD. But none of Young's other recordings offer this perfectly timed glimpse into the transition between swing and bebop.

The Bebop Era (Columbia/Legacy) gathers a baker's dozen tracks that show the evolution of swing to bop from the perspective of the late forties—*after* bop had already established itself. This apparent contradiction stems from the fact that, while musicians and aficionados would soon accept bebop as the next step in the evolution of jazz, the general listening public did not immediately share their zeal. But as Swing Era bandleaders such as Woody Herman, Gene Krupa, and Cootie Williams (all heard here) started to incorporate elements of bop into their own music, they helped the jazz world at large make the leap as well. This collection includes two tracks from the big band led by Claude Thornhill, a dance-band leader of the thirties who secured his place in jazz history by concentrating on the more impressionistic side of bebop, with the help of his arrangers Gil Evans and Gerry Mulligan (see chapter 4). It also includes tracks by Parker, Gillespie, and the young Miles Davis.

chapter three

Everybody's Boppin'*
1941–1955

There was neither a palace coup nor a ruling council—unless you want to count the unofficial junta of pianist Thelonious Monk, trumpeter Dizzy Gillespie, and saxist Charlie Parker. No bombs fell—except for the crisp, dark explosions dispatched from the drum sets of Kenny Clarke, Art Blakey, and Max Roach. And the closest thing to a rallying cry came in such nonsensical mottoes as "Oop-Pop-a-Da" and "Ool-Ya-Koo"—which, one has to admit, lack the reasoned indignation of "Give me liberty!" or "Remember the Alamo!"

But like any revolution, the bebop movement of the 1940s left the surrounding landscape strewn with smashed illusions and discarded icons. It had its champions and it created players of both major and minor roles. It fostered confusion too, and it battered egos among the old guard. Like any *successful* revolution, however, bebop also left behind fresh forms and modern constructs—as well as the newly discovered tools with which others could explore the idiom's legacy.

Boston served as the official birthplace of the American Revolution; for bebop, it was Minton's Playhouse, a jazz supper club in Harlem. Later accounts of the club suggest a smoky basement dive rife with new music and heroin. But Miles Davis, whose career took hold during the first flush of bebop's popularity, recalled that Minton's was in fact a "first-class" place

---

*"Everybody's Boppin'," written by modern jazz's "poet laureate," Jon Hendricks, was first recorded in 1959 by the vocal trio he cofounded, Lambert, Hendricks & Ross. Postdating the creation of bebop by nearly twenty years, it gives you some idea of bop's lasting effect on this century's music.

that drew "the cream of the crop of Harlem's black society." These people flocked to hear the swing artists who played there in the late thirties. But the music changed significantly after 1940, when a bandleader named Teddy Hill was hired to manage Minton's. Hill brought along some of the musicians with whom he had recently played—Dizzy Gillespie and Kenny Clarke among them—and then hired as the house pianist a largely self-taught musician with the unlikely cognomen of Thelonious Sphere Monk. After that, everything seemed to fall into place—particularly in the after-hours jam sessions that drew musicians from all over New York.

At these nightly events, the house musicians, along with Charlie Parker and such frequent visitors as the bassist Oscar Pettiford and the guitarist Charlie Christian, experimented with the new ideas and fresh formats that would coalesce into bebop—"the music of the future," as its exponents crowed in the modern-living euphoria that swept the USA after World War II. Because a nationwide recording ban had prevented the release of any new jazz for nearly two years, bebop evolved in relative secrecy from listeners outside New York. When records by Gillespie and Parker began showing up in 1945, it sounded to many as if this music had sprung full-blown from the head of Zeus. Nonetheless, history has come to view bebop as equal parts revolution and evolution. (See previous "transition" section.)

For one thing, most of the beboppers had gained their first experience and earned their living in the big swing orchestras. Parker had grown up in Kansas City as a groupie of the Count Basie Orchestra, and Gillespie had played in one of the most famous bands of the day, led by Cab Calloway. And although their improvisations took a radically different turn, the boppers still based their solos on such Swing Era staples as the blues and the popular songs of the day. Even their approach to rhythm, as set down by Kenny Clarke, had its roots in the style used by Basie's drummer, Jo Jones. Jones had transferred the basic beat to the cymbals from the bass drum, which he then used for explosive accents. The bebop drummers dramatically magnified this technique—their frequent use of those bass-drum accents became known as "dropping bombs"—while also inventing several new combinations of rhythms.

In fact, despite their real rebelliousness, the beboppers maintained a great respect for those members of the old guard who had inspired them, and for those who judged this new music on its own merits instead of its reputation or the mere fact that it offered something different. These sage elders included Lester Young, whose recorded solos the young Charlie Parker had learned by heart; pianist Art Tatum and saxist Coleman Hawkins, whose fearsome command of chords and their variations offered a treasure chest of ideas for the boppers; Count Basie, whose band starred Lester Young and Jo Jones, and whose own uncluttered keyboard style sowed the seeds of the bop piano style; and the unassailable Duke Ellington.

However it got there, bebop still represented a radically different music from the big-band swing that preceded it on the jazz family tree, and in several important ways.

- First, in place of the big bands—those sleek behemoths of the Swing Era—the beboppers used the smaller, quicker, and far more flexible combo as their primary vehicle. It most often featured five or six instruments: trumpet and saxophone (and sometimes trombone or a second sax), backed by piano, bass, and drums.
- Instead of the plush, consonant chords that supplied the harmonic underpinning for swing arrangements and even for swing's smaller groups, bebop harmonies had a stark and exciting edge. The bebop players stretched the harmonic envelope by using alternate chords as substitutes for the original harmonies. These chords were usually more complex, and they emphasized lively, colorful new combinations of notes that previous listeners considered too dissonant for jazz.
- The solos themselves relied more heavily on the harmonic foundation of each song than on the melodic structure built upon that foundation. In swing, an improviser usually spent most of his solo exploring variations drawn from the song's original melody—although he would ground his solo in the song's chord progression (the "changes," in musician's slang). But in bop, the musicians quickly abandoned a song's melody after playing it through once, instead basing their solos entirely on the underlying, previously "hidden" framework of chords. This allowed them to explore the relationships between

the chords—as well as the extended implications of the chords themselves—to a greater degree than their predecessors. The result was a startlingly new but perfectly logical approach to jazz improvisation.

- Instead of smooth and hummable melodies designed for dancing, the beboppers created angular tunes with unexpected accents and irregular phrases—and they expected people to listen, rather than jitterbug, to these songs and to the solos that followed. The boppers emerged as jazz's first "angry young men." They saw themselves as artists first and entertainers second, and they demanded that others respect them and their music accordingly.

One other aspect of bebop provided the most glaring difference between this new music and its ancestors. The boppers played at breakneck tempos—and they then played their improvisations faster still.

During the Swing Era, the music had kept to a basic pulse of quarter notes. In other words, if you patted your foot to the music, you'd most often settle on the central rhythm of four beats per each measure of music. The solos would double the rhythm to eighth notes, with the climactic moments finally reaching the level of sixteenth notes (that is, sixteen distinct notes within the measure of four beats).

But in bebop the music *started* with eighth notes. Most bebop songs sail along at a basic rhythm of eight notes to the measure (or "bar," in musician's slang). Even the written melodies that precede the solos contain some of those quicksilver sixteenth notes. In their solos, the musicians once again doubled the stakes, establishing sixteenth notes as the coin of the realm— and regularly making the leap to even faster notes in moments of breathtaking virtuosity.

The great swing-style tenor man Ben Webster reportedly confronted Charlie Parker, the first time he heard him, by grabbing away Parker's saxophone and exclaiming, "That horn ain't supposed to sound that fast!" And pianist/arranger Mary Lou Williams, a respected doyenne of the Swing Era, later remembered that "it sounded like Dizzy [Gillespie] was playing a million notes in one bar." Yet even at high speed, these musicians raised the art of musical allusion—the insertion into their solos of recognizable phrases from familiar songs—to new heights.

The beboppers proved that, in music and especially in jazz, "speed thrills." They used their hard-won ability to play fast tempos as a musical weapon, and also as a shield to fend off the less talented and the more old-fashioned players who sought to join their ranks. But mostly, they were adhering to the adage that artists serve as "the antennae of the [human] race." In the early 1940s, with the United States' entry into World War II, the pace of daily life began to accelerate, everywhere and forever. Because of the war effort, manufacturing, communications, the whole business of living, became faster and more furious. The world—especially the USA, and specifically New York City— had caught a buzz, and the beboppers picked up on it before almost anyone else.

The world had also started to shrink, and bebop reflected this as well, with the importation of exotic rhythms from other cultures, most notably the Afro-Latin rhythms of the West Indies (including Cuba and the Virgin Islands). Dizzy Gillespie deserves the credit for this development, having encountered such music sitting next to the Cuban-born Mario Bauza in the trumpet section of Cab Calloway's orchestra. When he formed his own big band, Gillespie included the spellbinding conga player Chano Pozo as part of the rhythm section.

Earlier, the simple two-step of traditional jazz had matched the hedonistic twenties, and the carefully regulated foursquare swing beat had fit the harder times of the thirties (while also providing the racy and elegant sound track with which one might escape the Depression). In the same way, bebop emerged as a response to the increasingly urban and faster-paced forties. Charlie Parker was actually recalling his introduction to a life-long heroin habit when he said, "The panic was on," but he might just as well have applied that description to bebop. And as Gillespie would comment years later:

"Music reflects the time in which you live. My music emerged in the war years, and it reflected those times in the music. Fast and furious . . . it might have looked and sounded like bedlam, but it really wasn't."

No lie there. In fact, later generations have come to regard bebop as "the academy"—the place a young musician goes to learn the technique and discipline for performing later styles of jazz. In much the same way that classical pianists study Bach and violinists start with Mozart and Haydn, few modern jazz musicians reach the point of breaking the rules before they have first *learned* the rules as laid down by Clarke, Gillespie, Parker, and Bud Powell (the piano genius who arrived at Minton's as a teenage protégé of Thelonious Monk).

Notice that Monk himself does not appear on this list. Although he stood witness at bebop's creation and wrote one of the idiom's most popular songs (the ballad " 'Round Midnight"), Monk and his music actually exist separately from bop. An iconoclast even among the rebels, Monk played in a quirky, herky-jerky, technically constrained style—a marked contrast to the standard bebop piano style of racing virtuosity and fluid filigrees that Bud Powell exemplified. Sounding in some ways like a throwback to prebop jazz styles (and even to pre*jazz* piano styles, such as blues and ragtime), Monk's playing has affected every important jazz musician since—even though few pianists have chosen to copy his technique. Rather, it is his body of compositions—more than a dozen of which have become essential components of the modern jazz repertoire—and the esthetic they represent that have made Monk one of the most enduring personalities in jazz.

The radical new sounds of bebop led to two quite different "reactionary" movements. The first of these saw a rekindling of interest in the very first jazz, the New Orleans style (by now known as Dixieland to all but its truest believers). More conservative listeners returned to the music of Louis Armstrong and the Chicago School, "discovered" previously little-known contemporaries of Louis Armstrong, and reveled to the sounds of revival bands of younger musicians playing in the older style— such as trumpeter Lu Watters and his influential Yerba Buena Jazz Band.

The second distinct reaction to bebop doesn't fit the definition of *reactionary* quite so easily: it offered a contemporaneous alternative, rather than a nostalgic return. In Chicago, the blind pianist, composer, and theorist-teacher Lennie Tristano began to attract a small coterie of students in the mid-forties. Tristano admired and even recorded with Charlie Parker, but his music eschewed many of the signal characteristics of bebop. Instead of jagged rhythms, it relied on evenly accented thematic lines and an understated beat. In place of vivid instrumental colors,

Tristano used two saxes and guitar to achieve smooth, unruffled textures. Tristano's "minimalist" approach allowed his musicians (and listeners) to focus on smaller shifts in rhythmic emphasis, and subtler shadings of melody, than would have been appropriate for bop. Nonetheless, they played at bop's fast tempos (and with a greater and stunning precision in Tristano's highly complicated ensemble passages). Introspective, less frenetic, and more cerebral than bop, Tristano's music was already headed toward the future, where it would become a cornerstone of the 1950s movement called cool.

The Discs

Charlie Parker, the soul of bebop—and in the opinion of many, the single greatest improviser in jazz history—played with unprecedented imagination on unexpected chord progressions at unimagined tempos. (Small wonder that after his death, the word went out, in conversation and scrawled on alley walls, that "Bird lives!" No one who had ever heard his dazzling music could reasonably accept his death.) Parker made virtually all of his records for three labels. Each has reissued these seminal recordings in a sometimes bewildering variety of packages aimed at a wide variety of listeners. The following offer the best introduction.

Yardbird Suite: The Ultimate Charlie Parker Collection (Rhino). If you buy only one collection of Parker's music, make it this double CD, which draws from five distinct sources to present the best-rounded portrait of Bird's music ever assembled. Half the tracks come from Parker's "middle period" (1946–48), when bop was no longer new but had not yet gained full acceptance from the jazz public. But this chronologically arranged set starts with a dozen classics from the dawn of bebop, such as the durable "Donna Lee," "Chasing the Bird" (one of dozens of titles that make reference to Parker's nickname, Bird), and "Koko," with a solo often considered Parker's masterpiece. You'll also find a half dozen of the classic collaborations—for instance, the lickety-split "Salt Peanuts" and the anthemic "Groovin' High"—recorded under Dizzy Gillespie's name; a few songs from Parker's last years; and three tracks, featuring Gillespie and Bud Powell, recorded at Birdland (the club named for Parker) and previously unavailable on CD. The studio-date sidemen include the young Miles Davis, stellar pianists from John Lewis to Duke Jordan to Dodo Marmarosa, guitarist Barney Kessel, and drummer Max Roach. Simply spectacular.

If you don't start with the above set, you'll want *The Legendary Dial Masters* (Stash), which contains the master take of almost every song Parker recorded for Dial Records during his "middle period" (half of which appear on *Yardbird Suite*). Parker's collaboration with the L.A.-based label mostly featured his working band of the time, but also fostered intriguing West Coast relationships with such musicians as pianist Erroll Garner and the fiery but somewhat overlooked trumpeter Howard McGhee. The thirty-five tracks on this double disc offer a cornucopia of legendary bebop melodies—"Relaxin' at Camarillo," "Dexterity," and "Moose the Mooche" (named after an L.A. heroin connection)—with solos as rich and varied as anything Bird ever recorded. And then there's the famous recording of Dizzy Gillespie's exotic "A Night in Tunisia," one of the most played of bebop themes. On it, Parker begins his solo with a flurry of notes so densely compressed that it seems to defy time: a star turn so remarkable that the company later issued these few measures on a separate track, so that listeners could more easily turn directly to them.

Confirmation: Best of the Verve Years (Verve). Parker died at the age of thirty-four (in 1955), a victim of the hard living that resulted from his huge appetites for food, liquor, drugs, and sex. Because of that, his "mature period" follows his "middle period" by just a couple of years. In the late forties, Parker began recording for the producer Norman Granz, who placed him in many different contexts. But whether fronting big bands or a quartet, backed by a vocal choir or the "legit" accompaniment of orchestral strings, heard with Afro-Cuban percussion or reunited with Gillespie and Monk, Bird's sculptured sound and juggernaut musicianship defined the occasion. On this double CD, you hear Parker in total command of the style that he cofounded, and every solo flows like liquid platinum. You also get the greatest ornithological variety: a panorama of Bird, in all of the contexts just mentioned. (If you're on a tight budget, about a third of these tracks can be found on the single-disc

Bird's Best Bop on Verve, which sticks to the small groups and omits the Afro-Cuban tunes.)

Ella Fitzgerald, *Ella at the Opera House* (Verve). Fitzgerald achieved her first stardom in the Swing Era, and in the 1950s, she extended that reputation to become a household name—even in *non*jazz households. In between these periods came bebop; but Fitzgerald had no trouble adapting her scat-singing abilities to the new idiom. This CD brings together two separate jam-session concerts featuring Fitzgerald with other swing icons respected by the beboppers—such as Coleman Hawkins and Lester Young—performing tunes that had inspired the musicians of both idioms. The complexity of bop actually brought a new demand for Fitzgerald's improvisatory genius. And her willingness to meet that demand made Fitzgerald the only major vocalist to bridge swing and bebop, unique in her ability to match musical wits with Benny Goodman and Duke Ellington on one hand, and Charlie Parker and pianist Oscar Peterson on the other. (Just one other singer in the 1940s, the slightly younger Sarah Vaughan, earned the same measure of respect for her bop musicianship.)

If the brilliant and messy Charlie Parker provided bebop's soul, the crafty and disciplined John Birks "Dizzy" Gillespie was its head. Diz himself called Bird "the other half of my heartbeat." (Jazz had seen only a couple such partnerships: Louis Armstrong and Earl Hines, Django Reinhardt and Stephane Grappelli, and Billie Holiday and Lester Young.) For his great early bop records, see the Parker sets described above; but because he lived and continued to perform into the 1990s, Gillespie's discography offers a great deal more to choose from. Nonetheless, his music did not evolve substantially after the early sixties, making most of his later dates valuable primarily for the appearance of Gillespie with other jazz giants or in innovative contexts, such as his multicultural United Nation Orchestra of the 1980s.

The Complete RCA Victor Recordings (Bluebird). Gillespie's nickname and antics made him the public face of bebop, but beneath the clowning beamed a trumpet virtuoso almost without peer in the history of jazz. This double disc provides a great place to start and to experience some of the full-blown excitement of bebop. While it features a few of Gillespie's earliest recordings, from 1937 and 1939, it concentrates on the sensational big band that he organized in 1946. (The recordings that paired Gillespie and Parker, and that actually served as bebop's birth announcement, are available under Parker's name.) Fueled by arrangements from some of the brightest young writers, Gillespie's big band burned with the accelerated solos from future bebop legends James Moody (tenor sax), Milt Jackson (vibraphone), and Cecil Payne (baritone sax). Gillespie himself could combine his penchant for high-speed, high-note solos with his lifelong love of the orchestral setting.

The Champ (Savoy). For a brief time after the demise of his second big band, Gillespie ran one of the first musician-owned labels—Dee Gee Records—where he recorded several songs that would remain in his repertoire for decades. Among them were the title song from this album of 1951 sessions and the simple but catchy blues line called "Birks' Works," one of his most popular tunes. On these tracks, you hear bebop in full flower. It had achieved status as the jazz idiom for the fifties, and with the inclusion of some entertaining vocals and even some standard tunes from earlier eras, Gillespie confidently assumed his place among the great movers and shakers in jazz. The cast of characters features Milt Jackson, Art Blakey, guitarist Kenny Burrell, and a twenty-four-year-young John Coltrane. In general, the Savoy reissues restrict themselves to the original vinyl records' contents, making the CDs surprisingly short—this one runs about thirty-five minutes—but this is reflected in a lower-than-average list price.

For Musicians Only (Verve). On this 1956 session, Gillespie shared the microphone with two of the bop era's most brilliant soloists: saxist Sonny Stitt (on alto), whom some considered the keeper of Charlie Parker's flame, and the unique tenor man Stan Getz, who brought the melodic purity of previous eras to his interpretation of bebop. Perhaps spurred by the memory of Parker, who had died nineteen months before this recording, they challenged each other on every hell-bent solo. And they spent plenty of time doing so. The advent of the long-playing album (in 1953) did away with three-minute records and the concomitant two-chorus solos. The tracks on this session average ten minutes each, allowing for extended expression and some of the most spectacular examples of bebop improvisation anywhere.

Dizzy's Diamonds: The Best of the Verve Years (Verve) offers the best overall picture of Diz, even though it's not all bebop. This three-CD set divides into one disc of small-group recordings and all-star collaborations; another featuring tracks from the several big bands Gillespie led during the decade (1954–64) he recorded for Verve; and a third CD that focuses on recordings influenced by Afro-Cuban and South American music. Gillespie doesn't play the same way in each context. On such straight-ahead bop tunes as "Ool-Ya-Koo" and "Dizzy Atmosphere," he re-creates the distinctive, flamboyant melodic contours that contrasted with Parker's when they discovered bebop in the 1940s. But with the big bands, he often soars into the stratosphere like the lead trumpet player he once was, in the jazz orchestras of the thirties; and on the Latin material, his trumpet often seems to giggle and whisper as it saunters to the infectious rhythms. More than anyone else, Gillespie proved that the idiosyncratic details of bebop could find a home in many contexts for the rest of this century, and *Diamonds* provides a good chunk of the evidence.

Dexter Gordon, *The Chase!* (Stash). Dexter Gordon was among the first to adapt Charlie Parker's innovations from the alto sax to the deeper tenor saxophone, but "Long Tall Dexter" did more. (He stood six foot five inches, and the tenor sax often appeared to be just a large toy in his hands.) He based his style of playing on the two prevailing models of the 1930s: his huge sound and harmonic ingenuity reflected the playing of Coleman Hawkins, but his use of little (if any) vibrato, and the lean and whimsical quality of his melodies, recalled the quixotic grace of Lester Young. In fusing these two seminal influences, Gordon created a style that became the major influence on the *next* generation of tenor players (particularly John Coltrane and Sonny Rollins). He also made one of the bebop era's signature recordings, "The Chase" (with fellow bop tenorist Wardell Gray). It epitomized the competitive "cutting contests" in which bop musicians, like their Swing Era predecessors, took turns trying to outsolo each other. That tune and another "battle of the saxes" highlight this set of (unfortunately low-fidelity) 1947 recordings.

Dexter Gordon, *Our Man in Paris* (Blue Note). To a significant degree, Gordon's career proved the long-term possibilities of the idiom he had mastered. He never stopped playing bebop, but from the beginning, Gordon's relaxed, loping style lent itself to longer expositions (as in "The Chase"). Thus, like Dizzy Gillespie, he blossomed with the advent of the long-playing album. In addition, Gordon proved adaptable: as the 1960s progressed, his style borrowed some of the stylistic breakthroughs of the younger John Coltrane, who counted Gordon as a prime influence on his own playing. Gordon recorded widely for a number of labels from the 1960s till he died in 1990, but this foreign affair remains one of the most striking. It reunited him with pianist Bud Powell, and perhaps in honor of the occasion, Dex plays with a harder edge and a sharper focus than on most of his albums from this period. On the bop classic "A Night in Tunisia," his solo spirals up into one of his most impassioned and personal performances. While other albums project more of his deceptively carefree approach to improvisation (see chapter 4), you won't find a better example of Gordon's captivating power than this recording. The cover photo alone almost justifies the cost of the album—a lean, taut-skinned profile, taken shortly after Gordon had recovered from heroin addiction, that suggests a proud African prince of the realm. (This French connection helped prepare him for his Oscar-nominated role as an expatriate jazzman in the 1986 film *Round Midnight*.)

Woody Herman, *Keeper of the Flame* (Capitol Jazz). Woody Herman embraced bebop with sincerity and skill, transforming his excellent swing orchestra into a dynamic and innovative bebop big band. By 1947 he had incorporated a tough new sound that starred a tight-knit unit of three tenor saxophones (instead of the usual two) and the even deeper baritone sax—a sax section that took its nickname from their featured highlight, a song called "Four Brothers." That tune is found on another CD (see the transition section "Swing 2 Bebop," following chapter 2). This collection begins with sessions made two years later, but it presents what everyone called the Four Brothers Band, officially known as the Second Herd, in full stampede. Such songs as "Lemon Drop" became part of bebop legend, while the ballad playing of the young Stan Getz made him an overnight star. In addition, the writing of arranger Ralph Burns achieved a separate reputation for its symphonic overtones. Herman himself played a middling clarinet, sounded a little better on alto sax, and occasionally sang; he wrote only a few tunes, and even fewer arrangements. Nonetheless, he assembled one band after another of brilliant soloists and allowed hot young arrangers to shape their sound and direction into the 1980s.

Milt Jackson, *Opus de Jazz* (Savoy). As bebop began to filter down from alto sax and trumpet to the entire instrumental family, Milt Jackson arrived with a distant cousin: the vibraphone (the electrically enhanced version of the xylophone that Lionel Hampton had introduced to jazz in the 1930s). Jackson's transformation of his instrument into a vehicle for bebop remains the most pronounced of the era. He took the staccato, often clanky-sounding vibraphone and created a flowing, lyrical style that most people had never imagined possible on the instrument, dramatically expanding the vibraphone's interpretive range and emotional appeal. He did this by using softer mallets, a slower electrically produced tremolo, and solo phrases that "breathed" in the same places as the hornmen's. Beyond that, Jackson soon emerged as one of the greatest bebop soloists on *any* instrument, his improvisations providing a model of sustained development and the essence of unflappable cool. This famous album, recorded in 1955, shows off the then-new LP format with a thirteen-minute title track starring flutist Frank Wess (of the Count Basie band).

You can best describe Thelonious Monk as bebop's midwife: he assisted in the birth, but the baby didn't look much like him. As both composer and pianist, Monk was an iconoclast whose music stood outside the standard parameters of bebop. The quirky, cantilevered construction of his songs represented a high-water mark for bebop and made him the most important jazz composer after Duke Ellington. And his rigorous discipline, as heard in his minimalist solos, helped shape the talents of the musicians who played with him, including (most notably) the saxists John Coltrane, Sonny Rollins, and Johnny Griffin.

Genius of Modern Music, Vol. 1 (Blue Note) showcases fourteen different tunes. Monk wrote ten of them, including several that remain among his best-known and most-played tunes: "Well You Needn't," "Off Minor," the humorous "Thelonious" (where most of the melody line consists of one repeated note), "In Walked Bud" (a jaunty line named for Bud Powell), and

"Ruby My Dear." But these 1947 recordings are the originals, and in revealing how Monk first conceived these songs, they give the listener a striking sense of the creator's stamp—almost like receiving a phone call from Alexander Graham Bell. This is most evident on " 'Round Midnight," which in subsequent recordings by other musicians became a pristine paean to the night. Monk, however, plays it as a blowsy, roadhouse slow-dance, smoky and earthy at the same time. This disc and its companion (*Genius, Vol. 2*) contain almost all of Monk's important early compositions, each a miniature marvel of construction and originality.

Brilliant Corners (Fantasy/OJC). This irresistible album, released in 1957, had much to do with earning Monk a wider reputation among the general public. Shortly after recording it, he began an extended New York engagement with a quartet starring John Coltrane, which gave Monk a career boost that landed him on the cover of *Time* magazine for a 1962 article headlined "The High Priest of Bebop." The long-playing record made it possible for a great quintet—featuring Monk's former Minton's Playhouse colleagues Oscar Pettiford on bass and Max Roach on drums, along with the exciting young saxist Sonny Rollins—to stretch out on two new classics-to-be, "Bemsha Swing" and "Ba-lue Bolivar Ba-lues-Are." The LP format also allowed Monk to expand his compositional arena: the title track is a tempo-shifting, stop-start composition so tricky that the band never got it right all the way through. (The producer drew from some twenty-five takes to edit together the version heard on disc.) The cover photo—with Monk in beret and shades, folded into a child's wagon making a sharp turn—exhibits the same eccentric humor as the music itself.

Criss Cross (Columbia/Legacy) provides a wonderful glimpse of the quartet that Monk led throughout the sixties: his last important band, and perhaps the best band he ever had. It starred tenor man Charlie Rouse, whose improvisations had a looping logic that made them especially compatible with Monk's music. His predecessors in this quartet, Coltrane and Griffin, remain the larger figures in jazz history; but Rouse's start-stop phrasing and blunt tone made his style the saxophone analogue to Monk's pianistics. Both Rouse and Monk turn in trademark solos on Monk's "Rhythm-a-Ning"—a prototypical Monk composition in that it defines simplicity without being simplistic. The album also includes two examples of his quirky solo piano, a delightfully odd and unmistakable mix of stride style, blues tonality, modernistic harmonies, and ironic sentimentality.

Fats Navarro and Tadd Dameron, *The Complete Blue Note and Capitol Recordings* (Blue Note). The marvelous trumpeter Theodore "Fats" Navarro was another bebopper who died tragically young—at twenty-seven, from tuberculosis (augmented by the weakened condition that comes with heroin addiction). Navarro's slipstream virtuosity combined with his contemplative improvisations to make him a serious rival to Dizzy Gillespie as bop's greatest trumpeter. His broad, open tone, along with the forceful sweep of his solo lines, recaptured some of the decorum of Swing Era instrumentalists. So even though his music never wavered from the founding principles of bebop, it never sounded quite as frantic as that of his colleagues. After recording with Parker and Coleman Hawkins, Navarro worked most often (and most comfortably) in bands led by pianist Tadd Dameron, a major bebop composer whose long-lined tunes and relaxed tempos best suited Navarro's personality. This set presents spectacular examples of both Navarro's fluid soloing ("The Squirrel," "Lady Bird") and Dameron's gracious writing ("Our Delight," "Casbah"). There's also a session co-led by Navarro and Howard McGhee (another top-notch bop trumpeter), and an important Bud Powell date starring Navarro and the young Sonny Rollins. The inclusion of no less than thirteen alternate takes stretches this material to two discs and makes a pricey introduction to these musicians' work; but in terms of musical excellence and the clarity of sound, it gets the nod over anything else currently available.

Fiery, erratic, intense, and absolutely brilliant, Bud Powell brought to the piano the same ferocious technique that Charlie Parker brought to the saxophone. Indeed, Powell was the first bebop pianist to match the pyrotechnics of the great horn players. Because of that, some people see him as the man who "transferred" Parker's style to the keyboard, but that misses Powell's own distinctive musical persona. His compositions develop in ways different from his colleagues', and his solos never sound like "Parker on piano." They belonged *to* the piano and really couldn't reside in any other instrument. Powell employed the same musical language as Parker, but he used it to tell a much different story, and his solos reveal a strikingly unique musical intellect. His mad-hatter genius can take the breath away even today, more than three decades after his death at age forty-one.

The Best of Bud Powell on Verve (Verve). From 1949 through 1955, Powell's trio recordings on the Verve label cemented his reputation while producing some of the most spectacular piano music ever heard in *any* idiom, including classical music. On this collection, you can also hear how Powell's music encompassed both the promise and the threat of bebop. His daredevil arrangements of such songs as "Tea for Two" and his own compositions (the knuckle-busting "Tempus Fugue-It," in particular) pushed the bebop envelope, taking Powell to an almost anarchic musical frontier and hinting at a later development— "free jazz" (see chapter 5)—that would shatter bebop's principles. In Powell's music, more than that of any other musician, you can hear bebop sowing the seeds of its own obsolescence.

The Best of Bud Powell (Blue Note) gathers together recordings of Powell's earliest and later trios as well as of the quintet with which he recorded four famous sides in 1949. The early tracks come from the first recording session under his own name, when he was just twenty-two; not far removed from his best records, they show his stellar command of both the piano and bebop. But Powell had begun to evidence a progressive nervous disorder in his early twenties, and by the mid-1950s it had seriously affected his playing. Although still capable of great and even incisive music, he could no longer summon the superhuman technique of his days at Minton's Playhouse. These later recordings have a dark, dense quality: the ballads brood, and even buoyant up-tempo tunes have an inner gravity that speaks of the pianist's personal demons. No one counts such tracks among Powell's best, but they still carry a dramatic and distinct power.

Sonny Stitt, *Endgame Brilliance* (32 Jazz). From his earliest recordings, Sonny Stitt displayed a prodigious mastery of the bebop language, a full and flexible tone, and about all the technique you could ask for. But when he first arrived, in the 1940s, he played primarily alto sax, the instrument personified by Charlie Parker, and he suffered the predictable consequences of evoking comparison to a god. (Parker himself, shortly before he died, reportedly offered Stitt "the keys to the kingdom," signifying his passage of the bop-alto torch.) By the mid-fifties, Stitt was giving equal attention to his light and spectacular tenor playing—in part to deflect such comparisons, and in part because of his penchant for friendly two-tenor "battles" with his frequent partner, Gene Ammons. Although he received much-deserved respect throughout his career, Stitt's recordings of the fifties and sixties proved inconsistent (if often exciting)—which explains the inclusion of this album, from the early 1970s, in a chapter about the 1940s. *Endgame Brilliance* contains the contents of two extraordinary LPs—*Constellation* and *Tune-up!*—on which Stitt distilled and bottled his style. The album features old standby tunes, and his solos, on both alto and tenor saxes, offer the favored riffs and personal clichés that he had used for decades; but on these two records, he strung them together in perfect balance with breathtaking command. Gathered together on this single CD, they not only define Sonny Stitt, but go a long way toward defining bop lyricism as well.

Lennie Tristano & Warne Marsh, *Intuition* (Capitol/EMI). You can just about take your pick when it comes to classifying Lennie Tristano's music. By chronology, it surely belongs in a chapter on bebop, but considering the basic thrust of the music, it could as easily fit into the next chapter, which covers "cool jazz"; and two of the tracks on this collection qualify as the first true *unstructured improvisations*, predating the revolutionary "free jazz" of Ornette Coleman by a decade (see chapter 5). Those tracks—on which the musicians played without any pre-set melody, chord structure, or rhythm pattern—were recorded in 1949 by Tristano's extraordinary and influential sextet. The same group also took the more traditional approach to five of Tristano's densely packed compositions, with dazzling solo work by his leading students, alto saxist Lee Konitz and tenor saxist Warne Marsh. Konitz later joined with Miles Davis to usher in cool jazz. Marsh, a somewhat underrecognized soloist and teacher in his own right, maintained closer ties to Tristano and took part in the 1956 quintet sessions that make up the rest of this album. Both men had mellowed slightly in the intervening years. But thanks to the intense, long-lined piano solos, and the inspired interplay between Marsh and a second tenor saxist, you can hardly find a better exposition of the Tristano school.

Sarah Vaughan, *Swingin' Easy* (EmArcy). The best of all? No jazz singer ever possessed a better "instrument" than Sarah Vaughan's. With her huge range and dramatic interpretative abilities, she might just as easily have succeeded as an operatic diva. And with its smoky, almost three-dimensional texture, her voice hit with the startling immediacy of Charlie Parker's alto saxophone. Vaughan first popped up with the short-lived be-bop big band led by singer Billy Eckstine in the mid-forties. There she met Parker and Gillespie, with whom she recorded in 1944–45, at the dawn of bop. A decade later she recorded the session that forms the bulk of this album, with several more tracks done in 1957. All in all, fourteen of the most exuberant, exacting vocal performances you've ever heard; they nonetheless have a relaxed grace, thanks to Vaughan's rhythmic authority (which allowed her to swing with the best, and which few have equaled). And on such tunes as "Shulie a Bop," "If I Knew Then," and "All of Me," you can hear why Vaughan's scat improvising took a backseat only to Ella Fitzgerald's. While her astute musicality had gained her access to bop's inner circle, Vaughan's voluptuous style soon extended beyond bop, and by the late fifties she was earning fame, fortune, and eventually a congressional resolution for her pop-music allure. (Nothing can start the juices flowing like Sassy singing ballads backed by sentimental strings.) Nonetheless, the Divine Sarah (another of her nicknames) continued to sing jazz throughout her career, and even her nonjazz recordings gleam with subtle melodic turns, and not-so-subtle swoops and glides, that remind you of her spectacular improvisational abilities.

Rebop

The anthology *Bebop's Greatest Hits* (Rhino), part of the label's "Masters of Jazz" series, groups many of the specific performances described above. It includes seven tracks starring Parker and Gillespie; the famous "Chase" by Gordon & Gray; Monk's original recording of " 'Round Midnight"; gems by

Bud Powell, Lester Young, and George Shearing; and a couple of tunes that bridge bebop and the decade that followed.

You can also hear five of the greatest of these musicians—Parker, Gillespie, Powell, drummer Max Roach, and bassist Charles Mingus (who really belongs to the next chapter)—in an all-star quintet recorded at a 1953 concert in Toronto. It once bore the immodest title *The Greatest Jazz Concert Ever*; it now exists as *The Quintet: Jazz at Massey Hall* (Fantasy/OJC), usually listed under Parker's name.

As bebop burgeoned, so did the recordings of Ella Fitzgerald. (And her greatest popularity lay still further in the future: see chapter 4.) Much of the greatest jazz singing you'll ever hear takes place on these recordings of the fifties and early sixties: the studio dates *Clap Hands, Here Comes Charlie* and *Ella Swings Lightly* (featuring terrific arrangements for ten-piece band); the concert recording *Mack the Knife: The Complete Ella in Berlin Concert* (with a title-track scat solo that made it a top-selling hit); and the hypnotically romantic *Like Someone in Love* (all on Verve). *Pure Ella* (Decca/GRP) finds her in more intimate surroundings—just voice and piano—in the early fifties. A great place to start would be *First Lady of Song* (Verve), a three-CD compilation issued during the year-long celebration of Fitzgerald's seventy-fifth birthday in 1992.

Tenor saxist Stan Getz's unique contributions primarily belong to later chapters, but his early recordings—in addition to his work on Gillespie's *For Musicians Only* (mentioned above)—reveal a highly personal adaptation of bebop. *The Roost Quartets* (Roulette Jazz), recorded 1950–51, feature Getz's purest bebop outside of his solos with the "Four Brothers Band" of Woody Herman, while on *Stan Getz Plays* (Verve), recorded a year later, he led a quintet that helped establish Jimmy Raney, perhaps the most influential of bop-forged guitarists.

Dizzy Gillespie grew up in the big bands of the 1930s and never lost his love for that format, continuing to assemble and lead large jazz orchestras at various times throughout his life. The most exciting remain the earliest ones, imbued with the fresh spirit of bebop, as heard on the 1948 *Dizzy Gillespie and His Big Band in Concert* (GNP Crescendo). A decade later, Gillespie led an especially star-studded big band at the nation's premier jazz festival, captured on *At Newport* (Verve). In later years, his quintets mostly honed the mix of bebop and Latin jazz that he had crafted in the 1940s, as on *Dizzy's Party* (Fantasy/OJC). You'd also do well to consider *The Cool World—Dizzy Goes Hollywood* (Verve), which compresses two LPs by his fine early-sixties band onto one CD. As a soloist, he took part in several good all-star reunions, with *The Giant* (Accord)—featuring saxist Johnny Griffin and the archetypal bop drummer, Kenny Clarke—standing above the rest.

Dexter Gordon's *Dexter Rides Again* (Savoy) collects three studio sessions into a good (but short—just over thirty-five minutes) lesson in vintage bop tenor, ca. 1947. You can hear his progression from the early strictures of bebop to that idiom's second generation on *Daddy Plays the Horn* (Bethlehem). (Other albums by Gordon crop up in the next chapter.)

Gordon's contemporary, the Chicago tenor man Gene Ammons, has faded from latter-day scrutiny, but his broad soulful sound and advanced harmonies deserve better. *Young Jug* (Chess/GRP) features tracks from 1948–52 and shows him in great bop form. *Boss Tenor* lets him stretch out and features his pop-music hit "Canadian Sunset"; by the sixties, he was drawing from Chicago's rich blues scene to become a premier exponent of soul jazz, as heard on *The Gene Ammons Story: Organ Combos*. (Both of these are on Fantasy.)

Best vibes: Milt Jackson first recorded as a member of Gillespie's big band, and in the early 1950s, he joined with other members of that band's rhythm section to form the Modern Jazz Quartet (see chapter 4). Among the purest of bebop players, his melodic strengths have nonetheless proved adaptable to a number of subsequent developments, so you can't go wrong with such subsequent albums as his 1960 meeting with John Coltrane, *Bags & Trane* (Atlantic); his 1962 matchup with pianist Oscar Peterson, *Very Tall* (Verve); his 1972 flirtation with soft-core fusion music, *Sunflower* (CTI/Columbia); or his in-concert jam session *Montreux '77* (Fantasy).

So much Monk, so little time. *Plays Duke Ellington* introduced the general bop-loving public to the idea that Monk's music might not be too "way-out" for them after all. *Monk* is short in minutes, long on brilliance; *Monk With Coltrane* features the band that elevated Monk's profile while helping to change Coltrane's music and life; *Misterioso* chronicles a justly famous 1958 engagement at the Five Spot nightclub in New York, featuring tenor saxist Johnny Griffin. To hear Monk's highly stylized, almost semiotic solo work, it's *Thelonious Himself*. They're all on Fantasy/OJC, and also part of the fifteen-CD extravaganza *Thelonious Monk: The Complete Riverside Recordings* (Riverside).

For more of the band with Charlie Rouse, get *Underground* or *Straight, No Chaser* (the original mid-sixties album and not the film sound track of the same name). And the double CD *Big Band and Quartet in Concert* chronicles a 1963 program in which Monk's music was most successfully translated to large ensemble (actually, ten pieces including Monk at the piano).

One of the most talented and enduring boppers is reedman James Moody. After playing tenor sax in Gillespie's big band, he switched to alto on a recording of "I'm in the Mood for Love" (which became one of the era's biggest hits), and shortly after he became one of the first and best-ever jazz flutists. For Moody's early style, try *New Sounds* (Blue Note), filed under "Art Blakey & James Moody" (the album features both men's groups: ten tracks from Moody, five from Blakey). In the sixties, Moody worked on and off with Gillespie's bands, as on Gillespie's *Dizzy Gillespie in Europe* (RTE), where he stars on flute. Several years later he made one of his finest and most fiery recordings, *Feelin' It Together* (32 Jazz). His solos, clearly influenced by later developments in jazz, showed how far a vintage bopper could push the idiom while remaining true to it.

For more Parker, you don't have to look far: virtually every note he ever played in a studio as well as many bootlegged live performances have made their way onto disc. It all depends on how deeply you want to delve. *Bird: The Complete Charlie Parker on Verve* amasses all of Parker's appearances for the label on ten CDs totaling eleven hours of music. *The Complete Dean Benedetti Recordings of Charlie Parker* (Mosaic) contains the low-fidelity tapes made by a noted Parker groupie, who followed the saxist from city to city with a primitive portable recorder—turning it off whenever Parker wasn't soloing to save tape! (As a result, you hear only snippets of songs, spread out over seven CDs—worth studying for the devotee, and difficult to appreciate for everyone else.)

Other live sets make the listening less arduous. *Bird & Fats at Birdland* (Cool N' Blue) documents a 1950 gig in which Parker and Fats Navarro locked horns at the Manhattan jazz club named in honor of Parker. The justifiably famous *Jazz at the Philharmonic, 1949* (Verve) finds Bird onstage with his idol Lester Young and other Swing Era greats—in one of the jam-session concerts that swept jazz in the late 1940s and 1950s—and Parker rises to the occasion. One of the best live performances, *Boston 1952* (Uptown), features several remarkable solos from two radio programs done in 1952 and 1954.

The best single-session CD from the Verve years remains *Bird and Diz*, the 1953 reunion of bebop's cocreators: Parker, Gillespie, *and* Monk.

The two Bud Powell discs recommended above draw from larger collections, the five-CD *Complete Bud Powell on Verve* and the four-CD *Complete Blue Note & Roost Recordings* respectively. Both have their definite virtues, although both contain a fair amount of material that fails to meet Powell's own standards (as you'd expect in the work of someone plagued by personal and artistic inconsistencies). But also consider two other single discs. *Jazz Giant* (Verve) includes five of the tracks found on *The Best of Bud Powell on Verve*, but also a few gems that didn't make it onto that anthology. And *'Round about Midnight at the Blue Note* (Dreyfus), recorded in Paris in 1962, makes clear that even near the end of his life, Powell could occasionally show the old genius.

In 1946 the blind British pianist George Shearing moved to New York, completed his re-education as a bebop pianist, and helped popularize the idiom with his quintet. The band's lithe swing—along with its cool clustered mix of piano, guitar, and vibraphone—helped make bop palatable to almost everyone. All of the band's important work is now available on *Lullaby of Birdland* (Verve), titled for Shearing's best-known composition.

Frank Sinatra never lost his love for jazz, and it animates a couple of recordings that stand apart from even the best of his pop work. In 1963 *Sinatra & Basie* (Reprise) finally brought to-gether two of the most potent forces in postwar music—the Voice and the Count—for an album that stands out in each man's discography. And on *Frank Sinatra with the Red Norvo Quintet Live in Australia, 1959* (Blue Note), the intimate setting pushes Sinatra closer to real jazz than on any other recording.

Vintage Sonny Stitt includes the anthology under his name on the "Compact Jazz" series from Verve, with many of his best performances of the fifties, and *Stitt Plays Bird* (Rhino), an al-most impressionistic homage to Charlie Parker recorded in 1964. An equally exciting but largely forgotten alto man, Sonny Criss, barely recorded in the forties and fifties, but on the ap-propriately titled *Out of Nowhere* (32 Jazz), recorded in 1975, he made up for lost time.

On *Sarah Vaughan in Hi-Fi* (Columbia), eight tunes (and their alternate takes) tie the great singer to bebop more strongly than anything else available. Recorded in 1950, these tracks surround her voice with a bop-based big band (with guest soloist Miles Davis). *Sarah Vaughan (with Clifford Brown)* also conveys the spirit of the time, as she wraps her voice in a loose-knit sextet, while the double-disc *Sassy Swings the Tivoli*, recorded in 1963, shows her awe-inspiring onstage style; both are on EmArcy. The EmArcy material comes from the Mercury Records vaults, which spill onto no less than twenty-three CDs spread over four volumes of *The Complete Sarah Vaughan on Mercury*. Volumes 1 and 3 are best from a jazz perspective.

Like Ella Fitzgerald, Anita O'Day made a smooth transition from swing (she first sang prominently with Gene Krupa's big band) to bebop. *Pick Yourself Up* (Verve) showcases her sparkling improvisational instincts, the flirtatious sexuality of her cool phrasing, and her huge debt to Billie Holiday.

Other vocalists played a role in the development of bop, the most important being Eddie Jefferson, who began fitting lyrics to the recorded improvisations of Coleman Hawkins, Lester Young, and James Moody and thus invented the vocal idiom called *vocalese*. His album *The Jazz Singer* (Evidence) contains several fine examples. The vocalist known as King Pleasure had the most success with vocalese, and *Moody's Mood for Love* (Blue Note)—with the title track featuring Jefferson's words and James Moody's music, as well as Pleasure's "It Might As Well Be Spring"—shows you why. In later years, the trio Lambert, Hendricks & Ross (next chapter) and the pop quartet the Manhattan Transfer would keep this particular flame alive.

Finally, Billy Eckstine did much more than simply introduce Sarah Vaughan to the world. In the Swing Era, his deep velvet baritone served as the African-American equivalent to Frank Sinatra's sigh-inducing ballad style; but Eckstine's bottomless feel for the blues, along with his appreciation for bebop, made him a real jazzman. In 1944, he went so far as to form the first bebop big band, which at various times featured Parker, Gillespie, Miles Davis, Dexter Gordon, and Art Blakey. You can hear most of them in the post-1945 recordings collected on *Mr. B and the Boys* (Savoy). For Eckstine the crooner, it's either the single-CD *No Cover, No Minimum* (Roulette) or the rangy and delightful two-CD collection *Everything I Have Is Yours* (Verve).

chapter four

Cool Blues (Hot Blues)*
1953–1965

As those who grew up during the 1950s will recall (and students of history can discover), the visual iconography of that decade contained a couple of telling images. In one of them, a small dark circle sat at the center of several elongated ovals that depicted the elliptical orbits of electrons. At the other end of the scale, the world gaped with wonder at photos and illustrations of an eerily seductive cloud, shaped like a giant mushroom, on the far horizon. Viewed from supposedly safe distances by military and civilian observers, it manifested the glorious power signified by the smaller picture. Both were symbols of the new Atomic Age—an era when mankind's ability to pulverize the tiniest bits of matter would yield incredible benefits for all.

Now try replacing that little picture of the atom with the compact and mighty music called bebop. In the *musical* iconography of the fifties, the jazz of Charlie Parker and Dizzy Gillespie was akin to the atom, in that it contained an enormous amount of potential compressed into a small package. And as with the atom, the "splitting" of bebop—accomplished by jazz musicians of the fifties—released an unforeseen torrent of energy.

This energy generated an explosion of creativity and artistic excellence that eclipses all others in jazz history—a golden age

---

*In some releases, Charlie Parker's 1947 recording called "Cool Blues" has carried the parenthetical subtitle "Hot Blues." That's not how we know the tune today, but the original mislabeling furnishes a perfect metaphor for the 1950s, when bebop gave way to two distinct idioms: hard-bop, which emphasized the heated emotionalism of bebop, and the cool school, which evolved as a reaction *against* such extroversion.

in which the heirs to bebop collectively produced an astonishing array of music. (Small wonder this chapter runs twice as long as any of the others in the *Playboy Guide*.) The fifties and sixties saw dozens of important young jazz musicians rise to prominence, a who's who of modern jazz that included Miles Davis and Chet Baker, John Coltrane and Sonny Rollins, Dave Brubeck and Bill Evans, Jimmy Smith and Horace Silver. Many of these artists would survive and thrive well into the 1990s; in the case of others, their innovations and recordings continued to exert influence, even on musicians born after their death. While the bebop of the forties represented the first watershed development in jazz since its invention, it wasn't until the fifties—when musicians explored and expanded upon the material bop contained—that the idiom's implications became evident and concrete.

The tiny atom turned out to contain still smaller particles; in a similar manner, bebop soon splintered into two major offshoots, each having distinct characteristics. Perhaps not surprisingly, both could find inspiration in the music of Charlie Parker, whose horn came to resemble a cornucopia, pouring forth elements of both these styles.

- The idiom known as hard-bop, played either blisteringly hot or with a radiant smolder, seemed a good deal like bebop, only seen from a new perspective. The hard-boppers retained the essence of the mother tongue, but they calmed down the most frantic rhythms, and they returned to the music an earthy emotionalism—a quality that had sometimes escaped the boppers in their quest to gain recognition as artists rather than "entertainers." (This soulfulness had its roots in church and gospel music, which formed the first listening experience for many black musicians. It soon inhabited an immensely popular subgenre of its own, known as funky, down-home, or soul jazz.)

  Making use of the new long-playing record format, the hard-bop crowd also opened up bebop's Morse-code schematic. Instead of two-chorus solos packed into a three-minute recording, the hard-bop musicians stretched out in extended solos, on tunes that might run six, eight, ten minutes (or more). The most perceptive of these players, musicians such as Cannonball Adderley, Miles Davis, and Sonny Rollins, saw this as more than just a license to play more choruses. They understood that the expanded context allowed them to *reconceptualize* the jazz solo, creating improvisations that delved into large-scale thematic development—artistic statements of a depth and breadth rivaling that of classical music, but with the immediacy found only in jazz.

(A coincidence: the twelve-inch LP format that facilitated this development was introduced in 1955—the same year that Charlie Parker, master of the two-chorus solo, died.)

- The alternative to hard-bop, "cool" jazz, embodied a radically different sensibility—an approach to artistic expression that actually became the dominant mood in all American culture of the decade, from film to theater to art to literature. In jazz, the "cool school" enjoyed tremendous commercial success because it included a preponderance of white musicians, who wielded the most influence in our white-majority society. But beyond that, "cool" struck a pose of seeming indifference that spoke volumes to the teenagers and young adults of the fifties—many of whom felt the need to protest the cultural conformity fostered by the privations of World War II.

Instead of extroversion, cool jazz displayed introspection. Whereas hard-bop (like bebop) embraced the beat and swung from the heels, the musicians of the cool school emphasized the value of restraint: they kept a slight distance between themselves and the emotions that lay beneath the music. Specifically, they emphasized a cerebral interplay among the melody instruments, and in the rhythm section you heard little of the incendiary accents that bebop (and hard-bop) drummers employed. In the cool school, the A students—saxists such as Lee Konitz, Art Pepper, and Gerry Mulligan; brass men such as trumpeter Chet Baker and trombonist Bob Brookmeyer—all favored flat-textured, muted tones, with little or no vibrato to warm them up. Their improvisations maintained a similarly measured, unruffled stance. This was true even at fast tempos—and make no mistake, the cool-jazz players often engaged in the thrill-ride tempos of their hard-bop colleagues. They just seemed to make less of a fuss about it.

The cool-jazz musicians could point with pride to certain recordings by both Parker and Gillespie, since these archetypal boppers each managed to blend elements of hot and cool jazz within a single style. But the cool school was primarily prefigured by Lennie Tristano and his acolytes in the 1940s (see chapter 3), and you can trace its roots back even further. Lester Young, and before him Bix Beiderbecke, had prophesied this style with their reflective and iconoclastic music, each man a solitary voice amidst a forest of hot-jazz sounds.

The music of the fifties and sixties has probably generated as many Useful Lies as the rest of jazz history combined.

For instance, to read some histories, and to hear some people talk about this period, you'd conclude that "cool was cool and bop was hard, and never the twain did meet." Certainly, the hard-boppers and the cool school had their real musical differences, as reflected in radio and press debates, magazine readers' polls, and the occasional "battle of the bands." And yes, the artistic divide between them *was* the major distinguishing characteristic of life after bop. But listening now to their music, you realize that the two idioms still had a good deal in common, in terms of the grammar, syntax, and vocabulary of their musical language.

The differences lay in how those materials were interpreted; and in any case, the musicians in each camp often borrowed at least a little from each other. (When the West Coast saxist Bob Cooper later explained to author Ted Gioia, "I really didn't relate to it [the music of the fifties] as East and West," he was expressing the view of many of his collaborators.) In both camps, though, jazz responded to—and appealed to—the rhythms of postwar life, as America sought to rediscover balance and relaxation after the intensity of global conflict.

Another popular generalization held that cool jazz belonged to the white cats while hard-bop remained the domain of black hipsters. This distinction is indeed useful as a guiding principle, but vulnerable to several obvious exceptions. (For example, the wonderful black pianist Sonny Clark played regularly in the Lighthouse All-Stars, a beacon of cool jazz.) Similarly, anyone reading magazine articles of the time would have believed that all cool jazz musicians, from Dave Brubeck to Art Pepper, resided in California, or at least somewhere on the West Coast. Cool-jazz album covers played this up with pictures of the Pacific beachfront, woodies with surfboards on the roof, and the occasional bikini-clad California cutie.

The term *West Coast jazz* quickly became synonymous with *cool jazz*—just as *East Coast* served as a code phrase for the rough-and-tumble sound of hard-bop. But while the West Coast did harbor the majority of cool players, a Los Angeles address didn't automatically mean the jazz was cool; just look at Dexter Gordon, born and bred in L.A. but a pillar of hard-bop. By the same token, it's true that clubs in midtown Manhattan and uptown Harlem (and Boston and Philadelphia) hosted a preponderance of cutting-edge hard-bop. But the East Coast had plenty of cool-jazz players in residence too.

The truth at the core of such generalizations helps explain why many jazz commentaries place hard-bop and cool jazz in separate chapters of jazz history. But the common heritage of the two idioms—and the cross-references between them—really demand they be seen as opposite halves of the same coin. Otherwise, you would lose sight of the very real connections they shared; otherwise, you'd have a hard time explaining Miles Davis, the slightly built trumpeter who towered over the fifties and sixties.

By himself, Davis put the kibosh on just about all of these assumptions: a black musician living on the East Coast, he nonetheless emerged as a famous symbol of cool jazz. In fact, history credits him as the *founder* of the cool school. As a teenager, he had joined Charlie Parker's band of the mid-forties, where he played in a noticeably different (and diffident) style from that of most bop trumpeters. Then, a few years later, Davis assembled a nine-piece band that made a handful of recordings collectively known as "the Birth of the Cool"—a slim body of work that would exert more influence than any other on jazz of the fifties. Davis worked on this project with several other jazz composers interested in finding an alternative to bebop's dizzying freneticism: pianist John Lewis, saxist Gerry Mulligan, and Gil Evans, who played piano but worked primarily as an arranger. Their music grew out of theoretical discussions that took place at Evans's "salon," to use the early-twentieth-century term for such a hotbed of artistic revolution. In fact, it was a one-room, cold-water flat behind a Chinese laundry, where Evans lived with his cat, Becky.

The sides recorded by the Davis Nonet served as the manifesto for a cool new artistic persona, which resounded across the jazz world during the fifties and beyond. In addition, it established Davis as a primary force in jazz, a position he strengthened through subsequent records with his quintet—a crackerjack *hard-bop* ensemble, of all things—and as a soloist accompanied by innovative big-band arrangements at the decade's end.

Nonetheless, it wasn't Miles Davis who ended up on the cover of *Time* magazine in 1954; it was a veterinary student turned struggling musician named Dave Brubeck (who became only the second jazzman so selected by the newsweekly, after Louis Armstrong in 1949). In Brubeck's case, this honor arrived several years *before* the hit records he would produce with his quartet later in the decade. *Time* made him a cover boy on the basis of his popularity with college students, in a story on how jazz (and cool jazz in particular) was sweeping the nation's campuses. Although his own piano playing had a blunt expressionism that overshot the bounds of cool, the Brubeck Quartet, based in San Francisco, became a standard-bearer for the West Coast sound. Within a few years, it had grown into an international phenomenon, thanks to compositions stamped by Brubeck's studies in classical music, and to the mercurial interplay between Brubeck and his musical soul mate, alto saxist Paul Desmond.

Desmond and his fellow cool-schooler Art Pepper, and their hard-bop counterparts like Cannonball Adderley and Phil Woods, faced an extra challenge. They all played alto saxophone—the same instrument played by Charlie Parker. For them, Parker's genius on the horn was like a nine-hundred-pound gorilla: one could go around it or one could go over it, but no way could one ignore it. No way, that is, except to play a different instrument.

So the saxophone spotlight of the fifties shifted to the alto's bigger cousin, the tenor sax. The hard-bop tenor players used the instrument's broad, deep sound to give their music a burly edge and a weightier punch than bebop's alto-and-trumpet pairings. The cool-jazz saxists, playing with more restraint, pulled a smooth, dry, and slightly dour timbre from the tenor, taking their cue from Lester Young. The fifties saw the rise of John Coltrane and Sonny Rollins. Along with Stan Getz (who had made his name in the previous decade), these three represented a saxophone junta of equally forceful but wildly different players, whose separate stylistic streams would influence jazz tenor playing, and jazz in general, for decades. In one instance, Rollins and Coltrane recorded together, on a twelve-minute blues aptly named "Tenor Madness." Before long, that title would apply to the state of jazz in general.

All these factors, and several others, made the fifties and early sixties an extraordinary time for the music, both artistically and commercially. Jazz still enjoyed the residual popularity engendered by the Swing Era. The rapid development of bebop—the first truly new sound since the very invention of jazz—had supplied a booster shot of adrenaline. And the musicians who inherited this legacy worked for the most part in small combos or mini-orchestras (like the Miles Davis Nonet and a similar-minded octet led by Dave Brubeck). This freed them of the financial constraints felt by Swing Era bandleaders, who tried assembling big dance bands to present their variations on the bebop theme.

On top of that, these younger players often got to appear alongside their own idols (the bop musicians) and even the music's progenitors. Remember, such artists as Armstrong, Basie, Ellington, and Goodman had only reached middle age and still maintained full-time recording and touring careers. It's really no accident that the phenomenon known as the jazz festival—usually a multiday concert series that packed together a variety of bands, in order to encompass the full variety of the contemporary scene—took shape during the fifties. At such events, most notably the Newport (RI) and Monterey (CA) Jazz Festivals, one could enjoy a panorama of jazz's first half century, painted by artists still in their prime.

In the work of a few musicians, listeners confronted that panorama as depicted by a *single* artist. The rapid evolution of jazz inevitably meant that some players fell through the cracks—or, more specifically, they bridged the boundaries separating two or more idioms. The pianists Oscar Peterson and Erroll Garner each created styles that blended aspects of swing and bebop, hot blasts and cool breezes, into quite personal

idioms that resist hard-and-fast categorization. Not incidentally, each attained a level of popular appeal head and shoulders above that enjoyed by most of their colleagues.

Of course, despite the emphasis on a "jazz war" between
East and West, the fallout from bebop blanketed cities across
the nation as well. Detroit in particular became home to a remarkably fertile postwar jazz scene, where such artists as guitarist Kenny Burrell, trumpeter Donald Byrd, saxists Yusef
Lateef and Charles McPherson, and pianists Tommy Flanagan
and Barry Harris concocted a bluesy and flavorful recipe for
hard-bop. All these artists and many others soon moved to
New York, where their urban-soul sound quickly became a vital
and influential subgenre.

In Chicago, a healthy club scene and the city's strategic ge-
ography insured a steady parade of visiting stars from either
coast, who often worked and recorded with their Midwestern
peers, and the city's large black population welcomed hard-
bop and soul-jazz bands with wide-open arms. Nonetheless,
Chicago had relatively little influence—certainly less than its
smaller northern neighbor, Detroit—on the jazz of the fifties.
That would change dramatically as jazz underwent its next major upheaval.

The Discs

Cannonball Adderley, *Them Dirty Blues* (Landmark). Only a
handful of alto saxists had either the skill to pick up Charlie
Parker's torch or the vision to run with it, and Julian "Cannonball" Adderley led the pack. Adderley's skill lay in his effortless
mastery of Bird's technique, as well as his full-throated sound
and his blues-drenched lyricism. His vision allowed him to
build directly upon Parker's innovations without merely copying him. These attributes made Adderley one of the most popular jazz performers of the late 1950s—when musicians and
critics hailed him as "the new Bird"—and especially the sixties,
as jazz audiences flocked to hear his increasingly funk-filled
music. *Them Dirty Blues,* a 1960 recording, offers an excellent introduction to the quintessential Adderley sound. It stars pianist
Bobby Timmons and Adderley's brother Nat on cornet; each of
them added further to the quintet's reputation by composing

memorable songs that mined the soul-gospel vein. (Nat Adderley's hits included "The Work Song," which appears on this album, and "Jive Samba"; Timmons wrote "Dat Dere," heard on this recording, as well as "Dis Here" and the blues hymn "Moanin'.") While most of the hard-bop artists injected some down-home funk into their music, no one could get more down and dirty than Adderley. But he also shone in terms of his trained musicianship, and this duality gave his music a rare emotional power.

In rock and roll, Elvis Presley gained success as a white artist performing black music for a larger audience. Chet Baker did much the same thing in jazz. With his pouty good looks, reminiscent of the fifties screen idol James Dean, he offered a version of the brooding, ultracool trumpeter that proved popular with white audiences—more popular even than the original, Miles Davis. But this should not detract from his very real artistic validity and terrific musicianship, displayed in his heartbreaking solos and yearning, unaffected vocals.

Let's Get Lost (Blue Note) showcases the youthful Baker's vulnerable singing voice. With no evident training as a singer, Baker doesn't always hit the notes right on, and his technique—with its slight nasality, similar to that of his contemporary Marlon Brando—would never grace a conservatory stage. But Baker's voice packs a compelling emotional punch and, on this album's twenty tracks, the lithe spring of a gazelle—as opposed to the stunning, haunted weariness of his last years. (The career-long arc of his singing mirrors that of Billie Holiday.) Subtitled "The Best of Chet Baker Sings," this album draws from five recording sessions of the mid-fifties—all of which starred Russ Freeman, the prototypical West Coast pianist—to provide a definitive example of cool-school jazz. It helps that most of the songs also feature Baker's trumpet solos, recorded separately on a different track. "The Thrill Is Gone" places his trumpet *behind* his singing, which creates an unexpected and simpatico duet between Baker (the instrumentalist) and Baker (the vocalist). Besides the sprightly flirtation of the title tune, this collection includes Baker's vocal version of "My Funny Valentine," the song that had helped make him famous when he recorded it as part of the Gerry Mulligan Quartet in 1953—three years before Miles Davis recorded his own famous version of the tune.

(Don't confuse this album with the sound track from the documentary about Baker's life, also titled *Let's Get Lost*, on Novus.)

Baker would rate another recommendation under his own name if he didn't also play a costarring (and cobilled) role on two of the albums listed below. See the paragraphs for Gerry Mulligan and Art Pepper in this chapter.

Art Blakey started out playing piano in his native Pittsburgh. He became a drummer when a gangland club owner hired a second pianist for Blakey's own trio and "suggested" that he switch to the drums if he wished to remain employed and healthy. (That the "other pianist" was Erroll Garner didn't hurt; see below.) Blakey created his sensational, colorful drum style while recording with Charlie Parker and earning his stripes as a bebop pioneer. Then, in the mid-fifties, he created the Jazz Messengers, the hard-bop battalion he commanded until his death in 1990. The Jazz Messengers name quickly came to stand for professionalism, excitement, and the future, in that it served as a sort of farm system for young players on their way to personal stardom. (Just a handful of those who played in the Messengers: Freddie Hubbard, Keith Jarrett, Branford and Wynton Marsalis, Jackie McLean, Wayne Shorter.)

The History of Art Blakey and the Jazz Messengers (Blue Note) delivers what the title promises in three CDs. It includes the first Jazz Messengers quintet that Blakey co-led with Horace Silver; several of his other late-fifties bands; and two tracks from the early eighties, featuring the young Wynton Marsalis. Nonetheless, it rightly places most of the emphasis on his scintillating 1960s groups: the quintet that featured trumpeter Lee Morgan and saxist Wayne Shorter, and the subsequent sextet in which Shorter was joined by Freddie Hubbard (trumpet) and Curtis Fuller (trombone) in the front line. Playing such highlights as the infectiously funky "Blues March" and "Moanin'," as well as the Shorter compositions "Free for All" and "Ping Pong," these two bands concretized the Jazz Messengers' reputation. Along with a couple of excellent previous groups, they make this set well worth the price. Covering three and a half decades of an evolving yet cohesive oeuvre, these three discs give you the wide-angle view of Blakey's contributions.

While you could pick another half dozen albums and still not go wrong, *The Big Beat* (Blue Note) does perhaps the best job of representing the Jazz Messengers ethos on a single disc. The tunes include bluesy stomps, hard-bop burners, and one shot of modernism; the quintet, starring Lee Morgan, Wayne Shorter, and the soulful swing of pianist Bobby Timmons, would get many votes for the best Blakey band of them all; and the leader's own solos combine brains and brawn with even more than his usual élan. (In Blakey's hands the modern drum solo came to resemble a tornado, in the sense that even those frightened by its imminent arrival can't help but admire its power.) This 1960 album has two certifiable classics in "Dat Dere" and "Lester Left Town." But the whole thing rocks, from "The Chess Players"—the boisterous opener, written by Shorter— to the frisky finale, a lightly arranged version of the Depression-era hit "It's Only a Paper Moon." And the album's very title sums up the Messengers' approach to jazz.

Clifford Brown and Max Roach, *Alone Together* (Verve). Clifford Brown died at the age of twenty-five, but he had already left his mark on the jazz world and on his colleagues. He could spin phrases of brain-boggling length and complexity into solos as lyrical as birdsong, and he had a large and almost honeyed tone, which carried his exquisite lyricism out to the world. (In fact, his music sometimes grew *too* pretty and flirted with cuteness.) When drummer Max Roach—the veteran of Charlie Parker's classic recordings—formed his own quintet, he built it around "Brownie" and gave him cobilling. The partnership resulted in what was arguably the decade's most respected hard-bop unit. It relied on not only the blistering technique of the leaders, but also the deft and memorable arrangements crafted by the band's pianist, Richie Powell, the younger brother of bebop genius Bud Powell. (The band's famous version of "Cherokee"—the Swing Era love song that the beboppers remade into a musical racetrack—offers a fine example of all this, from its stereotypical "Injun" introduction to Brownie's measured virtuosity at an extremely fast tempo.) On this unusual anthology, disc one showcases Brown in several settings, including "The Quintet," which also starred tenor saxist Harold Land. Disc two follows the progress of what became the Max Roach Quintet after Brown's death. The list of excellent jazzmen who came to prominence in this band includes Hank Mobley (see below), trumpeter Booker Little, and saxist Stanley Turrentine, and they all play here.

Dave Brubeck's approach to jazz has inspired millions of fans, and almost as many arguments. Experimental visionary or dead-end populist? Stylistic innovator or repetitive bore? Brubeck, with his heavy debt to classical music and his literal-minded improvising, seems to permit no compromise in the mind of history. But in the 1950s and 1960s, a series of inventively conceived albums made him one of the world's four or five best-known jazz musicians, leading a quartet rightly considered the flagship of West Coast jazz.

The first jazz album to sell one million copies, *Time Out* (Columbia/Legacy) remains the best encapsulation of the Brubeck Quartet's sound and concept. The band cut a clean, spare profile, with the cloud-borne alto sax of Paul Desmond floating dryly over Brubeck's thick modern chords. This elegant balance gave Brubeck the leeway to experiment with various and unorthodox musical ideas. The title of this 1959 album refers to the innovative use of odd meters in most of the compositions, rather than the usual jazz time of four beats per measure. For instance, "Blue Rondo à la Turk" has *nine* beats per measure, and "Three to Get Ready" alternates measures of three and four beats. Still, the success of *Time Out* rested primarily on the cool-school anthem "Take Five" (five beats per measure)—the most famous Brubeck tune that Brubeck never wrote. It was actually composed by his alter ego, alto saxist Paul Desmond, whose presence vindicated the group in the eyes of many. Whatever they thought of Brubeck, critics had few complaints about Desmond's ice blue tone and gorgeously deliberate improvisations, which recalled such precursors of cool as Frankie Trumbauer (see chapter 1) and Lester Young (chapter 2).

Brubeck and Desmond enjoyed an almost telepathic communication on the bandstand, and an instantaneous connection with their audiences, which gave the quartet's in-concert recordings a separate cachet. *Jazz at Oberlin* (Fantasy/OJC)—recorded in 1954 at one of the college concerts that launched the quartet's career—remains perhaps the best example. The first tune, "The Way You Look Tonight," sets the table: the arrangement is thick with counterpoint, which leads to an incandescent alto solo. Then, with the audience still reeling, the band launches into the bebop-era favorite "How High the Moon," which features one of the most musically satisfying of Brubeck's fiercely percussive block-chord solos. Since it dates from the quartet's early years, a time before the group had filled its repertoire with original compositions, this album is one of the few Brubeck dates to feature only standards. And while the band retained its enthusiasm for the rest of its run—until 1968—this concert has an electrifying edge (which may have resulted from reported tensions among the individual members before the curtain went up).

John Coltrane attracted attention, as well as controversy, almost from the time he began soloing on record. (Even as more and more musicians began to pay attention, one reviewer called his tenor playing "antijazz.") His voracious harmonic imagination allowed him to create swirling, note-packed improvisations that reportedly led his employer, Miles Davis, to exclaim, "Coltrane, you can't play everything at once!" Throughout this decade, Coltrane seemed bent on proving that he could; in the next decade, he would use such techniques to tap a solemn spiritualism rarely heard in jazz.

Blue Train (Blue Note). The dynamic, phosphorescent character of Coltrane's tenor work placed him in great demand from the mid-fifties until he formed his own quartet in 1960. He recorded often (as both leader and sideman) for several companies, but only once under his own name for the famous Blue Note label. Nonetheless, many observers consider it his best album of this period, thanks in part to the Blue Note philosophy of scheduling an extra day or two for rehearsals. This 1957 date used a three-horn lineup, with Lee Morgan's trumpet and Curtis Fuller's full-voiced trombone. The presence of drummer Philly Joe Jones and bassist Paul Chambers (bandmates of Coltrane's in the Miles Davis Quintet) kept the pulse light but complex. *Blue Train* chugged along on only five tunes, and three of them eventually landed among Coltrane's best-known compositions. You needn't travel much beyond the title track—as Trane's tenor solo accelerates out of the simple blues theme—to understand the power and charisma of his music during these years. (If that doesn't work, his brawny, cascading solo on the famous "Moment's Notice" should do the trick.) Forty years later, this remains among the most popular albums of its time.

Giant Steps (Atlantic), recorded in the last weeks of 1959, did more than showcase the new quartet Coltrane would begin leading a few months later. It also provided a sort of apotheosis for hard-bop in general. Jazz musicians had spent the previous two decades perfecting solos based on the permutations and extensions of colorful, fast-moving chords. By now, in the words of the noted critic Martin Williams, they had begun to sound like "rats in a harmonic maze," running in more and tighter circles just to end up in the same place. On *Giant Steps*, Coltrane's "sheets of sound" brilliantly demonstrated that he had taken this process further than anyone else—with the connotation that it had no place else to go. The title tune, a proving ground for succeeding generations of jazz musicians, consists of a rather simple melody, with just two notes per measure. But almost every note has a different chord attached to it, and taken at a fast tempo, this results in one of the most challenging sets of "changes" ever designed for improvisation. (Coltrane navigates it with the slippery acumen of an expert skier.) This tune and others displayed the farthest reaches of hard-bop jazz, but the album also contained two of Coltrane's most memorable compositions—"Syeeda's Song Flute" and his famous ballad the lovingly lyrical "Naima"—which further helped it become an all-time treasure.

Chris Connor, *A Jazz Date with Chris Connor* (Rhino). With her understated delivery, her immaculate phrasing, and her smoky timbre virtually devoid of vibrato, Chris Connor could have changed her first name to Cool and no one would have batted an eye. Connor belongs to a lineage of female vocalists who came up via the Stan Kenton Orchestra. Anita O'Day (chapter 3) created the mold with her hip and knowing stance, which communicated a slightly reckless sexuality. Her replacement, June Christy, lacked O'Day's bebop sympathies and had none of her scat-singing capabilities; instead, she focused on the husky quality of O'Day's voice and her own restrained emotionalism to become a cool-jazz star. Connor, who joined the Kenton band in 1953, might have struck listeners of the time as just a Christy clone, but her musicianship easily outshone that of her predecessor. Her sparing command and ebullient swing provided a lively counterweight to the shrouded expressiveness that placed her so firmly in the cool camp. This CD brings together two LPs of the mid-fifties, *A Jazz Date* and *Chris Craft*, featuring both orchestra and small-group backing, with such songs as "Moon Ray," "Lonely Town," and "Driftwood" proving the jazz equivalent of *film noir*. If you find anything odd in the idea that cool jazz might cause one to melt, this album will end your confusion.

Miles Davis made a name for himself as Charlie Parker's acolyte in the mid-1940s. But not until the fifties did his importance as a trumpeter, bandleader, and jazz innovator come into full view. Davis himself presented an image of the quintessential "cool cat," but his music actually straddled the boundary between cool jazz and hard-bop. The handful of nonet sides that he recorded at the turn of the decade were enough to form a template for the cool-jazz sound, especially among West Coast musicians; yet the sextet he led in the late fifties starred several of the premier hard-bop players and remains one of the greatest of post-bebop bands. (In the sixties, he would establish two more stylistic schools of vital importance.)

Birth of the Cool (Capitol) assembles the dozen studio tracks recorded in 1949–50 by the legendary Miles Davis Nonet, sometimes called the Tuba Band because of the presence of that instrument in the lineup. The tuba anchored a radical array that employed French horn and trombone—along with Davis's dark trumpet tone—to create a round, burnished sound. These instruments also interacted with the two saxophones, alto and baritone, to create the translucent voicings. (The band had unusual depth for its size, thanks to the ingenuity of Gil Evans and Gerry Mulligan, who wrote most of the arrangements.) It wasn't just the instrumentation that left such enormous impact. The pastel harmonies, the purposeful restraint of the improvising, the reliance on midspeed tempos, the use of shorter solos in balance with the exciting ensemble work—everything about this music posed a viable alternative to the regimen of bebop. Nonetheless, *cool* did not mean "cold," and such indelible classics as "Move" and "Israel" cook convincingly even if they use a lower flame. Although this music would eventually change the face of jazz in general, it did not exert any influence to speak of until four years after its recording, when these sides finally appeared all together on one LP. Even then, other musicians found the arrangements fresh and forward-looking—an indication of how far ahead of their time they really were.

In 1955, after recovering from heroin addiction, Davis hired saxist John Coltrane and formed the quintet that would make them each a household name (at least, in jazz households). By immersing Coltrane's heated hard-bop excursions in the placid pools of his own muted trumpet, Davis had defined—within one band—the yin and yang of modern jazz. The results first streamed out on a series of 1955 recordings for the Prestige label, many of which feature extended jam tunes. But by the following year, when they recorded 'Round About Midnight (Columbia), the band had a more determined repertoire, and a mystique spelled out in Davis's timeless arrangement of the Thelonious Monk ballad " 'Round Midnight." (The album also contains now classic performances of "Bye Bye Blackbird" and "All of You.") The rhythm section was propelled by the great Philly Joe Jones on drums and the agile and highly influential bassist Paul Chambers. It also introduced the relaxed poise of pianist Red Garland, who, like many others who played in Miles Davis's bands, did his best work while under the trumpeter's direction. You can't go wrong with any of the studio dates by this band, but this makes an excellent starting point.

Kind of Blue (Columbia Jazz Masterpieces) has earned a place among the twentieth century's signal artistic achievements. Forty years after it appeared, it remains a cultural icon as well as a powerful musical experience. The compositions have a gracious simplicity, and the solos a chiseled economy, that communicate instantly with first-time listeners. And the convergence of such inspired improvisers as Davis, Coltrane, alto saxist Cannonball Adderley, and pianist Bill Evans gives the album both the breadth of a searchlight and the intensity of a laser. But *Kind of Blue* also lit the path to a paradigmatic shift in jazz thinking, thanks to the music's theoretical underpinnings. Davis designed the five pieces on the album around particular scales (a scale being any linear progression of notes—not always eight—that span an octave). The scales replaced the chord sequences that had provided the structure for most previous styles of improvisation, and this system forced the members of his sextet to look in unusual directions when it came time to solo. (To further spark innovation, Davis presented this new musical puzzle to his players just a few hours before the recording session—placing them on the spot, and thus increasing the challenge.) Davis's reliance on these scales—and the subsequent de-emphasis of chords—made *Kind of Blue* especially influential in the mid-sixties, as jazz musicians sought avenues of greater musical freedom than bebop seemed to allow.

Davis had one more trick up his sleeve in the fifties, and it reunited him with Gil Evans, his collaborator on the *Birth of the Cool* recordings. Together, they conceived a reinvention of the concerto form used in classical music, in which a soloist and the orchestra engage in a sort of running duet. On a total of four albums, Davis's trumpet (and the darker, more mellow flügel-horn) worked within the demanding confines of Evans's arrangements, which shaped, supported, and framed Davis's playing with unique sensitivity. Jazz had not previously wit-nessed writing like this. The liquid textures amplified the sound of the Davis Nonet for a much larger band; meanwhile, each album arrived as a symphonic-length suite that linked the individual songs to those around it. This comes through most clearly on the first of these albums, *Miles Ahead* (Columbia), in which Evans weaves ten otherwise unrelated tunes into a seam-less story of varying moods. Before this 1957 recording, no jazz musician had made such innovative or authoritative use of the LP format: such a project would have been unimaginable only five years earlier. The Davis-Evans collaboration would reach its zenith in the smoldering intensity of "Sketches of Spain" a few years later, but with its wide-ranging scope and its stamp of the new, *Miles Ahead* is the place to start.

Bill Evans, the pianist who played an important role in Miles Davis's group of the late 1950s, would soon emerge as one of the most popular and important musicians of his time. (After his death in 1980, musicians as diverse as hard-bop saxist Phil Woods and fusion guitarist Pat Metheny wrote compositions in his honor.) Evans combined hard-bop melodicism and the balanced restraint of the cool school, and he perfected a de-centralized approach to the piano, in which neither right-hand melodies nor left-hand harmonies dictated to the other. He was criticized for his understated beat, but musicians quickly per-ceived it as a deceptively propulsive force of enormous swing. And in eschewing the showy fireworks of bebop, he crafted a lyrical profile that left an enormous impact on the next two generations of pianists.

Sunday at the Village Vanguard (Riverside/OJC)—one of two albums recorded in performance on June 25, 1961—brims with history as well as extraordinary music. It marks the first time the Bill Evans Trio recorded at the Vanguard, the storied jazz spot in New York's Greenwich Village, which remained the pianist's favorite venue throughout his career. The albums also document the last performance of bassist Scott LaFaro, whose death in a fiery car crash ten days later shook the jazz world in general and Evans in particular. In this trio, Evans sought and achieved a true trialogue among the instruments, a musical conversation in which no one instrument would dominate the others. LaFaro's astounding virtuosity proved vital to this effort, as did his ability to hear beyond the normal constraints imposed on his instrument. This evolution of the trio—from a group that mainly frames the piano solos to one that weaves a fabric from three instrumental threads—constitutes a huge part of Evans's legacy, and this recording represents the full flowering of that concept and of this, his first great trio. It also demonstrates how the pianist had transformed cool jazz into a personal romantic esthetic, especially on ballads. (A second volume from the same recording date, titled *Waltz for Debby* after one of Evans's best-known compositions, is every bit as good.)

While Evans's new concept of the piano trio was strong enough to withstand changes in personnel, it still placed unusual demands on sidemen. As a result, he didn't replace members of his trio quickly or carelessly. But the ones he chose usually stayed quite a while, since his music proved such a rewarding challenge. Several years after LaFaro's death, Evans established his longest-lasting trio—and the second most important of his career—featuring bassist Eddie Gomez and drummer Marty Morell. Gomez in particular brought a new dimension to the trio, having taken LaFaro's innovations to another level. Gomez's speedy, rhythmically creative lines and featherweight tone suggested a deep-voiced guitar rather than an instrument standing six feet tall, and his solos still provide a benchmark for technical prowess. *The Tokyo Concert* (Fantasy/OJC), recorded onstage in 1973, has about everything you would want in one CD by this trio: a couple of well-known standards; tunes that had helped define the Evans sound through the years ("Up with the Lark" and "Gloria's Step"); a solo-piano lullaby that conveys the intense romance Evans could achieve; and a contemporary foray (folksinger Bobbie Gentry's "Morning Glory") of the sort Evans made throughout his career. Most important, this CD gives you a near-perfect portrait of Evans's piano in action: assured, unmistakable, brimming with ideas, and yet just one actor in a three-man play.

Erroll Garner, *Concert by the Sea* (Columbia/Legacy). Another album's title refers to "the most happy piano" of Erroll Garner, and therein lay the secret of his popular appeal. The diminutive Garner managed to transfer his thousand-watt smile and pixie personality to the keyboard, creating a style of perky rhythms, colorful chords, and frolicking melodic devices that danced from one end of the keyboard to the other. He became one of the best-known jazzmen of any era (appearing frequently on TV in the fifties and sixties). A completely self-taught musician who never learned to read music, Garner crafted elaborate piano arrangements that made him a second cousin to Art Tatum. And like Tatum, he created a style out of time. The insistent pulse of his four-to-the-bar rhythms had more to do with swing, but his harmonies borrowed from bebop and classical impressionism. Meanwhile, he made a trademark of richly voiced full-chord improvisations that brought new dimension to ideas first presented by Earl Hines in the twenties. Garner's introduction to a song might have the grandiose air of operetta (as on this album's "I'll Remember April") or the playful jaunt of a clever kid ("Where or When"), and the key-tickling arpeggios heard on "Autumn Leaves" and "April in Paris" became grist for less talented cocktail pianists everywhere. Recorded in 1955 in Carmel, California, *Concert by the Sea* is quintessential Garner in its mix of spice and schmaltz, and it became one of the best-selling albums in jazz history. It lacks only his famous composition "Misty," written some years after this concert took place.

Stan Getz, *Stan Getz at the Shrine* (Verve). The great tenor saxist had come of age when bebop did, playing in the Woody Herman "Four Brothers" band (see chapter 3), which combined elements of swing and bop into a viable big-band commodity. In the fifties, Getz himself combined these two idioms into one of the most personal, popular, and artistically successful saxophone styles in jazz. His limpid but energetic sound effectively defined the cool-jazz esthetic, especially when surrounded by like-minded musicians—such as at this concert recorded on the West Coast (appropriately) in 1954. It featured the short-lived quintet that matched Getz with another important cool-jazz figure, the trombonist and composer Bob Brookmeyer. Soloing in fast and furious counterpoint, they recalled the contrasting lines of New Orleans jazz while proving that *cool* didn't *have* to mean "relaxed." Getz's resplendent, transportive lyricism resulted from his three great gifts: his passionate and velvety tone, his genius for pure melody, and his seemingly fragile but in fact indestructible sense of swing. In its bittersweet evocation of pain and joy, his playing elicited awe from both his fellow musicians and the general public. (John Coltrane reportedly once commented, "We would all play like Stan Getz if we could.") His style proved immensely versatile; it filled the goblet of ballads as well as the crucible of bebop barn burners; it shone in intimate duos, in star-studded collaborations, and in front of string orchestras. To top it off, his greatest success would come as an unlikely pop-music star in the next decade. (See the transition section "From There 2 Here.")

Dexter Gordon, *Doin' Allright* (Blue Note). Although he caught the public ear as a pioneering bebopper (see chapter 3), Gordon remained adaptable throughout his career. His instantly recognizable, confident, and casual style allowed him to try out newer idioms and ideas, yet always end up sounding just like himself. On this 1961 recording, Gordon hooked up for the first time with the young trumpeter Freddie Hubbard and had no trouble settling into the relaxed grooves often associated with the hard-bop style. You can also hear inklings of John Coltrane's innovations. Even though the younger tenor man had used Gordon as a model for his own music, Gordon proved an astute enough observer to admire and borrow from his "student" in return. This entire album ranks among the most satisfying examples of post-bebop playing, laid-back and energized at the same time, and filled with grand solos by both hornmen. Above them all stands Gordon's vibrant, hard-edged improvisation on "It's You or No One" (a song that would become a staple in his repertoire for the next three decades). It epitomizes his vivid storytelling approach to improvisation.

Freddie Hubbard, *Hub-Tones* (Blue Note). Arriving in New York from Indianapolis in the late 1950s, the young trumpet phenom Freddie Hubbard came armed with a flamboyant tone, an abundance of improvising savvy, and the confident attack of a tiger in its prime. Such qualities caught the ears of many important and established hard-bop musicians, who quickly moved to either hire him or recommend him to others. As a result, Hubbard plays such an important role on several other albums recommended here—by Blakey, Gordon, and Herbie Hancock and Oliver Nelson (see below)—that one could justify the omission of his own albums from a hard-core list of hard-bop listening. But on his recordings of the mid-sixties, Hubbard did more than simply exercise his bright, brash, and playful approach to jazz. Of course, you'll hear plenty of that in his solos; you won't find many better examples than on this date's title track and the song "Prophet Jennings." But Hubbard combines this aspect of his music with hints of an exploratory bent—a leaning that led him to participate in the startling free jazz experiments of Ornette Coleman and John Coltrane (see chapter 5). As such, *Hub-Tones* represents both the heights of hard-bop and its future. It stars Hubbard's fellow native Hoosier reedman James Spaulding, and their fellow Midwesterner Herbie Hancock (of Chicago).

Ahmad Jamal, *Ahmad's Blues* (Chess/GRP). Addition by subtraction: the trio led by pianist Ahmad Jamal added much to the musical discourse of the fifties, largely by leaving notes out. Bebop, hard-bop, and even cool jazz showcased skeins of notes, as if the musical space always needed refilling. But Jamal's solos ignored this tendency, following the upside-down advice "Don't just do something, stand there!" and making a structural element of the space itself. He thus allowed his music to breathe freely in a relaxed, airy setting, which became a new hallmark of cool. In 1958, this aspect of his music—along with his delicate phrasing, and the irresistible beat he created for the song "Poinciana"—made him a top-selling recording star. But even earlier, Jamal's career had received a substantial boost from Miles Davis, who publicly credited Jamal's music with inspiring his own (and then "borrowed" Jamal's arrangements when recording some of the same tunes). Here, Jamal himself borrows from the example of Nat "King" Cole—whose piano stylings so clearly influenced his own—on "Autumn in New York" and "Stompin' at the Savoy." Experienced jazz lovers may howl at the choice of this album over *At the Pershing: But Not for Me* (Chess/GRP), which contained "Poinciana" and climbed to no. 3 on the pop-music charts. But while that album does emblematize Jamal's music, it clocks in at barely over thirty minutes. *Ahmad's Blues*, recorded nine months later, gives you the same trio, the same quality of performance, and twice as much music.

Stan Kenton Orchestra, *The Best of Stan Kenton* (Blue Note). Few jazzmen of any era have raised as many hackles as Stan Kenton, whose music often wasn't jazz at all. By the early forties he had started looking beyond dance-band boundaries, christening both his orchestra and his musical philosophy with the high-minded moniker Artistry in Rhythm. Soon he began to gather talented arrangers who, like their leader, gravitated toward huge compositions for huge orchestras. (One such project numbered forty-three musicians!) With pounding brass that remind many of nineteenth-century symphonic music (Teutonic division), these works had a solemn, self-important, and decidedly "serious" cast to them and at times would forgo even the illusion of such attributes as swing and improvisation. But when Kenton stayed on the jazz side of the artistic divide, his sold-out concerts provided exposure for the cool-school giants he hired, while his well-documented obsessiveness—he made sure his musicians crossed each *t* and dotted every *i* in the arrangements—resulted in performances of power and precision. Kenton's music exhibited the self-analysis of cool jazz but not its emotional introspection; it had the ballsy strut of hardbop, but not its soul-drenched warmth. It really qualifies as sui generis. Nonetheless, he either launched or boosted the careers of many important soloists (Maynard Ferguson, Lee Konitz, Shelly Manne, Art Pepper), writers (Bill Holman, Johnny Richards, Pete Rugolo), and vocalists (Anita O'Day, June Christy, Chris Connor). This set touches several bases, including the band's admirable intrigue with Cuban music.

* * *

Lambert, Hendricks & Ross, *The Hottest New Group in Jazz* (Columbia/Legacy). Imagine the thrill of singing the solos improvised by some of jazz's greatest soloists; then multiply by three, and you can understand why the music of Lambert, Hendricks & Ross had such a kicky exuberance. L, H & R raised vocalese—the art of carefully fitting words to previously recorded improvisations—to new heights. Their debut album featured vocalese versions of arrangements from the Count Basie songbook, and it made them overnight celebrities. But this excursion into the Swing Era was just a side trip. L, H & R reveled in the cool jazz and hard-bop of the fifties and found their greatest inspiration in the solos of such players as trumpeter Art Farmer, pianist Bobby Timmons, and especially Horace Silver. Their voices had a bright, edgy blend; the hip, often wiggy lyrics caught the bohemian spirit of the era's underground; and with three singers, they could pay their respects to several solos from a given tune. (On their version of Silver's "Come on Home," for example, Ross sings the leader's piano solo, Lambert takes on Blue Mitchell's original trumpet improvisation, and Hendricks covers the tenor solo first played by Junior Cook.) As they celebrate and "translate" the original solos, these vocalese performances also have musicological value: they can help a listener discern the structure of an improvisation through the "story" told by the lyrics. *The Hottest New Group in Jazz* compresses three of the group's early-sixties LPs onto two CDs and includes virtually all of their best work. On a budget, get *Everybody's Boppin'* (Columbia/Legacy).

Howard Rumsey's Lighthouse All-Stars, *Sunday Jazz à la Lighthouse* (Fantasy). The East Coast made Birdland its fortress of hard-bop; on the Pacific, a club called the Lighthouse served as bastion for the West Coast sound. At least, that's how critics approached it. In reality, the Lighthouse gave cool-jazz players a chance to bust loose in regular jam-styled sessions, and this blurred the lines between hard-bop and cool more than ever. The sessions—and the band that grew out of them—sprang from the fertile mind of bassist Howard Rumsey. In 1949 he convinced the owner of the Lighthouse, a bar in Hermosa Beach (adjacent to Los Angeles), to host loosely organized Sunday-afternoon sets. By 1953, when this recording took place, the "regulars" had come to include such cool-jazz icons as trumpeter Shorty Rogers, saxist Bob Cooper, and drummer Shelly Manne. Yet the band heard here also features Maynard Ferguson, whose searing high-note trumpet work had nothing to do with cool jazz; and later the same year, Rumsey enlisted be-bop's master drummer Max Roach to join the group. Even without these additions, the All-Stars had a decidedly East Coast tinge in their emphasis on pure blowing, long solos, and sketchy arrangements. But they retained their cool-jazz reputation, thanks in part to album covers that played up their West Coast heritage. (One featured a photo of an actual lighthouse; another showed the band members, with instruments at the ready, standing on the beach with the ocean behind.)

The bassist Charles Mingus, one of the most intriguing figures in jazz history, could fill a book on his own. (And he did: his autobiographical *Beneath the Underdog* revealed many of the demons and godheads that drove him.) His remarkable technique made him one of the true innovators on his instrument, but even that distinction paled in comparison to his abilities as a composer and bandleader. Like Thelonious Monk, one of his idols, Mingus wrote and recorded music too individualistic for categorization: he belongs to, but is not really *of*, the hard-bop period. And like his other self-professed idol, Duke Ellington, Mingus achieved an instantly recognizable sound whether writing for a handful or an army of musicians. More than any of his contemporaries, Mingus envisioned a wider canvas for jazz, then used the basic materials of hard-bop to fill it up.

You can't do any better than *Mingus Ah Um* (Columbia/ Legacy) from 1959. Its nine tracks include four certifiable Mingus masterpieces. Many of his compositions related directly to hard-bop, though he often turned to earlier forms of jazz; in each case, he offered a unique take on a given idiom's generic elements. Thus, while Art Blakey and Horace Silver had popularized the "churchy" sound of gospel-influenced jazz, Mingus's "Better Git It in Your Soul" pushed that style over the top: the double-time drumming and urgent theme transform church service into revival meeting. Similarly, "Boogie Stop Shuffle" rewrites the basic boogie-woogie beat with a manic, almost dangerous ferocity. On "Fables of Faubus"—heard here without the lyrics that, in later versions, ridiculed the notorious segregationist governor Orville Faubus of Arkansas—Mingus revisits the minstrelry of vaudeville to find inspiration for his satirical melody. And while his threnody for Lester Young, "Goodbye Pork Pie Hat," is not a blues, Mingus used phrases *from* the blues to create one of the most moving ballads in jazz history—the perfect springboard for a famous tenor solo by Booker Ervin. No wonder so many discussions of Mingus start here.

The double-CD anthology *Thirteen Pictures* (Rhino) offers an unusually wide-ranging survey of Mingus's many masks. Even though it begins with a twenty-eight-minute Latin-jazz work recorded in 1977, it still emphasizes his work of the 1950s and early 1960s, with a hard-to-beat assemblage of many important (and delightful) compositions. One of them, the 1956 trailblazer "Pithecanthropus Erectus," served notice of Mingus's ability to tackle more serious musical questions than hard-bop had previously addressed. Along with the "Haitian Fight Song" (which became a subject of ridicule in the film *Jerry Maguire*) and the rollicking "Hora Decubitis," this set also includes the monumental "Reflections on Integration," a twenty-two-minute composition for twelve-piece band, recorded at the 1964 Monterey Jazz Festival, that clearly links hard-bop and the sixties' push toward improvisatory freedom. Of the "thirteen pictures" displayed here, only two originally appeared on *Mingus Ah Um* (above), so both albums can easily coexist in your jazz gallery.

Not only did Mingus write indelible music for a wide variety of ensembles, he also led a series of working bands, from the 1950s until his death in 1979, that introduced innovative soloists testing their creative mettle against his challenging music. In sponsoring these important young players—saxists Eric Dolphy and George Adams, trombonist Jimmy Knepper, pianists Roland Hanna and Don Pullen, drummer Dannie Richmond—Mingus solidified his credentials as a savvy bandleader. By setting these musicians loose on his sprawling compositions, he presided over concert performances of epic length and impact. Luckily, several of them are preserved on disc, including *At Antibes* (Rhino), recorded at the 1960 Antibes Jazz Festival on the Côte d'Azur. For this concert, Mingus led a lean, pianoless quintet that included Richmond, trumpeter Ted Curson, saxist Booker Ervin, and the exhilarating Dolphy (on alto sax and bass clarinet). Their solos leap with passion and power, thanks in part to the short, bristling riffs played behind each soloist by the other hornmen (in the manner of Swing Era big bands). These riffs, along with Mingus's audible instruction and encouragement, helped push this performance into the pantheon of live recordings.

Modern Jazz Quartet, *European Concert* (Atlantic). Formed from the rhythm section of Dizzy Gillespie's mid-forties big band, the MJQ developed into one of the best-known jazz ensembles of its or any other time. But labeling the band as either cool or hard-bop is a fool's errand. While pianist John Lewis and vibraphonist Milt Jackson (the MJQ's two principals) had arrived during the first flush of bebop, they both gravitated toward the cooler end of the spectrum—Lewis by temperament, Jackson by virtue of his instrument's liquid-nitrogen timbre. Nonetheless, a real dichotomy existed within the band: Jackson's voluptuous improvisational style versus the restrained formality of Lewis's compositions and minimalist piano solos. This creative tension fueled the MJQ (and eventually caused them to disband for several years in the seventies). Acting as the MJQ's musical director, Lewis followed his sensibilities to create some noteworthy "theme" albums, but the *European Concert*, recorded in Sweden in 1960, furnishes your best introduction. This lengthy CD, originally issued on two LPs, presents a compilation of many MJQ classics—including Lewis's "Django" and "Vendome" and Jackson's great blues tunes "The Cylinder" and "Bags' Groove"—but it retains the integrity of a unified album recorded at a single setting. And it has the advantage of presenting the MJQ in their natural habitat, the concert hall. Champions of the view that jazz deserved the same respect as classical music, the quartet preferred this venue (where they always appeared in tuxedos) to the nightclub.

Wes Montgomery, *The Incredible Jazz Guitar* (Fantasy/OJC). Like his jazz-guitar predecessors Django Reinhardt and Charlie Christian, Wes Montgomery inspired something close to deification—even *before* his premature death (at age forty-three). That seems appropriate, since Montgomery borrowed something from each of those giants in forging a sound and style that would influence jazz guitarists for decades. Montgomery's magic began with his innovative technique. By using his thumb (instead of a pick) to pluck the strings, Montgomery gained additional control over his articulation, giving his melody lines a textural variety usually reserved for horn players; yet he still played with more speed and intensity than most other guitarists of the time. And because he didn't curl his whole hand around a guitar pick, he could use the fingers to create various rhythmic and melodic devices. The most notable of these involved improvising in octaves (playing a solo line in two areas of the guitar's range simultaneously). This tricky device, which only Reinhardt had previously accomplished, became a Montgomery trademark. So did his tone, which rang roundly but had echoes of a country-swing twang and a healthy touch of the blues; and his habit of incorporating Latin and funk rhythms gave his music an extra shot of adrenaline. Montgomery led several small bands before moving into large-scale formats that insured his commercial success. But this quartet date is generally considered his single best recording.

Lee Morgan, *The Best of Lee Morgan* (Blue Note). You can trace the prevailing lineage of jazz trumpet players from Louis Armstrong to Roy Eldridge to Dizzy Gillespie, whose potent bebop presented a model for Clifford Brown. But Gillespie handed the baton quite literally to Lee Morgan, who joined his big band as a seventeen-year-old trumpeter in 1956. After that, Morgan completed his education as a member of Art Blakey's Jazz Messengers (see above). By the time he started recording under his own name, his style had become a logical evolution of Gillespie's, and his solos came to stand among the most tuneful and still exciting statements in the hard-bop idiom. In addition, he established fruitful partnerships with the tenor saxists Joe Henderson and Hank Mobley, each of which continued to evolve over several albums; and he showed a natural inclination for the "soul" side of hard-bop. The best example is "The Sidewinder," a bouncy boogaloo-beat blues that in 1964 became one of the decade's biggest jazz hits. The album on which it appeared (also called *The Sidewinder*) remains a perfect documentation of the mid-sixties jazz scene, worth owning for that reason alone. But since this *Best of* collection includes both "The Sidewinder" and its sequel, "The Rumproller"—along with enough other crème-de-la-crème selections to fill more than seventy minutes—it really constitutes a much better buy.

* * *

Baritone saxist Gerry Mulligan occupies a threefold place in jazz history. First, he employed a buoyant bounce and a dry, breezy tone that established the most popular sound for his instrument. Second, his clarified arrangements and light but swinging compositions—written for the Miles Davis Nonet (see above) and later for his own Concert Jazz Band—helped create and solidify the cool jazz ethos. Finally, he broke new ground as a bandleader with his pianoless quartet; along with bass and drums, it featured two horns, often in counterpoint, and introduced a clean new sound to jazz.

That particular band also launched the career of the second most influential cool-jazz trumpeter, as you can hear on *The Best of the Gerry Mulligan Quartet with Chet Baker* (Pacific Jazz), which contains tracks recorded in 1952 and 1953. The Mulligan compositions—busy, catchy tunes such as "Freeway" and "Nights at the Turntable"—pick up where he left off in his writing for the Miles Davis Nonet; they have the same buoyancy as his own saxophone playing. (This quality also extends to his clever treatment of such standards as "Love Me or Leave Me.") Thanks to his arranger's skills, Mulligan could voice the two horns in such a way as to suggest the presence of a third, and his composer's sensibilities inform his improvising: virtually all of his solos are so organized, with such unfettered forward movement, that they almost sound as if he'd written them the night before. The youthful Baker made an excellent partner in this enterprise. Obviously inspired by the sound and phrasing of Miles Davis, he plays with a rounder but still slightly puckered tone. His solos on this set rarely waver from his own standards of crisp melody and measured phrasing, and his dramatic evocation of "My Funny Valentine" still shouts calmly across the gulf of five decades. Later editions of the Mulligan Quartet starred trumpeter Art Farmer or trombonist Bob Brookmeyer in lieu of Baker, and these bands also have much to offer. But this is the original item.

Since current availability—or really, the lack thereof—makes it tough to recommend a suitable album of Mulligan's big-band writing, *The Gerry Mulligan Songbook* (Pacific Jazz) will have to do. But even though it features only a big-band saxophone section, with neither trumpets nor trombones on hand, it has much to recommend it. The five saxes provide some of the impact you'd get from a small jazz orchestra and allow Mulligan to show off his tight harmonies and plein-air voicings. The men playing those saxes—Lee Konitz, Allen Eager, and Al Cohn and Zoot Sims (two of Woody Herman's "Four Brothers")—make up an all-star ensemble of cool-jazz exemplars. And the seven Mulligan compositions include three of his best in "Turnstile," "Disc Jockey Jump," and "Venus de Milo" (which Mulligan had written for the original Miles Davis Nonet). In addition to those seven tracks, this CD reissue tacks on four previously unissued tunes recorded at the same sessions in late 1957. Written not by Mulligan but by such peers as Horace Silver and Tadd Dameron, these songs find Mulligan in an unusual chamber-jazz setting with plenty of strings attached; the instruments are violin, cello, guitar, bass, and drums.

Art Pepper, *The Return of Art Pepper* (Blue Note). If you want to expose the Useful Lie about West Coast cool jazz, head straight for the last track on this 1957 album—a superheated sprint through Pepper's theme song, "Straight Life." (An ironic title: he battled narcotics addiction his entire life.) A native Californian, Pepper played alto and occasionally tenor sax with the light tone and measured phrases associated with the Pacific shore, and his five-year stay in the Stan Kenton band completed his West Coast pedigree. Yet his solos, and the tempos at which he played them, had much of the emotional fire that distinguished the best hard-bop players. In fact, his early-fifties recordings would really qualify as pure bebop. On *The Return*, this aspect of Pepper's personality comes to the fore in such tunes as the percolating "Mambo de la Pinta" and "Pepper Returns" (based on one of his favorite chord sequences, "Lover Come Back"). But Pepper remained the most individualistic of the West Coast saxophonists even in the cooler settings that dominate this album. All in all, it offers a truly three-dimensional example of the California sound. Give the credit to Pepper's smoldering reserve; the counterpoint and harmonies between Pepper and trumpeter Jack Sheldon; the semidetached lilt of the sparse piano chords; and the light, crisp timekeeping of the irreplaceable drummer (and later club owner) Shelly Manne.

Chet Baker and Art Pepper, *The Route* (Blue Note). Not only does this 1956 recording feature two of the most distinctive leaders of West Coast jazz in Baker and Pepper, it also stars an all-star L.A. rhythm section, as well as the lesser-known but excellent tenor saxist Richie Kamuca (whose ancestors were from Hawaii—*way* out West). You can't find a finer exposition of the California concept than the five numbers on which they all appear. But even though Baker's name appears first, and he plays with spirit and sunlight throughout, the spotlight stays on Pepper. He steals the show with his solos on the sextet performances, and he also performs several tunes without the other hornmen; two of these tracks use a pianoless rhythm section (just bass and drums), a format still considered somewhat experimental at the time. The bassist, Leroy Vinnegar, became a fixture of the L.A. jazz scene for the next three decades. The marvelously understated drummer, Stan Levey, had previously played with Charlie Parker and Dizzy Gillespie in New York, and his dry, clean strokes have the contours of bebop, though not its inspired anarchy. The entire album serves as a reminder that the West Coast sound, while a direct descendant of bop, had a different personality from that of its parent.

Oscar Peterson, *The Jazz Soul of Oscar Peterson* (Verve). Pianist Peterson came out of his native Canada in the late forties, armed with a towering technique second only (and very likely equal) to Art Tatum's. This granted him easy access to bebop's inner sanctum and gained him legions of fans, which made him one of the true jazz monomials: as with Louis, Ella, Lester, and Miles, Oscar's first name alone supplies instant identification. The sheer number of Peterson albums in print (approximately 80 at last count) argues against selecting just one to open a window on his style; on the other hand, his remarkable consistency mitigates this problem. Peterson's virtuosity has been a source of both praise and complaints throughout his career. His detractors carp that because Peterson can and often does play *so much* in any given solo, these solos may actually have little to do with the songs that launched them; in that case, they become interchangeable (and thus superficial). Peterson fans counter that (*a*) they don't either, and (*b*) to whatever extent the criticism *does* hold true, the solos themselves remain at the pinnacle of technical accomplishment. In any case, Peterson at his best can blow away all but the most strident reductionists. On this CD, which contains the material from two LPs recorded in 1962, the pianist created an individualistic context for each song, and he displayed unusual care in inventing solos that grow out of the thematic materials (rather than sounding superimposed on them). He also made some jaw-dropping in-concert discs, which are discussed below.

The extraordinary musical maturity of tenor saxist Sonny Rollins had something to do with the neighborhood in which he grew up. Bud Powell and Thelonious Monk lived nearby, while Jackie McLean and the highly regarded drummer Art Taylor were classmates. But it had more to do with Rollins's ability to seize the implications of Charlie Parker's music and develop them further. As a result, his style of improvisation became more richly textured, thematically unified, and rhythmically intrepid than almost any other. In their surprising twists and turns, nearly every one of his solos overflowed with imagination, intellect, virtuosity, and a dry humor (which some people read as irony or satire)—all of which make him one of the half dozen most important tenor players in jazz history.

Saxophone Colossus (Fantasy/OJC), his 1956 masterpiece, left listeners limp and critics agape at Rollins's command of both his instrument and the map he drew for the future. The album includes Rollins's most-played composition, the island-flavored "St. Thomas," featuring not one but *two* distinct tenor solos, sandwiched around a remarkably melodic drum break by Max Roach (Rollins's former boss). Then there was the saxophonist's solo on "Moritat," better known as "Mack the Knife": eight choruses, linked together in intriguing ways, that count as one of the most cogent and balanced improvisations in all of jazz. Yet when the album first came out, those tunes didn't receive the greatest attention. Instead, it was the jaunty and mysterious "Blue 7" that inspired a famous article in *The Jazz Review*—which called for nothing less than a totally different approach to jazz analysis! (Indeed, "Blue 7" remains one of Rollins's most provocative and satisfying performances. It gains some of its effectiveness by seeming to exist in two different keys at the same time.) With this album, Rollins established his genius for spontaneous composition of the highest order and also showed that modern jazz could support such lofty concerns as compositional form and structural development. What's more, the whole album swings like Tarzan.

Rollins's exploratory nature—and his ability to suggest

entire harmonic schemes with just his own improvised melodies—soon led him to record without a pianist. On the 1957 recording *A Night at the Village Vanguard, Vol. 2* (Blue Note), his open-sided trio included bassist Wilbur Ware (solid as bedrock) and the scintillating drummer Elvin Jones (who would later join John Coltrane). Without a piano accompaniment to shape the chord sequences—or in this case, to limit them—Rollins could send the music wherever his fervid creativity took him. And his ability to craft lengthy, continually inventive solos obviated the need for a second horn in the band. The sustained quality of these performances places this album among Rollins's best. The music has the spare texture of *Waiting for Godot* (the contemporaneous play by Samuel Beckett); but in Rollins's voluptuous improvising, it presents a melodious and dramatic language closer to Shakespeare. (*Vol. 1* of these sessions contains several tracks just as spectacular; it runs ten minutes shorter.) Partly because of Rollins's success in this context, pianoless trios gained more acceptance in the 1960s, eventually becoming the preferred format for many younger horn players in the eighties and nineties.

In the early sixties, Rollins took one of several celebrated sabbaticals from the music business. Not wanting to disturb his neighbors with late-night practicing, he took his saxophone out to the middle of the Williamsburg Bridge and played there—a situation that caught the public eye when it inspired a short story published in the music magazine *Metronome*. Rollins's 1962 album *The Bridge* (Victor Jazz) takes its name from this incident, but it might also apply to the ways in which he spans the gap between his hard-bop roots and the freer musical landscape that beckoned from just over the horizon. As with his trio recordings (above), the album features no piano; instead, it adds guitarist Jim Hall, renowned for his ability to create flexible new harmonies while accompanying a soloist. The presence of Hall allowed Rollins to range far and wide in his improvisations without chordal constraint; more to the point, Hall's simpatico harmonies tend to form a counterline that enhances and enriches the saxophone flights. And those flights remain among Rollins's most exciting. They're leaner and lighter than his work of the fifties, with a gimlet quality that would mark his work for the next few years. Deservedly considered one of Rollins's very finest discs, *The Bridge* features four standards and two Rollins tunes, with the title track pointing directly toward his more overt attempts at free jazz in the mid-sixties.

Horace Silver, *Best of Horace Silver Volume One* (Blue Note). The career of Horace Silver has much in common with that of Art Blakey, with whom Silver debuted the Jazz Messengers concept in 1954. Both went on to channel a steady stream of promising young musicians through their bands, while adhering to the basic musical architecture of hard-bop. The main difference is that Silver's bands have always concentrated on Silver's compositions—memorable, seemingly simple songs that in fact supply unerring guidance for his soloists, without dictating the direction they take. Silver's piano solos have a similar "simplicity": without flamboyance or any overt virtuosity, he distills the essence of each song and also the spirit of hard-bop itself. Plain-spoken but elegantly organized, his solos have a graceful and natural melodic arc—a quality that made them perfectly suited for the vocalese lyrics sung by the trio Lambert, Hendricks & Ross, who augmented the popularity of several Silver songs. Silver's music has two other ingredients that make it so appetizing to jazz listeners: the earthy gospel spice in many of his compositions, and a taste for Afro-Latin rhythms inherited from his father, who emigrated from the Cape Verde Islands (a Portuguese colony off the west coast of Africa). Silver's "Song for My Father"—his best-known composition—pays homage to that influence. It appears not on this album but on the also excellent *Best of Horace Silver Volume Two* (drawn from five of his 1960s LPs).

Jimmy Smith, *Cool Blues* (Blue Note). If the electric organ had not existed when Jimmy Smith started playing jazz, he would have had to invent it. Not since Lionel Hampton encountered the vibraphone in the 1930s had a new jazz instrument found such a well-matched champion. (Because of this, some of us still get a slight shiver of authenticity when we hear Smith play—as if, say, the woman serving the beef turned out to be Mrs. Wellington.) In his first recordings, Smith laid out the principles that would define the jazz organ for the next fifteen years. He emphasized its capacity for excitement, taking advantage of the organ's electronics to create quick, skittering melody lines, and punctuating them with keening cries from the upper register. Smith also introduced to jazz the organ trio—which included guitar and drums, with the leader playing bass lines on the organ's foot pedals—that had developed in the black neighborhoods of such urban centers as Chicago, Detroit, and Philadelphia (near Smith's hometown). This soul-rich sound, originally associated with rhythm and blues, proved perfect for the earthier blues lines of hard-bop, and Smith became one of the most popular jazz artists—first with trio recordings, then in lengthy jam-session settings featuring star hornmen, and eventually backed by big-band arrangements in the 1960s. A 1958 nightclub date, *Cool Blues* finds Smith at his most heated and inspired.

Just Warming Up?

The entrenchment of cool jazz and hard-bop led to a proliferation of great recordings by individualistic young artists, making the fifties and early sixties a golden age for modern jazz. Many of these recordings appeared under the names of musicians barely mentioned above. But several of them deserve serious consideration when it comes to expanding the scope of your jazz library.

The pianist Sonny Clark, a young victim of fatal drug abuse, could fit his lean and muscular attack into both hard-bop and cool-jazz situations—witness his excellent work on recordings by Sonny Rollins on the one hand and the Lighthouse All-Stars on the other. *Cool Struttin'* (Blue Note), a quintet date starring trumpeter Art Farmer and saxist Jackie McLean, gets a nod for both the integrity of the solos and the indelible lilt of the title track.

Perhaps because of his similarities to Sonny Rollins, tenor saxist Hank Mobley slips under many listeners' radar. Nonetheless, he offers a terrific summation of hard-bop saxophone. *Soul Station* (Blue Note) best represents his mix of emotive swing and melodic intricacy and also features his composition "This I Dig of You"—one of many Mobley tunes much admired by other musicians then and now. The album was recorded in 1960, just after Mobley had left Art Blakey (who appears here) and shortly before his year with Miles Davis.

Herbie Hancock gets plenty of attention in later chapters, thanks to his seven-year association with Miles Davis, his rapid development as a composer and improviser, and, from the seventies on, his successful forays into fusion jazz and dance pop music. But it would be a shame to omit his debut as a leader, *Takin' Off* (Blue Note)—and not just because it features his delicious funky blues "Watermelon Man." Two of his other compositions, and the dynamic contributions of Dexter Gordon and Freddie Hubbard, also make this one a minor must.

Oliver Nelson scored a hit with *Blues and the Abstract Truth* (Impulse/GRP), which continues to captivate new generations with its surprising blend of Nelson compositions and stylistically diverse soloists: reedman Eric Dolphy, pianist Bill Evans, trumpeter Freddie Hubbard, and Nelson himself. The opening track, "Stolen Moments," has been recorded dozens of times en route to becoming a jazz standard (and occasional cabaret choice, thanks to the slightly noir lyrics, which came later).

Few improvising vocalists have taken risks equal to those of the great instrumental soloists, and that alone would make Mark Murphy stand out—even if he didn't sing in a strong and malleable baritone, swing authoritatively, and boast superb interpretative skills. His audacious adventurousness would have great influence on jazz singers from the sixties through the nineties. The first half of *Rah* (Fantasy/OJC), his ironically titled 1961 gem, features several attractively sung standards; but the bop tunes and vocalese in the album's second half are the real focal point here.

The soul-jazz side of hard-bop had its roots in the church, and on *A New Perspective* (Blue Note), trumpeter Donald Byrd went to the source: he enlisted a gospel choir to accompany his septet, which featured saxist Hank Mobley and guitarist Kenny Burrell (see below), on tunes that incorporated both traditions. Sensitive arrangements made this unusual project successful, and one track—the haunting "Cristo Redentor" (Portuguese for "Christ the Redeemer")—made it a cult hit.

The creative explosion of this period also resulted in scores of albums by young musicians who *are* mentioned in the main part of the chapter—as sidemen on albums by such famous talent incubators as Art Blakey, Miles Davis, and Charles Mingus. In most cases, the albums recommended for these leaders allow you to adequately sample the contributions of these "young lions." In some cases, their greatest importance really belongs to later chapters (Joe Henderson, Wayne Shorter, McCoy Tyner). Since most of these artists recorded for the Blue Note label, they made up an informal "stable" of innovative players who frequently worked on each other's records—thus creating a welter of albums with virtually the same personnel but issued under the names of different leaders. The list below should cut through the confusion.

(By the way, the painstaking craftsmanship that characterized the Blue Note label—and especially the fact that the company almost always hired the extraordinary recording engineer Rudy van Gelder to capture the music—had much to do with the success of these albums. Together, they created the "Blue Note sound," a warm, resonant presence that itself became an integral part of the music.)

The solos of guitarist Grant Green emphasized his heavy-lidded, innately sensual style. He drew a fat sound from the instrument and played with an unflappable technique, and he used these to create bright, uncluttered, driving melodies that influenced hard-bop hornmen as well as his fellow guitarists. In addition, Green's R&B roots, and his early experience as the lead voice in organ trios of the fifties, were always peeking around the corner. *The Best of Grant Green Volume 1* provides the best introduction, since it includes a standout track from each of six albums (including his wonderful *Idle Moments* and *Solid*).

McCoy Tyner gained his great fame as a member of John Coltrane's monumental quartet (see chapter 5), which quickly led to trio records under his own name. Tyner hammered his heavily percussive chords and clipped articulation into a pulsating, force-of-nature piano style. It proved as fresh as it was influential, and by the end of the sixties, aspects of his style were heard not only in younger pianists but in Tyner's own contemporaries. You can see why on *Today and Tomorrow* (Impulse/ GRP), which also features some of his early writing for horns.

Even though his greatest acclaim would come in the nineties, the originality of tenor saxist Joe Henderson placed him in heavy demand among his fellow "young lions" of the sixties. In fact, no other Blue Note horn player showed up on as many excellent records of the period as did Henderson. His hooded tone and the undeniable lyricism of his pretzel-logic solos left an indelible mark on important albums by Kenny Dorham, Lee Morgan, Horace Silver, McCoy Tyner, and vibraphonist Bobby Hutcherson. Henderson's debut album, *Page One*, is the appropriate place to start. (But if you spend the bucks on the four-CD *The Blue Note Years*, you won't go wrong—especially since it includes tracks by all the leaders just mentioned.)

Like Henderson, Wayne Shorter forged a distinctive variation on hard-bop saxophony. With a hard, bright sound, Shorter spun away from Coltrane's dominant influence to create solos that satisfied both emotionally and intellectually. And his compositions—musical changelings that avoided almost every formula and cliché—gained him additional and well-earned respect. Shorter received wide exposure first with Art Blakey and then with Miles Davis as the trumpeter moved his bands beyond hard-bop entirely (see chapters 5 and 6). In between, he recorded *Speak No Evil* (Blue Note), featuring some of his finest solo work and starring Hancock and Hubbard.

You'll find what may be Cannonball Adderley's most polished and imaginative solos of this period on *Somethin' Else* (Blue Note), which includes *the* definitive jazz arrangement of "Autumn Leaves." But it also features a studio rhythm section (rather than his own band) and the strong stamp of Adderley's employer, Miles Davis, who plays on it—making this an atypical (though excellent) Adderley album. Meanwhile, the Adderley brothers' first records, made just after their 1955 arrival in New York, are available on CD, but not under their own names. They performed, as new kids on the bop, on the album *Bohemia After Dark* (Savoy), a jam session led by drummer Kenny Clarke.

Other fine choices: the self-explanatory *Cannonball and Coltrane* (EmArcy), featuring the Miles Davis sextet of the fifties minus Miles; *Dizzy's Business* (Milestone), featuring Adderley's sextet of the sixties with the young Joe Zawinul on piano; and *Mercy, Mercy, Mercy* (Capitol), the title track of which became a runaway hit single.

Even after his death, Charlie Parker served the 1950s as a guiding light. In addition to Adderley, two other alto saxists found individualistic ways to pursue Parker's stylistic innovations; and although both Jackie McLean and Phil Woods are best appreciated from the perspective of later chapters, they still deserve mention here. (The pursuit of Parker's muse had more than academic interest: through the music of such saxophonists, the graffiti manifesto "Bird Lives," which had appeared after Parker's death, came searingly true.)

Jackie McLean performed the most radical surgery on Parker's body of work, wielding his brittle, slightly sour tone with broad strokes of color and attack. You can hear the way he both simplified and built on Bird's style on *New Soil* and *Bluesnik* (both Blue Note). The main body of his work belongs to the next transition section, as he spent the sixties and seventies extending the boundaries of hard-bop; but in the eighties he crafted an updated version of his hard-bop roots, making the recent albums *Rites of Passage* (Triloka) and *The Jackie Mac Attack Live* (Verve) relevant to the discussion here.

In the case of Phil Woods, the 1974 quartet album *Musique du Bois* (32 Jazz) extends and updates the basic principles of hard-bop architecture, with marvelous, full-scale solos throughout. Also consider *Rights of Swing* (Candid); more of the period (it was recorded in 1961), it showcases Woods's arranging skills for an octet that resembled Miles Davis's "Birth of the Cool" band in its instrumentation. Woods remained especially true to Parker's spirit, thanks to his fat tone, his lovingly smeared inflections, and his sometimes stupefying interpolation of musical quotations from other tunes.

Chet Baker's cult status quickly escalated to full-time stardom and led to a bewildering array of records, most of them available on CD. *Chet Baker & Crew* presents some of his best playing—his solos have an almost beatific glow—while *Quartet: Russ Freeman and Chet Baker* has just trumpet and rhythm, no other horns, and matches Baker with a leading pianist of West Coast jazz. (Both are on Pacific Jazz.) On *Baker's Holiday* (EmArcy) he delves into the repertoire of Billie Holiday, a kindred spirit. His first session with an "all-star" supporting cast, *Chet* (Fantasy/OJC), also makes the list. Finally, Baker's career is bookended by a couple of large-ensemble albums: *Chet Baker Big Band* (Pacific Jazz), from the early fifties, which drops his quintessential cool into the middle of charts written by several esteemed arrangers; and *The Last Great Concert, Volume 1: My Favorite Songs* (Enja), recorded with orchestra in a concert just two weeks before Baker's death.

The best way to dive further into Art Blakey's music is to drum up the best albums by his best bands. Both volumes of *A Night at Birdland* (Blue Note) document the birth of the Jazz Messengers: in-concert performances from the quintet co-led by Blakey and Horace Silver, and starring Clifford Brown on trumpet. *The Jazz Messengers* (Columbia/Legacy) features two line-ups from 1956, one with Donald Byrd and Hank Mobley, the other starring Jackie McLean. The following year, the wonderful tenor saxist Johnny Griffin joined (see below), and the band recorded a memorable collaboration in *Art Blakey's Jazz Messengers with Thelonious Monk* (Atlantic). The subsequent band, with Lee Morgan and Benny Golson, sounds great on *1958—Paris Olympia* (Mercury). From the sixties, go for *Three Blind Mice Volume 1* or *Indestructible* (both on Blue Note), but only if you *didn't* buy the three-CD set recommended above; and *Kyoto* (Fantasy/OJC) or *Free for All* (Blue Note) even if you did. Blakey's later work, including the band that introduced Wynton Marsalis, pops up in chapter 8.

On four CDs, *The Complete Blue Note and Pacific Jazz Recordings* (Blue Note) contains much of the music Clifford Brown recorded before joining Max Roach in 1954—including the live quintet date that led to the creation of the Jazz Messengers (see previous paragraph). Sonny Rollins joined the Clifford Brown–Max Roach Quintet in 1956, briefly adding a solo voice as strong as Brownie's own. For a full hearing of this extraordinary partnership, get *Study in Brown* (EmArcy). For a glimpse of Brownie's relaxed command in a live setting, try the three long jam-session tunes included on *The Beginning and the End* (Columbia/Legacy). They carry an extra punch when you learn they were recorded just hours before the auto accident that took his life.

More for Brubeck fans: *Gone with the Wind* includes several famous Quartet favorites; some of Brubeck's most persuasive writing lights up his *Jazz Impressions of Eurasia*; *Dave Digs Disney* is the first jazz album devoted to songs from Disney films (more would follow, but not for three decades); and the wacky *The Real Ambassadors* offers a surprising and delightful collaboration with Louis Armstrong and others. (All are on Columbia/Legacy.)
Octet (Fantasy) features the music that Brubeck wrote and

recorded in the 1940s, resembling (but predating) the repertoire of the Miles Davis Nonet. *Last Set at Newport* (Atlantic) adds fellow cool-school alumnus Gerry Mulligan to Brubeck's 1960s trio. Of Brubeck's many later albums, I like *Moscow Night* (Concord), *New Wine* (Music Masters), which features string orchestra, and *Young Lions & Old Tigers* (Telarc). And the four-CD retrospective *Time Signatures* (Columbia/Legacy) does an extraordinary job of tracing his entire career, validating his significant (if oft-ignored) innovations and contributions.

No guitarist of this period played on more sessions than Kenny Burrell, whose busy studio schedule attested to his popularity among musicians as well as listeners. Burrell's exceptionally mellow tone and easygoing solo style lead the way on *Blue Lights* (Blue Note) from 1958, a full-priced double CD of extended tracks. It stands as a leading example of the jam-session-styled albums that proliferated in the LP age. Lesser-priced alternatives include the single discs *All Day Long* and *All Night Long* (both on Fantasy/OJC). Also, *Kenny Burrell & John Coltrane* (Fantasy/OJC) documents a quite rewarding occasional collaboration with the famous saxist. Burrell's post-sixties recordings, exemplified by *Moon and Sand* (Concord) and *Sunup to Sundown* (Contemporary), find him increasingly contemplative.

In general, the two distinct and much-recorded phases of Coltrane's career—his hard-bop period and the subsequent avant-garde years—make it especially hard to narrow his music to a handful of albums. But the marvelous double-CD anthology *The Last Giant* (Rhino) includes collaborations with Miles Davis and Thelonious Monk; tracks from both *Blue Train* and *Giant Steps*; and even an example of his searching, extended soloing (a twenty-five-minute version of "My Favorite Things"), which really belongs to the music covered in chapter 5. Those who've never heard a note of Coltrane's music should start here.

Other notables from this period: *Soultrane, Standard Coltrane,* and *Bahia,* with trumpeter Donald Byrd (all on Fantasy/OJC), and the album with Monk mentioned in the previous chapter; plus *Coltrane Jazz, Coltrane's Sound,* and the album with Milt Jackson mentioned in the previous chapter (all on Atlantic). Trane's entire career on Atlantic (including *Giant Steps*) fills the seven-CD box *The Heavyweight Champion* (Rhino/

Atlantic Jazz Gallery), and since this covers a high-water mark in Trane's career, it's worth saving for.

Given the number of successful and influential albums recorded by Miles Davis during these years, it would be easier to simply list the albums *not* to buy. Nonetheless: *Miles Davis and the Jazz Giants* (Prestige) culls seventy minutes of music from the years 1951–56, focusing not on his working bands but rather on rare collaborations with the likes of Monk, Rollins, Blakey, and Charlie Parker (playing *tenor* sax instead of alto). It draws from such important albums as *Blue Haze*, *Walkin'*, and *Bags' Groove*.

For Davis's regular quintets, try *Workin'* (Fantasy/OJC) with Coltrane and *Saturday Night at the Blackhawk* (Columbia/Legacy) with Hank Mobley. The sextet with Adderley shines on their debut *Milestones* (Columbia/Legacy). By the early sixties, the Davis band had begun its metamorphosis into something quite different from hard-bop *or* cool (see transition section "Free 2 Roam"), and you can hear the change beginning with *Seven Steps to Heaven* (Columbia/Legacy) and the exquisite *Miles in Antibes* (Sony, available only as an import, but worth the hunt).

To hear more of Davis with Gil Evans, go next to *Sketches of Spain* and then *Porgy and Bess*. Everything they recorded together in the late fifties and early sixties, along with a voluminous array of extra takes and rehearsal material, is on the multiple-Grammy-winning *The Complete Columbia Studio Recordings*, which really aims at serious students of jazz. You can sample the entire set on just one disc, *The Best of Miles Davis and Gil Evans* (which contains selected material from all their collaborations. (All on Columbia/Legacy.)

Evans himself followed these ideas further on his own *The Individualism of Gil Evans* and also in his settings for guitarist Kenny Burrell's album *Guitar Forms* (both on Verve).

You can pursue the *other* Evans—pianist Bill—in the following trio dates: *New Jazz Conceptions* and *Explorations* (both on Fantasy/OJC); *Empathy/A Simple Matter of Conviction*, which finds his trio in transition, and *The Best of Bill Evans Live* (both Verve); and *Consecration I* (Timeless), recorded in the two weeks before Evans's death in 1980 and featuring his last trio—the best of his bands since the first one. Evans also recorded in even smaller formats and came up with two classics: *Undercurrent* (Blue Note), an album of piano/guitar duets with Jim Hall; and *Conversations with Myself* (Verve), an album of piano duets, with Evans playing both parts (using double-track recording).

In general, few artists have inspired the snowballing adulation that followed Evans's death, as reflected in the presence of no less than *five* multidisc sets devoted to his work—culminating in an eighteen-CD behemoth released in the fall of 1997. His earliest works fill twelve discs on the more manageable *Complete Riverside Recordings* (Riverside). Still too much too soon? Then consider *The Secret Sessions* (Milestone), an eight-CD set of bootlegged performances (legally cleared with the Evans estate) made between 1966 and 1975 at the Village Vanguard. The sound quality is hardly pristine but is quite serviceable, and it provides an excellent overview of Evans's trio with Gomez and Morell.

Erroll Garner just kept recording, and the recordings keep coming out. For his best early work, it's *Body and Soul* (Columbia/Legacy) and the double-disc *Solo Time!* (EmArcy). *Mambo Moves Garner* (Mercury), an effortless wedding of Garner's own rhythm impulses with the fifties' Latin dance fad, avoids camp thanks to Garner's limitless ebullience. *Dancing on the Ceiling* (EmArcy) features excellent, previously unreleased tracks from the early sixties. *That's My Kick & Gemini* (Telarchive) is probably the best of several recent releases that each contain the music from two LPs (in this case, from 1967 and 1972) on a single CD.

"As good as Stan Getz": *The Best of the West Coast Sessions* (Verve) runs a little cooler than the tenorist's Shrine concert (above), making it even more representative of his playing during the fifties. Other excellent Getz albums in this vein span the decades, including his 1980s quartet albums *Pure Getz* (Concord) and *Serenity* (EmArcy). But Getz kept seeking new contexts for his consistently splendid improvising: *Nobody Else but Me* features his intriguing quartet of the mid-sixties, which employed the young vibraphonist Gary Burton instead of a pianist; the double-disc *Dynasty* from 1971 finds Getz joining up with a Parisian organ trio for some of his most forceful extended soloing; and *Focus*, from 1961, remains one of the most inventive examples of orchestral writing in a jazz context, thanks to Getz's conception and the arrangements of Eddie

Sauter. (These last three are all on Verve.) Other Getz albums appear in subsequent chapters.

By the way, you can get a good dose of both Bill Evans *and* Stan Getz on one of the two albums they recorded together, which bears the unsurprising title *Stan Getz & Bill Evans* (Verve).

Dexter Gordon didn't make *any* bad records for Blue Note, and you can only fault a few of his later albums for other labels. Among the Blue Notes, the hard-bop spirit most effectively animates *Clubhouse* (1965) and *Go* (1962), while *Gettin' Around*, Dex's 1965 collaboration with the young vibraphonist Bobby Hutcherson, has a lighter touch. (Or you can pop for the six-CD set *The Complete Blue Note Sixties Sessions* and get them all.) *Homecoming* (Columbia/Legacy), the dual-disc documentation of Gordon's 1976 appearance at the Village Vanguard, pairs him with trumpeter Woody Shaw and paved the way for Gordon's return to the United States. The saxist also recorded one of the finest examples of soloist plus strings in all of jazz: *More Than You Know* (SteepleChase).

The soulful spectre of Grant Green hovers over several often overlooked gems. *Sunday Mornin'* goes to church and *The Latin Bit* heads for Mexico and the Caribbean. Together they prove the guitarist's heavy-lidded style could complement almost any kind of music.

The diminutive tenor saxist Johnny Griffin came out of Chicago to earn praise as the "fastest gun" on the prairie, combining the hottest elements of swing phrasing and bebop harmonies to craft solos of amazing speed but also plenty of soul. *Introducing Johnny Griffin* (Blue Note) opens the door; also consider the albums on which he played in Thelonious Monk's band (see chapter 3). Griffin's current work, recorded forty years later (such as *Dance of Passion*, on Verve), shows absolutely no diminution of his skills. Griffin also took part in a famous "saxophone summit" with fellow hard-bopsters Coltrane and Mobley, called *A Blowing Session* (Blue Note).

Griffin's fellow Chicago tenor men John Gilmore and Clifford Jordan matched up on a similar project, *Blowing in from Chicago*—also on Blue Note, and also a whole lot of fun. Other tenor tag teams chose to institutionalize their partnership by recording and performing semiregularly. These included Gene Ammons and Sonny Stitt, heard on *Boss Tenors—Straight Ahead from Chicago 1961* (Fantasy/OJC); former Woody Herman saxmen Al Cohn and Zoot Sims (aka Al & Zoot), *From A to Z . . . and Beyond* (Bluebird); and Griffin again, with Eddie "Lockjaw" Davis (Griff & Jaws) on *Tough Tenor Favorites* (Fantasy/OJC).

Don't forget that Freddie Hubbard took part in several albums already described in this chapter. For more under his own name, *The Best of Freddie Hubbard* (Blue Note) offers a nice survey (but be careful, since a Pablo Records album bears this same title). *Ready for Freddie* and *Breaking Point* (both Blue Note) will take you deeper, as will *The Artistry of Freddie Hubbard* (Impulse/GRP). *The Night of the Cookers* (Blue Note) pairs Hubbard with trumpeter Lee Morgan, his direct predecessor in the lineage handed down by Dizzy Gillespie.

That giant whooshing sound you hear—really, the collective inhalation of the Stan Kenton brass section—energizes the albums *Kenton in Hi-Fi* (featuring his forty-three-piece "Innovations in Modern Music Orchestra"), *Adventures in Time*, and *West Side Story*, where Kenton's theatricality finds its match in the music-drama of Leonard Bernstein's score. *Cuban Fire* focuses on the locale of the title, always a hot spot in the Kenton repertoire. The four-CD anthology *Retrospective* does a terrific job of capturing the key Kentonian moods. These discs all appear on Capitol Jazz. Ever the iconoclast, Kenton actually recorded most for his own label, Creative World Records; these only began to appear on CD in 1996, and you're on your own in terms of quality and value.

Digging into the other important big-band developments of this period poses problems. Trumpeter Shorty Rogers became more famous for his arrangements, a staple of the West Coast sound. The best examples are out of print, but you'll do okay with an Art Pepper album, *The Artistry of Pepper* (Pacific Jazz), which surrounds Pepper's sax with Rogers's arrangements. The most important big band to emerge in a hard-bop context, the Thad Jones–Mel Lewis Orchestra, has *no* individual albums now in print. *The Complete Solid State Recordings* (Mosaic) contains almost all their great work, but at seven CDs, it makes a pretty pricey introduction.

The absence of any Lee Konitz discs above is due largely to his presence on other important recordings: those led by Lennie Tristano (chapter 3), Miles Davis, and Gerry Mulligan. But the ongoing stylistic evolution of the saxist—who has continued to work and record up to the time of this writing—offers a study in the relentless purification of such cool-jazz attributes as the use of space and the de-emphasis on flamboyant technique. The 1949 tracks that make up Konitz's *Subconscious-Lee* (Fantasy/OJC), give you more of the cool manifesto; the dual CD *Live at the Half-Note* (Verve) finds him in 1959 with his old Tristano-days partner Warne Marsh and pianist Bill Evans; a fascinating late-sixties album, *The Lee Konitz Duets* (Fantasy/OJC), foreshadows later duets and unaccompanied solos (the ultimate in intimate formats); and the recent *Rhapsody* (Evidence) mixes and matches musical elements to create a miniature musical odyssey.

Charles Mingus's prolific imagination led to a labyrinth of now reissued recordings. Mingus himself considered his 1957 album *Tia Juana Moods* one of his best; now issued as *New Tia Juana Moods* (RCA Victor), it should be your next destination. The earlier *Pithecanthropus Erectus* and *The Clown* (both on Atlantic) are also certifiable classics, with several masterpieces between them. *Blues & Roots* (Rhino), recorded a couple years later (1959), expands upon their spirit. Or you can get all three—along with *At Antibes* (recommended above) and Mingus's two other late-fifties Atlantic albums—as part of the six-CD collection *Passions of a Man* (Rhino), which also includes a seventy-five-minute interview with the always outspoken bassist.

Mingus stretched the hard-bop ethos much further on his strikingly original *The Black Saint and the Sinner Lady*; it and the more conventional *Mingus Mingus Mingus Mingus Mingus* are both on Impulse/GRP. Later gems include *Changes One* and the underrated *Mingus Moves* (both on Rhino). If you enjoy large-scale, classically oriented compositions, the darkly impressive *Let My Children Hear Music* (Columbia/Legacy) introduces you to this side of Mingus's talent.

* * *

The remarkable consistency of the Modern Jazz Quartet led to the creation of many equivalently good albums, including *Django* (Fantasy/OJC), the film score *No Sun in Venice* (Atlantic), and *Odds Against Tomorrow* (Blue Note). *The Comedy* (Atlantic) is a multipart suite inspired by the sixteenth-century Italian improvisational theater form called commedia dell'arte, and it represents John Lewis's most ambitious attempt to move beyond the traditional confines of jazz music. A great live recording from around this same period—the double-disc *Dedicated to Connie* (Atlantic)—features songs from *The Comedy* and has much more to offer. For the big picture, I highly recommend the anthology *MJQ 40* (Atlantic), an admirable condensation of the band's four decades onto four CDs.

For the best overview of Wes Montgomery's music, pop for the double CD *Impressions: The Verve Jazz Sides* (Verve). It has several examples of his collaborations with organist Jimmy Smith, several of the commercially successful tunes featuring big-band orchestrations, and then throws in *all* of what is probably his best live recording—a 1965 quartet date originally (and aptly) titled "Smokin' at the Half Note." If that doesn't do the trick, try *So Much Guitar* and *Wes Montgomery Trio* (with organist Melvin Rhyne), both on Fantasy/OJC. Montgomery also guest-stars to great effect on *Cannonball Adderley and the Pollwinners* (Landmark).

Lee Morgan's late-fifties *Candy* and mid-sixties *Search for the New Land* flank his soul-jazz successes and help round out the picture of this delightful player. Especially good is his sextet date *The Procrastinator* from 1967. It reunites the trumpeter with his Jazz Messengers cohort Wayne Shorter—by this time a key figure in modern jazz via his work with Miles Davis (see the transition section "Free 2 Roam")—and also gains from Herbie Hancock's dense chords and Bobby Hutcherson's impressionistic vibes playing. They're all Blue Notes.

More Mulligan: The quartet featuring trombonist Bob Brookmeyer shines on *At Storyville* (Pacific Jazz). Mulligan often collaborated with other saxophonists, contemporary and otherwise, most notably on *Gerry Mulligan Meets Ben Webster* and *Blues in Time* with Paul Desmond (both on Verve). He also undertook an unexpected but interesting collaboration with Thelonious Monk, *Mulligan Meets Monk* (Fantasy).

Unfortunately, the only available album by the Concert Jazz Band, *Night Lights* (Phillips), runs barely over a half hour. But the strength of this early-sixties orchestra should validate the double-disc price of *Gerry Mulligan and the Concert Jazz Band en Concert* (RTE), which captures a 1960 concert in Paris featuring Brookmeyer, Zoot Sims, and drummer Mel Lewis.

A lifelong drug addict, Art Pepper was inconsistent as a recording artist. *The Art of Pepper* (Blue Note) and *Smack Up* (Fantasy/OJC) will just about cover you for this period of his career. But Pepper remained a searcher, digging ever deeper into his battered psyche. His later recordings—influenced by John Coltrane and Ornette Coleman (see chapter 5)—led him to some of the most naked and searing musical admissions ever heard in jazz. Try *The Trip, Friday Night at the Village Vanguard*, and *Tête-à-Tête*, an album of sax-piano duets (all on Fantasy/OJC).

Oscar nominations (for pianist Peterson, of course) include *At the Concertgebouw*, which stars his drummerless trio (bass and guitar) and turns out *not* to have been recorded anywhere near the Amsterdam auditorium named in the title (don't ask); *The Trio* or *Night Train*, both excellent examples of Peterson's trio with the invaluable drummer Ed Thigpen; and *The Gershwin Songbooks* (all on Verve). *Trio + One* (EmArcy) adds the influential trumpeter Clark Terry. Another album called *The Trio* (Pablo) dates from 1973 and stars two players with almost as much technique as Oscar, guitarist Joe Pass and the Danish bassist Niels-Henning Ørsted Pedersen. Between 1963 and 1968, Peterson made a series of superb solo and trio records in Germany, now available as the four-CD *Exclusively for My Friends* (Verve)—a marvelous compendium of what he can do.

In the nineties, a stroke left Peterson with limited use of his left hand, but since his right hand always did the work of a whole pianist anyway, he soon returned to performing. (Still, you should know that the later recordings lack the textural variety of his pre-illness recordings.)

* * *

The trio format used by Sonny Rollins at the Village Vanguard first showed up some months earlier on the legendary *Way Out West* (Fantasy/OJC), where a surprising repertoire ("I'm an Old Cowhand," "Wagon Wheels") complemented the oddball humor of the cover photo (Rollins in the desert, dressed in suit and tie, gunbelt, and ten-gallon hat). *The Essential Sonny Rollins on Riverside* (Riverside) lives up to its name, and *Sonny Rollins Volume 2* (Blue Note) is a classic. The Rollins-Coltrane "battle" mentioned in the chapter introduction appears on the album *Tenor Madness*, and Rollins led one of the last recordings by his bandmate Clifford Brown on *Sonny Rollins plus Four* (both now on Fantasy/OJC). For those with deeper pockets, all ten of the LPs Rollins made originally for the Prestige label—including those last two titles, plus music he recorded under the leadership of others—can be found on the unbeatable seven-CD set *Sonny Rollins: The Complete Prestige Recordings* (Prestige). *All the Things You Are 1963–64* (RCA Bluebird) features his meeting with past tenor great Coleman Hawkins, a seminal influence on Rollins and others.

If you can't find Jimmy Smith's *Cool Blues* (see above), don't hesitate to pick up the equally fine *Open House/Plain Talk* (Blue Note), a 1960 session with trumpeter Blue Mitchell and saxist Jackie McLean originally released as two LPs but now contained on a single CD. Smith's continued prowess makes good buys of such later albums as *Midnight Special*, *I'm Movin' On*, and *The Master* with Kenny Burrell (all on Blue Note); *Organ Grinder Swing* (Verve), featuring Grant Green; and *Sum Serious Blues* (Milestone).

On the subject of organists, several other keyboardists followed Smith's lead and began to work with the new instrument, creating by their efforts a subgenre—organ jazz—that proved especially popular as a medium for the soul-and-funk sounds of the period. Great examples would include Jack McDuff's *The Honeydripper* and *Live!* (featuring a hot young guitarist named George Benson), both on Fantasy/OJC; Richard "Groove" Holmes's *Groovin' with Jug* (Pacific Jazz); and Lonnie Smith's *Drives* (Blue Note), recorded in 1970 but still illustrative of this trend.

* * *

The best jazz vocal work of this period does not have much to do with a discussion of hard-bop and cool jazz. (In fact, from this point until the mid-eighties, the leading vocalists would mostly perform in styles established prior to the decade in which they sang.) Ella Fitzgerald and Sarah Vaughan, the two greatest virtuosos ever to sing jazz, had both metamorphosed into major pop-music stars. Neither of them really adapted the period's innovations to their own styles. Their successor, Carmen McRae, brought a tougher edge to her singing, but she didn't really sail the pervasive musical currents of the fifties, and in fact gained her renown in later decades. And Dinah Washington, who outdistanced them all in terms of popularity, was truly sui generis. Even though she made many excellent jazz sides, her recordings also included rhythm and blues, pure blues, and symphonically arranged love songs. Before she died at age thirty-nine, her style had begun to influence not only other pop singers, but also the early stars of rock and roll.

Carmen McRae Sings Lover Man and Other Billie Holiday Classics (Columbia/Legacy) offers a fine introduction to a complicated and brilliant singer. McRae's voice had more salt than sugar, and as the years passed, sentimentality became an increasingly rare contrivance for her. (In her worldly, dramatic, and sometimes defiant interpretations, she suffered fools not gladly, not sadly—just not at all.) Because of this, her singing was a perfect match for the music of her close friend Thelonious Monk. *Carmen Sings Monk* (Novus), one of her last recordings, speaks for itself. The double-disc nightclub recording *Great American Songbook* (Atlantic) remains the best encapsulation of her music and her personality.

By the time of that recording, the "great American songbook" had already become a much-used phrase to describe the trove of sophisticated popular-music compositions left by writers such as Irving Berlin, Harold Arlen, Richard Rodgers and Lorenz Hart, and others. The person most responsible for gaining new attention for these songs was Ella Fitzgerald, in a series of eight albums. Each was devoted to the work of a different songwriter, and each placed Ella's crystalline voice in front of large ensembles, with improvisation taking a backseat. Ella thus became the only jazz singer to reinvent herself not once but twice—as swing songstress turned bop chick, turned pop-music diva. To hear how and why, go for *Best of the Songbooks* and *Best of the Songbooks: The Love Songs*, which compile songs from all eight albums, or delve more deeply with *Ella Fitzgerald Sings the Duke Ellington Songbook* (a three-CD box), then the double discs *Gershwin Songbook* and *Cole Porter Songbook* (all on Verve).

Sarah Vaughan also did some songbooking, on the strings-laden discs *Sarah Vaughan Sings George Gershwin*, volume one of which gets the nod here; *The Rodgers & Hart Songbook*; and teaming up with Billy Eckstine on *The Irving Berlin Songbook* (all on EmArcy). In the seventies, she recorded two volumes of *The Duke Ellington Songbook* (Pablo), with sparkling small-group accompaniment. Other recordings helped make Vaughan one of the most famous pop-music stars, although her interpretative abilities remained indisputably jazz. You can find the best of them on *The Roulette Years, Volumes One and Two*, compressed onto a single CD (Roulette/Blue Note).

To experience the unmistakable sound of Dinah Washington, the anthologies *Compact Jazz* and *Dinah Washington Sings Standards* (both on Verve) will get you started. The sultry *Blue Gardenia* and the waggish *Fats Waller Songbook* (both EmArcy) are each terrific for completely different reasons. But the absolutely best introduction will cost you a little more: the three-CD box that constitutes *Vol. 4* (recordings made between 1954 and 1956) of the massive reissue project *The Complete Dinah Washington on Mercury*.

One vocalist who really does embody this period—from hard-bop to cool to Beat poetry to the Camelot administration of JFK—is Mark Murphy. Nonetheless, his best recordings were still to come. After *Rah* (mentioned above), the indisputable best buy is the double-disc *Stolen . . . and Other Moments* (32 Jazz), which anthologizes the great series of records he made in the seventies and eighties. Since the original albums that supplied this material are out of print, and since this set comes at a discounted price, you really have no excuse.

Born 2 Be Free: Intimations of Liberation

In the 1960s, as described in the next chapter, jazz attained a new liberation, characterized by sweeping changes in the relationships that connected the most basic elements of music—melody, harmony, and rhythm. To many listeners, this "free jazz" represented a wholesale abandonment of everything they believed about jazz and improvisation. As such artists as Ornette Coleman, John Coltrane, and Cecil Taylor sought and found a new land, it appeared as if the sky had impetuously fallen on the old homestead.

But appearances notwithstanding, few artistic developments take place overnight, and clues to the free jazz revolution lay scattered among key recordings of the 1950s and early 1960s. On these discs, recorded during the same time as mainstream masterpieces such as *Kind of Blue* and *Blue Train*, you can clearly hear the changes under way. In some cases, such albums simply anticipated the gathering storm; more often, they held a definite and discernible sway over later events.

Like a plant growing toward the sunlight, jazz has steadily thirsted after more freedom. You can hear this in the evolution of big-band swing into bebop, and from there to the dual idioms, hard-bop and cool, that defined the fifties. The replacement for those idioms emerged more quickly than many expected, but the seeds had already been planted in the urgent and relentless questing of such musicians as Charlie Parker and Bud Powell—both of whom could well have burst through the bebop confines had they lived longer or healthier lives. As young artists cultivated those seeds, they grew rapidly, leading to the music described below. It sets the stage for the even more challenging events covered in the next chapter.

The short career of woodwind virtuoso Eric Dolphy— who spent only six years as a recognized recording artist before dying (of diabetes and insulin shock) at age thirty-six—cannot camouflage his impact on contemporaries and his influence on later musicians. Dolphy did not leap wholly into free jazz, but he pushed the hard-bop envelope to the point of blurring the line between the two idioms. Similarly, on all three of his instruments—alto sax, flute, and the relatively rare bass clarinet—Dolphy pushed against conventional boundaries of technique. He challenged prevailing notions of expressivity and beauty, while attaining a stylistic voice that often seemed to mimic the variety and nuance of the *vox humana*.

Far Cry (Prestige) brilliantly exploits Dolphy's ability to apply still-developing musical concepts to the hard-bop idiom and thus extend it in a significant way. The best examples come on the ballad standards "Tenderly" and "It's Magic." The first features his keening alto sax, in an unaccompanied rendition that overflows with imagery and detail; on the second, his speech-inflected bass clarinet employs stylistic devices that would later be called "avant-garde." Both songs bend to accommodate Dolphy's expansive improvisational theory, which made room for notes once considered "wrong" within a given key or harmonic structure. (Dolphy himself said, "I hear [these notes] as proper.... Every note I play has some reference to the chords of the piece.") The remaining songs, written by Dolphy or his pianist Jaki Byard, work in much the same way: they allow the reedman and his alter ego, the graceful and daring trumpeter Booker Little, to confront familiar formats and structures armed with brand-new weapons in jazz's constant war against complacency. (Just listen to Dolphy's fluttery, discursive flute work on "Ode to Charlie Parker.") Dolphy recorded *Far Cry* on December 21, 1960—improbably, the same day that he took part in the groundbreaking Ornette Coleman project entitled "Free Jazz" (see next chapter). Together they provide spectacular evidence of the ease with which he moved both within and beyond the jazz tradition.

Dolphy made his last studio recording, *Out to Lunch* (Blue Note), just four months before his death in 1964, and even today it whets the appetite for what might have followed. By this session, familiar song structures—such as standards and the blues—had all but disappeared; in their place stood a gleaming new sonic architecture, labyrinthine and open-ended at the same time. The songs and solos on *Out to Lunch* rely on rhythmic motifs as well as melodic development; the solos roam far and wide, finding pockets of total freedom within the boundaries of the compositions. For this session, Dolphy did away with the piano, as would many free jazz exponents of the sixties (see chapter 5). But rather than completely jettison the harmonic underpinnings supplied by the piano, he replaced it with the vibraphone— another instrument capable of playing chords, but with an airy and less restrictive sound. The youthful Bobby Hutcherson is the vibist, playing wildly imaginative solos and bold accompaniments that shape and prod the horn solos. The album also features a gloriously unleashed Freddie Hubbard on trumpet. As for Dolphy, his alto cries joy, sadness, and even panic, while his bass clarinet becomes an octave-leaping dervish on the mock-martial "Hat and Beard" (a tribute to Thelonious Monk). On the cusp of hard-bop and the new freedom of the sixties, *Out to Lunch* serves as a fitting epitaph to Dolphy's creativity.

Dolphy also figures prominently in recordings by Charles Mingus and Oliver Nelson (chapter 4), and Ornette Coleman and John Coltrane (chapter 5).

Jackie McLean, *One Step Beyond* (Blue Note). Even during the fifties, when he reigned as one of the hard-bop successors to Charlie Parker, the playing of Jackie McLean showed glints of the future. His alto saxophone had a hard attack and plastic timbre, with which he could manipulate the sound in blunt and sometimes even harsh ways; and he often spiced his playing with touches of the modal theory that Miles Davis had employed as a first step away from the shackles of bebop harmony. Like Eric Dolphy, McLean helped to open up the jazz mainstream from within; and like Dolphy, he also made an album with the high priest of free jazz, Ornette Coleman. But McLean never really abandoned his hard-bop roots, despite his obvious attraction to the jazz style that supplanted it. *One Step Beyond*, one of his most ambitious albums, sits squarely at the junction of hard-bop and free jazz, with a clear view of both camps but leaning toward neither. Like Dolphy's *Out to Lunch*, it features Bobby Hutcherson on vibes and the even younger Tony Williams on drums. It also stars a potent and open-minded trombonist named Grachan Moncur III, whose broad strokes and bop-based phrases made a fine complement to McLean's own soloing. Recorded in 1963, several years after Ornette had cut his swath across the jazz landscape, this album bridges the music of the fifties and the avant-garde developments of the late sixties.

(You can fine-tune your exposure to McLean's genre-spanning music. The 1959 *New Soil* is a straight-ahead hard-bop album with only a hint of modal improvisation; *Destination Out*, recorded six months after *One Step Beyond*, moves the bar a notch; and *New and Old Gospel*, McLean's meeting with Ornette Coleman—here playing trumpet!—finds McLean in his fullest embrace of free jazz ideas. All are on Blue Note.)

Sun Ra and His Solar Arkestra, *Visits Planet Earth/ Interstellar Low Ways* (Evidence). Jazz people use the word *outside* to describe the avant-garde, and no one was more outside than Sun Ra. For starters, he claimed the planet Saturn as his place of birth; he then draped his band (variously called the Cosmic Arkestra, the Astro Infinity Orchestra, and Le Sony'r Ra's Myth-Science Arkestra) in capes and headgear; and he wrapped his music in an evolving philosophy that combined ancient Egyptology with modern myths about space travel and alien visitation. For all that, the record shows that Sun Ra came into the world as Herman Blount and acquired the nickname Sonny as a jazz arranger and bandleader in 1950s Chicago. Meanwhile, his *records* show that his use of the electric piano predated its arrival in mainstream jazz by a full decade—and that by the early sixties he had already figured out how to balance written music and avant-garde improvisation within the setting of a small jazz orchestra. On *Planet Earth/Low Ways*— comprising sessions from 1956, 1958, and 1960—you can hear for yourself the transformation of Sun Ra's concept. The earliest tracks offer conventional hard-bop writing, although Sun Ra's melodic twists and modal chords provide surprises even in this setting. More exotic experimentation comes on such songs as "Planet Earth" and "Overtones of China," as the music begins to blossom with unusual song structures and dissonant techniques. By the last session—on titles such as "Interstellar Low Ways" and "Rocket Number Nine Take Off for the Planet Venus"—Sun Ra could incorporate sections of free improvisation while still retaining his idiosyncratic approach to bebop, blues, and swing. Few albums provide such a clear picture of jazz in transition.

(Others to consider: Sun Ra's *Jazz in Silhouette,* a delightful album from 1958 that features some of his early band's best work; and *Angels and Demons at Play/The Nubians of Plutonia,* which combines two earlier LPs and features more 1956–60 recordings, with many compositions rich in African rhythms and imagery. Both albums are on Evidence.)

Cecil Taylor, *Jazz Advance* (Blue Note). The crashing chordal polyphonies and hyperactive jabs of Cecil Taylor's piano music can still leave listeners at a loss for words. We can only guess at their effect on the average jazz fan in 1957, when this album reached the stores. It remains among the most dramatic recording debuts in jazz history. In subsequent years, Taylor would create his own large-scale compositional structures. These fit hand in glove with his new approach to improvisation, which breaks the music into jagged, disconnected beads of sound that the pianist recombines with the skill of a genetic engineer. But on *Jazz Advance,* he used this philosophy to deconstruct songs by Cole Porter, Duke Ellington, and Thelonious Monk, and hearing the transformation of these tunes forecasts the events to come. In most cases, Taylor and his trio lurk around the form of the piece; but he quickly moves beyond the initial theme to create careening new melodies with only a tangential relationship to the original. (On Porter's "You'd Be So Nice to Come Home To," the relationship between that song and Taylor's solo remains a matter of faith.) His knuckle-busting virtuosity is impressive in its own right, offering a peek at what the next generation would know as "extended technique" (see chapter 5). But Taylor needed every ounce of it to realize his stupefying concept of jazz in general and the piano in particular, using rapidly dancing rhythms, gnarled and knotted motifs, and keyboard-spanning leaps to forge a brand-new alphabet for the language of jazz.

Various Artists, *The Birth of the Third Stream* (Columbia/ Legacy). Originally contained on two LPs recorded in 1956 and 1957, the music here represents the attempt to fuse the two streams of American art music—classical composition and jazz—into a "third stream" that would embody the strengths of both. The third-stream movement, spearheaded by the Modern Jazz Quartet's John Lewis and composer/ conductor/writer/educator Gunther Schuller, never quite developed into the rushing river its champions hoped for. But these first attempts did employ a variety of avant-garde ideas and techniques, especially in compositions by George Russell ("All About Rosie"), Charles Mingus ("Revelations"), and Schuller himself ("Transformations" and "Symphony for Brass and Percussion"). And by gathering together works from both the jazz and classical schools (and moreover giving them a label), these records promoted the exalted concept that jazz could embody such elements as harmonic dissonance and shifting tempos, both of which would distinguish the avant-garde jazz of the late sixties.

chapter five

Freedom Now*
1959-?

In 1949—the same year that the Miles Davis Nonet assembled to give birth to the cool (chapter 4); the same year that Lennie Tristano's sextet recorded the first unstructured improvisations (chapter 3)—Ornette Coleman got beat up for playing his music.

Then a nineteen-year-old saxophonist from Fort Worth, Texas, Coleman was touring with a rhythm-and-blues dance band. Such bands, prevalent in the South and Southwest during the forties and fifties, constituted most of Coleman's early professional experience. The band had reached Baton Rouge, Louisiana, and midway through his featured solo, he decided to work in some of the new musical ideas he'd been experimenting with in his own practice sessions. Coleman had discovered and gravitated toward the "modern jazz" of that period, bebop; and if he had simply dropped a typical bebop phrase à la Charlie Parker or Dexter Gordon, it would probably have caused *enough* of a stir. But every indication suggests that Ornette's bebop didn't sound like anyone else's; indeed, in less than a decade the music world would both hail and revile him for the same iconoclasm he had exhibited as a teenager. (He certainly didn't *look* like many other musicians. He wore his

---

*When drummer Max Roach gave the title "Freedom Now" to his extended suite of 1960—a work that appeared on the album *We Insist!*—he was thinking of the composition's strong civil-rights message. But the phrase might also describe the musical message that turned jazz upside down in the sixties: the message that new avenues of expression lay beyond the prevailing ideas of melody, harmony, and rhythm.

hair too long and had an unfashionable beard, and he didn't swagger.)

After his solo, Coleman received word that some local musicians wanted to meet him outside. There he received a vicious beating from a half dozen large African-American men who mocked his appearance and apparently resented his music: they wrecked his saxophone by tossing it down the street. Clearly, despite the label Ornette's music would soon receive, he wouldn't get to play "free jazz" without paying a price.

The term *free jazz* emerged in the early sixties, after the release of Coleman's influential album of the same name. To many, this new music had a tumbling, almost violent forcefulness and a slapdash immediacy—qualities that would also describe the "splatter" paintings of the artist Jackson Pollock (one of which appeared on the cover of the album *Free Jazz*). The saxist actually sought to do just what the name suggested: to "free jazz" of the formulas and clichés that had permeated bebop and stolen much of its rebellious spirit.

Although it accurately described Coleman's approach, the term would soon become a prism for several different but compatible approaches to jazz improvisation, focusing them all into a deceptive monolith. It had other names as well: "the avant-garde," "the New Thing," and "that free crap" (to dyed-in-the-wool beboppers who believed the "free" players lacked proper training and all sense of esthetics). And by the late sixties—when a second wave of the avant-garde did away with the steady tempos and flowing improvisations that still marked Ornette's music—free jazz represented the most abstract, inclusive, and unpredictable genre in jazz history.

To liberate jazz melody, Coleman took aim at the harmonic patterns that had dictated the structure of jazz improvisation since the 1920s and then destroyed them. His compositions arrived with no predetermined harmonies whatsoever. And without the limitations imposed by such harmonic patterns, his solos—and those of trumpeter Don Cherry (the Dizzy to his Bird)—could freely travel into, out of, and between musical keys. As Coleman wrote in the liner notes for his first album, "I think one day music will be a lot freer. Then the pattern for a tune, for instance, will be forgotten and the tune itself will be the pattern."

Since his music did not depend on predetermined harmonies, Coleman saw no need for his bands to include a piano. After all, the primary function of that instrument in a jazz ensemble is to play the chords that reinforce a song's harmonic structure. (Not until the nineties did Ornette work with a conventional pianist-led rhythm section.) Gerry Mulligan had pioneered this pianoless-quartet format in the early fifties, but his band played tunes that *did* contain harmonic progressions, and the members of his quartet maintained that structure as the foundation for their solos. By contrast, in Coleman's band the only guide to improvisation lay in his bouncy, propulsive melodies; after that (to paraphrase his statement above), each solo became its own pattern.

Whatever harmonies this music exhibited were either implied by the soloist or else they resulted from the intersection of simultaneous melodies played by the sax, trumpet, Charlie Haden's bass, and at times, even Billy Higgins's drums. Sound familiar? It should. These intersecting lines hearkened back to the polyphony of the first jazz, created in New Orleans and exemplified by the early records of King Oliver and Louis Armstrong. Not since the twenties had a jazz style relied so little on chords and harmony; and not coincidentally, the freewheeling melodies and raucous energy of Coleman's music recalled the lively strutting of Armstrong's Hot Seven. Free jazz was the first jazz style to significantly *reduce* the importance of harmony in jazz. To free jazz of its bad habits, Coleman went back to a time before those habits had accumulated.

What's more, Coleman and Cherry—along with such contemporaries as Albert Ayler and Eric Dolphy (see previous transition section)—shared something else with their long-ago counterparts. The first jazz had developed, in part, from a desire to bring instrumental music closer to the expressive capabilities of the human voice. This became a vital concern to these musicians as well (but in ways that Armstrong might never have imagined).

Coleman and Cherry both played instruments that produced a less polished and more visceral sound than the precision-crafted horns used by most jazzmen. Cherry played a *pocket cornet*, sometimes called a toy trumpet, because it did indeed resemble a child's version of the real thing. It allowed Cherry to more easily mold his tone into puckered smears and human-sounding exclamations. Rather bizarrely, Coleman himself preferred a student-model alto sax made of plastic (unlike any other professional saxist in jazz history). It facilitated his remarkably plastic tone, which ranged from slippery/oily to passionately keening, now fulsome, now astringent, and always bearing the strong blues stamp of his Southwest upbringing.

Coleman had assembled his revolutionary ensemble in Los Angeles, where he had gone to live in the mid-fifties. Shortly after their first recording—the appropriately titled *Something Else!*—his star began to rise. At the decade's end, by which time the quartet had taken up residence in New York, their intellectually exciting, furiously emotional music created a sensation of admiration and controversy. Bohemians and artistic thrill-seekers rubbed elbows with the jazz press and curious musicians when the band debuted at the Five Spot Café. Afterward, almost everyone agreed that Coleman had hit on something new. What it was, and whether it would last, were matters of significant disagreement.

Those disagreements could grow quite heated. Ornette claims that after hearing the band, Max Roach—no stranger to the concept of freedom, and himself a rebel when he helped create bebop a generation before—came up and punched him in the mouth. A decade had passed, and Ornette's music could still get him beaten up.

The sixties would witness the tumultuous collapse of barriers that had stood for decades. The hard-won successes of the civil rights movement meant greater freedom (in theory) for people of color; a booming economy gave many a greater freedom to indulge in hobbies and recreation; the sexual revolution meant more freedom to indulge, period. On transistor radios, pop music mirrored the nation's sense of optimism and potential. But beneath this veneer, the changes in American life had begun to buck and roil, and free jazz caught those rhythms— just as swing and bebop had anticipated the changes in their own eras.

From a narrower perspective, the evolution of such a radically different music shouldn't have surprised the jazz world. The widespread success of bebop had created a comfortable, often predictable idiom and an artistic environment ripe for rebellion—in exactly the same way that the plump, cushy sounds of the Swing Era had invited the sharp prick of bebop.

In fact, careful listening reveals that bebop had sown the seeds for its own replacement. On live recordings, in the spiraling intensity of their extended solos, Charlie Parker and Bud Powell would occasionally break through the tyranny of harmony for brief but illuminating moments, foreshadowing the music of Ornette Coleman and pianist Cecil Taylor.

In addition, even mainstream musicians were starting to reduce their dependency on complex harmonic schemes, thanks largely to Miles Davis. Remember that on his popular and influential album *Kind of Blue* (chapter 4), Davis had done away with chord patterns as the basis for improvisation, replacing them with the particular scales called modes. The concept of *modal improvisation* gained many adherents among those musicians looking to burst out of bebop's box, but unwilling to go as far as Ornette Coleman. The most prominent of these musicians, John Coltrane, had performed on *Kind of Blue*. Shortly later he turned to modal improvisation as his primary vehicle, riding it for epic and at times apocalyptic improvisations that made him the most visible proponent of the "avant-garde."*

Coltrane and others also adapted the hyperexpressionism found in Ornette's playing, and especially in that of Albert Ayler: guttural growls, fluctuations in pitch, and piercing shrieks that extended the saxophone's upper range beyond its inventor's design. These devices all enlarged the music's tonal palette, and along with other unorthodox sounds that fall somewhere between traditional music and random noise, they became an important weapon in the avant-garde arsenal. The term *extended technique* covers the specific virtuosity needed to create and control such utterances. It applies mostly to saxophonists for the simple reason that reed instruments lend themselves more readily to these innovations. But the insect screams generated by trombonist George Lewis at the top of his range; the skittering pizzicati of the British guitarist Derek Bailey; the athleticism used by Cecil Taylor when he smashed his dense

---

*This phrase has always generated confusion. *Avant-garde* roughly translates as "ahead of the pack," so its meaning shifts from era to era. Louis Armstrong's mastery of the jazz solo made him avant-garde with relation to King Oliver, and bebop qualified as the avant-garde of the forties. Nonetheless, the phrase stuck like glue to the music following in Ornette's wake. It became a proper noun tied to a historical style and period, thus losing its effectiveness in describing any new jazz movements that would follow.

piano chords together with enough force to create echoing overtones—all these would earn the denotation *extended technique* as well.

Before long, Taylor had brought the concepts of free jazz *and* the avant-garde further than almost anyone else: his music, which frequently took the form of episodic, hour-long improvisations, came to incorporate his own obscurantist poetry along with Tourette's-like shouts from the keyboard and balletic dance movements (inspired by tai chi) away from it. His difficult, self-contained art predates even Coleman's (see the transition section "Born 2 Be Free"), and in his prolific recording career he has generated currents that both jazz and classical artists have tried to navigate. Among his other achievements, Taylor liberated the jazz piano, transforming it from the chord-wielding arbiter of tonality to a paragon of *pantonality* (a musical system that makes all the scales, and the keys they correspond to, simultaneously available to the composer or improviser).

The theatricality of Taylor's performances did not go unnoticed—certainly not in the Midwest, where Ornette Coleman's manifesto had stirred up a number of young musicians centered in Chicago and St. Louis. These artists constituted the "second wave" of the avant-garde, building upon Coleman's innovations to create a thunderous cornucopia of new music. Working within two musicians' collectives—Chicago's Association for the Advancement of Creative Musicians (AACM) and the Black Artists Group (BAG) in St. Louis—they nourished the concepts of free jazz and explored its implications. The results ranged from bleak or tender interludes of intimacy to the cacophonous joy of polyphonic improvisation. The musicians also nourished each other: the collective produced and supported its members' concerts when no club owners would promote their radical and sometimes confrontational creations.

The AACM grew out of the Experimental Band, a rehearsal orchestra that pianist Muhal Richard Abrams organized in 1962 to work on new musical concepts. In 1965, he and three others from this circle obtained the legal charter for the AACM, which they envisioned as a community service organization as well as a musicians' collective. Indeed, these musicians saw music itself as a community service, and they shunned the alcohol and drugs that had devastated previous generations of African-American jazzmen. To this end, they established a music school, where Abrams and his peers taught many of the artists who would carry the AACM's concept into the seventies and eighties, among them saxists Chico Freeman, Douglas Ewart, and Edward Wilkerson; trombonist George Lewis; and percussionist Kahil El'Zabar.

But none of these musicians had as much impact as those who formed the Art Ensemble of Chicago, which in 1969 took up residence in Paris and spread the AACM gospel. Combining music, costumery (including African face paint), and performance art, the AEC became an overnight sensation. Their first recordings, made in Europe, ping-ponged their reputation back across the Atlantic. The band included trumpeter Lester Bowie, saxophonists Roscoe Mitchell and Joseph Jarman, bassist Malachi Favors, and drummer Famoudou Don Moye—five of the most accomplished and innovative musicians the avant-garde has produced (although only Mitchell and Bowie would go on to enjoy equal fame beyond the band). They still appear semiregularly thirty years after the AEC's formation, making it one of the longest-running acts in jazz history.

From their Parisian base, the Art Ensemble—along with the remarkable saxist and composer Anthony Braxton, who had traveled with them—built a strong and long-lasting European audience for the avant-garde. Never again would audiences automatically conjure the images of Louis Armstrong and the Austin High Gang when they heard the words *Chicago jazz*—at least, not without such unlikely musical heirs as Bowie and Jarman hovering behind them.

In the meantime, the sounds of Chicago's avant-garde began to infiltrate New York through the music of such players as Braxton, the Art Ensemble, trumpeter Leo Smith (originally from St. Louis), and violinist Leroy Jenkins. For the most part, this music was presented in loft spaces different in every way imaginable from the smoky cellars and tricked-out nightclubs that housed most live jazz; in some cases, these lofts doubled as living spaces for their owner/entrepreneurs. Because of these locales, the term "loft jazz" soon came into the lexicon to improbably describe this second-story underground music.

But despite its message of liberation, the abstract structures and unorthodox sounds of most avant-garde jazz actually isolated this music from the general public, many of whom reacted with horror, disdain, and bereavement for what they perceived as a lack of beauty and the loss of swing.

The Discs

Although three other musicians joined him in founding the AACM, Muhal Richard Abrams was first among equals. A bandleading pianist and theorizing composer, he quickly assumed the additional role of teacher—imparting lessons about both music and life to AACM members (most of whom were younger than Abrams)—and served as the organization's conscience and guiding light in its first years.

Abrams's earliest recordings are also his most abstract, using the license provided by free jazz to weave their way in and out of defined rhythms, tempos, and tonalities. His first two albums contain lengthy, atmospheric compositions that make heavy use of tintinnabulating percussion sound. They also showcase Abrams's own piano work, which can build intensifying tension with dense, pointillistic textures. This aspect of Abrams's music informs the second of two twenty-minute tracks that make up his 1969 recording *Young at Heart, Wise in Time* (Delmark), starring trumpeter Leo Smith and violinist Leroy Jenkins. But Abrams's piano can also dance with grace and lull with beauty, as on the solo piano excursion that constitutes the first half of this recording. This piece, "Young at Heart," traverses the history of jazz piano, with touches of stride and bebop, romantic balladry and spiky "freebop." It serves as a reminder that in his leadership of the AACM, Abrams always stressed the importance of knowing the music's history as well as mapping its new directions (in keeping with the AACM motto, "Ancient to the future").

Abrams moved to New York in the mid-seventies and steadily established his reputation as a superlative composer, writing for groups that ranged from sextet to big band. In fact, his compositions of the eighties and nineties mark him as a "portmanteau" composer of the avant-garde, summing up the free jazz accomplishments of the sixties and seventies and placing them in the larger context of all jazz history. (As such, Abrams embodies one of the signal characteristics of the mature avant-garde: having extended the boundaries of improvisation with his earlier achievements, he no longer finds it necessary to restake those boundaries with each and every note.) His 1989 *The Hearinga Suite* (Black Saint), which features an eighteen-piece big band, provides perhaps the best example of his luminescent compositional style. Still abstract, in some ways still experimental, *The Hearinga Suite* also showcases the hearty lyricism that always coexists in Abrams's art. Like most of his albums in the last decade, it remains accessible even to those who decry the avant-garde. One of Abrams's best works, it also stands among the most inventive orchestral-jazz albums of the last quarter century.

Air, *Air Time* (Nessa). Since the cooperative trio called Air didn't emerge until the mid-seventies, most people consider it a "second-generation" AACM group. But one of its members—the late Steve McCall, a remarkably sensitive and subtle drummer—helped Muhal Abrams found the AACM; and saxist/flutist Henry Threadgill, the group's primary motivating force, had played in Abrams's seminal Experimental Band. (The third Air man, bassist Fred Hopkins, got involved with the AACM in the late sixties.) Air confounded expectations at almost every turn. Saxophone-led trios often rely on sax solos with accompaniment, but every member of Air played an equal role in the group's dynamic, translucent music. McCall's highly lyrical drum solos were just as prominent as Threadgill's improvisations, and Hopkins's fleet, singing bass lines allowed him to play a pivotal role throughout, acting not only as rhythmic fulcrum but also as a second melody instrument. Without histrionics, Air maintained a distinct theatricality in their music, a result of their carefully worked-out arrangements, and a by-product of Threadgill's interest in Japanese culture; their most stylized pieces made strong use of empty space and came to resemble an avant-garde jazz version of No drama. A powerful soloist and provocative composer, Threadgill went on to form an exciting, exacting septet in the 1980s; since those discs are all out of print, his Air shift provides virtually the only glimpse of his earliest work.

Note: Although *Air Time* is the best example of Air's music, most stores will have to order this album, since they rarely stock it. You may have an easier time finding the worthy alternative *Live Air*, on the Black Saint label.

Fred Anderson, *The Missing Link* (Nessa). The title of this 1979 album refers to tenor saxist Fred Anderson's important place in the Chicago avant-garde arena of the mid-1960s. Anderson's burly sound and his heroic, tumultuous style of improvisation provided a link between the music of Ornette Coleman and that of the musicians who would form the AACM. Anderson's music is a bridge from the pantonality of the first free jazz to the furious atonality associated with the avant-garde's "second wave." He had already been working on new forms of jazz expression in the late fifties, when recordings of Ornette's work validated his own. Along with the rarely recorded trumpeter Billy Brimfield (not heard on this CD), Anderson pushed his soloing past Ornette's relatively linear lyricism, filling his improvisations with long cul-de-sac passages—like little set pieces within a larger solo—and recurring rifflike motifs. These devices, along with the marathon lengths to which Anderson's solos might run, became important components of the music then under development by younger Chicago avant-gardists; when they formed the AACM in 1965, Anderson was a charter member. Anderson's music would gain increased attention in the nineties when a new generation of free jazz Chicagoans paid homage to his work—often in person, performing at the Velvet Lounge, the tavern/nightclub he runs on Chicago's near South Side.

Art Ensemble of Chicago, *Full Force* (ECM). The flagship of the AACM, the Art Ensemble of Chicago struck some observers as a ship of fools. But given the band's respect for the figure in African folklore known as the Trickster, and their use of humor in general, they may not have objected to this characterization. The Art Ensemble's first triumphs don't exist on CD at this time; the only available recordings from their earliest years were made in concert, where the music boasted a rampant theatricality that translates poorly to disc (unless you've actually seen them perform). So *Full Force* provides a solid and rather accessible introduction—even though it dates from 1980, some thirteen years after the AEC's formation, and after the band had institutionalized many of its once startling trademarks. The twenty-minute "Magg Zelma" is a fine example of the sort of piece that made the Art Ensemble famous: it progresses from inchoate percussion sounds to sirens, then horns, eventually a pulse from the bass, and finally a full-tilt group improvisation that pours out sound and fury. Earlier such performances had an unvarnished quality, but "Magg Zelma," like the rest of *Full Force*, combines the thrill of creation with the sheen of experience. So does a supersonic track called "Old Time Southside Street Dance," which brims with the soloists' use of extended technique. And the free-form title track offers a crash course in the Art Ensemble's ability to transform abstract musical elements into concrete (and even funky) communication. This one only gets better with age.

Albert Ayler, *Love Cry* (Impulse/GRP). After three decades, Albert Ayler's uncompromising music still raises eyebrows and confuses initiates. So start with this album, a sort of retrospective made a few years after his highest-impact recordings. An enigmatic and visionary saxophonist, Ayler expanded upon the speechlike playing of Ornette Coleman and Eric Dolphy. He affected an almost operatic vibrato, simultaneously romantic and satiric, which would become part and parcel of avant-garde improvising. He also filled his solos with gruff honks, double-edged attacks, guttural shadows, yodel-like trills, and liberating screeches from the top register. These solos often occurred against a backdrop of totally free rhythm supplied by drummer Sunny Murray, who abandoned traditional ideas of "swing." Instead, he supplied an elastic and episodic series of pulses that infused the proceedings with remarkable vitality. (Such music earned the name "energy playing"; it applied not only to Ayler but to anyone spewing high-wattage solos without a predetermined structure or even a steady beat.) Ayler's frenetic and mysterious solos avoided melody as we know it, substituting patterns of sax shouts and squeals. They had an equally mysterious flip side in his pointedly simplistic compositions, which resembled early American folk songs and bore such titles as "Ghosts," "Spirits," "Saints," and "Witches and Devils." Never popular with audiences, Ayler died (quite possibly by his own hand) in 1970 at age thirty-four, but he has continued to influence free-music adventurers to the present.

Even among the iconoclasts of the AACM, Anthony Braxton stands out. In the sixties he supported himself as a chess hustler. He professes allegiance not only to the expected free jazz influences (Ornette Coleman, Eric Dolphy) but also to cool-jazz altoists Paul Desmond and Lee Konitz and pianist Lennie Tristano. Instead of conventional titles, he used mathematical diagrams (and later cartoon drawings) to identify his vast array of compositions. The second recording under his own name was a double album of unaccompanied saxophone solos. He then initiated a series of pieces for ensembles of up to thirty-five players and once talked of writing music for antiphonal orchestras situated around the globe and on the moon. The MacArthur Foundation awarded him a "genius" grant in 1994.

In some ways, Braxton's early quartets seem almost conventional; his music has a rigorous if iconoclastic structure, which limits the open-sky freedom exemplified by his colleagues in the Art Ensemble. Thus, while no one would deny Braxton's avant-garde status, you won't find many people calling him a "free jazz" player, either. On *Performance (Quartet) 1979* (Hat Art) you can hear a spectacular concert featuring the young trombone star Ray Anderson and drummer Thurman Barker, an exciting but detail-minded AACM drummer. Braxton's later bands (see below) introduced a complex, multi-tiered method of composition, but this quartet places more emphasis on the individual soloists and their interplay with the rhythm section. Anderson is one of several avant-garde trombonists who have extended the instrument's range through their mastery of extended technique. And Braxton proves himself an innovative stylist on alto sax, his main instrument, with discursive solos that show his clipped attack, seismographic leaps in the melody line, and almost obsessive virtuosity. Not that he restricts himself to that one instrument; on this set Braxton, an eclectic collector of sounds, also plays soprano sax, clarinet, and the contrabass saxophone—a rarely seen behemoth, with a range *below* that of a tuba, that remains on a small scaffold when played (because of its enormous weight).

Braxton's skill as a performer and improviser sometimes seems to disappear behind his accomplishments as a composer of works for large ensemble. (His interests in compositional organization have brought him closer than most jazz musicians to modern classical music.) Tossing blocks of sound around like playthings, he creates densely layered yet unusually clear passages. These often set off the plaintive cry of a single instrument or the impassioned squabble of a small group. In 1989 he performed eight works with a progressive-minded big band, the Northwest Creative Orchestra in Oregon, releasing them two years later as *Eugene (1989)* (Black Saint). Despite the complexities of his small-group compositions, and despite the radically different demands of the big-band format, Braxton transfers his music to the large ensemble with remarkable fidelity. Yet his command of the idiom, and his compulsive regard for tonal colors, prevent these works from sounding like bloated versions of his quartet music. This album makes an excellent introduction to Braxton's compositions, but if you can't find it readily, go right to *4 (Ensemble) Compositions—1992* (Black Saint). A little denser, the music still shines, thanks to the talents of his handpicked New York ensemble.

Everything about Ornette Coleman's music seemed tailormade to shake up the jazz establishment. There was his non-Western approach to melody and pitch ("I realized you could play sharp or flat in tune"). There was his insistence on implying, rather than stating, an entire *range* of tonalities (instead of sticking to just one). Even his use of that plastic saxophone left jazz insiders scratching their heads. But the proof of Coleman's vision lies in the fact that most of his early albums—the very recordings that puzzled and even angered so many contemporaneous listeners—today sound relatively tame. As his concepts gained acceptance, they became part of the overall language of jazz.

Though not his debut album, *The Shape of Jazz to Come* (Atlantic) was the first to introduce Coleman's fully formed concepts to an unready jazz world, and it remains the best introduction. The song "Lonely Woman"—a bleak, beautiful ballad with a roiling rhythmic undercarriage—became the best known of his compositions, thanks to dozens of recordings by other instrumentalists and vocalists. "Congeniality" has boppish phrases and a fanfare introduction reminiscent of the bebop classic "Parker's Mood," providing a perfect link between bop and Coleman's innovations. And the fast tune called "Eventually" challenges past assumptions with its sheer audacity, in much the way Parker's "Koko" established a high-water mark for the boppers, but also offers plenty of wit (most notably in Coleman's detailed imitation of a whinnying horse that appears toward the end of his solo). On these tunes, you get a clear view of bassist Charlie Haden's extraordinary harmonic perception: as the solos of both Coleman and trumpeter Don Cherry skitter in and out of different keys, Haden emerges as Charlie on the spot, his racing bass lines sensing and instantly reacting to the music's shifting tonality. At once innocently playful and mysteriously elusive, the music on this 1959 recording provides the same rush as your first panorama of a new land.

Fourteen months and two recording sessions later, the Coleman Quartet had a new drummer in Ed Blackwell (although Billy Higgins would return to play alongside Blackwell shortly later—see next paragraph). Blackwell's style was less polished and more intuitive than that of Higgins, who brought a crisp professionalism and lightning reflexes to Coleman's music. Blackwell poured more emotion into the enterprise; he also favored a darker sound to his drum setup, but matched this with a buoyant beat that echoed the street parades of his native New Orleans. The best album by this band (titled *This Is Our Music*) is not a separate CD at this writing, but *Ornette!* (Atlantic) runs a close second. Instead of the several shorter tracks found on the saxophonist's previous dates, this one features only four— and three of them run ten minutes or longer. Accordingly, you get to hear Coleman solo at length and with greater complexity than on his earlier recordings, while Cherry—whose individual contributions sometimes disappear behind his skills as a collaborator—claims his full measure as a delightful and continually surprising player.

Ornette's revolution reached an early peak with the daring experimentation of *Free Jazz* (Atlantic), an album-length, thirty-seven-minute piece by his "double quartet." This group comprised two pianoless bands, one on each stereo channel, with Coleman and Cherry at the head of one and Eric Dolphy (on bass clarinet) and trumpeter Freddie Hubbard fronting the other. Each hornman used a different scrap of written melody as the jumping-off point for his solo; meanwhile, the two bassists and two drummers (Billy Higgins and Ed Blackwell) played throughout as a four-piece rhythm section. If it all sounds too forbidding, think again; despite the risk of musical chaos, this steaming, boisterous masterpiece succeeds as a model of balance. The bright, swaggering Hubbard trumpet stands opposite the introspective tone of Cherry's explorations; the fluid mastery of bassist Scott LaFaro courses around and through the earthy bass lines of his friend and roommate Charlie Haden. There's balance, too, within the solos themselves: the hornmen managed to perch themselves between the superego (the improviser's need for control) and the id (giving oneself completely over to the enveloping rhythmic polyphony). More than Coleman's preceding albums, *Free Jazz* exhibits a weakening of traditional barriers between melody, rhythm, and yes, even harmony—a process intrinsic to what Coleman would later dub his Harmolodic Theory of music.

Although John Coltrane would become the most visible symbol of the jazz avant-garde, he engaged in actual free jazz—improvising with neither harmonic guidelines nor recurring structure—on relatively few recordings. Coltrane soaked up the innovations of Albert Ayler, Ornette Coleman, and Eric Dolphy; he then applied them to his increasingly open-ended modal pieces, in which the piano accompaniment and the steady-swinging rhythm section nonetheless maintained their traditional roles. Trane's monumental solos, filled with atonal note clusters and piercing high-note passages, pushed against his instrument's range and his own endurance. Small wonder his music inspired such widespread admiration, which sometimes verged on cultish adulation.

In the autumn of 1961, Coltrane took his quartet into the Village Vanguard for what now ranks among the greatest events in the history of that storied New York nightspot, captured on *Live at the Village Vanguard* (Impulse/GRP). The saxist had just established what would be his working quartet for the next four years—pianist McCoy Tyner, bassist Jimmy Garrison, and drummer Elvin Jones—and here augmented it with Eric Dolphy on bass clarinet. Coltrane also used the occasion to reintroduce the soprano saxophone, an instrument that had all but disappeared from jazz during the previous three decades. Its somewhat nasal, exotically Eastern timbre proved perfect for the trancelike solos that soon began to distinguish his music. (The band grew again to include the oud—a Middle Eastern instrument described in chapter 7—on the song "India," included here. The title signaled Trane's burgeoning interest in Eastern spirituality.) This CD shows Coltrane profoundly influenced by the new music of Ornette Coleman: on each of the five tracks, Tyner's piano drops out for long stretches, leaving Coltrane to solo with a suddenly pianoless rhythm section (à la Ornette). It results in some of the liveliest free jazz in Coltrane's entire discography, and one of the early sixties' truly representative recordings.

Note: this single-disc album draws from the *four*-CD collection of Coltrane's performances from that first week of November 1961—the excellent (if expensive) and long-anticipated *Complete 1961 Village Vanguard Recordings*, released in the fall of 1997.

A Love Supreme (Impulse/GRP) quickly became one of the most popular recordings in the Coltrane discography—indeed, one of the most famous jazz albums of all time—thanks to its pungent melodies, the strength and conviction of the leader's performance, and the album's bold concept. The title piece makes up the entire disc and is dedicated to the Creator, its four movements tracing the steps toward spiritual enlightenment. A chantlike devotional poem, written by Coltrane himself, dominates the liner notes. And Coltrane's billowing solos have the plaintive allure, the naked sincerity, and the incantatory fire of the sincere pilgrim. By the time of this 1964 recording, his rhythm section had played together for three years; their eddying interplay and storm-force intensity gave the music an aura of destiny. The album also showed the gamut of emotion that a master soloist such as Coltrane could wring from the potentially monotonous stratagem of modal improvisation; yet the work coheres as a unified (and overwhelming) single statement. *A Love Supreme* exemplifies not free jazz per se, but rather a more liberated approach to improvisation—a free-*er* jazz, if you will—and forms the heart of an especially creative period (1963–65) in Coltrane's music.

The Gentle Side of John Coltrane (Impulse/GRP). Although Coltrane's main impact during these years stemmed from the fulminating power and tradition-shattering adventure of his avant-garde performances, he also made two classic recordings in an altogether different vein. On the 1963 releases *Ballads* and *John Coltrane and Johnny Hartman* (his only collaboration with a vocalist), Coltrane presented a passionate, voluptuous voice that updated the ballad work of his early idols Coleman Hawkins and Ben Webster. (The Hartman album gained new converts in the nineties when several tracks were used in the hit film *The Bridges of Madison County*.) Totally free of free jazz, these remain two of the most romantic, devastatingly sensuous albums in all of jazz, and while they have little to do with the thrust of this chapter, they represent an important side of Coltrane's music. Both CDs run only about thirty minutes, so instead consider *The Gentle Side of John Coltrane*. This compilation runs close to seventy minutes and includes two tracks from each album (plus two more from Coltrane's meeting with Duke Ellington—see chapter 2). The value of *The Gentle Side* goes beyond bargain-hunting, though; this CD also features seven tracks from other, more progressive recordings of the period, showing that Coltrane's contemplative side could find expression in even his most ferocious discs.

Joseph Jarman, *Song For* (Delmark). The reedman and poet Joseph Jarman gained renown as a member of the Art Ensemble of Chicago, under whose auspices he has done most of his recording. Nonetheless, the few discs under his own name have a distinctive identity—none more so than this 1966 septet date, one of the very first AACM recordings. The material ranges from the rough-and-tumble brawn of the tunes "Little Fox Run" to the title track, a sprawling, free-form garden that blossoms from a few seeds of percussion and random noise. And the remarkable and centered "Non-Cognitive Aspects of the City"—which revolves around Jarman's recitation of his own poetry—recalls experiments by Charles Mingus, but at the same time foreshadows the all-out theatricality that the Art Ensemble would later employ. The album counts among its virtues the recording debut of several important AACM members—including trumpeter Billy Brimfield, bassist Charles Clark, drummers Thurman Barker and Steve McCall, and especially tenorist Fred Anderson—making it a valuable snapshot of the vital and uncompromising Chicago avant-garde in the mid-sixties. The cloistered nature of that scene, with its hothouse rehearsals on Chicago's south side and musician-supported concerts at or near the University of Chicago, had paid off: despite the iconoclastic music and the complex demands of unstructured improvisation, this album has marvelous cogency, as well as the passionate warmth of the most communicative hard-bop.

Steve Lacy, *The Condor* (Soul Note). Steve Lacy, who won a MacArthur "genius" grant in 1992, presents a challenge to new listeners because he occupies several artistic platforms. He gained notice through his interpretations of Thelonious Monk's music—at a time (the mid-fifties) before those compositions had gained general acceptance—and he still plays programs devoted to Monk. During the fifties, he also perfected his use of the soprano saxophone, becoming the first jazzman in a half century to focus entirely on this small, straight horn—about a decade before John Coltrane popularized the instrument. In addition to large-scale compositions and crystalline trio work, Lacy also excels as an unaccompanied saxist, a context which by its very nature probably qualifies as avant-garde. And on several occasions he has collaborated with modern poets. His sextet of the eighties and nineties presents the best-rounded picture of Lacy's skills, and out of the albums available by that group, this one shines strongest. Lacy achieves a dense, confrontational ensemble through his interplay with fellow saxist Steve Potts, pianist Bobby Few, and especially the violin and voice contributions of his wife, Irene Aebi. (If you're put off by harsh, expressionist vocals, you'll want to skip this album in favor of the terrific pianoless-quartet date *Morning Joy*, on Hat Art.) One of the two or three undisputed soprano kings, Lacy has always sought the rough-hewn tone and texture associated with Monk's piano. But Lacy has also built upon other Monkish attributes in his unmistakable music—respect for the melodic quirks and structural integrity of a theme, and the ability to worry an individual motif into full-blown flight.

Archie Shepp, *Fire Music* (Impulse/GRP). Influenced by John Coltrane and by Cecil Taylor (in whose early-sixties bands he worked), Archie Shepp quickly found his way onto almost every jazz fan's radar. His gruff and throaty tenor-sax exclamations brought a fresh perspective to the extramusical sounds Albert Ayler had introduced. Besides that, he became something of a spokesman for the avant-garde, giving ardent and articulate explanations to the press. And his willingness to use the music to promote political viewpoints—specifically related to civil rights and racial prejudice—made the spotlight only brighter. Shepp could handle it, however: like many of his contemporaries, he brought elements of theater into his music, but unlike most of them he came by it naturally, having studied dramatic literature in college. On *Fire Music,* Shepp's sextet sounds like a much larger band, thanks to the high-impact horn motifs that weave in and out of the music. Sometimes they set up the solos, à la Ornette Coleman's "Free Jazz," and sometimes they provide a concertolike backdrop for Shepp's virile, screaming saxophone. The album highlights several elements of Shepp's art. "Malcolm, Malcolm—Semper Malcolm" uses poetry to memorialize slain civil-rights leader Malcolm X; Shepp's version of Ellington's "Prelude to a Kiss" shows his ability to mix sentiment and irony; and you'll never hear a stranger solo to the bossa nova hit "The Girl from Ipanema" (see the transition section "From There 2 Here,") than Shepp's, with fragile and then urgent cries rising above a tough-samba beat.

Sun Ra and His Intergalactic Solar Arkestra, *Space Is the Place* (Evidence). The music of the Saturnian-American keyboardist and composer Sun Ra (see previous transition section) continued to evolve up until the early seventies, arriving at a dense, mysterious plateau that fully encompassed African rhythms, avant-garde horn solos, space-traveling mumbo jumbo, and section writing left over from his days as a Chicago show-band arranger. Even though Sun Ra became a cult figure via several albums recorded for the ESP label in the mid-sixties, it's the music he made in the following decade that thrilled and befuddled listeners around the world, establishing his legacy. (In the 1980s, he concentrated on repackaging his past achievements in admittedly attractive, quite user-friendly albums.) *Space Is the Place*—the title taken from the band's signature tune—gives you seventy-five minutes of music recorded for a terrific film about Sun Ra and his band. As you can imagine, his unique philosophy, costumery, and the band's communal living arrangements gave the filmmakers plenty to work with. In addition to containing several of the Arkestra's better-known songs, including "Satellites Are Spinning" and "We Travel the Spaceways," this album features some of Sun Ra's most evocative electronics—on "Cosmic Forces" and "It's After the End of the World"—and also a seventeen-minute romp through the band's forest of instrumental colors and key soloists. Imaginative, hallucinatory, and utterly without precedent, this music is so vivid, you don't need a projector to see the film.

*   *   *

Poet, mystic, martial-arts dancer, and—oh, yes—galvanic pianist, Cecil Taylor has mesmerized and/or angered audiences since his recording debut in 1956 (see previous transition section). Whether leading small groups of enormous energy and complexity, or transferring those qualities to the solo-piano idiom (which he first undertook in the early seventies), Taylor relentlessly burrows into the darkest heart of his music; simultaneously, he soars on its intensely beating pinions. He is another recipient of a MacArthur Foundation "genius" grant, thanks to his wildly idiosyncratic and essentially inimitable body of work.

Taylor's bands over the years have epitomized the panoramic range of his musical vision. The quintet he led on his 1966 recording *Conquistador* (Blue Note) ranks with his best and welcomes you into his at times forbidding sphere. The album comprises two long compositions, each of which extends from the first chattering phrases of Taylor's piano. In that sense, the individual solos—by alto saxist Jimmy Lyons and the overlooked trumpeter Bill Dixon—resemble variations on a theme; but Taylor's thick chords and darting countermelodies are light-years away from the distinct accents and harmonic carpet rolled out by previous pianists. Often polyphonic on its own, the pianist's in-your-face "accompaniment" joins with the soloists to create maelstroms of improvisation. The rhythms of Andrew Cyrille's drumming and not one but *two* bassists undergird the music and propel it further when necessary. Much of this music's magic lies in Taylor's ability to ignore or defy all normal rules of compositional form, but still create improvisations that establish their own intuitive logic. As he comments on the album's notes, "There is no music without order ... but that order is not necessarily related to any single criterion of what order should be." This album—a vital achievement in Taylor's music, and one of the first to expose him to a larger public—is a perfect illustration of that philosophy.

Taylor's unaccompanied piano concerts have become the stuff of legend: lengthy, unyielding performances of superhuman strength and keyboard agility, filled with herky-jerky phrases and jackhammer rhythms, dense pummeling chords and spiky, skittering, keyboard-vaulting sorties. In his best solo recordings, such as *Silent Tongues* (Freedom), he often presents a recurring motif that anchors his most expansive ideas. Even when he doesn't, his absolute command of attack and technique allows him to paint a detailed and engrossing picture of his wild inner landscape. *Silent Tongues* makes the best introduction to Taylor's piano praxis: one of Taylor's most impressive solo outings, it is also one of the most musically accessible. Unlike many of his later albums, this one divides the forty-five-minute title work into five distinct movements that allow you to digest it in smaller pieces if necessary. (The album also includes two short encores.) Unfortunately, the Freedom label may prove somewhat less accessible in terms of distribution; if so, dive into *Air Above Mountains* (Enja), an equally clearheaded performance that features *two* large-scale improvisations totaling seventy-six minutes of music.

World Saxophone Quartet, *Live in Zurich* (Black Saint). The name of this band tells the whole story: four saxophonists, period. The WSQ was born in New York in 1976, when three of those who had spearheaded the avant-garde movement in St. Louis—alto/soprano saxists Julius Hemphill and Oliver Lake, and baritone saxist Hamiet Bluiett—joined forces with the sensationalistic young tenorist David Murray. (Each man played several other saxes and clarinets too, providing an enormous cache of instruments.) The mercurial Hemphill became a de facto leader, using the band as a platform for his highly charged blend of soul and space. But the others also had deep blues roots as well, giving the WSQ's abstractions a firmly grounded core. With no bassist or drummer, these highly individualistic players shared the rhythmic responsibilities among themselves. They often relied on a bass line originating in the baritone sax (a technique borrowed from rhythm and blues) and also found inspiration for their arrangements in the four-part vocal groups of sixties soul music. But thanks to their experience with free improvisation—particularly as members of the Black Artists Group, the St. Louis counterpart to the AACM—their simultaneous improvisation led to constantly shifting textures that winked in and out of the music. The WSQ always emphasized the entertainment quality of their challenging idiom; in performance they would begin their theme song in the wings, then strut onstage (in full formal wear) while continuing to blow their horns. *Live in Zurich* transmits the electric shock of their concerts and shows off several of their better-known tunes.

Feel Free

In the sixties, progressive musicians in Europe began to tackle some of the same musical issues that drove their avant-garde counterparts in the United States. The problems in locating many of these artists' albums—small overseas labels, low inventory, poor distribution—limit their value (but not their relevance) to this discussion. For starters, consider any albums you can find by the following musicians.

British saxophonist Evan Parker—a Zen-level master of extended technique—and the fire-breathing German reedman Peter Brötzmann have both recorded widely, and in a few cases for U.S. labels, improving your odds of finding their work. Another giant of extended technique, the German trombonist Albert Mangelsdorff, developed a facility and range on his instrument that have left listeners agape since the 1960s. In the bad old USSR—perhaps the last place you'd expect to hear intimations of liberty—the trio led by pianist Vyacheslav Ganelin attracted attention in the West after their tapes were smuggled out to a Russian émigré living in London, who produced their albums (on the Leo label). And the Italian pianist and composer Giorgio Gaslini has built a brilliant career on his measured, unbound piano style and his unhurried, analytical explorations.

The Netherlands has spawned a fertile new-music scene centered in Amsterdam. Reedman and composer Willem Breuker infuses his music with the irony and slapstick that are both part of his national heritage. He has led his Kollektief (a little big band) for the better part of three decades, and strains of everything from military marches to Dutch music-hall ditties, stylized tangos to pantomime, can find a place in their performances. His countryman Han Bennink plays drums with the precision of a surgeon and the uninhibitedness of a lunatic, and any album on which you find his name will expand your horizons about his instrument—that is, unless you *already* know of a percussionist who (literally) builds small fires in his hi-hat cymbals, using their up-and-down action to fan the flames and send smoke signals out across the audience.

* * *

Muhal Richard Abrams has turned out a diverse series of recordings since the 1980s. For large-scale orchestra writing, you'll want *Blu Blu Blu* or *Rejoicing with the Light*; for smaller groups, try *Mama and Daddy* or *Colors in Thirty-Third*, which uses a sextet with violin and cello. To appreciate Abrams's ability to blend hard-bop roots with avant-garde exploration, get the lovely *Sightsong*, a duet recording with the Art Ensemble bassist Malachi Favors. The above albums are all on Black Saint. Eventually, find your way back to Abrams's debut, *Levels and Degrees of Light* (Delmark)—still his most challenging work even after all these years.

The most potent example of the Art Ensemble's early work is *Live at Mandel Hall* (Delmark), two LPs compressed to a single CD that documents a 1972 homecoming concert at the University of Chicago, where many of their original performances took place. Don't start here, but definitely find your way to it. A later concert recording, *Urban Bushmen*, does a better job of communicating the band's onstage magic, while the studio date *Nice Guys* presents a solid if somewhat restrained view of their repertoire; both are on ECM. The AEC's latest work appears on the Japanese label DIW (import only); go for *Ancient to the Future* and their collaboration with a five-man South African vocal group entitled *Art Ensemble of Soweto*.

The Art Ensemble's individual members are well represented on a number of albums. Trumpeter Lester Bowie has built the largest discography; it includes the hospitable *The Fifth Power* (Black Saint) and several albums by his other band, the Brass Fantasy (start with *Serious Fun* on ECM), which takes a semi-ironic and crowd-pleasing approach to its material. Roscoe Mitchell, the most rigorous and scientific improviser in the AEC, created an important early AACM album in *Sound* (Delmark). His two main ensembles of the eighties share the program on *Roscoe Mitchell and the Sound & Space Ensembles* (Black Saint). Joseph Jarman and drummer Famoudou Don Moye have recorded several albums together; try *The Magic Triangle* (Black Saint), a resonant trio date with pianist Don Pullen (see the next transition section). Jarman's unusual and rewarding duo date with Anthony Braxton, *Together Alone* (Delmark), is now out on CD.

Most of Albert Ayler's better (and stranger) recordings came earlier in his career: find *Vibrations* and *Witches & Devils* (both on Freedom) if you can. Once you've acclimated yourself to his music, go for *Live in Greenwich Village* (Impulse/GRP), which many experts feel is the best overall portrait of his playing.

The Canadian-born pianist Paul Bley had an early appointment with free jazz: he hired Ornette Coleman's first quartet to perform under his name (as the Paul Bley Quintet) shortly after Coleman had arrived in Los Angeles, where Bley then lived. His subsequent recordings revealed an important composer and a highly organized avant-garde improviser. Go for the early *Footloose* (Savoy), the midcareer solo date *Tango Palace* (Soul Note) and the trio date *Paul Bley with Gary Peacock* (ECM), which stars Bley's frequent partner on bass. Also, *Time Will Tell* (ECM) matches Bley in an unusual collaboration with British avant-gardists Evan Parker (saxes) and Barre Phillips (bass).

Anthony Braxton's occasional forays into other composers' music—*Six Monk Compositions (1987)* (Black Saint) and the double-disc *Charlie Parker Project* (Hat Art)—provide perhaps the best way into his work for many listeners. Basic Braxton would also include *Four Compositions 1983* (Black Saint), with the mind-boggling AACM trombonist George Lewis; *Six Compositions: Quartet* (Antilles); and if you can find it, *Creative Orchestra (Koln) 1978* (Hat Art), a double album documenting some of Braxton's earliest big-band writing. Starting in the early eighties, Braxton's quartet adopted the conventional format of piano-bass-drums and an utterly *un*conventional method of multilayered improvisation. To hear this music at its best, you'll have to pop for the expensive four-CD set *Wilisau (Quartet) 1991* (Hat Art).

That last package stars pianist Marilyn Crispell, one of the most exciting and individualistic pianists in all of jazz, and one of the few avant-garde keyboardists to move beyond the example of Cecil Taylor. If you can find the British imports *Gaia* or *Santuerio* (both on Leo), grab them; otherwise, get *Live in San Francisco* and *Marilyn Crispell Trio on Tour* (both on Music & Arts). In 1997, Crispell undertook a change in direction with a double CD that quietly examines the music of sixties new-jazz composer Annette Peacock: *Nothing Ever Was, Anyway* (ECM).

To be Ornette? The free jazz pioneer debuted his music on *Something Else!*; this album, as well as *Tomorrow Is the Question*, give you an early insight into Ornette Coleman's radical thinking (both albums on Fantasy/OJC). *Change of the Century* (Atlantic) makes a perfect follow-up to *The Shape of Jazz to Come* (recommended above). *All* the music Ornette recorded for Atlantic (including *This Is Our Music*, unavailable on its own) fills six discs on the marvelously documented *Beauty Is a Rare Thing* (Rhino).

Coleman later led an exciting trio on the two equally good volumes of *At the "Golden Circle," Stockholm* (Blue Note); in the seventies, he tackled fusion jazz in typically idiosyncratic fashion (see chapter 6); and by the eighties, his importance was so widely accepted that he recorded and toured with the top-selling jazz-rock guitarist Pat Metheny (*Song X*, on Geffen) and collaborated with Jerry Garcia (*Virgin Beauty*, Columbia). In the nineties, Coleman became more prominent in unusual formats, at least for him: both his quartet album *Sound Museum: Hidden Man* and his duo album *Colors* feature piano. They're both on Harmolodic/Verve.

Ornette's alter ego, trumpeter Don Cherry, became an effective hybridizer of avant-garde jazz and world music (see chapter 7) when he went off on his own. First, though, he recorded the wide-ranging 1966 *Symphony for Improvisers* (Blue Note), with a handpicked band that included new-music stars-to-be Gato Barbieri and Pharoah Sanders on saxes.

Onrushing Trane: John Coltrane's fecund creativity and widespread popularity led to many important recordings in the sixties. *The Complete Africa/Brass Sessions* (two CDs) bathed Coltrane's quartet in the burnished glow of a large ensemble dominated by French horns and trumpets; the music is unforgettable. *Newport '63* documents a fine concert in which Coltrane's second favorite drummer, bebop veteran Roy Haynes, played instead of Elvin Jones. Two other live dates—the 1963 *Coltrane Live at Birdland* and *The John Coltrane Quartet Plays . . .* (from 1965)—join the reflective masterpiece *Crescent* in rounding out this extraordinary phase of Trane's career.

From then on, Coltrane worked in increasingly unfettered surroundings as he homed in on total freedom. *Meditations* augmented his quartet with drummer Rashied Ali and saxist Pharoah Sanders, a Coltrane protégé. And *Interstellar Space*, recorded less than five months before Trane's death in 1967, contains six duets with Ali, whose drumming was described by Coltrane as "multidirectional rhythm." All these albums are on Impulse/GRP.

A little more Lacy: If you haven't already purchased *Morning Joy* (mentioned above), do so now. The early-sixties recording *School Days* (Hat Art) is a cult classic among new-music fans, featuring the incisive and swinging trombonist Roswell Rudd and a slew of Monk tunes. The double CD *The Way* (Hat Art) dates from 1979, when Lacy's sextet was fairly new, includes the poetry and readings of Brion Gysin, and is a fine survey of the band's early sound. *Troubles* (Black Saint) offers some wonderfully outré performances, with chanted refrains by the band used as musical riffs. For Lacy's solo soprano work (and loads of Monk), the albums *Only Monk* and *More Monk*, both on Soul Note, are contemplative and purifying.

Sonny Rollins had already incorporated elements of freedom in his pianoless trio of the 1950s. In 1966 he took a stab at the "new thing" on *East Broadway Rundown* (Impulse/GRP). Not wholly successful, the title track still validates the purchase with its powerful tenor solo—a reminder that not even the beckoning frontiers of the avant-garde could dull his intense lyricism.

Archie Shepp's large discography is marred by uneven quality, especially in his later records. *Four for Trane* (Impulse/GRP) and *Steam* (Enja) won't let you down, and *New Thing at Newport* (Impulse/GRP)—on which Shepp's band shares the stage with the quartet led by his mentor, John Coltrane—also makes a good introduction. Of his post-seventies music, your best bet is the unusual duo date featuring electronic keyboardist Jasper van't Hof, *Mama Rose* (SteepleChase).

Early in his career, Sun Ra recorded extensively for his own Saturn label, and these LPs now appear on Evidence Music, which has graciously packaged many of them as handsome "twofers" (two LPs on one extravagantly illustrated CD). Check out *Fate in a Pleasant Mood/When Sun Comes Out* and the disc that contains the LPs *Cosmic Tones for Mental Therapy* and *Art Forms of Dimensions Tomorrow*. The mid-seventies *Concert for the Comet Kohoutek* (ESP Disk) has special purpose and structure and boasts some of the band's most focused work. The best of Sun Ra's later recordings is *Live in Japan* on the Japanese DIW label. You may have an easier time finding *Mayan Temples* (Black Saint) and certainly *Strange Celestial Road* (Rounder), neither of which will disappoint in the least.

Taylor-made: Cecil Taylor's other noteworthy discs include the landmark *Unit Structures* (Blue Note), the recording of which directly preceded *Conquistador* (above); the earlier *Cell Walk for Celeste* (Candid); *3 Phasis* (New World), an excellent work by his late-seventies sextet featuring Ronald Shannon Jackson on drums; and the wholly astonishing large-ensemble album *Winged Serpent (Sliding Quadrants)* on Soul Note. For more of his extravagant solo work, *For Olim* (Soul Note) shows how his command of this idiom had evolved in the dozen years since he first unveiled it to the world.

Besides the World Saxophone Quartet, a few other four-reed lineups became important players on the free jazz scene, most notably the ROVA Saxophone Quartet (the name is an acronym of the members' surnames). If anything, this San Francisco–area band employs a more rigorous approach and a different but equal measure of humor. You should start with their 1985 recording *The Crowd* and also consider the party-crashing *Saxophone Diplomacy*, an exercise in détente (it documents their 1989 tour of what was then the USSR); both are on Hat Art. Also, *Beat Kennel* (Black Saint) remains an especially good collection of their work.

For more of the World Saxophone Quartet, try *W.S.Q.* (Black Saint) and some of their later albums, which often concentrated on themes or individual composers. The best are *World Saxophone Quartet Plays Duke Ellington; Rhythm and Blues*, with the quartet's versions of tunes made famous by Otis Redding, the O'Jays, Marvin Gaye, and others; and *Metamorphosis*, on which the quartet teams with a trio of African drummers. They're all on Elektra/Nonesuch.

The individual members of the WSQ each bear more listening on their own. Julius Hemphill's great dates of the early seventies are not in print, but you can get some of their flavor from a 1977 trio album, *Raw Materials and Residuals* (Black

Saint). He leads a saxophone sextet on *The Fat Man and the Hard Blues* (Black Saint) and a jazz orchestra on the intriguing if badly recorded *Julius Hemphill Big Band* (Elektra/Musician). Oliver Lake stretches out nicely with two quite different quintets, first on the 1980 *Prophet*, featuring trumpet, then on the 1985 *Expandable Language*, with the *Tonight* show's Kevin Eubanks on guitar (both from the mid-eighties, both on Black Saint). In 1981, baritone saxist Hamiet Bluiett led a sparkling ensemble on *Dangerously Suite* and a decade later scored with *Sankofa/Rear Guard* (both Soul Note). And alto saxist Arthur Blythe, who would replace Hemphill in the WSQ in 1990, can and should be heard on *In Concert: Metamorphosis/The Grip* (India Navigation)—the album with which he established his reputation as a gutsy musician able to reconcile the avant-garde with lessons learned from such past giants as Johnny Hodges and Charlie Parker. His early-nineties date *Hipmotism* (Enja) is a beauty.

The remaining WSQ founder, David Murray, has recorded so often—some might even say indiscriminately—the choice bewilders even his fans. (He also has his share of detractors, who voice exception to his flood of recordings and to his hyperexpressive take on past stylistic devices.) His breakthrough came on *Live at the Lower Manhattan Ocean Club* (India Navigation), recorded when he was just twenty-two. Highly recommended are the albums in which he places his tenor sax and bass clarinet in contexts different from the standard trio and quartet. He leads his exciting octet on the wonderful *Home* and *Ming* (both Black Saint) and an organ quartet on *Shakill's Warrior* (DIW). In the late eighties, he recorded several albums with a well-grounded quartet starring pianist Dave Burrell: go for *Deep River* or *Ballads* (DIW). Murray has also done some of his best work with the Chicago percussionist Kahil El'Zabar, specifically the hard-to-find *Golden Sea* (Sound Aspects) and *A Sanctuary Within* (Black Saint).

El'Zabar, a former president of the AACM, spurs discussion of some later avant-garde developments in Chicago, the launching pad for so much of the music inspired by Ornette Coleman's discoveries. El'Zabar's Ethnic Heritage Ensemble, featuring his percussion and two hornmen (no bass, no piano) has emerged as his main vehicle over the last two decades. *Live from Stockholm* (on the Swedish label Silkheart) and the 1997 *Continuum* (Delmark) convey the message. El'Zabar's other main band, the Ritual Trio, features Art Ensemble bassist Malachi Favors and the strong sax work of Ari Brown: check *Renaissance of the Resistance* on Delmark. A frequent bandmate of El'Zabar's, saxist Ernest Dawkins, leads a band almost as old, the New Horizons Ensemble, which in the mid-nineties emerged as one of the best latter-day AACM groups; either *South Side Street Songs* or *Chicago Now, Vol. 1* (both on Silkheart) will do the trick.

Others of note include saxists Edward Wilkerson and Ken Vandermark, both discussed in chapter 9. Some of the latter-day Chicagoans combine the influence of the AACM with lessons taught by the quirky, focused, and sometimes wonderfully silly music of the late multi-instrumentalist Hal Russell—a contemporary of the AACM founders. His album *The Hal Russell Story* (ECM) makes for a humorous and painless introduction to free jazz and the avant-garde in general.

Free 2 Roam: Echoes of Liberation

While the extremities of the avant-garde left many listeners (and even most older jazz musicians) in the lurch, others heard and understood the new sounds and concepts trumpeted by Ornette Coleman, John Coltrane, Cecil Taylor, and the Chicagoans. Primarily members of the same generation (or younger), these open-minded players chose not to abandon harmony and form completely; instead, their music reflected the innovations of free jazz within a fairly traditional context. Most often, these echoes of liberation served as the catalyst for later developments of a more experimental nature.

Miles Davis provides the primary example of this process. In the sixties, he began to replace various members of his quintet; by 1963 he had finally arrived at a viable and malleable group that followed a steady trajectory toward the jazz-rock fusion he would lead at the decade's end (see chapter 6). The albums in the middle of this trajectory—such as the one listed below, and several others recorded by his sidemen (represented here by Herbie Hancock's *Maiden Voyage*)—have the trappings of hard-bop. But you can't ignore the breath of freedom that blows through them, sweeping away the habits and clichés that had begun to accumulate. Often, these albums get lumped in with the earlier styles played by their leaders. But in truth, the music recommended below fits comfortably under no existing label.

In later years, revisionist commentators and historians would attempt to bury free jazz entirely, characterizing it as a cul-de-sac in the evolution of jazz, and pointing to its failure to win converts among musicians and listeners. But anyone looking at the music of the sixties can find evidence to the contrary. The majority of progressive musicians did not fire their pianists, learn extended technique, and compete to see how many songs without harmony they could include in their repertoire. But in carrying the message of freedom back to their own idioms, they immediately validated the work of their more experimental contemporaries. And they insured that the "mainstream" of jazz would slowly (but inexorably) seek a new path.

* * *

George Adams–Don Pullen Quartet, *Earth Beams* (Timeless). Few bands did as good a job as this one when it came to the essential work of the seventies—broadening the mainstream by applying lessons learned from free jazz. And why not? The quartet's coleaders, tenor saxist George Adams and pianist Don Pullen, first met as sidemen with one of jazz's original freedom fighters, the iconoclastic Charles Mingus. (They formed the band in 1979, the year Mingus died, and recorded *Earth Beams* in 1980. The participation of drummer Dannie Richmond, Mingus's longtime drummer and protégé, only strengthened the sense that they were continuing on in Mingus's footsteps.) Pullen's tightly wound chord clusters reminded some listeners of Cecil Taylor, but he used them to surround rather than escape a song's harmonies; and while his phrasing could be jagged or flowing, the concept of swing remained central to his playing. Similarly, Adams's tenor flights usually took him into the high-note stratosphere previously explored by Albert Ayler and John Coltrane, but he used these "screech" notes in a more conventional manner: he wove them into the fabric of his solos, instead of using them to make a statement about liberation. Their mastery of both hard-bop and avant-garde idioms made the Adams-Pullen Quartet effective and exciting on a wide range of music. Not even the New Orleans funk of "Sophisticated Alice" (a Pullen composition with an irresistible Bo Diddley beat) proved immune to the pianist's barreling tone-poetry or the saxophonist's fluttery expressionism.

Betty Carter, *The Betty Carter Album* (Verve). She sings the slowest ballads of the century, with elongated phrasing that can sometimes lag a whole *sentence* behind the beat—not just a syllable or a word (as previous singers had done). Then she scats at tempos faster than most vocalists would even attempt. Either way, Betty Carter's exaggerated and expressionistic style has remained daring into the late nineties, three decades since it fully evolved. Each song, whether a standard or one of her own quite original compositions, quickly becomes a launchpad for her extravagant melodic shape-shifting. In most cases, if you didn't know the tune going in, you probably won't know it after hearing Carter's version. (As if in explanation, a later album would be titled *It's Not About the Melody*.) Carter incorporated into her style the careening freedom that proliferated among her contemporary instrumentalists—in much the same way that Ella Fitzgerald exemplified the swing style of the thirties, and Sarah Vaughan translated the innovations of Dizzy Gillespie and Charlie Parker in the forties. And Carter's smoky, chocolaty timbre makes a compelling complement to both her edgy solos and molasses ballads. This 1976 album, originally released on Carter's self-owned label, features compact versions of "Sounds," "Tight," and "I Can't Help It," her three best-known compositions. On later recordings, these songs stretch out to thrice the length heard here.

(While the recommendation of this album fits the historical range of this chapter, Carter has continued to make terrific albums. Certainly consider 1988's *Look What I Got* and the aforementioned *It's Not About the Melody* from 1992. If money's no object, a double disc called *The Audience with Betty Carter*—a 1980 concert recording—is the best choice. They're all now on Verve.)

Miles Davis, *Miles Smiles* (Columbia/Legacy). The music made by the Miles Davis Quintet in the mid-1960s has *transition* written all over it. In fact, it rests so clearly at the intersection of idioms that no one has ever figured out exactly what to call it. Hard-bop? Not really—even though four of the players made their reputations as masters of that style. And it's certainly not free jazz—even though the insistent, chatty rhythms of drummer Tony Williams utilize some techniques favored by free jazz drummers, and even though the looser song structures and harmonic schemes reflect a similar yearning for liberation. Free-bop? No; that name suggests the two distinct idioms this music studiously avoids. Some people called it "progressive jazz"; almost everyone has come to regard it as brilliant, and *Miles Smiles* stands as perhaps the best album ever recorded by what was arguably Miles's greatest band. Credit the almost telepathic communication within the rhythm section (Williams, bassist Ron Carter, and pianist Herbie Hancock). Credit also the oblique and subtly textured approach to improvisation that Davis and saxophonist Wayne Shorter had developed: their solos seem to float above each song's harmonies, using the chords as aerial landmarks rather than anchoring tethers. And the choice of material didn't hurt, either: Shorter's "Footprints," the Eddie Harris composition "Freedom Jazz Dance," and "Gingerbread Boy" (written by Miles's old friend saxist Jimmy Heath), all became jazz standards as a result of this recording.

Von Freeman, *Never Let Me Go* (SteepleChase). Von Freeman's unique role on the postwar Chicago scene makes him difficult enough to pigeonhole; then there's the matter of chronology. Since he had already established himself by the fifties—after which his hyperexpressive sound and improvisations began to influence future members of the AACM—one might wonder why he doesn't belong in the previous transition section, along with his contemporaries. Unquestionably, Freeman's voluminous and conversational solos, which make radical departures from a song's written harmonies, helped shape the thinking of younger Chicago sax men, such as Eddie Harris, Joseph Jarman, and even Anthony Braxton. (Freeman's solos have a prodigal, almost spendthrift quality, tossing off a dozen ideas in the space where he might easily explore any one of them.) What's more, his unique sound—cloaked and reedy, slightly wounded, with a sweet-and-sour twist—anticipated the range of intonation used by all the AACM saxists. In turn the freedom explosion of the sixties finally opened a worldwide window on Freeman's own playing. He didn't lead his first record until the early seventies, and not until the following decade did he begin to reap the attention of international jazz critics and audiences, so here he stands. This quartet date, recorded in 1992 (a few months shy of Freeman's seventieth birthday), shows Freeman's remarkable vitality and boundless bonhomie; it also stars pianist Jodie Christian, a cofounder of the AACM.

(While this is the best introduction to his work, the long-gone but recently digitized *Have No Fear* [Nessa] probably features the finest Freeman solos on disc. His most recent date, *Walkin' Tuff!* [Southport], is a bit windy but won't disappoint.)

Herbie Hancock, *Maiden Voyage* (Blue Note). Jazz is not renowned for its theme albums, but on this 1965 date—only Hancock's third recording as a leader—the thematic undercurrent pulled in a masterpiece. It helped that Hancock chose for his topic the ocean—a fount of mystery and poetry throughout the ages. It helped even more that the album's five tunes (all by Hancock) include two that became certifiable jazz standards, and one more that approaches that stature. The title track uses a modal harmonic structure; serene on the surface and motile beneath, it opens up into saxist George Coleman's gorgeous call to the open sea, followed by Freddie Hubbard's continually cresting trumpet solo. The finale, "Dolphin Dance," further clarifies Hancock's genius for jazz composition: graceful and relaxed, it has inspired more than twenty recorded versions by other artists. In between, the lesser-known "The Eye of the Hurricane" captures the storm's buoyancy as well as its power and yields a series of archetypal hard-bop solos. Meanwhile, "Survival of the Fittest" has moments that are virtually indistinguishable from avant-garde free jazz of the period. Hancock's own solos—pearly, fleet, incisive—don't dominate, but rather complement both his hornmen and his compositions. And by importing his rhythm-mates from Miles Davis's band (Ron Carter and Tony Williams), he insured smooth sailing throughout.

Andrew Hill, *Judgment* (Blue Note). Born in Chicago, pianist and composer Andrew Hill began to attract attention in the early 1960s with his disciplined but catchy music. His startlingly original Blue Note recordings—which often starred saxist Joe Henderson and introduced vibist Bobby Hutcherson to many jazz listeners—utilized discoveries made in free jazz, and they still strike many listeners as avant-garde. But Hill eschewed the blank-verse poetry of Ornette Coleman's music, which sounds wide-open while Hill's finely detailed improvisations remain within the lines of his knotty compositions. Like one of his piano heroes, Thelonious Monk, Hill fills his music with slightly skewed, subtly tart harmonies. From the example of another idol, Art Tatum, he honed a solo style of unexpected leaps and asymmetrical phrases, driven by tumbling, herky-jerky rhythms. Taken together, they allowed Hill to update blues tonalities (as did Ornette), and to explore much of the "freebop" territory surveyed by his fellow Chicagoan Muhal Richard Abrams (see chapter 5). On *Judgment*, recorded in early 1964, Hill used the same instrumentation as the famous Modern Jazz Quartet—rhythm section and vibraphone (here played by Hutcherson)—but to much different purpose, nudging the hard-bop format away from its strictures while presenting accessible yet challenging new music.

Keith Jarrett, *The Survivors' Suite* (ECM). Keith Jarrett is one of the four most influential pianists—and among the most important jazz composers—of the last quarter century. He brings an impressive depth (informed by his intense classical training) and a single-minded commitment to his music. Of the many varied formats in which he has worked, the quartet he established in 1973 remains the most complex—and perhaps the most ambitious. At the time, as you'll read in chapter 6, the idea of free jazz had lost its hold on jazz experimenters. Few mainstream jazz musicians—and Jarrett's work with Charles Lloyd (see below) and on the ECM label (chapter 6) had made him just that—would have invited a direct comparison with free jazz guru Ornette Coleman. But Jarrett did so happily, crafting a personal idiom that, like Coleman's, placed its greatest emphasis on strong melody. What's more, Jarrett's quartet included two of Coleman's former sidemen, bassist Charlie Haden and saxist Dewey Redman. Jarrett's accomplishment in this band lay in his ability to combine the demands of free jazz with the weighty romanticism found in his own solo-piano music; the result was a new jazz expressionism quite his own. (Indeed, no one would confuse the intense lyricism of his piano with the astringent prickle of Coleman's saxophone.) He himself has portrayed this quartet as an experiment in democracy: "four sort of radical individualists who were willing to play together," which helps explain the integrity of the music. This album, which consists of a single forty-nine-minute piece, documents a concert performed shortly before the band's demise in 1976.

(For a more representative and in-depth look at this band, the five-CD set *The Impulse Years, 1973–1974* compiles the recordings that made up their first four LPs, along with many alternate takes and previously unreleased songs.)

Rahsaan Roland Kirk, *Rip, Rig & Panic/Please Don't You Cry Beautiful Edith* (EmArcy). A blind musician playing up to three reed instruments simultaneously (two of them, the manzello and the stritch, being bizarre saxophone mutants that he reclaimed from the scrap heap), while punctuating his music with sirens, whistles, shouts, and such invented devices as the nose flute, Roland Kirk sounds like a work of fiction rather than an artist at work. Kirk—who adopted the name Rahsaan after it came to him in a dream—confused many listeners with what appeared to be mere gimmickry. But on closer inspection, his music had roots firmly planted in ancient jazz soil. His unshakable rhythmic impulse and velvety ballad playing had more to do with the Swing Era than with free jazz, and he even used his unorthodox instrumentation to re-create classic reed harmonies. Still, he gave them a rougher edge, and he effortlessly spiced his music with the acerbic cries and trickster whispers that revealed his kinship with the avant-garde. He also applied a combination of post-bop irony and genuine respect to contemporary pop tunes of the sixties and seventies, mimicking their simplistic beat and then humming through his flute to create a rasping, surrealistic timbre. (No one else could have brought such impact to the music of Burt Bacharach, as Kirk would do a few years later; more important, no one else would even have tried.) This CD includes two well-respected LPs of the mid-sixties. Those with deeper pockets should pop for his endlessly surprising concert date, the double-disc *Bright Moments* (Rhino) from 1973.

Charles Lloyd, *Forest Flower/Soundtrack* (Atlantic). On the most basic level, you can regard the reedman Charles Lloyd as a popularizer of John Coltrane's innovations. Indeed, had he done nothing more than make Coltrane's extended technique and expansive concept more user-friendly, he would belong here to indicate the avant-garde's influence on mainstream jazz. But thanks largely to "Forest Flower"— a seventeen-minute piece that moves seamlessly between its two main themes ("Sunrise" and "Sunset")—Lloyd cuts a considerably stronger profile. The album of the same name—recorded at the Monterey Jazz Festival—has become an all-time favorite among jazz listeners, and his quartet enjoyed about three years of worldwide success. Lloyd softened the brunt of Coltrane's attack, with a slightly muffled, almost shy sound on tenor sax, and he reassembled Trane's scrambled scales and modal melodies into a smoother, invitingly lyrical style. (Lloyd actually reserved his more outré side for his flute features, such as the rollicking, vaguely Latin "Sombrero Sam" on this CD.) Within this esthetic, the piano solos of the then twenty-one-year-old Keith Jarrett already have the sharp definition, and a hint of the mountaineering bravado, that would mark the rest of his career. *Forest Flower* catapulted all the members of

Lloyd's band—Jarrett, bassist Cecil McBee, and drummer Jack DeJohnette—to jazz stardom. This CD brings together that record and the LP *Soundtrack*, another concert recording (made two years later), which includes an updated and noticeably tougher version of "Forest Flower."

Pharoah Sanders, *Karma* (Impulse/GRP). What the Jefferson Airplane did for rock, tenor saxist Pharoah Sanders did for jazz. After his stint with John Coltrane (see chapter 5), Sanders bore the imprimatur of the avant-garde's high priest. Wearing that mantle, he made a series of albums that blended free jazz innovations and the burgeoning idiom of psychedelic pop and layered the whole mixture with flower-child philosophizing. The thirty-three-minute piece titled "The Creator Has a Master Plan" is the best example, and it made this 1969 album his most famous. Characterized by a broad and meaty tenor sound similar to Coltrane's—and the occasional emphasis supplied by the guttural split-tones that Trane and Albert Ayler had brought to the music—Sanders's improvisations open up at a loping, unhurried pace. On "Master Plan," he plays two main solos, which both extend across a sonic landscape-in-motion painted by the five-man rhythm section, flute, and French horn; one solo portrays relative serenity, while the other achieves the fury of creation. The various percussion colors provide strong echoes of Africa and the Orient, incorporating the awareness of "world music" (see chapter 7) just starting to percolate at this time. The presence of vocalist Leon Thomas, using the yodel effects that became his signature, adds another ingredient to the stew. The length of "Master Plan" almost insures self-indulgence, but it remains a minor classic.

Woody Shaw, *The Moontrane* (32 Jazz). Of all the musicians mentioned here, the late Woody Shaw stands the greatest chance of disappearing from the consciousness of future listeners. This has everything to do with timing. When Shaw joined Horace Silver's band in 1965, he quickly emerged as the leading inheritor of the trumpet legacy that runs from Louis Armstrong through Roy Eldridge to Dizzy Gillespie and his "children," Lee Morgan and Freddie Hubbard. What's more, Shaw infused his solos with more of the crisp, chess-move logic that distinguished the trumpeters Fats Navarro (chapter 3) and Clifford Brown (chapter 4). But this occurred in the late 1960s and 1970s, when that particular branch of the jazz mainstream was all but engulfed by the avant-garde and fusion; by the time listeners began paying renewed attention to the music Shaw exemplified, a young superstar named Wynton Marsalis (see chapter 8) had hit the scene, stealing the thunder that might once have belonged to Shaw. A tremendously forceful improviser, and a savvy and accessible composer, Shaw wove together the two preeminent strains of the sixties, hard-bop and free jazz, moving his music "outside" the usual harmonies at will, and effortlessly returning to home base moments later. He recorded *The Moontrane*, named for his most famous composition, in 1974, and it largely established his place on the modern jazz scene. (For an excellent second purchase, try the discount-priced two-CD collection called *Dark Journey*, also on 32 Jazz. It traces Shaw's career over a twenty-year period, including key records on which he appeared as a sideman.)

Wayne Shorter, *Adam's Apple* (Blue Note). The saxist and composer Wayne Shorter's featured role in the Miles Davis Quintet—exemplified by the album *Miles Smiles* (see above)—afforded him a great deal of visibility. But on his own albums, Shorter could quite naturally play more of his own compositions and direct them his own way. (A case in point: "Footprints," taken here at a radically different tempo and meter from the version on *Miles Smiles*.) Shorter's tunes, as mysterious and captivating as beautiful ghosts, had already secured his reputation among fellow musicians and savvy listeners. In these pieces, Shorter effortlessly folded in echoes of the liberation then swirling through jazz. His own saxophone revealed very little of these echoes, since he had already begun paring his improvisations toward what would become a famously elliptical solo style, and one quite at odds with the free jazz approach. Shorter pops up several times in the middle chapters of this book; nonetheless, you'll probably want one of his own albums from this period, which serve as a sort of personal diary vis-à-vis the music he played with the Davis Quintet. (For another worthy choice try *Schizophrenia*, also on Blue Note, which reunites Shorter with his old cohort, trombonist Curtis Fuller, in a three-horn sextet. It suggests, then quickly expands upon, their days in Art Blakey's Jazz Messengers.)

McCoy Tyner, *Sahara* (Fantasy/OJC). After leaving John Coltrane's band in 1965, McCoy Tyner strove to find a direction that would reflect his experience with the great saxophonist yet still stand on its own. (Since the powerful and percussive chords from his piano had played such an important role in Coltrane's quartet, Tyner's music would always bear a certain resemblance to that of his former employer.) The pianist made several fine recordings in the late sixties, but not until the 1972 album *Sahara* did he claim fertile musical ground—ironically, on an album named for a desert. With a twenty-three-minute title track, along with several other gut-stirring compositions, this album unveiled the matrix that Tyner would follow for most of the next decade and a half: crashing piano figures that establish the rhythm, mood, and often the theme of a piece; aggressive, colorful drumming; and horn solos indebted to the high-energy avant-garde that Coltrane had come to represent. Here, the drummer is Alphonse Mouzon, who would soon flash his flamboyant stick work with fusion guitarist Larry Coryell (see next chapter). Saxist Sonny Fortune pours out his solos with splintering force but no loss of control. And Tyner himself uses his brittle, steel-trap technique to splay arpeggiated solos across the keyboard. By this time, the pianist had nurtured the denser thickets of Bud Powell's piano into a pointillistic forest of dark textures, percussive accents, and sharply angled melodies. The results were hard, loud, and featured large sections of almost total jazz freedom.

(Tyner's long and satisfying career has yielded many excellent discs, which is only fitting: he stands with Keith Jarrett, Herbie Hancock, and Chick Corea as one of the most important post-sixties pianists. Highly recommended albums include *Song for My Lady*, the big-band date *Song of the New World*, and the trio CD *Trident*, all on Fantasy/OJC; *McCoy Tyner Quartets 4 × 4* [Milestone]; *Live at Sweet Basil* [Evidence], with his long-lived working trio of the eighties and nineties; and the 1991 solo piano date *Soliloquy*, on Blue Note. In the late eighties, he also began recording a big-band project he conceived years earlier, and *The Turning Point* [Verve] is your ticket here.)

chapter six

Plug Me In*
1967–1984

Fusion. The word itself conjures an image of scientific skulduggery and experimental hybridization: wires, tubes, and of course some newly discovered source of mysterious power. (Lightning? The atom? Alchemy?) This B-flick setting is only slightly more preposterous than applying the term *fusion* to *any* specific idiom of jazz, since jazz has always defined itself through its synthesis of disparate elements: folk and art music, improvisation and composition, and quite literally, even black and white (in the melding of African and European musical traditions).

As it turns out, *fusion* didn't arrive as the vague one-word label we've come to know. It was shortened from *jazz-rock fusion,* a term coined by music journalists in the late sixties to describe what they saw happening around them: jazz musicians toying with elements of popular culture (in this case, rock rhythms and song structures), and rock bands employing jazz hornmen to give their efforts more weight. But *fusion* came to connote something else. To listeners and many musicians, it soon meant the spectacle of jazz musicians actively incorporating the artistic ethos, electric instruments, and even the sartorial fashions of rock and roll, their supposed archenemy.

In other words, the jazz players of the sixties and seventies, aware of the luster and lucre that rock musicians enjoyed, chose

---

*Eddie Harris, the Chicago saxist whose use of the electric saxophone anticipated the jazz-rock fusion, used the title *Plug Me In* for one of his less memorable albums of the early seventies. But it perfectly describes the dominant ethos of the period, as the synthesizer and the wah-wah pedal—along with the electrifying energy of rock and roll—became integral parts of jazz.

to abandon their principles, reach out to the pop audience, and rake in some loot.

As you've by now come to expect, this Lie contains some Useful truths.

Yes, jazz faced some tough times in the 1960s. The far-flung rigors of the avant-garde had turned the music's leading edge away from entertainment: people could not even snap their fingers to free jazz, let alone dance to it. Most casual listeners found it forbidding and disturbing, and many came to identify *all* jazz with long, screaming sax solos and tunes lacking discernible melody. A lot of them found a suitable replacement at the top of the charts. So in the sixties, rock and roll—along with its black counterpart, soul music—siphoned off some of those who had previously enjoyed the funkier side of hard-bop. Small wonder that mainstream jazzmen, watching shaggy-haired Brits fill Shea Stadium while their own audience dwindled, blamed the hard times on the Beatles. (But at the same time, they acknowledged the strength of that band's repertoire by covering such songs as "Yesterday" or, in the case of guitarist George Benson, reconstructing the entire *Abbey Road* album, tune by tune.)

And yes, a fair share of jazz musicians tried to reverse their sagging fortunes by going after the money. Used-LP shelves would soon overflow with ill-conceived attempts to tap the youth audience by incorporating rock, then disco beats, and then treacly pop romance. But it wasn't only the lure of financial success that drew jazz to the harder rhythms, higher volume, and simplified chords of rock. The upstart idiom had also become more sophisticated and had began to attract attention among adventurous improvisers seeking new avenues of expression. In the 1967 Summer of Love, the harsher style called acid rock began etching its way onto the national consciousness, using electronics and amplification as new tonal colors. Some jazz musicians saw this technique as a means of expanding their own musical palette. Meanwhile, the raw power of rock held a separate sociopolitical appeal: it arrived via brash, indelicate rhythms that captured this era's heady mix of violence and euphoria, societal permissiveness and protest marches, and such issues were certainly not foreign to jazz artists.

Most of the musicians who found rock and roll intriguing

belonged to a new breed in jazz—young, white improvisers who had grown up listening to rock and roll as well as jazz. For such emerging players and bandleaders as Gary Burton, John McLaughlin, and Mike Nock, *Beatles* was not a dirty word. But these young, white musicians weren't the ones who brought the gestating jazz-rock fusion to full term. Instead, it took a middle-aged black man—an icon of straight-ahead jazz in the minds of the American public—to deliver the goods. For the fourth time in his career, Miles Davis placed himself at the vanguard of a new direction in jazz and remained virtually unchallenged as its leader.

Davis started moving in this direction with the more blatant rhythms and increasingly open-ended musical forms heard on such albums as *Miles in the Sky* and *Filles de Kilimanjaro* (both on Columbia/Legacy), recorded four months apart in 1968. Davis and his men—notably Wayne Shorter and Tony Williams, and later keyboardists Chick Corea and Joe Zawinul—relied less and less on such traditional jazz cornerstones as harmony and linear development. Instead, they concentrated on investigating other aspects of the music, such as pure melody and tonal color. By this time Davis's band had begun using the elemental sound of the instruments themselves as a basis for improvisatory interaction. This represented something entirely new in music; you could almost say that they were playing off the colors instead of the chords.

Davis received and deserves the greatest share of the credit—or blame, in the minds of jazz purists—for the jazz-rock fusion. But you can't really claim that he invented it out of whole cloth, or that he alone saw the potential in taking jazz into the electronic age. Earlier, such hard-to-classify bands as the Fourth Way and Soft Machine (the latter name taken from writer William Burroughs's metaphor for the human body) had created heavily improvised music using guitars and electric keyboards, and based on rock rather than jazz composition. Frank Zappa presented a better-known example: his intricate and complex instrumental pieces had at least as much to do with jazz theory and harmony as they did with rock-and-roll hooks.

The first real fusion credit, though, belongs to vibraphonist Gary Burton. He started early, leading a family band in his native Indiana before reaching his teens, and making his first record at age seventeen, as a sideman with country-and-western guitarist Hank Garland. This experience helped convince Burton that jazz could work well with other, supposedly incompatible, types of music. But when he left Stan Getz's band to form his own quartet in 1966, he had more on his mind than just "flavoring" jazz with some country twangs. Burton sought to *fuse* jazz, country, and rock and roll into a style different from each of them. It was this conscious (and conscientious) effort to synthesize something new that separated Burton's genre-bending from previous crossbreeding. In those earlier cases, the musicians exploited the influence of pop, classical, or Caribbean idioms, but the performances remained unquestionably jazz.

What's more, Burton and his youthful band—which starred a converted rock guitarist named Larry Coryell—had the right look for this new music. They had all grown up appreciating not only rock and roll but also the accompanying clothes and hairstyles that screamed rebellion as loudly as the music. Press reports of the time devoted almost as much attention to what the quartet wore as to what they played. Burton's bell-bottom pants, vividly colorful body shirts, shaggy mustache, and shoulder-length hair—photographed as the band played rock palaces such as the Fillmore West—made him the poster boy for the jazz-rock fusion. Miles Davis, a noted fashion plate throughout his career, was not far behind; and when he abandoned his classy suits and understated ties for outsize sunglasses and leather pants, he again set the pace.

A 1969 album entitled *In a Silent Way* (Columbia/Legacy) served as the calm before Davis's sonic storm. A sensuous unfolding of propulsive rhythms, pastel-electronic timbres, and simplified melodies, it filled each side of the original LP with a single performance almost twenty minutes in length. The music extended the concepts of Davis's previous few albums and also toured a no-man's-land bordering jazz, rock, and what would in the nineties be called trance music. But the real breakthrough came on Davis's next recording, the double album *Bitches Brew*, which managed to combine ingredients of jazz and acid rock into a well-stirred and mystical concoction—as the title said.

The musicians who performed with Davis went on to create no less than four distinct subgenres of fusion jazz. Cofounding the quintet Weather Report, Wayne Shorter and Joe Zawinul emphasized the carefully orchestrated colors and strength of composition found on *Bitches Brew*. The second subgenre developed as John McLaughlin and Tony Williams took the pure rock energy they had brought to *Bitches Brew* and made it the centerpiece of their own bands, the Mahavishnu Orchestra and the stunning power trio Lifetime (respectively); a little later, Chick Corea also adopted this approach with his band, Return to Forever. In a third direction, the slippery soul rhythms that formed the molten undercurrent of Davis's music became the basis for Herbie Hancock's groups—although Hancock would add increasing layers of technological gimmickry and strait-jacketing rhythms, eventually arriving at a machine-heavy funk sound that had little if any relation to jazz. Meanwhile, Miles himself moved ever closer to a new form of instrumental soul music, inspired by such rockers as Jimi Hendrix and Sly & the Family Stone.

In their reliance on hard-rock rhythms and the rapid-fire flow of acid-rock melodies, none of these bands really "swung"—at least, not in the sense that jazz had come to know and accept. The loping bounce of earlier jazz forms was replaced by trippy swirls of percussion in some cases, the staccato bursts of rhythm in others. The complex harmonic schemes that characterized bebop and its heirs also disappeared; and with the popularization of electronic keyboards, so did many of post-bop's trademark timbres, such as sax and trumpet, tenor versus tenor, piano and bass fiddle, or big-band sax section. This development forced an odd back-formation in vocabulary. Suddenly, listeners began to see album-credit references to "acoustic piano," a new term created to differentiate the traditional instrument—which musicians had used since Beethoven's time—from the various electric pianos that had suddenly become ubiquitous.

At the same time, however, a number of prominent white jazzmen began to offer a quietly powerful alternative to the fusion barrage. A few of these musicians had worked with Davis, and the majority of them recorded for a new label in Germany called Editions of Contemporary Music (ECM). The music released by ECM mostly eschewed electronics. Even when an ECM album did feature guitar or synthesizer, the instruments were usually part of a grand romantic scheme, as opposed to the rock-spawned machinism that increasingly took hold of fusion.

These artists included some familiar faces: Gary Burton, who had prefigured the fusion esthetic, but whose band in the seventies took a less frantic approach to the idiom; Chick Corea, whose frankly romantic ECM recordings preceded his embrace of hard rock; and Keith Jarrett (see previous transition section), whose main experience with electronic keyboards had come on one Miles Davis album, and who quickly returned to the acoustic piano, which better suited the textural range of his music. The roster expanded to include many artists in northern-European countries that had rarely been considered hotbeds of jazz, including saxist Jan Garbarek and guitarist Terje Rypdal (of Norway), the Swedish pianist Bobo Stenson, the German bassist and composer Eberhard Weber, and trumpeter Kenny Wheeler of Great Britain.

Their music, created in reaction to fusion's heated flamboyance, soon rivaled and eventually outlasted its electrified contemporary. As with Blue Note Records in the fifties, ECM presented its own recognizable esthetic, which contributed greatly to the music's success. The label's founder, Manfred Eicher, emerged as a jazz auteur who, like the film directors who have earned that title, paid diligent attention to every aspect of his productions—from the choice of songs to the reverb in the studio to the gorgeously photographed landscapes and still lifes that gave the LP covers an understated mystique. These decisions helped convey the same shrouded emotion and oblique implication as the music. The ECM label became home to a "new cool school," which—despite a spiritual connection to its namesake—differed radically from the smoldering passions that Miles Davis had captured twenty-five years earlier.

Although fusion jazz began in the late sixties and came to dominate the seventies, that didn't render other styles of jazz extinct. They merely went underground, lying in wait for the eighties—by which time fusion had largely spent its serious musical influence, and the term itself had come to denote diluted mixtures of jazz with pop music of almost any stripe.

The Discs

Gary Burton created an entirely new style of playing the jazz vibraphone. His agility at using two or even three mallets in each hand allowed him to play full chords and adopt a truly pianistic approach to the instrument—at times performing without any accompaniment. Throughout the 1970s, he straddled the two dominant jazz camps, bringing something of each to the other. With his quintet, he offered a toned-down version of electric fusion; in his duo and even solo recordings, he brought a highly charged virtuosity to the "new cool" (see this chapter's second section, which starts on page 192).

While it would stretch the point to call Burton's jazz-and-country experiments the first real fusion music, he left no doubts with the band he assembled in 1967 after leaving Stan Getz. On *Lofty Fake Anagram* (One Way), Burton and his quartet consciously sought to infuse jazz with elements of rock and roll, the youth-oriented sound track for the explosive sixties. (The reasons were obvious: Burton himself had recently turned twenty-four, and the old man of the group was Steve Swallow, at twenty-seven.) Some of the band's songs had a bouncy, evenly accented rhythm more characteristic of the Beatles than the Beats; the use of occasional folk-rock textures recalled the Byrds instead of Bird. You could still hear references to country-western music, particularly in several of Larry Coryell's guitar solos. On the other hand, the Coryell composition "Lines" foreshadowed the intricate unison playing that would later mark such fusion exemplars as the Mahavishnu Orchestra and Coryell's own Eleventh House. This and the Burton Quartet's previous album, *Duster*—along with their popularity among young white audiences attuned to rock—gave an accurate forecast of the coming musical storms.

Burton's band kept evolving during the next decade. The rhythm section continued to pivot around Swallow—who had traded in his bass fiddle for the electric bass guitar—but different guitarists moved into the front line, each one changing the sound and direction of the band. (These included a future star in John Scofield.) The most important of them, Pat Metheny, had longed to work in Burton's band since junior high school. As a teenaged guitar instructor, he eventually joined Burton on the faculty of the Berklee College of Music; and although Burton's quartet already had a guitarist, the band soon expanded to make room for Metheny. On *Dreams So Real* (ECM) this two-guitar lineup—a rarity in jazz (though not in rock)—matched up with exceptionally strong material: seven works by the imaginative and idiosyncratic composer Carla Bley, whose music has always occupied a favored shelf in Burton's library. You can't really say that Burton's own solos on this album outshine his other work, because throughout his career his improvising has remained remarkably consistent in its brilliant blend of technique and structure. Nonetheless, the Bley compositions seemed to elicit an incandescent logic, placing this among the more memorable albums of the decade.

Stanley Clarke, *Children of Forever* (One Way). By the time Stanley Clarke recorded this, his debut album as a leader, the twenty-one-year-old bassist had already served notice of his wunderkind abilities. He had demonstrated his groundbreaking technique on tour with Stan Getz and on record with Dexter Gordon, playing the bass fiddle with the agility of a guitarist. He had also left listeners agape at his innovative *electric* bass work in Chick Corea's band Return to Forever. The title of this album shouts out its genealogy. So does the instrumentation, with its emphasis on flute instead of saxophone, and the presence of Corea himself seals the deal. But despite this comparative lack of originality, *Children of Forever* offers an appealing variation on the theme, as well as a solid example of the genre. Clarke's infectious "Bass Folk Song" is the only instrumental composition. The other four tracks feature extensive vocal work by the veteran Andy Bey and a youthful Dee Dee Bridgewater, cementing Clarke's lifelong ties with pop and light rock. (Both singers would gain renewed fame in the 1990s.) And Clarke created a fusion epic with "Sea Journey," which added vocals and orchestration to the Corea composition originally titled "Song for Sally" (see Corea's *Piano Improvisations* in this chapter's second section) and inspired several other recordings of the song.

Chick Corea, *Return to the 7th Galaxy* (Verve). His fellow keyboardist Herbie Hancock scored a hit with the song "Chameleon," but that title would have better fit Chick Corea. By the summer of 1972, he had already led a free jazz band, acted as musical director for Stan Getz's mainstream quartet, and helped catalyze Miles Davis's electronic experiments. In 1972, Corea assembled the first of the two distinctly different fusion bands—both of which he called Return to Forever (RTF)—that appear on this dual-CD anthology. The first band starred flutist-saxist Joe Farrell and bassist Stanley Clarke and had a relatively light sound. It also had a distinct Latin tinge, thanks to Corea's Iberian-flavored compositions, and to the Brazilian musicians in the band—percussionist Airto Moreira and vocalist Flora Purim (husband and wife). In the second RTF, Corea took his cue from the Mahavishnu Orchestra of John McLaughlin. He got rid of the horns and voice, replacing them with a stinging electric guitar and his own use of the Moog synthesizer. The phaser-strength drumming of Lenny White ratcheted up the energy level even further. Corea's unique and influential compositions remained a consistent strength, but by 1975—shortly after guitarist Al DiMeola joined—RTF had evolved into something close to a true hard-rock band, with only vestigial traces of jazz improvisation. This collection stops just before that point and includes virtually all the tracks from RTF's most interesting recording, *Where Have I Known You Before*.

Larry Coryell, *Introducing the Eleventh House* (Vanguard). Although Larry Coryell qualifies as one of the first fusion players—before joining Gary Burton, he had played in a jazz-influenced rock band called the Free Spirits—it took a while for the guitarist to form his own electric jazz band. The Eleventh House perked up some ears nonetheless. For one thing, Coryell led one of the only fusion bands to employ trumpet, which gave the music a bright, splashy bravado. A technically gifted player, Coryell balanced rock-guitar moans, precision-tuned skeins of notes, and exotic textures from India and Spain, while the hyperkinetic keyboardist Mike Mandel could summon a loopy, anarchic energy that matched Coryell's own. And the nonstop barrage from drummer Alphonse Mouzon expressed both the sleek power and rampaging excesses that fusion could attain. The Eleventh House's best albums aren't currently available, but this 1974 debut gives you an idea of their skill and direction. It lacks the more original thinking of their later work, but serves as a sort of road map to the fusion landscape, with scenic detours into territories already staked out by such bands as Weather Report (on a song called "The Funky Waltz") and the Mahavishnu Orchestra ("Low-Lee-Tah," "Yin"). Several other tunes display the band's real distinction: a lighthearted, pop-rock sensibility missing in most other fusion bands. (The band's name referred to the position of the astrological sign Aquarius—as in "Age of.")

Miles Davis, *Bitches Brew* (Columbia/Legacy). Despite the many significant musical events leading up to it, the original release of this album still represents the birth of fusion—the moment when the gestation ended and the baby started wailing. Appearing first as a double LP and now available as a dual CD, *Bitches Brew* picked up where *In a Silent Way* left off, with long, wandering pieces that emphasized sound and texture. But the presence of an extra percussionist, two bassists (one playing bass violin, the other bass guitar), and no less than *three* keyboardists—Chick Corea, Joe Zawinul, and Larry Young—allowed Davis to better exploit the possibilities for complex interaction and musical drama. And with the addition of Bennie Maupin's wraithlike bass clarinet, the music gained a spooky air of foreboding. Davis's "new directions in music" (the phrase emblazoned above the album title) followed a new map—one where colors and melody provided the main landmarks, instead of the chords and rhythms of bebop and its offspring. And indeed, virtually everything about this music *was* new, from the startling psychedelic cover illustration, to the lead voice provided by guitarist John McLaughlin, to the complete abandonment of traditional jazz structures. Only one element really remained unchanged: the sound and the improvisational conceits of Davis himself, which nonetheless attained a much different glow in this bubbling sonic cauldron.

Miles Davis, *Dark Magus* (Columbia/Legacy). Davis's electric band went through a rapid evolution, partly because of a steady supply of new sidemen flowing through it, and partly due to the leader's habitual need to push his music further and further. By 1974, when the music on *Dark Magus* was recorded at Carnegie Hall, his band featured not one but three electric guitarists, who built a thicket of rhythm and effects behind the horn soloists (Miles and saxist Dave Liebman). In addition to the powerful drummer Al Foster, the band also carried a separate percussionist, whose colorful accents on primitive instruments—such as log drum and thumb piano—contrasted with the guitar technology and Davis's own use of the electric organ. This music emphasized polyrhythmic, Africanized rock beats, and the combination of instruments gave the music a layered, woolen texture. (The previous edition of Miles's band had included Indian instrumentalists playing sitar and tabla, and the music retained traces of that influence as well.) The Fusion Father's version of his creation became increasingly rougher, tougher, and more confrontational. In concert, the music simply exploded to a start, usually with only the hint of an actual theme; rumbled along (often with sensationalistic splashes) for forty or sixty minutes, hardly even pausing to shift gears for a new piece, challenging the listener to give in to the hypnotic pulse and the dense wall of sound; and then imploded to a halt. This double CD, unavailable in the United States until 1997, presents an especially cohesive version of this experience. (Play it loud.)

Gil Evans & the Monday Night Orchestra, *Live at Sweet Basil* (Evidence). As far back as the 1940s, and especially in his collaborations with Miles Davis (see chapter 4), arranger Gil Evans had seized attention with his provocative tonal colors and instrumental textures. So it should come as no surprise that fusion—with its range of new sounds, from electronic timbres to rock rhythms—would propel his imagination. Evans did not lead a regular performing ensemble until his big band of the seventies; the best of that band's albums don't exist on domestic CD, but this 1984 date captures their spirit of adventure. His arrangement of "Parabola," a song by Wayne Shorter, shows Evans's penchant for not just orchestrating but actually rewriting an extant composition. And the presence of two Jimi Hendrix tunes shows the strong influence of acid rock on this music—as well as similarities between the Grateful Dead's "space" jams and Evans's drifty, often chilling ballads. Like some sort of space-age polymer, these arrangements became increasingly malleable, granting an extraordinary freedom to such soloists as trumpeter Hannibal Marvin Peterson, saxist George Adams, and guitarist Hiram Bullock. From the keyboard, Evans conducted his arrangements to make them conform to the solos, instead of the other way around. As a result, even the written passages sound improvised, creating unusually fluid big-band performances. This album gets the slight nod over *Live at Sweet Basil Vol. 2*, which contains more material from the same sessions.

Herbie Hancock, *Head Hunters* (Columbia/Legacy). Of all the fusion bands to evolve out of Miles Davis's music, the one led by Hancock (who incidentally did *not* play on *Bitches Brew*) retained the strongest ties to African-American music. In Hancock's hands, the jazz-rock fusion became the jazz-*soul* fusion, incorporating the sinewy rhythms and thickly sweet textures of contemporary black pop music. It all arrived with a healthy helping of funk, provided by wah-wah guitar and fuzz-tone bass and the sexy, sultry sound of backbeat drumming (which places the heaviest accent on the second and fourth beats of the measure). Small wonder that Hancock titled one of the album's songs for Sly Stone, among the funkiest and most influential pop musicians of the time. Hancock had recorded three earlier fusion albums, but this 1973 album was his breakthrough. It grabbed listeners' ears (and feet) with the sixteen-minute "Chameleon," the blistering, bluesy march that became a funk-fusion staple. For balance, a tune called "Vein Melter" recaptured the dreamy textures of his earlier fusion albums. And on a remake of his most famous composition, "Watermelon Man," Hancock borrowed a riff from Pygmy tribal music, using it to key a radically reharmonized arrangement—and thus spelled out the connection between his own past and future directions. Few albums paint a better picture of the fusion phenomenon.

Eddie Harris, *The Electrifying Eddie Harris* (Rhino). Some people would place the Chicago saxist Eddie Harris in this chapter simply because of his early use of the electric saxophone attachment—an amplifier/modifier with which Harris could manipulate and mask the sound of his horn. (This despite the fact that his tenor sound was among the most recognizable in jazz.) But besides his pioneering experiments in electricity, Harris belongs here for incorporating soul-rock rhythms and a distinct "street" sensibility into his virtuosic improvisations. By the time of these 1967–68 recordings, he had learned to bounce his angularly phrased compositions and solos—both of which had an almost mathematical precision—against tough, syncopated shuffle rhythms. Harris himself suggested, with his tongue only partly in his cheek, that his infectious recording of "Listen Here" represented the "invention" of fusion. In any case, the song sold more than a million albums, and it certainly did presage the coming decade's fascination with funk. (In the seventies, Harris recorded his share of funk, then turned his shrewd sense of humor on the fad—thus creating priceless bits of socio-musical satire, even as he made money by exploiting it!) This disc presents a mixed bag of straight-ahead jazz, some pop nonsense, and several pre-fusion classics, including his irresistible tunes "Listen Here" and "Sham Time." It actually contains two complete LPs, *The Electrifying Eddie Harris* and *Plug Me In*—a good thing, since together they add up to just under sixty minutes of music.

Ronald Shannon Jackson and the Decoding Society, *Man Dance* (Antilles). The Texas-born drummer Ronald Shannon Jackson injects his music with a supercharged dose of country blues and a psychedelic vision of two-beat swing. In addition to his spectacular energy, though, Jackson's uncanny control of his instrument amended the rules of jazz drumming: the basic pulse now seemed to come not from any one part but from *all* of the drum kit, as multiple rhythms simultaneously battled and fed each other. Like several other fusion leaders, Jackson emphasized composition as much as improvisation, with an endless flow of his own well-conceived pieces. But more than earlier fusion bands, the Decoding Society—which wasn't formed until 1979, after the heyday of punk rock and the emergence of hip-hop—had a wildly liberated sound, even within the strictures of carefully composed music. You can trace some of this to the absence of high-tech keyboard clutter, and some credit goes to the sweet-and-sour guitar of Vernon Reid, who would later become a full-fledged rock star. Even more credit goes to Ornette Coleman's Prime Time Band (in which Jackson had played)—a band that smeared the line between lead instruments and rhythm section into a thick layer cake of sound. Jackson took this concept still further. On some tunes, you hear three distinct melody lines vying for the spotlight, with the leader's colorful and lyrical drum work supplying the essence of a fourth.

Mahavishnu Orchestra, *Inner Mounting Flame* (Columbia/ Legacy). Shortly after his seminal work on Miles Davis's *Bitches Brew*, guitarist John McLaughlin became a disciple of the meditation guru Sri Chinmoy, adopting the spiritual name Mahavishnu and drastically changing his diet and lifestyle. (Well, it *was* the sixties.) But even knowing none of this, you might have guessed that some form of religious fervor had grabbed hold of the music: all it takes is one hearing of this album's opening track, with its mystical overtones and frenzied rhythms. The Mahavishnu Orchestra played with an almost supernatural energy, hammering out intricate ensemble melodies with incredible precision at breathtaking tempos; at times, the dizzying intensity suggested the motion of Sufi dervishes. The music mirrored the high-voltage power of McLaughlin's guitar style, primarily in the machine-gun drumming of Billy Cobham—which established a new standard in its mix of speed and brawn—but also in the swirling keyboard chords of Jan Hammer and the enraptured solos of a classically trained rock violinist, Jerry Goodman. The quintet recorded three albums before Goodman was replaced by violinist Jean-Luc Ponty, a fusion star in his own right. This resulted in an unstable "supergroup" that grew to the size of a small orchestra before it succumbed to clashing egos. In any case, none of their later albums eclipsed the exuberant wonder of this, the band's debut recording.

Pat Metheny Group, *Travels* (ECM). Metheny's platinum lyricism and laser-focus virtuosity have made him the most influential jazz guitarist of the last quarter century. When he left Gary Burton to form his own band in 1977, Metheny joined forces with Lyle Mays, a keyboardist who shared the guitarist's interest in a music driven primarily by strong composition. Both players were (and remain) capable of extensive and at times epic solos. But in this band's songs—as in those of Weather Report—the improvisations became less important as individual statements than as building blocks of a larger musical edifice. (Eventually, their pieces came to suggest an especially sophisticated brand of instrumental rock. The music thus differed from earlier jazz idioms, or even such bands as John McLaughlin's and Miles Davis's, which often had the open-ended spirit of a jam session.) The Missouri-bred Metheny and the Wisconsin-born Mays shared something else: a Midwestern esthetic that honored folk-rock and country-western music in addition to post-sixties jazz. This "prairie" sound became immensely popular on pieces such as "Phase Dance," "San

Lorenzo," and a long tone poem called "As Falls Wichita, So Falls Wichita Falls," all of which are contained on *Travels*. For all the stiffness that marked the original studio recordings of these pieces, the band always opened them up in concert, making this double disc—recorded on a 1982 tour—the most satisfying document of their early work.

Weather Report first took shape in 1970 as a quintet co-led by saxist Wayne Shorter, the Czech bassist Miroslav Vitous, and the Austrian-born keyboardist Joe Zawinul (who had held the spoon as Miles Davis stirred his "bitches brew"). Representing fusion's finest hour, Weather Report offers a study in balance. The band placed Shorter's tantalizingly elliptical solos against Zawinul's sharply stamped compositions. It also used the natural ("acoustic") sound of Shorter's tenor and soprano to warm the space-age timbres launched by Zawinul's growing electronic arsenal. As in Miles Davis's group, Weather Report broke down the traditional line between solos and accompaniment. Most important, they combined rock mechanics and a jazz sensibility like no other band, eventually adding the exotic world-music sounds of Asia and Africa as well.

Their eponymous first album, *Weather Report* (Columbia/Legacy), issued sounds unfamiliar to listeners of either jazz *or* rock. Expanding upon the "Twilight Zone" aspect of the music they had made with Davis, Zawinul and Shorter created an album in which traditional musical elements—such as linear melody and familiar chord progressions—took a backseat to tonal colors and instrumental textures as the driving force. The quieter and more contemplative tracks still have a pristine aura of spacey new beginnings. Other compositions (notably Vitous's "Seventh Arrow") appropriated rock's pile-driver rhythms, but still retained an otherworldliness in their fragmented melody lines. In the original LP's liner notes, Zawinul described the music as "a sound track for your imagination," a phrase very much in sync with the cool psychedelic mix of natural and electronic sounds. And more than on any of the albums that would follow, some of these tracks even hint at "new [classical] music" of the period—a reminder that conservatory composers had, only a few years earlier, begun using the synthesizer in their own concert-hall efforts.

In the band's fifteen-year life span, Weather Report moved

increasingly toward the rock-music side of the jazz-rock equation. Zawinul's compositions became more concrete, the rhythms gained flamboyance and definition, and Shorter's solos grew—well, shorter. Their fourth album, *Mysterious Traveler* (Columbia/Legacy), finds the band midway through this process, combining the best of both worlds. With its UFO sound effects and stop-start rhythm, the title track carries the same slightly sinister thrill as the cover illustration (a meteor falling through the night sky). But the entire album plunges into depths of tightly compressed sound, with Shorter's tenor and soprano carrying a gamut of emotions. Zawinul's keyboards gave breadth to the electronic orchestrations that dominated rock music in the seventies; and on this album, with his use of advanced recording techniques, he began to incorporate the studio itself as a "sixth member" of the quintet. Yet the album also makes room for an acoustic duet by Shorter and Zawinul, and their interactive communication proves as impressive as the Louis Armstrong–Earl Hines duets of five decades earlier. The imminent arrival of electric bassist Jaco Pastorius would provide a new source of inspiration on the band's next album and later help define their best-known song ("Birdland"). But *Mysterious Traveler* remains their masterpiece—the best album by the Band of the Decade.

With an encyclopedic command of rhythms from Central and South America, Pastorius added an extra layer of percussion to the band's increasingly global esthetic. His accompaniment work had a bristling authority, and his improvisations revealed a spectacular, even unique technique. Pastorius adapted the model of Steve Swallow (see Gary Burton, above) in using a fretless electric bass, an instrument that, in terms of concept, sound, and design, is closer to the bass fiddle than to the conventional bass guitar. Pastorius reinvented the role of the electric bass in jazz. In so doing, he helped Weather Report chart a new direction, as Zawinul modified his writing to accommodate this powerful new presence. The music became increasingly concrete, replacing the subtle mystery of earlier albums with a masterly command of pop-music focus; yet the band retained the intricacies and variety of jazz. The best example is *Heavy Weather* (Columbia/Legacy), and particularly "Birdland," which brilliantly juggles the cheery melody, Zawinul's keyboard orchestrations, the startling virtuosity of Pastorius, and a searing tenor solo by Shorter. But the album also shines for two of Pastorius's own compositions, and for the Caribbean flavor of several other pieces, which indicated both the bassist's influence and the talents of percussionists Alex Acuna and Manolo Badrena.

Tony Williams Lifetime, *Spectrum: The Anthology* (Verve). As a teenaged drummer, Tony Williams had solidified the Miles Davis Quintet and left his mark on musicians throughout jazz. In 1969, still in his early twenties, Williams became the first member of Davis's circle to embrace the jazz-rock fusion with his own group. He called this power trio Lifetime, and it strongly reflected Williams's appreciation of such to-the-wall rock artists as Jimi Hendrix, Cream, and the MC 5. But Lifetime—which starred the soon-to-be-famous guitarist John McLaughlin and the iconoclastic organ player Larry Young—remained the black sheep of fusion music. Employing gritty vocals, as well as song forms that were unequivocally rock based, Lifetime made few friends in jazz. On the other hand, rock audiences admired but could barely appreciate the complexities of McLaughlin's solos, let alone the startling new voicings and rhythms that Young brought to the organ. More than any of his colleagues, Williams envisioned a band that incorporated the aggressive anarchy as well as the liberating power of rock music, and Lifetime's performances—especially on their first album, *Emergency*—had a dangerous, unpredictable energy. (Other fusion bands played on concert stages, but Lifetime always seemed to belong in a rough-edged rock-and-roll bar.) This excellent double CD traces Lifetime's brief lifetime, 1969–73, originally documented on four separate LPs.

The New Cool

Gary Burton and Chick Corea, *Crystal Silence* (ECM). Steel and ivory, polished to a high sheen: this groundbreaking album, one of the earliest released by ECM Records (in 1972), quickly became a hallmark of the "new cool." Its unorthodox instrumentation of vibraphone and piano captivated listeners in retreat from the fusion barrage. So did the now rocking, now ethereal interaction between two of modern jazz's uncontested virtuosos, both devotees of Bill Evans's music. (Not incidentally, Burton and Corea had both starred in quartets led by Stan

Getz, another Evans admirer.) The title track, one of Corea's most haunting compositions, has a rarely recaptured mixture of fragrance and foreboding. Meanwhile, the tunes that bookend the album—"Senor Mouse" and "What Game Shall We Play Today"—provide fast and furious showcases for technical fireworks, primarily on the part of Burton. The impressionistic bent of the entire album made it virtually unforgettable to contemporaneous listeners, and even today it retains an almost totemic impact. *Crystal Silence* initiated a collaboration between Burton and Corea that has lasted to the present, heard on several more recordings. In truth, all of those are more ambitiously conceived and technically accomplished than this original meeting. But none of them—and few recordings by any other artists—so precisely captures the quiet revolution of the new cool.

Chick Corea, *Piano Improvisations, Volume 1* (ECM). Like Gary Burton, Chick Corea straddled electric fusion and the new cool, exerting an even greater influence over the music of his time and beyond. But despite the flashy synthesizer voicings and powerhouse style of his seventies bands (see above), the true extent of Corea's contribution comes across in his glassy acoustic-piano stylings and unmistakable compositions. On this solo-piano album (and, to a lesser extent, its companion, *Volume 2*), Corea unspools a voluptuous, Romantic impressionism. The music has the yearning precision of Chopin's mazurkas and polonaises, and the watercolor harmonies of Ravel and Debussy. The individual performances reveal distinct charms, while the entire album made a strong case for the solo-piano idiom in general, helping open the floodgates for such recordings by a host of keyboardists. Aside from their presentation, the compositions themselves give this album an extra dimension, turning it into something of a Rosetta Stone for subsequent recordings by Corea. Such exquisite pieces as "Noon Song" and "Ballad for Anna" contain the lyric essence that would inform much of his writing for the next thirty years. And in "Song for Sally," Corea presented a brooding, Byronic tone poem that later found new life in fusion as the monumental "Sea Journey" (see Stanley Clarke, above). This song also hints at the Spanish and Brazilian influences that would lead Corea to write such new jazz standards as "La Fiesta," "Spain," and "Sometime Ago" (the first recording of which appears on this CD).

Keith Jarrett, *Köln Concert* (ECM). The albums recorded by Keith Jarrett in the early and middle seventies did more to popularize the solo-piano idiom than anyone else's, and his *Köln Concert*, recorded in Germany in 1975, had the greatest impact of all. This did not represent Jarrett's initial foray into unaccompanied recording. It wasn't even his first stab at creating a concerto-length, multisectioned improvisation, in which (by his own explanation) he came onstage with absolutely no preconceived idea of what he would play. But at Köln, Jarrett unloosed a masterpiece of the idiom: rich with elegant, emergent themes, rollicking sections of highly charged rhythm, and rubato passages of nearly overripe romance. The concert set the pattern for Jarrett's solo performances over the next two decades. These concerts (which reached their apex with a Japanese tour that produced the six-CD set *The Sun Bear Concerts*) typically contained two pieces separated by an intermission. Usually thirty-five to fifty minutes each, these pieces arose from a fairly fixed repertoire of techniques and devices. The success of all these performances depended not so much on some newly unveiled idea or direction, but rather on the explorations Jarrett undertook into a frontier of his own creation. More than any other manifestation of his career—which includes composing, interpreting classical music, and leading top-notch ensembles—these solo works have secured his reputation and expressed his musical character.

Keith Jarrett, *Belonging* (ECM). In addition to his unaccompanied concerts and his domestic quartet (see previous transition section), Keith Jarrett also led a second and distinctly different quartet during the seventies. He hooked up with three Scandinavian musicians—the Norwegians Jan Garbarek (saxophones) and Jon Christensen (drums), and the Swedish bassist Palle Danielsson—to make music that was less democratic and more hierarchical than that of his American band. Garbarek in particular benefited from his association with Jarrett; already well known in Europe, he now attained a heightened profile in the United States as well, thanks largely to the broad brocade of his tone and his effective extension of John Coltrane's more involuted phrase-making. But despite Garbarek's spotlit role, and the attention that audiences lavished on his opulent sax stylings, the band remained firmly under the command of Jarrett, who used it to explore a clearly defined European romanticism. You can hear this best on the title track, and on "Solstice," both of which brim with the jazz equivalent of deep-felt lyric poetry: Jarrett's improvisations well up from deep within the piano, following a crisp, inexorable melodic impulse. Yet two up-tempo Jarrett compositions—the rollicking "Spiral Dance" and "The Windup," which has something of a silent-movie chase-scene quality—make clear that the new cool precluded neither speed nor passion.

Oregon, *Winter Light* (Vanguard). While most fusion bands contented themselves with hybridizing rock and jazz, the all-acoustic quartet Oregon merged jazz improvisation, chamber-music instrumentation, folk-rock sensibilities, and the percussion traditions of India and Africa into an indelible body of work. The band's unusual sound derived from the combination of Ralph Towner's classical (unamplified) guitar, reedman Paul McCandless's oboe (an instrument that had never before provided the leading voice in a jazz ensemble), and the late Colin Walcott's percussion setup of tablas, congas, and sitar, which replaced the tom-tom drums and cymbals that make up the typical jazz drummer's equipment. Only the sound of Glen Moore's bass provided a hint of normal jazz sonorities. The clockwork complexity of Oregon's music reveals the same intrigue with exotic colors and imagery heard in most of the fusion bands. But Oregon's airy and extremely centered music conjures up mountain streams and forests, as opposed to the spaceships and pageantry of the electric bands. Oregon's music has the aura of meditation but avoids the drift into mere New Age noodling—even on an album with so atmospheric a title as *Winter Light* (1974). It contains a number of the best and best-known pieces in their repertoire: "Tide Pool," "Ghost Beads," "Rainmaker," and "Witchi-Tai-To." Their spinning melodies and intensely focused improvisations disproved the idea that all-*acoustic* would have to mean "dull"—or even "quiet"—in the electric age.

Terje Rypdal, *Odyssey* (ECM). In the hands of Norwegian guitarist Terje Rypdal, the new cool turned positively frigid.

Most of the compositions on this epic album concentrate on the slow drift of wintry chords and thick electronic clouds of sound. Yet Rypdal's own playing—with its manipulation of relatively few notes into wailing, screaming solos—sounded as if he had lifted it directly from the crucible of acid rock. Rypdal had indeed started out in rock music, and he continued to hone a rock-guitarist's fascination with timbre and texture. But in marrying these solos to the bleak beauty of his wide-angle compositions, he created an artistic voice both bold and introspective. On *Odyssey*, recorded in 1975, the music is often chilling, but you can't deny the passionate revelations of Rypdal's guitar in the leading role. It sometimes seems as if the great Norwegian dramatist Henrik Ibsen had come back as a musician. Like his countryman Jan Garbarek, Rypdal helped create the portrait of a new romanticism in modern music. But the versatile Rypdal managed to mirror his homeland's harsh landscapes even on bubbling melodies at sprightly tempos—such as a tune called "Over Birkerot" on this album, and all of the music on a subsequent album (*Waves*, also on ECM). These songs not only reflected his rock roots, in their busy but especially well-crafted solos; they also revealed his capacity to play tough fusion jazz à la Miles Davis.

More Juice?

The new possibilities offered by fusion—plus the premium that jazz musicians have always placed on evaluating and adapting the latest "new thing"—led several established musicians to enlist in the electronic revolution. In some cases, the results were surprisingly effective.

Ornette Coleman entered the fusion fray with a band that featured two drummers, two bass guitarists, and two electric guitarists in addition to his clarion alto sax. But as you might expect, Ornette's version of fusion proved different from all the others, which is clear from *In All Languages* (Verve). In fact, the use of electric instruments provided Ornette with the vehicle for his Harmolodic Theory of music, which seeks to equalize traditional distinctions between melody, harmony, and rhythm.

Two albums by trumpeter Freddie Hubbard—*Red Clay* and *Straight Life* (both on CTI/CBS)—show how musicians less adventurous than Miles or Ornette could still use elements of fusion creatively. In Hubbard's case, that meant employing Herbie Hancock on electric piano and opening up the title tracks to modal improvisation and rock rhythms. The Brecker Brothers—trumpeter Randy and saxist Michael—took this further. Having played together in Horace Silver's quintet, then spearheading a wild early fusion group called Dreams (currently unavailable on CD), they formed their own band. They played hard-edged funk, combining dance rhythms with splashy jazz solos (some of them by a young David Sanborn); *The Brecker Brothers Collection Vol. 1* (Novus) will clue you in.

Guitarist John Abercrombie—a charter member of the group Dreams—recorded frequently and well, covering several parts of the musical map. On *Timeless*, he offered a new take on the "organ trio" format with an album that flits between kick-ass fusion and the introverted ballads familiar to ECM listeners. His solo album *Characters* and his trio *Gateway* come down more firmly in the new-cool camp and help trace the guitarist's growing importance as a romantic stylist.

Gary Burton's music would demand further attention if only for its variety of concept and consistency of execution. *Duster* (Koch Jazz), the best-known album by his first quartet, featured veteran drummer Roy Haynes, which gives the music a more jazz-grounded base. Burton's first collaboration with the noteworthy composer Carla Bley resulted in the extraordinary *A Genuine Tong Funeral* (RCA); and the relatively freewheeling *Passengers* (ECM) makes a fine counterpart to *Dreams So Real* (recommended above). You can hear Burton in the format of a more traditional rhythm section—piano, bass, and drums—on *Whiz Kids* (ECM). You can also follow the further adventures of Burton and his two most simpatico collaborators: Pat Metheny, on the 1990 *Reunion* (GRP), and Chick Corea, on the duo album *In Concert, Zurich, 28 October 1979* (ECM.)

For more of Chick Corea's *first* Return to Forever—the Brazilian-influenced, semi-acoustic band—get the album of the same name, *Return to Forever* (ECM). Also consider *Tap Step* (Stretch/Concord) and *Voyage* (ECM), both recorded after his foray into the formulaic hard rock of his second RTF. But Corea's electric inclinations did find a suitable home in the nineties with a quintet called the Elektric [sic] Band, *Eye of the Beholder* (GRP) being the best example; meanwhile, his 1994 outing *Expressions* (GRP) reiterated his command of the solo-piano idiom.

Miles Davis's *In a Silent Way* remains one of the most purely sensual jazz albums ever released; it still leaves listeners searching for adjectives and questing for more. After *Bitches Brew*, Davis recorded an in-concert follow-up, *Black Beauty*, at the rock palace Fillmore West; his next studio date, *Live-Evil*, began to make the shift to a harder, louder, and even more confrontational brand of fusion, which reached an apocalyptic apotheosis with *Pangaea*—dense, intense, and not to everyone's taste. (They're all double CDs from Columbia/Legacy.)

After the furor he had unleashed in the seventies, Davis left the public arena for almost seven years, returning to records and concerts in the mid-eighties with bands that played a formulaic funk program. But within that format, he still managed to create the occasional gem, and throughout this period, he employed a number of excellent younger musicians. The best examples of this music are *Amandla* and *Live Around the World* (both on Warner Bros.).

One note of caution. Miles's last album, *Live at Montreux* (Warner Bros.), features Quincy Jones leading a band playing the classic 1950s arrangements of Gil Evans. It all sounds too good to be true, and it is—a victim of the sloppy ensemble work and impoverished trumpetry by Davis, who died less than three months after the concert. Avoid it at all costs.

Before *Head Hunters*, Herbie Hancock made two of the subtlest albums in the fusion genre, *Mwandishi* and *Water Torture* (both on Warner Bros.). Each featured a marvelous sextet with a three-horn front line—fusion's answer to the Jazz Messengers. These two LPs, plus one pre-fusion date, also make up the double CD *Mwandishi: The Complete Warner Bros. Recordings*: somewhat inconsistent, but still worth owning. Of his later electric recordings, only *Thrust* (Columbia/Legacy) still bears much resemblance to jazz as we know it.

Eddie Harris's pop successes always overshadowed his innovative vision, but the double-disc anthology *Artist's Choice*

(Rhino) presents a comprehensive survey of his early career (1960–77). A later album, the delightful *Eddie Who?* (Timeless), features plenty of his acrobatic, yodel-like scat vocals, while his return to all-acoustic music is best heard on one of his last albums, *There Was a Time* (Enja).

Harris also took part in a recording that came to symbolize the early seventies when he sat in with the bluesy pianist-vocalist Les McCann at the 1969 Montreux Jazz Festival. The resultant *Swiss Movement* (Rhino) contains several rock-ribbed jazz jams, but became a gold-record hit—and remains among the most popular albums in jazz history—largely because of the infectious protest song "Compared to What," a product of the period's turbulent political waves.

If you enjoyed Keith Jarrett's "Scandinavian" band, *My Song* and the in-concert *Personal Mountains* pick up the thread. For more of his solo-piano work, the revelatory double CD *Staircase* is the next step, followed by the much later *Vienna Concert* (1992). Jarrett's *Köln Concert* left big shoes to fill, and that happens only on *The Sun Bear Concerts*—a six-CD set documenting a 1976 Japanese tour. They're all on ECM.

Pat Metheny's quartet began to evolve into a new band that reached its full stride a bit later (see chapter 7); *Offramp* is the best studio album from this transition period. During these years, he also broadened his scope to emphasize his straight-ahead jazz background, on such albums as the dual-disc *80/81*—with saxists Michael Brecker and Dewey Redman—and *Rejoicing*, which featured two musicians (Charlie Haden and Billy Higgins) who had gained fame playing with an unlikely Metheny hero, Ornette Coleman. (All on ECM.)

The Oregon trail led to *Distant Hills* (Vanguard) and *Roots in the Sky* (Discovery); it also led to the inclusion of electronics, in the form of synthesizers, on their later albums. After the devastating death of percussionist Colin Walcott in a car accident, Oregon worked with the Turkish percussionist Trilok Gurtu—*Ecotopia* (ECM) and the 1997 release *Northwest Passage* (Intuition) are arguably the best—and sometimes as a percussionless trio.

In addition, the most accomplished of Oregon's members,

Ralph Towner, has made several albums that have become hallmarks of the "new cool." Of these, *Solstice* (1975) and *Solo Concert* (1979), both on ECM, get the nod.

The jazz-pop fusion found one of its strongest practitioners in saxist Grover Washington, Jr., who brought a sure-handed technique and a populist lyricism to smooth rock rhythms and easy-to-absorb tunes. *Mister Magic* (MoJazz) was his breakthrough; a more insightful use of these same elements occurs on *Reed Seed* (Motown).

Many commentators consider Weather Report's second album, *I Sing the Body Electric*, their best; comprising both studio tracks and an early in-concert performance, it does provide an excellent if somewhat atypical view of their music, but not the best introduction. W.R. presented a somewhat different face in performance, elaborating upon and illuminating their studio-tweaked compositions: the 1979 double album *8:30* is a fine example, and also the "jazziest" album in their discography. In addition, the studio album *Tale Spinnin'* shows the band making the transition from the space-age inspiration of *Mysterious Traveler* to the worldly delights of *Heavy Weather* (all on Columbia/Legacy).

At the same time that he joined Weather Report, Jaco Pastorius debuted his own short-lived career with one of the most stunningly assured first albums in modern memory. On *Jaco Pastorius* (Epic) he wove a seamless tapestry that included several fusion tracks, an evocation of Cuban religious music, traditional R&B, and mainstream jazz, all focused on his phenomenal new conception of the fretless electric bass.

Germany's Eberhard Weber played an important part in crafting the ECM sound with distinctive bass solos, high-concept compositions, and a spectacular sensitivity to the tonal palette. *The Colours of Chloe* and *Fluid Rustle* top the list of his available albums.

The development of a high-fidelity amplification device for the violin made that instrument more audible—and thus more visible—in jazz; and because this occurred in the 1960s, several violinists turned to fusion. Two of the best fusion fiddlers were the Polish violinists Michal Urbaniak and Zbigniew Seifert, but neither man's albums of the period have come out on CD; the best known, Jean-Luc Ponty, electrified the French jazz-violin tradition that began with Stephane Grappelli, first in a classic collaboration with Frank Zappa entitled *King Kong* (Pacific Jazz) and then, in the seventies, *Upon the Wings of Music* (Atlantic). Ponty's successor as the young gun on violin, Didier Lockwood, maintained the French fusion tradition with some excellent fusion albums beginning in the 1980s and is best heard on *Didier Lockwood Group* (JMS).

Finally, although the fusion torch dimmed not long after it was lit, it continues to burn in the hearts of several contemporary groups. One of the best of these "neo-fusion" groups is the Yellowjackets, whose music grew from distinctionless trivia to solid improvising in the mold of Weather Report, as on *Live Wires* (GRP). In the early nineties, the saxophonist Bill Evans— no relation to the pianist (although both played with Miles Davis)—joined with several others who had come of musical age in the 1980s to record the solid and exciting *Petite Blonde* (Lipstick Records). Another saxist, Jane Ira Bloom, added what she called "live electronics" to her music, as heard to great advantage on *Art & Aviation* (Arabesque); her percussionist on that project, Jerry Granelli, later assembled a two-guitar band called UFB and recorded the excellent mid-nineties album *Broken Circle* (Intuition). All of them give fusion a life it seemed to have lost long ago.

From There 2 Here: A Short Look at the Long History of Foreign Influence

As it turned out, the two new strains of jazz that appeared in the early seventies did have something in common. Both the electric fusioneers and the new-cool-school players showed a strong interest in different musical traditions from around the world. You might have trouble naming two bands more different from each other than Weather Report and Oregon, yet both of them looked east—the one toward Africa, the other toward India—for key ingredients in their sonic recipes. In the case of Chick Corea, it was the lure of Spain and Brazil that proved strongest. Some of his Brazilian-flavored songs, originally written for his sun-dappled acoustic band, made sense even when played by the dark knights of his electric group.

All of this helped create an increased awareness of other musical cultures among jazz musicians, paving the way for the emphasis on "world music" in the late seventies and eighties. And while the resulting hybridization differed in substance from earlier such fusions—as discussed in the next chapter—that's not the point here. Rather, it's that previous such hybrids even *occurred*. They did, and rather often; but you could easily lose sight of that fact, blinded by the skyrocketing popularity of world music that has taken place in the last two decades.

What's more, the very term *world music* presupposes a certain sort of cultural as well as chronological myopia. As a label, it draws a division between "us" and the undifferentiated "everyone else." It suggests that the quite different traditions of, say, Arabic and Argentinian music belong in the same category—for no other reason than that they're both *not* American.

In the eighties, jets and Concordes delivered world music to our doorsteps more efficiently than ever. Earlier generations had to rely on packets from Paraguay and slow boats to China, but as the recordings listed below will testify, the messages still got through—in one case, with spectacular clarity. When Stan Getz made his bossa nova records of the sixties, he initiated a fad that swept the music world:

for the first time since the Swing Era, the newest jazz sound and the nation's favorite pop music were one and the same.

These recommendations travel not just around the globe but also through time, touching on many of the eras already discussed. When you consider jazz's much-heralded status as our only indigenous artistic achievement, you might wonder that jazz musicians would leave themselves so open, and for so long, to these "un-American" sounds and styles. But it was exactly that kind of influence—in the form of African rhythms and European harmonies—that created jazz in the first place; and ever since its birth, jazz has thrived as a sort of mongrel breed, absorbing, transforming, and usually ennobling what it borrows from other sources. Jazz has always kept a light in its window for the different, the "exotic"—the *foreign*. For proof, go back to such early jazz tunes as "St. Louis Blues" (with its introductory tango rhythm) and Jelly Roll Morton's "Tia Juana"—as well as Morton's famous statement that jazz music needed to have a little "Spanish tinge" to succeed.

The "fusions" in chapter 7 involve not rock and synths but mazurkas and *berimbaus*; but unlike electronics, these foreign elements did not appear in jazz overnight. So think of these albums less as a historical transition between two jazz styles and more as a means of filling in the historical gaps. In a very real sense, you can also think of them as being ahead of their time.

The Original Mambo Kings: An Introduction to Afro-Cubop (Verve). The musicians of earlier eras used the rhythms of the Caribbean mainly as seasonings; in bebop, these rhythms took their place as a vital part of the menu, thanks mainly to the efforts of Dizzy Gillespie. This anthology gathers recordings made between 1948 and 1954 and includes several noteworthy illustrations of the Afro-Cuban impact on bebop. Featuring Gillespie, Charlie Parker, and other mainstream soloists in collaboration with Latin-jazz big bands, these pieces opened the door for the south-of-the-border beats found in so much of the hard-bop jazz that followed. Even though you'll find this album in the bins under "various artists," it largely belongs to two Cuban-born musicians. The first, Francisco Grillo—known professionally by his nickname, Machito—leads his Afro-Cuban Orchestra on most of the tracks heard in this collection and was the first to successfully merge jazz and Latin music. The second Cuban giant, Chico O'Farrill, composed and/or arranged such large-scale works as "The Afro-Cuban Jazz Suite" (with guest soloists Parker and tenor man Flip Phillips) and "The Manteca Suite" (for Gillespie); these two pieces make up nearly half this CD. Parker, Erroll Garner, and others made entire albums using Latin rhythms, and Gillespie in particular wrote and recorded many examples of "Afro-Cubop" (some of which appear on the album *Dizzy's Diamonds*, discussed in chapter 3). But *Mambo Kings* gives you the best synopsis of this important intersection of jazz and Hispaniola.

Yusef Lateef, *Eastern Sounds* (Fantasy/OJC). Yusef Lateef revealed his debt to Eastern culture in both his music and his name (which he chose when he converted to Islam). Coming of age on the bustling jazz scene of 1940s Detroit, Lateef played a heady brand of bop tenor, but his fascination with non-Western musical traditions led him to other instruments and modes of expression. Among the first jazzmen to play flute, he found its tone perfect for simple melodies of Middle Eastern origin. When he introduced the oboe to jazz, he presaged by several years the nasal, Indian timbre that became popular after John Coltrane adopted the slightly less alien soprano saxophone. (Lateef has also recorded with the unwieldy bassoon and several wind instruments from Asia and Africa.) Nothing demonstrates Lateef's approach better than this album's "The Plum Blossom," which spins an exotic fantasy starring two ancient instruments from the East: the Chinese globular flute and the *rabab*, a two-string Arabian precursor to the bass fiddle. His interest in Middle Eastern music also led him to employ a raft of colorful percussion instruments, again years before these became a standard weapon in the jazz drummer's arsenal. *Eastern Sounds* intersperses such Lateef titles as "Blues for the Orient" and "Ching Miau" with jazz standards and the evocative themes from *The Robe* and *Spartacus*, two films set in the Mediterranean and Middle East. In creating this attractive mix of jazz roots and the seeds of other cultures, Lateef followed his own muse, but anticipated the call of world music by two decades.

Mongo Santamaria, *Mongo's Greatest Hits* (Fantasy). Relatively few congueros have such an individualistic sound that you could pick them out of a crowd, but Ramon "Mongo" Santamaria does. He emphasizes the darker timbres of his congas, and he hangs back a bit from the beat to create a remarkably swinging brand of Afro-Cuban drumming. But if he played with only half the skill he commands, the Havana-born Santamaria would still have left an indelible influence on jazz. After playing in the Afro-Cuban jazz band led by vibraphonist Cal Tjader, Santamaria started his own group. Almost immediately, his early-sixties recording of Herbie Hancock's "Watermelon Man" (see chapter 4) became a national hit, calling attention not only to the performer but also to its young composer. And Santamaria himself wrote the simple, mysterious "Afro-Blue," which became a signature tune for John Coltrane in 1963, and subsequently a jazz standard. What's more, Santamaria's bands have provided early experience for several jazz musicians who later established their own careers, such as Chick Corea and flutist Hubert Laws. This collection delivers just what it promises: Mongo's best-known recordings of the early 1960s, including the two mentioned above; his tune "Sabroso"; and his version of the Dizzy Gillespie evergreen "Manteca."

(For an equally good collection—but from more of a cool-jazz perspective—there's *Cal Tjader's Greatest Hits*, also on Fantasy, which features several different lineups led by drummer and vibraphonist Tjader. After Dizzy Gillespie, Tjader was perhaps the leading early advocate of Afro-Cuban jazz. His sidemen on these tracks include not only Santamaria but also percussionist Willie Bobo and the popular pianist Vince Guaraldi, best known for composing the music used in the various *Peanuts* television specials.)

Stan Getz, *Getz/Gilberto* (Verve). The indelible "Desafinado" and "The Girl from Ipanema" placed this among the most famous jazz albums ever—although by the time he recorded it, Stan Getz had *already* attained the stature of a pop star, thanks to three previous albums of bossa nova. The saxophonist did not initiate the seamless blend of his legendary lyricism with this "new beat" from Brazil; guitarist Charlie Byrd, who first heard the bossa nova on a tour of South America, brought it to his attention. But Getz was clearly its greatest beneficiary, making five widely respected bossa nova albums in a row. The bossa nova gained from this association too: it likely would never have conquered the United States (and from there, the globe) without the poetry of tone and the perfectly weighted solos that Getz provided. Invented in the fifties by the Brazilian composers Luiz Bonfa and Antonio Carlos Jobim (one of the twentieth century's undisputed musical geniuses), the bossa nova was itself a serendipitous hybrid: a light, delicate blend of Brazilian rhythms derived from the sultry samba, crossed with the cool-jazz sensibilities embodied by Miles Davis, Gerry Mulligan, and Getz himself. The "Gilberto" in the album title referred to singer/guitarist Joao Gilberto, the first great interpreter of bossa nova, but after the runaway success of "The Girl from Ipanema" it also meant his wife, Astrud. She made her recording debut singing an English translation of the lyrics in a fragile, waifish voice and became one of the decade's unlikeliest stars. This album represents the first meeting between Getz and the Brazilians who had inspired him—including Getz's soul mate Jobim, who plays piano on the album.

(Given the impact that Getz's bossa nova records had on jazz—as well as the entire pop-music world—it's worth noting a couple of other albums from this period. The Stan Getz/Charlie Byrd record *Jazz Samba* [Verve], which set the bossa nova loose in the States, remains a favorite for many; *Getz/Bonfa* [Verve] actually has much more to offer. Cannonball Adderley recorded a bossa nova date that marked the first meeting of U.S. and Brazilian jazzmen; *Cannonball's Bossa Nova* [Landmark] finds him playing with Brazil's Bossa Rio Sextet, which featured a young pianist named Sergio Mendes, better known in later years for his band Brasil 66. And Miles Davis hooked up with Gil Evans to create nocturnal magic on the album *Quiet Nights* [Columbia/Legacy].)

Duke Ellington, *The Far East Suite Special Mix* (Bluebird). In his later years, the Maestro Ellington increasingly turned his attention to composing extended suites. In all, he wrote more than two dozen of them (most in collaboration with his musical twin, Billy Strayhorn). Arguably the best of his later big works, with an overarching form and some of his most exotically evocative writing, *The Far East Suite* also revealed Ellington's keen eye (and ear) for cultural reportage. The piece began to take root during a tour of the Middle East undertaken by the Ellington band in 1963 and sponsored by the U.S. State Department, but Ellington didn't write the music during that journey. He let his impressions "roll around, undergo a chemical change, and then seep out on paper" and finally recorded it some three years later. The music surveys impressions garnered in Delhi and in Lebanon; at a Japanese jam session and a post-concert feast in Jordan; at the Taj Mahal ("Agra") and the former capital of ancient Persia ("Isfahan"). Throughout the piece, Ellington's portraiture seems to capture the smells and shadows as well as the sounds. Previously, those jazz musicians who borrowed from the Middle and Far East had mostly done so for mere effect. Ellington used these foreign elements to spur and enhance his imagination and came up with a work that proved faithful to both his source material and his own oeuvre. As such, it represents exactly the kind of synergy that later world-music experimenters would aim for. (By the way, the "special mix" designation is not part of the suite's title: it refers to a 1995 remastering meant to improve the original album's sound balance.)

Charlie Haden, *Liberation Music Orchestra* (Impulse/GRP). As a member of Ornette Coleman's original quartet, bassist Charlie Haden was certainly no stranger to the concept of liberation; but in the band he assembled for this 1970 recording, the word carried a meaning more political than musical. An ardent proponent of left-wing causes, Haden began cobbling together a repertoire that would eventually include the freedom songs of oppressed peoples from around the world. This first album, however, featured just one labor-movement song from Germany and three antiwar songs from Spain. Others, written by Haden and Carla Bley (who arranged all the music), carried more modern political messages celebrating the U.S. civil rights movement and the protesters who were beaten and arrested at the 1968 Democratic convention in Chicago. This doesn't really qualify as a typical "world music" album. But in reaching out for a universal message of freedom, Haden did introduce elements from other cultures; and the presence of the Argentine saxist Gato Barbieri, as well as the globe-trotting trumpeter Don Cherry (Haden's colleague from Ornette's quartet), added more foreign seasoning to the mix. Note, however, that this album might just as easily qualify as "avant-garde."

chapter seven

Letter from Home*
1973–1998

Perhaps it was that evening in the mid-seventies at the Village Vanguard, when the members of the Thad Jones–Mel Lewis Orchestra put down their horns and picked up toys, that crystallized the historical moment.

Jones and Lewis led a no-nonsense big band; themselves alumni of the Count Basie and Stan Kenton bands, they had filled their award-winning orchestra with some of the finest and most committed jazz musicians in New York City. Yet here they were, veterans of the bebop wars and icons of mainstream jazz, putting down their trusty (and expensive) Selmer saxes and Stradivarius trumpets and switching to shakers and sticks, triangles and cowbells, tambourines and *au-go-go*—the little instruments that musicians call percussion "toys." Suddenly, for a brief interlude in a modified samba written by Thad Jones, the entire band had turned into a faux-Brazilian rhythm section.

No one could have asked for a clearer indication that the world of music had again expanded as the world at large was shrinking—or that jazz had embraced the panoply of exotic musical styles that characterize the last quarter century of life in the United States.

In the 1970s, an influx of foreign influences—in the form of artists and recordings that would only later be described as

*Guitarist Pat Metheny gave this name to the title song of the 1989 album with which he first attained a truly *American* fusion of jazz and world music. Balancing a variety of musical elements from both Americas—North and South—his work on this and subsequent albums offered an exhilarating testament to the influence of foreign cultures upon jazz in the eighties.

"world music"—provided jazz musicians with another palette from which to work. As the preceding transition section suggests, the shapes, colors, and especially the rhythms of the world's older musical traditions had always found a welcome mat at jazz's door. What's more, progressive musicians of the sixties found extra inspiration in the example of John Coltrane, who experimented with world-music possibilities on the song "India" and the album *Africa/Brass*, and whose towering musical presence added credence to such experiments. But the earlier use of foreign beats and alien instruments had been only an occasional side trip; here in the seventies, the exploration of other cultures' music became a wide-ranging phenomenon. And in the eighties, this phenomenon reached unprecedented proportions, as jazz made the pursuit of internationalism a goal in itself.

In previous generations, musicians usually had a fairly narrow agenda for incorporating the sounds of other cultures. They might have warmed to a particular Latin American song form or gravitated to the rhythmic tradition of a certain African people. Impelled by religious or spiritual concerns, they might have experimented with instruments unique to India or the Middle East. But now the jazz community seemed intent on the *idea* of adding outside elements; the choice about which ancient culture to tap sometimes seemed like an afterthought.

This trend in jazz—which has ebbed and flowed up till the present day—presaged and then mirrored the larger societal movement known as multiculturalism. Remember, the United States in the eighties had a consuming interest in not only the ideas and artifacts of other countries and traditions; Americans became fixated on the very existence of these other ideas and artifacts, and then on the value of mixing and matching them to find their common denominators. School curricula emphasized cultural diversity; so did fashion and art and theater and cuisine.

So the energizing polyphonic rhythms of multiple percussion instruments began to creep into jazz recordings. Soon came the pungent pinched timbres of the Middle East, the hard bright sun of Brazilian compositions, the stately tonalities of traditional Japanese scales and modes, and the occasional rumbling snore of the Australian didgeridoo. Cuba supplied the greatest amount of foreign trade—shocking when you consider the current U.S. embargo on that nation, but hardly surprising given the impact that Cuban music had made on American jazz since the bebop years. But Brazilian musicians left their mark as well: the bossa nova might have faded in its homeland, but it had become a staple of jazz musicians, and they seemed especially eager to make use of the subsequent Brazilian styles. And Africa—the source of rhythm, whose peoples had instigated not only jazz but also the various idioms of Cuba *and* Brazil—remained a treasury of musical riches.

Some artists, such as Randy Weston and Dizzy Gillespie, simply continued to explore areas they had already pioneered, only now their efforts received heightened attention. Others (such as Pat Metheny) gravitated toward world music for the first time or—as with Chick Corea and Wayne Shorter—got the chance to delve more deeply into idioms they had previously only scratched. And in many cases, the artists exemplifying this jazz-world fusion fit into none of these categories, being South American or African or Asian or Eastern European themselves.

You can't really speak of an overall "world music" style, at least not in the sense that we discuss bebop or free jazz. In each of the descriptions accompanying this chapter's recommended CDs, you'll find more details about the specific culture (or cultures) at work in the music. And it's important to note that jazz's movement toward multiculturalism coexisted with other jazz idioms, which continued to evolve and even flourish and in many cases reflected international influence. For instance, the onrush of world music overlapped with the maturation of fusion jazz, most obviously in the persons of Chick Corea, Miles Davis, and John McLaughlin; their electric music of the seventies often bore the mark of (respectively) Brazilian, North African, and Indian music.

But you must remember this (as Dooley Wilson sang in the film *Casablanca*, one of the most memorable examples of foreign intrigue): the world itself can never really agree on a universal concept of world music. The term is a self-referential invention of the United States and Europe: it defines the "world" as everything outside one's own borders, and that causes some obvious problems. For example, the extraordinary singer-songwriter Milton Nascimento, a celebrated world-music star, carries no such distinction in Brazil, one of the world's most music-savvy nations—for the simple reason that Milton is himself Brazilian. The *Brazilians* don't think of Milton's music as "world music"; only the rest of the world does that. Similarly, only listeners from someplace other than Finland would find anything "worldly" or exotic about Karelian folk singing. It depends entirely on where you stand.

Whatever the terminology, however, the trade winds blew through jazz with gale force in the seventies and eighties, and the music shows the effects of that storm to this day.

The Discs

Airto, *Seeds on the Ground* (One Way). In concert, the inventive and energetic Brazilian percussionist Airto Moreira would often teach audiences to correctly pronounce his first name by pointing to body parts as he enunciated: "Eye. Ear. Toe. A-ir-to." His best music conveys the same mixture of simplicity and cleverness, plus a musical esthetic rooted in the organic sounds of shells, stones, and sticks—the basic matériel in his arsenal of percussion sounds. *Seeds on the Ground* opens with the distinct sound of the *berimbau*, the bow-shaped Brazilian instrument that serves as a crude zither, and quickly introduces a jazz-rock drumbeat and wordless, chanting vocals; a minute later, the entrance of a deep, throaty flute finishes setting the essential elements in place. Airto recorded *Seeds* in 1970–71, a couple years before this chapter "officially" begins; for that matter, having moved to the United States in 1968, he had already performed with Miles Davis and on the debut album by Weather Report (see chapter 6) before this album even appeared in stores. But it took until 1972, when they joined Chick Corea in the band Return to Forever, for Airto and vocalist Flora Purim (his wife) to attract widespread attention. Their newfound fame led listeners to seek out the previously overlooked *Seeds*, which also stars the uncategorizable Hermeto Pascoal (see below). This album first appeared as a normal-length LP; the addition of new material swells the CD to more than seventy minutes of aromatic Brazilian jazz.

Gato Barbieri, *Latino America* or *Chapter Three* (Impulse/ GRP). The tenor saxist Leandro "Gato" (Cat) Barbieri left Argentina to play free jazz in Europe in the 1960s. Returning home in the seventies, he took a different tack, steering his wide-toned lyricism into the rhythmic currents of his homeland. Acknowledging both the tango (an urban invention) and the percussive music of Argentina's indigenous rural peoples, Barbieri offered simple tunes played simply, with a minimum of ornamentation. This allowed him to focus attention on his opulent and impassioned tone—a sweet, yearning sound that made frequent use of the guttural rasp that most saxists use only for occasional emphasis. Barbieri's best recordings place his sweeping melodies against distinctively Argentine backgrounds. Rather than the heat of Brazilian samba or Cuban *son*, it is the loping bolero of the Pampas, or the seductive march of tango dancers in Buenos Aires nightclubs, that supplies the music's long-limbed smolder. (Barbieri's saxophone style achieves a similar effect by juxtaposing his laconic phrasing with the sultry warmth of his tone.) These sets, recorded in the early seventies, remain the most fully realized examples of Barbieri's musical chauvinism. The double CD *Latino America*, the more adventurous of the two, has wilder solos, a thicket of percussion, and bands that include aboriginal harps and flutes. The single disc *Chapter Three: Viva Emiliano Zapata* finds Barbieri's sax framed by the excellent big-band arrangements of Chico O'Farrill, who had written for such icons of Afro-Cuban jazz as Dizzy Gillespie and Machito. (If you want to sample selections from both projects, go for the Barbieri entry in Impulse's *Priceless Jazz* series.)

Pierre Dørge & the New Jungle Orchestra, *Brikama* (Steeple-Chase). On paper, the concept of the New Jungle Orchestra seems too goofy to actually work; in practice, the Danish guitarist Pierre Dørge concocted (and continues to lead) a witty and exciting blend of United States, African, and European musical traditions. Dørge—whose previous recordings had revealed the influence of Arabic and Balkan music, as well as the compositions of Thelonious Monk—first visited the Gambia region of western Africa in 1982. Captivated by what he heard, he returned to Copenhagen and assembled a thirteen-piece band of Danish musicians to realize the new music inspired by that trip. By the time of this 1984 album, recorded after Dørge's second trip to the Gambia, he had brought several African musicians into the fold, notably the South African bassist Johnny Dyani.

The music also gained authenticity from Dørge's use of his guitar to mimic the distinctive sound of the *kora*, the twenty-one-string African gourd harp. But the key to the New Jungle Orchestra's music lies in their name: it reflects not only Dørge's studies in Africa, but also his love for the early music of Duke Ellington (whose success in 1920s Harlem came with the band called the Jungle Orchestra). His respect for history allows Dørge to mix and match his sources with wild and woolly results, as on the whimsical "Monk in Africa," or his intercontinental arrangement of "St. Louis Blues," one of the first jazz tunes. They provide a grand introduction to this effervescent band.

Paquito D'Rivera became a symbol of the new jazz internationalism in 1980, when he defected from his native Cuba and settled in the United States (leaving his wife and son in Havana at the time). In Cuba, D'Rivera had starred with the pioneering modern-jazz band Irakere (see below); in New York, he quickly joined Dizzy Gillespie's combo and then became a charter member of the United Nation Orchestra that Gillespie assembled later in the decade. In the meantime, D'Rivera was establishing a solo career of his own, with recordings that infused jazz with distinctively Cuban elements, and also toyed with the electronic timbres and rapid-fire rhythms of fusion.

D'Rivera's earliest U.S. albums have gone out of print, so *A Taste of Paquito* (Columbia/Legacy) makes the best introduction to his style; it includes a dozen tracks, culled from five albums recorded between 1981 and 1985. D'Rivera's playing can be exuberant, and sometimes overbearing. On both alto and soprano saxophones, he sports a Day-Glo tone and the flamboyant technical prowess that seems endemic to Cuban music. His groups almost always feature a conga player (in addition to a jazz drummer well versed in Latin rhythms), and his compositions have a pressure-cooker recklessness. D'Rivera has a full command of the U.S. jazz tradition, but he filters almost everything he plays through the lens of his homeland; so even when he plays a bop blues or a pop standard—such as "Green Dolphin Street," the first tune on this collection—his heritage comes through in the crisp accents and jumpy contours of his solos. *A Taste* also includes a rousing update of Dizzy Gillespie's Cubano bop classic "Manteca," and two frenetic and catchy tunes that became D'Rivera signatures in the eighties: "Why Not" and "Just Kidding."

In the 1990s, D'Rivera (like several of his contemporaries) undertook a more conscientious investigation of his musical roots, including a return to the music he remembered playing with dance bands as a child prodigy in 1950s Havana. On *Portraits of Cuba* (Chesky), D'Rivera worked with the imaginative arranger Carlos Franzetti to recast classic Cuban compositions in the light of modern jazz, and to create new works capturing the flavor of D'Rivera's knowledge and experiences. A man of immense good humor, D'Rivera has no qualms about including, and reclaiming, such clichéd impressions of Cuban culture as "The Peanut Vendor"—a hit for the Stan Kenton band in the forties—and the theme song from TV's *I Love Lucy* (remember, Desi Arnaz led a Cuban dance band on that program). Every song on this 1996 album reflects the impact big-band jazz has left on Cuban music. It also displays D'Rivera's maturity as an improviser, as well as jazz's continually evolving appreciation of the "Spanish tinge"; and it presents one of the happier consequences of the West's fin-de-siècle fascination with revisiting twentieth-century art.

Jan Garbarek, *I Took Up the Runes* (ECM). In the 1970s, Jan Garbarek of Norway established himself among the most original-sounding tenor players in jazz. Even before that, the saxophonist's chill tone and forceful improvisations, utterly unbeholden to the bebop canon, had placed him at the center of the new cool school of jazz emerging in Scandinavia and Germany (see chapter 6). Although Garbarek's music has often referenced the measured melodies and stately rhythms of his native folk music, it was not until 1976 that he devoted an entire album to exploring this tradition—the introspective and starkly beautiful *Dis* (ECM), which utilized a Norwegian-made aeolian harp (a large stringed instrument driven by the wind to create random harmonies and textures). Garbarek's concern with Scandinavian roots reached maturation with his 1989 album *Rosensfole* (ECM)—featuring music based on medieval Norwegian songs—and 1990's *I Took Up the Runes*, on which he augmented traditional Lapp melodies with electronics and added the blunt, throbbing rhythms of African-French drummer Manu Katché. More than most such hybrids of jazz and non-American music, *Runes* has an almost universal simplicity that encourages comparisons to other traditions. One moment it echoes Native American melodies, then a harmonic scheme from central Europe or Japan, while this or that rhythmic pattern might recall the classical music of north India (another preoccupation of Garbarek's). But the music retains a distinctively Scandinavian quality of passion under wraps.

Stan Getz, *Best of Two Worlds* (Columbia/Legacy). When Stan Getz made the bossa nova the most popular sound in the United States in the 1960s (see previous transition section), he found himself spearheading the first assault by world music on jazz—this, before terms like *world music* even existed. So it only made sense for him to revisit those sinewy rhythms and bittersweet melodies in the seventies, when the music of other cultures had become an increasingly pervasive influence on jazz. Having eschewed Brazilian music since his hits of a decade earlier, Getz effortlessly reprised the formula that had insured his previous success. He again teamed up with the unflappable Joao Gilberto; he added a female vocalist to sing the lyrics in English (in this çase, the exquisite Heloisa Buarque de Hollander); and he assembled a repertoire that included indelible songs from the pen of Antonio Carlos Jobim, including the now-famous "Waters of March." (But while the music carried the same lilt as in the sixties, some of the tunes now had a slightly heavier beat—an indication of the rock influence that had by then begun to supplant the bossa nova in Brazilian music.) The material again propelled Getz to the pinnacle of his romantic lyricism, with solos so simply constructed, and so well suited to the songs, that he might have composed them in the leisure of his study instead of improvising them in a pressure-filled recording studio. But his darker tone and harder swing also reflected jazz's development in the years since his first encounter with Brazilian musicians.

Paul Horn, *The Attitude of the Sun* (Black Sun/Celestial Harmonies). The arc of Paul Horn's career might serve as a metaphor for this entire chapter: Jazz Discovers the World and Embraces It. A mainstream saxist and flutist in the 1950s, Horn studied in India in the late sixties and emerged as an avid world-music experimenter (as well as a teacher of meditation). His fascination with other cultures led him to incorporate music from India, Africa, and even the world of the oceans, using whale songs as inspiration. Meanwhile, his search for the perfect resonating chamber led him to record inside such structures as the Taj Mahal and the Great Pyramid of Cheops. Although he's not regarded as a strong jazz player, these unusual projects made Horn a well-known figure in contemporary music, and his espousal of world-music influences carried more weight because of his populist appeal. In any case, one can't find fault with the music on this disc, which comprises two LPs that came out in the seventies. The first, originally titled *Nexus*, covers Afro-Brazilian territory, emphasizing a wide array of percussion instruments to excellent effect; the second, originally titled *Altura do Sol*, proved absolutely revelatory. On it, Horn played a program of compositions by the brilliant young Brazilian Egberto Gismonti, and for most listeners, it offered a first glimpse of Gismonti's extraordinary talent (see below). This seventy-seven-minute CD speaks to Horn's prescient anticipation of new sounds and forthcoming trends: neither African music nor the "new wave" Brazilians of Gismonti's generation would become big news for several years.

Abdullah Ibrahim, *Water from an Ancient Well* (Tip Toe). When Hollywood films *The Abdullah Ibrahim Story*, they won't have to dress up the plot: the facts will do just fine. They can start with the pianist's birth (1934) and childhood in South Africa, where he was known by his given name of Dollar Brand; then move on to his self-exile in Europe and the United States, his mentoring by no less than Duke Ellington, his conversion to Islam, and his triumphant return to post-apartheid South Africa in the nineties. Ibrahim didn't waste his time away from home: working in a variety of formats, he compiled a quite large discography, weaving the songs of his homeland with the American jazz that first captivated him during his teenage years. The pianist couches his compositions in the rolling rhythms and unhurried chord structures of traditional South African music. Then he expands this format with the curiosity and experimentation native to jazz: he complicates the music in ways that deepen and extend it. Ibrahim has recorded several fine solo piano albums and duo projects, and he has led excellent quartets, both in concert and on disc. But his smoothly arranged sextet and septet dates best convey his musical "dual citizenship" as they combine South African high-life melodies,

Ellingtonesque saxophone shadings, traditional and modern rhythms, and extensive solos by noteworthy American players. This album features an excellent selection of typical Ibrahim moods, from a remake of his lovely ballad "The Wedding" to the jaunty and joyous "Mandela."

Irakere, *Misa Negra* (Messidor). In the 1970s, this Cuban band struck a profile similar to that of Horace Silver's bands of the 1950s. Irakere featured infectious rhythms and ear-grabbing soloists; and, like Silver's bands, they played a repertoire of well-crafted compositions from their pianist-leader. Irakere gained international acclaim as a Cuban *jazz* band, rather than a Cuban band that happened to play some jazz; and even after cofounders and star soloists Paquito D'Rivera (saxes) and Arturo Sandoval (trumpet) had emigrated to the United States, Irakere retained the dynamic spirit and hybrid wizardry that had wowed audiences from the start. Much of the credit goes to pianist Jesus "Chucho" Valdes, who cofounded the band in 1973 and shepherded its development while earning an international reputation of his own. Unlike most Cuban jazz bands—in fact, unlike many of the Cuban– and Puerto Rican– oriented jazz bands in the United States—Irakere always offered a fair amount of distinctively *non*-Latin music, such as their straight-ahead version of Dave Brubeck's "The Duke" on this 1986 album. (Of course, from the Cuban perspective, straight-ahead American jazz would have to be considered a "foreign influence.") But *Misa Negra* includes two tracks that showcase their mix of hard-bop horn lines and Latin-and-jazz rhythm, as well as the four-movement title work—an ambitious depiction of rites celebrated in the Yoruban religion, which African slaves brought with them to Cuba in the seventeenth century.

Jon Jang & the Pan-Asian Arkestra, *Self-Defense!* (Soul Note). Asian audiences, specifically those in Japan and India, have warmly welcomed American jazz since the 1950s. But Far Eastern culture did not really flow the other way until the mideighties, when a number of Asian-American musicians began using jazz to explore their ethnic identity. Grouped under the banner of Asian Improv Arts, they have continued to create a pungent and stirring body of work, exemplified in the music of

Chinese-American pianist Jon Jang and his Pan-Asian Arkestra. (The important Asian-American players are primarily of Chinese ancestry, including baritone saxist Fred Ho and tenor man Francis Wong, who appears on this album. Nonetheless, the Pan-Asian Arkestra encompasses musical traditions of not only China but also, quite prominently, Japan, Korea, and the Philippines.) *Self-Defense!* emphasizes Jang's own compositions, which inventively recombine the essences of jazz and Chinese music—as in the thirty-minute "Concerto for Jazz Ensemble and Taiko," named for the Japanese barrel drum used throughout. The best introduction to Jang's methodology comes in his arrangement of the traditional melody "Butterfly Lovers Song," which undergoes a subtle metamorphosis via the sonorities of the modern jazz orchestra. He turns this strategy around when he inserts echoes of Chinese martial music into his version of the bebop classic "A Night in Tunisia." Bebop reflected a growing sociopolitical consciousness among African-Americans in the 1940s, and a half century later, Asian-American jazzmen address similar concerns of their own. Jang's works boast titles such as "Reparations Now!" (recalling the World War II internment camps for Japanese-Americans) and "Tiananmen."

John McLaughlin, *Shakti, with John McLaughlin* (Columbia/Legacy). You can describe the 1970s music of John McLaughlin in terms of a Zen koan: after the breakup of his Mahavishnu Orchestra in 1975, the guitar guru found himself doing the same thing, and also something entirely different. He continued to perform with almost superhuman speed and stamina, but his path took him from the heights of electronics to the low-tech instrumentation of the group Shakti, where he explored one of the world's oldest musics. A few other Western performers had previously acknowledged the influence of India, prime examples being John Coltrane, Yusef Lateef, and the Beatles; McLaughlin himself had included Indian instruments on his 1970 album, *My Goal's Beyond*, and had used his studies in Buddhist meditation to energize the Mahavishnu Orchestra. But until Shakti, no one had tried to create a true fusion of jazz and Indian classical music—a discipline that, like jazz, emphasizes improvisation. Just as he had in the Mahavishnu Orchestra, McLaughlin again matched wits with a virtuosic violinist (in this case Lakshiminarayani Shankar); but his now unplugged guitar joined a trio of percussionists playing the ancient Indian drums tabla and mridangam, instead of electric bass and keyboards. The first of Shakti's three albums (and the only one now available), *Shakti* was recorded live and features two lengthy tracks—sort of like jazz ragas—as opposed to the shorter and more accessible pieces on their other recordings. But the often hypnotic improvisations draw the listener deep into this refreshing musical hybrid.

Pat Metheny Group, *Still Life (Talking)* (Geffen). In Pat Metheny's music of the mid-1980s, the "world" in *world music* got smaller than ever. His quartet—which still featured his longtime partner, pianist Lyle Mays—grew to include three vocalists, and they began to incorporate high-energy rhythms and lyric melodies from South America, primarily Argentina and Brazil. But Metheny and Mays reshuffled these elements to arrive at a unique hemispheric fusion that embraced the music of both continents in nearly equal amounts. (Usually, when we speak of "American music," we refer to music made in the United States; Metheny's albums pinpointed the chauvinism in such usage.) This immensely popular phase of Metheny's career started with *First Circle* in 1984 and would later explode in a riot of colorful beats and textures on 1989's *Letter from Home*; in between, the music hit its full stride with *Still Life (Talking)*, the most cohesive of these recordings. At once familiar and foreign, intensely visual and vibrantly rhythmic, this near-masterpiece strikes few false notes. Its most famous track—the folkish anthem "Last Train Home"—is actually the least compelling, once you consider the seamless internationalism that characterizes the rest of the album. In addition to Metheny's unique take on world music, his use of electronics bucked the neoclassic jazz trend of the eighties and nineties (see chapter 8). He thus reminded listeners not only that the seventies jazz-rock fusion had taken place, but also that it could evolve and grow in the right hands.

Eddie Palmieri, *The Sun of Latin Music* (MP Records). No musician has eclipsed Palmieri in moving beyond the stereotypical parameters of Latin jazz. Commentators have called him salsa music's answer to Duke Ellington, high praise indeed; and true to Ellington's famous encomium, Palmieri has consistently reached "beyond category" in his restless explorations. At the beginning of his career, he built a bridge between the music of Cuba and his Puerto Rican heritage, connecting salsa and Afro-Cuban music by way of his bebop-influenced piano. (Like his music in general, Palmieri's piano is romantic and iconoclastic: it broods and exults, slashes and burns, and can even grab center stage from the surging big bands he has led throughout the years.) He has undertaken other challenges as well, such as his 1990s octet, which wedded salsa to the hard-bop stylings of Art Blakey's Jazz Messengers. But his most exciting and illustrative work appeared on several big-band albums of the seventies. These contained a few unorthodox concerti, in which Palmieri's piano engaged the salsa-jazz orchestra in an evenly matched dialogue. The wildest of these pieces, "Un Día Bonito," appears on *The Sun of Latin Music*. This album also has the best selection of shorter works, in which easily identified elements of Afro-Caribbean music—such as the heartfelt crooning of a male vocalist and the asymmetric pulse of the claves—are successfully transplanted to the hothouse of progressive big-band jazz.

(Note: While both this album and its successor, *Unfinished Masterpiece*, are available on CD, they appear on the small and poorly distributed MP label. You can probably find these discs through mail-order services; if not, try the Columbia CD *Lucumi Macumba Voodoo*, a notch or two below the others.)

Hermeto Pascoal, *So Nao Toca Quem Nao Quer* (Intuition). In most cases, the musicians in this chapter achieved a fusion of jazz and world music by first playing jazz and then incorporating the traditions of other cultures. Hermeto Pascoal of Brazil has done just the opposite: a prolific composer and virtuosic multi-instrumentalist, he has applied lessons *from* jazz to the indigenous music of his own culture. Known by his first name only (like many Brazilian musicians), Hermeto celebrates a culture far removed from the bossa nova beaches of Rio or the street-corner sambas of Salvador. Hailing from the poor, parched region of northeastern Brazil, he builds his music around such traditional styles as the emotion-packed *choro*—a precursor of the samba—and lively folk-dance rhythms such as the *frevo* and *baiao*. (Baiaos are traditionally played on accordion, one of the several instruments that Hermeto commands like a wizard.) In investigating these older styles, Hermeto uses the jazz techniques of improvisation and modification to dissect the melodies, alter the harmonies, and magnify the rhythms. The uncompromising modalities of his music echo the ancient tunes of Brazil's native peoples, but Hermeto pushes them as far as they can go. In his arrangements, even a chorus of flutes can spin off on logical but extreme tangents of dissonance and danger. Such devices give this remarkable album the manic power of a Frank Zappa set, but also an otherworldliness all its own. (By the way, the Portuguese title roughly translates as "Only if you don't want it, you can't do it"—a good motto for Hermeto's limitless imagination, and for jazz in general.)

Tito Puente and his Latin Ensemble, *El Rey* (Concord Picante). The title means "the king," and for decades the Puerto Rican–American drummer and vibraphonist Tito Puente has worn the crown, primarily by virtue of his popular Latin dance bands. But from the 1980s on, he has established a toehold in jazz, leading one of the best of several Latin-and-jazz combos that came together during these years. (See below.) Puente's bands effortlessly mix Latin percussion, rhythms from throughout the Greater Antilles—specifically Cuba and Puerto Rico—and jazz improvisation, writing an irresistible recipe for both mind and body. And Puente himself has attained the stature of a jazz giant, thanks in part to his longevity (born in 1920, he has recorded more than one hundred albums), and mostly to his collaborations with such elder statesmen of jazz as Woody Herman and Dizzy Gillespie. The 1984 concert recording *El Rey* opens up with "Oye Como Va," a staple of salsa and Afro-Cuban bands since the fifties, best known via the rock group Santana's hit record in the early seventies, and a tune written by Puente. But the program includes a couple of pop standards widely used in jazz ("Autumn Leaves" and "Stella by Starlight") as well as two John Coltrane compositions ("Giant Steps" and "Equinox")—making the album illustrative of the rangy repertoire Puente covers with this band. Refashioned with mambo, cha-cha, and merengue beats, these songs become as fresh as an elegant old house after a new coat of paint. It certainly doesn't hurt to have improvisers as accomplished as the ones on this album, such as saxist Mario Rivera, trumpeter Ray Gonzalez, and the late Argentine keyboardist Jorge Dalto—some of whom had worked in Puente's bands for many years.

Claudio Roditi, *Slow Fire* (Milestone). A permanent member of Paquito D'Rivera's bands during the 1980s, trumpeter Claudio Roditi brings a rare combination of brain and virtuosic brawn to the trumpet, all of it bound up in a tone inspired by Dizzy Gillespie, another of his former employers. In fact, Roditi deserves respect not as a "great *Brazilian* trumpeter" but for being such a spectacular hornman and improviser, period (and nationality be damned). Roditi represents a special case among international jazz musicians. Although he was raised in Rio, his music has relatively few followers in Brazil, largely because sambas and *forros* take a backseat to his impeccable jazz solos. But although he has lived in the United States since the seventies, and has established his jazz credentials in a variety of contexts, Roditi's repertoire still shows the strong influence of Brazil's sunny rhythms and melodies. Thus we in the United States still consider him a "Brazilian musician"; on the other hand, Brazilian listeners tend to regard him as a quite "American"-sounding expatriate jazzman. Perhaps this paradox best explains Roditi's ability to combine the music of the two continents into something that reflects both of them, yet fully belongs to neither. *Slow Fire*, recorded in 1989, dives headfirst into Roditi's native heritage—with fast bossa beats and slow themes that unwind the subtle twists unique to Brazilian songwriting—but it still sprouts solos as American as apple pie.

Wayne Shorter, *Native Dancer* (Columbia/Legacy). Floral, mysterious, seductive: few albums of the 1970s have had such enduring impact as this enchanted meeting of musical traditions. A decade earlier, Stan Getz had introduced the United States to a new sound by recording with Brazilian musicians, and Wayne Shorter accomplished exactly the same thing on this album. But in Getz's case, the "new sound" was bossa nova; on *Native Dancer*, Shorter showcased the "next wave" in South American music as represented by the shining Afro-Brazilian songwriter Milton Nascimento. Nascimento's inspiration comes from a unique set of sources, including the roots music of Minas Gerais (his native state in Brazil); the elevated poetry of folk-rock musicians in the United States; and the hard-rock energy that helped distinguish *tropicalismo*, which succeeded bossa nova as the prevailing idiom in Brazilian music. Nascimento's compositions engaged Shorter in a different way from those of Shorter's own band, Weather Report. At times, the saxist's powerful solos even tapped the complex emotion the Brazilians call *saudade* (a sort of happy melancholy). Nascimento sings in a voice at once ardent and angelic, and as it entwined Shorter's soprano saxophone, they created lush and exotic sounds that might have originated in the myth-laden Amazonian jungle Moto Gross Feio (which had provided the inspiration and the title for an earlier Shorter album). *Native Dancer* also starred pianist Herbie Hancock and a slew of Brazilian jazzmen, including percussionist Airto Moreira and the keyboardist Wagner Tiso.

With his towering height (around six feet six inches) and noble bearing, Randy Weston might easily pass for a transplanted Watusi prince—even if he *didn't* favor African garb, or had never written the African-inspired compositions that gained him fame in the fifties and sixties, or hadn't been among the first jazz musicians to visit Africa (eventually settling in Morocco in the late sixties). His experiences there allowed him to consummate the fusion of jazz and African music that he had undertaken in the United States. By combining the rhythmic and melodic impulses of African music with the harmonic language of hard-bop, Weston constructed a style both dark and lithe, which he has used to enliven formats from the piano trio to expansive big bands.

Weston recorded the big-band date *Tanjah* (Verve) in 1973, shortly after returning to the States from his first sojourn in Africa. On the album he reprised two of his best-known compositions from the fifties: the moody minor-key waltz "Little Niles" and the sprightly "Hi-Fly," both influenced by African music. He also reestablished his association with Melba Liston, who had made her reputation by arranging Weston's compositions for his smaller bands of the fifties and sixties. The presence of several percussionists—not to mention an oud player (see the section on Rabih Abou-Khalil, below)—swelled the band on this recording to nineteen instrumentalists. They included such famous players as trumpeters Jon Faddis and Ernie Royal, saxists Budd Johnson and Billy Harper, and bassist Ron Carter. A potentially sour note is the occasional use of the electric piano, a jazz staple of the 1970s; but Weston makes it sound as natural to his music as the rollicking beat and energetic melodies. The potboiler title track presents a barely controlled bacchanalia of color and rhythm, guaranteed to transport you to a Moroccan Saturday night in full fever.

While many of his seminal recordings from the fifties have disappeared from the catalog, Weston recaptured their sensibility on the 1992 double CD *Spirits of Our Ancestors* (Verve)—perhaps the best overall presentation of his art and craft. His rugged, percussive phrases lead the way as the pianist offers a multipart panorama of African impressions, all filtered through a jazz perspective—from village dances to the mournful muezzin's call of Islam (reminding the listener that part of the Middle East in fact sits on the African continent). On the first track, a fast solo blues, Weston not only displays his two main piano influences—Ellington and Monk—but also shows you the thread that connects them. When the entire ten-piece band joins in, such previously recorded compositions as "African Cookbook" and "Blue Moses" gain new power from the contributions of three tenor-saxophone savants in Billy Harper, Dewey Redman, and Pharoah Sanders. Dizzy Gillespie, no stranger to world music (see previous Gillespie entries), appears on "African Sunrise," a Weston piece that starred Gillespie when it was commissioned by and performed at the Chicago Jazz Festival in 1984. Once again, Melba Liston's arrangements bring impressive depth to the compositions, juggling African polyrhythms among the brass and reed instruments and juxtaposing her potent big-band textures with the five-piece rhythm section. (For those on a budget, a single-CD abridgment of this album—entitled *African Sunrise*—now exists as well.)

More Flights

A relative latecomer to the internationalist jazz scene, the Lebanese musician Rabih Abou-Khalil emerged in the nineties as a master of the oud. This small lute has a sweet, throaty sound and is as common in Middle Eastern music as the modern guitar (a descendant of the oud) is in the West. Abou-Khalil collaborates with noted Western jazzmen—saxist Sonny Fortune, bassist Glen Moore, and harmonica virtuoso Howard Levy—but keeps the rhythms and harmonies almost entirely within the guidelines of Arabic music. *Blue Camel* (Mesa) from 1992 and *The Sultan's Picnic* (Enja) from 1994 are the most fully realized of his albums, although the soulful *Al-Jadida* (Enja) has much to recommend it.

As the seventies progressed, Airto Moreira aligned himself with the electric fusion music he had played earlier in the decade. *The Best of Airto* (Columbia/Legacy) gives a good look at this double-layered hybrid (jazz-rock fusion *plus* world music), although the music doesn't wear as well as his earlier work. Airto's wife, Flora Purim, soon became the bigger star, with a number of well-known jazz artists (George Duke, Joe Henderson, McCoy Tyner) gracing her albums; *Butterfly Dreams* and *Stories to Tell*, both on Milestone, are the best known (and deservedly so).

Toward the end of his life, the great Cuban trumpeter Mario Bauza—the same Mario Bauza who had introduced Dizzy Gillespie to Afro-Cuban rhythms in the 1940s—recorded three big-band albums that reintroduced his mastery to a new generation of listeners. *Tanga* (Messidor), by Bauza and his Afro-Cuban Jazz Orchestra, provides the best introduction to his creative command of the idiom he helped create. You also won't go wrong with *944 Columbus* (Messidor), the last album he made (at age eighty-two).

Another legendary figure in Cuban jazz is the bassist Cachao (also known by his given name, Israel Lopez). Credited with inventing the mambo (!) back in the 1930s, Cachao also created the *descarga*, or Latin jazz jam session, in which the instrumentalists solo over simple, repetitive chord progressions and the most basic of Cuban rhythms. He became a presence in the jazz mainstream in the nineties, primarily via the album *Master Sessions, Vol. 1* (produced by film actor Andy Gonzalez, who also plays congas on this all-star recording).

After leaving Ornette Coleman, trumpeter Don Cherry became a sort of geo-musicologist, sampling and collecting sounds and traditions from all over the world. Good examples include *Dona Nostra*, recorded with Scandinavian musicians; and the album (and group) *Codona*, the name being an acronym formed from the first letters in the names of its members: sitarist and percussionist Collin Walcott, Don Cherry, and percussionist Nana Vasconcelos (both on ECM).

One of Cherry's loveliest and liveliest world-music projects, *Multikulti*, is out of print on CD but available as a video.

Chick Corea helped initiate jazz's embrace of world music with the Brazilian- and Iberian-influenced music of his first Return to Forever band (see chapter 6). Corea made his own return to this arena with *My Spanish Heart* (Polydor), which uses the sultry melodies of Andalusia and the rhythms of flamenco music for inspiration.

If you like Pierre Dørge's *Brikama*, you should also enjoy the New Jungle Orchestra's late-eighties tribute to bassist Johnny Dyani, *Johnny Lives* (SteepleChase). But this band just keeps getting better, and it's worth searching for both of their late-nineties masterworks, *Absurd Bird* on the Danish label Olufsen, and *Music from the Danish Jungle* (Da Capo).

The album *Manhattan Burn* (Columbia) gets you a little deeper into Paquito D'Rivera's music of the eighties, and the 1991 CD *Reunion* (Messidor) brings D'Rivera together with trumpeter Arturo Sandoval, his former comrade in the Cuban band Irakere; the album was recorded a month after Sandoval defected to the United States, in 1990. Also note *Havana Café* (Chesky), which features an excellent and musically multilingual sextet. A bit later, D'Rivera joined with two mallet players—vibist/marimbist Dave Samuels and the jazz steel-drum player Andy Narell—to form the Caribbean Jazz Project, best heard on *Island Stories* (Heads Up). D'Rivera also reassembled the last big band led by Dizzy Gillespie, the heavily Latin-oriented United Nation Orchestra; their 1997 Valentine's Day concert makes up *Live at MCG* (Blue Jackel Entertainment).

Sandoval, by the way, learned jazz by listening to Gillespie and Clifford Brown, and his style revels in high-note sensationalism and rambunctious but immaculate improvising. On the GRP album *Danzon* (*Dance On*), recorded in 1993, he surveys several rhythms in a measured and educational tribute to Cuban music.

In 1976, the same year his compositions inspired Paul Horn to record them, Egberto Gismonti began his ongoing association with the ECM label, where he performed with stunning virtuosity on both piano and the unusual eight-string guitar. Best bets: the unaccompanied *Solo*, the duo date *Dança das Cabecas*, and the double album of solo and quartet performances called *Sanfona* (all on ECM).

The sheer number of recordings by Abdullah Ibrahim insures a few losers, but also some extraordinary successes. *Africa: Tears and Laughter* (Enja) tops this list. *African Sun* (Kaz), an import worth looking for, is close behind: recorded during Ibrahim's brief return to South Africa in the 1970s, it features several other giants of African jazz. If you enjoy *Ancient Well* (see above), try the tradition-oriented *African Marketplace* (Discovery) and *African River* (Enja), the latter showing more of a pure jazz edge. A fine and famous example of Ibrahim's solo piano work is *Anthem for the New Nations* (Denon).

Eastward Ho: Born in China and raised in Japan, pianist Toshiko Akiyoshi came to the United States in the 1950s to study jazz and went on to cofound one of the finest big bands of the 1970s. From the beginning, her writing for the band included pieces that interwove her Asian heritage with postbop jazz, in terms of both musical themes and the colorful orchestrations that conveyed them. *The Toshiko Akiyoshi/Lew Tabackin Big Band* (Novus) includes several of these works as part of an excellent cross-section of their mid-seventies recordings.

Jon Jang's album *Tiananmen* (Soul Note) further explores the multicultural premise of his Pan-Asian Arkestra, while his sextet recording *Two Flowers on a Stem* (Soul Note) concentrates on Chinese roots alone (but also stars two wide-ranging jazz soloists in James Newton and David Murray).

Chinese music in particular, along with an edgier political agenda, have motivated saxophonist/composer Fred Ho (aka Fred Houn), who has proved himself the equal of his frequent bandmate Jon Jang in terms of culture-spanning creativity. *Fred Houn and the Afro-Asian Music Ensemble*, recorded in 1988, exemplifies this side of his work, and *The Underground Railroad to My Heart* (1994) is musically perhaps the strongest effort from this group. They're both on Soul Note. He also engages his avid interest in Chinese folklore on albums featuring "the Monkey Orchestra"; start with *Monkey Part One* (Koch Jazz).

Two other noteworthy Asian-American jazz experimenters:

saxist Francis Wong, who, more than any of his Asian Improv colleagues, shows the influence of such avant-garde musicians as John Coltrane and the AACM saxists; and pianist Glenn Horiuchi, who uses Asian-sounding themes in the conventional jazz quartet format. You can hear them both on Horiuchi's album *Oxnard Beat* (Soul Note), while Wong's *The Great Wall* (Asian Improv) is probably the easiest way into his work.

In the nineties, some musicians also began to tap the legacy of Vietnam. Saxist Michael Blake's *Kingdom of Champa* (Intuition), inspired by a visit to that nation, blends East with West and ancient with modern. And on the elegant and moving *Tales from VietNam* (ACT), the Vietnamese-French guitarist Nguyên Lê leads an octet that includes horns, synths, and traditional Asian zithers.

Astor Piazzolla, the much-admired Argentine composer and virtuoso of the *bandoneon*, became famous for his reinvention of the traditional tango as a vehicle for serious composition. (The *bandoneon* is a button accordion that differs from its better-known cousin—the one you see in polka bands—largely in that it has no piano-style keyboard.) Although Piazolla's music doesn't qualify as jazz, its strong rhythms and striking harmonies have entranced many jazz players and even led to some spectacular collaborations: the 1975 *Tango Nuevo* with baritone saxist Gerry Mulligan, and *The New Tango*, his 1986 Montreux Jazz Festival concert with vibraphonist Gary Burton (both on Atlantic).

Tito Tito: Some other Tito Puente albums worth grabbing include *Goza Mi Timbal*, *Sensacion*, and *Out of This World*, which features one of Puente's hottest small groups; and *Un Poco Loco*, which also features a sixteen-piece big band. They're all on Concord Picante.

Puente's Latin Ensemble was one of several Latin jazz groups to establish themselves in the eighties. One is led by his contemporary, the marvelous conguero Mongo Santamaria (see previous transition section). Although less active in recent years, Santamaria still scores on *Mambo Mongo* (Chesky) and *Mongo Returns* (Milestone).

Another conguero, the much younger Mexican-American Poncho Sanchez, apprenticed with Cal Tjader's groups in the late seventies. After Tjader's death, he carried on their spirit with his own fine group, which boasts a higher percentage of solid jazz blowing than any of the others. You might start with *Papa Gato* or *Fuerte* from the eighties, or go right to Sanchez's 1995 tribute to his mentor, *Soul Sauce: Memories of Cal Tjader*. And *Para Todos* offers an extra treat in the presence of the soul-meister Eddie Harris on tenor. They're all on Concord Picante.

One more Latin-jazz group of note belongs to Hilton Ruiz, a pianist of Puerto Rican heritage whose first notice came as a pure-jazz improviser in Rahsaan Roland Kirk's band of the mid-seventies. His own albums have gone back and forth between mainstream and "the Spanish tinge"; of the latter, the best available are *Manhattan Mambo* (Telarc), *Live at Birdland* (Candid), and *Hands on Percussion* (Tropijazz).

For more of Randy Weston's soulful intercontinental blend, go for *Monterey '66* (Verve), a grand festival recording by a septet that featured percussionist Big Black and as special guest, the Charles Mingus sideman Booker Ervin on tenor. The early-seventies *Carnival* (Freedom) features saxist Billy Harper and stretches out to capture the lazy expanse of the Serengeti, while Weston's classic solo piano date *Blues to Africa* (Freedom) serves as a bridge between Morocco and Manhattan. The more recent solo album *Marrakech in the Cool of the Evening* (Verve) does some of this as well.

Note: The album called *The Splendid Master Gnawa Musicians of Morocco* (Verve), under Weston's name, sounds promising enough. He produced it, but the album in fact features almost nothing of Weston's playing and no jazz. It's a fine world-music document, but don't expect anything else.

The Japanese pianist Yosuke Yamashita towers above most other Japanese jazzers, for both his history-spanning command of the piano and the strength of his artistic vision. Start with *Dazzling Days* (Verve). While the album never attempts the riveting cross-cultural fusion of Yamashita's *Sakura*—now out of print but definitely worth seeking in used-CD stores—a couple of the tunes still display his ability to transform uniquely Japanese materials into a source for jazz improvisation.

chapter eight

Hesitation*
1982–1998

The thrust of jazz in the 1960s and 1970s had taken the music far afield, to exotic locales both real and imagined. The message of liberation proffered by Ornette Coleman had opened the flood-gates; new sounds flowed in from the southern continents (world music), from distant planets (fusion), and from inner space (in the measured abstractions of the avant-garde). The eighties would take modern jazz in an old direction that seemed suddenly quite new—back to its roots in bebop and the music that bop spawned in the golden age of the fifties.

To a large degree, this movement arose in reaction to specific events within jazz. The move toward rock in the sixties and sev-enties had sent legions of faithful jazz listeners underground: it left them at first angry, and then simply resigned to their fate, waiting out the infidels until the real music might return. For many of these hard-core faithful, the incorporation of world music only compounded the problem. After all, to those who longed for the pure sweet strains of hard-bop and cool jazz, the answer hardly lay in the sitars of India, the aboriginal rhythms of Brazil, or the highlife vocals of South Africa.

Meanwhile, as much of the jazz public hungered for a more traditional approach, a new generation of well-taught musi-cians appeared to reprise it. In the sixties, many colleges and even high schools had created jazz-education courses and stu-

*"Hesitation" is the name of a particularly effective track—described below—from the first album by the then twenty-year-old trumpeter Wynton Marsalis. Presum-ably, he chose the title to describe the start-and-stop nature of the melody line. But it also summarizes the 1980s, when jazz stopped moving forward to look back, and around, and decide where to go next.

dent jazz bands, and these programs had now matured; so had their alumni. The music world suddenly brimmed with thousands of highly trained young musicians, with a broad knowledge of jazz history, who could intelligently survey jazz styles from the past in deciding what they would play in the future.

But this return to roots—or *neoclassicism*—also reflected larger concerns within the entire society. Modern history shows us that as the denizens of one century begin to approach the next, they begin yearning for and reexamining the past. Perhaps this serves as a hedge against an unknown future, made distressingly distinct by an impending century. One hundred years ago, the French came up with an adjective for this mind-set; they called it *fin de siècle*, which simply translates as "end of the century." But the phrase has come to connote a great deal more in terms of behavior, fashion, and art. By the early 1990s, for example, fin-de-siècle America exhibited movies based on old TV shows, clothing based on styles of the twenties and thirties, a fascination with the "hip" philosophy of the fifties (with a renewed celebration of the Beat poets)—and we still had a whole decade to go.

The artists, and especially the jazz musicians, anticipated these events by several years. The twentieth-century poet and essayist Ezra Pound called artists "the antennae of the [human] race," alluding to their ability to sense and translate new developments in society and among its members. As the century began to wind down, Wynton Marsalis and those who followed were undoubtedly responding, at least in part, to this fin-de-siècle sensibility as they thirsted for a return to older forms and idioms.

Most of these younger musicians gravitated toward bebop, the cornerstone of virtually all postwar jazz styles, and to the hard-bop and cool idioms that grew out of bebop in the fifties. What's more, these players started out with quite specific role models. The alto saxist Kenny Garrett had a special affinity for Cannonball Adderley, although he worked through that to establish his own voice. A younger altoist named Jesse Davis came along with a dead-on impression of Charlie Parker. The playing of trumpeter Wallace Roney bore an uncanny likeness to Miles Davis's kind-of-blue persona; the British tenor player Courtney Pine wore John Coltrane's influence like an insignia; and a teenaged altoist named Chris Hollyday used the style and unique sound of Jackie McLean as his template. With his arioso tone and suave but muscled technique, the young bassist

Christian McBride stood up to comparisons with the once peer-less Ray Brown, who essentially invented the sound of modern jazz bass. The drummer Winard Harper formed a band with his younger brother Philip, a trumpeter, that even sought to re-create the experience of Art Blakey's Jazz Messengers—even though Blakey was still alive and the Messengers remained as active as ever. By the late eighties, it seemed that every month brought another twenty-something artist, with a new recording contract in hand, and all of them trying to carve out their niche as a modern version of this or that hard-bop icon.

A few years later, I started using the nickname "wannabe-boppers" to describe these musicians. Obviously talented, and just as obviously well schooled, they mustered a precise, compli-cated, and often exciting version of the music that had prolifer-ated more than a quarter century earlier. But except in the hands of the most accomplished and imaginative players—such as those recommended below—the music had a peculiar hollowness about it. Bebop had derived much of its vitality from responding to the tumultuous events of the 1940s (remember, "the antennae of the race"), and this gave it a specific relevance—not only to its time, but also to those listeners who had experienced the same events that had helped forge it. That vitality cuts through the in-tervening half century in a way that listeners can still hear today.

The neoclassic jazz of the 1980s could revisit the songs, the styles, and the formats of that era. But it couldn't hope to capture that same cutting-edge sensibility, because the music did not truly belong to its time. Nonetheless, this neoclassic movement proved enormously popular, and in the process it gave jazz—unelectrified, nonfusion jazz—a new profile. Suddenly, the music began to generate more attention than it had received at any time since the early sixties. The neoclassicists touched a nerve in the generation looking to rebel against their hippie parents—a gen-eration that couldn't wait to grab something from the storied fifties and sixties for their very own. But the neoclassicists reached an audience beyond their contemporaries. Playing clean, concise solos, concerning themselves less with new questions than with rediscovering answers, they also delighted those listeners who had grown up with this style of music the first time around and had been hoping against hope to see it reborn. And eventually, the best of these young musicians began stretching, adapting, and seeking new directions of their own.

As explained, the hard-bop era inspired these neoclassicists, not just in the music they played but also in the clothes they wore and the quiet dignity that many of them projected. But an odd fact is that their leader, Wynton Marsalis, had less to do with hard-bop—or even with bebop—than any of them. As the years have passed, he has gravitated steadily to the music of Duke Ellington as his true artistic inspiration.

Wynton made his first splash as a precocious trumpet virtuoso, a teenager equally adept at jazz improvisation and classical interpretation. While still a nineteen-year-old student at the prestigious Juilliard School in New York, he joined Art Blakey's Jazz Messengers, and by the time he started his own band two years later, he had already made his classical recording debut as well. But by the early nineties his trumpet playing had largely retreated into the shadows cast by his roles of composer, con-ductor, educator, and self-appointed jazz spokesman: the man who would be Duke.

There are two good reasons for referring to Wynton by his first name. First, there's its distinctiveness: after all, you won't find many people having to ask which Wynton you're referring to. There's also the matter of specifying which of the many *Marsalises* you're referring to. Merely saying "Marsalis" might lead one to think of saxist *Branford* Marsalis, Wynton's older brother, who followed Wynton into jazz and film scoring, and who eventually eclipsed him in terms of mainstream popularity (by virtue of his nightly appearance as the first bandleader for Jay Leno on *The Tonight Show*). Or you might be referring to *Delfeayo* Marsalis, a trombonist better known for producing sev-eral of Branford's albums. These days, the name might also lead one to think of *Jason* Marsalis, a sparkling drummer who has per-formed with a number of well-known leaders. And in their hometown, New Orleans, you'll probably still find people who hear "Marsalis" and think first of pianist *Ellis*, the patriarch of this clan and a respected jazz educator who has made nearly a dozen albums under his own name or with his sons.

Like the great bandleaders he admires and after whom he has patterned himself—Ellington, Blakey, Armstrong—Wynton has encouraged, hired, and/or launched the careers of many young musicians who have made significant contributions to this stylis-tic period. Several of them—Terence Blanchard, Cyrus Chestnut, Roy Hargrove, and Marcus Roberts—are discussed below. You might call these artists "Wynton's children"; like the generation that grew up on Charlie Parker's music and considered him their musical "father," these young players point with pride at their source and mentor. From his first appearances and recordings with Blakey—who named him the band's musical director less than a year after hiring him—Wynton has set the tone, direction, and even the sartorial style (snappy suits, crisp shirts, expensive ties, clean-shaven appearance) for the decade to follow.

(Wynton also threw down the gauntlet at anyone who challenged, either by word or deed, the doctrine he espoused. His philosophy started with a statement of artistic humility: in interview after interview, he explained that musicians of his generation needed to "learn the basics," as laid down by the music's past giants, before trying to innovate on their own. But this reverence for the "main line" of jazz development came with a steep price tag. The cost? Anyone who sought to move the music in some other direction—including even those past giants themselves—was suddenly suspect of heresy. In short order, Wynton attacked Miles Davis for his turn to fusion, then went after Lester Bowie, the leading free jazz trumpeter, for straying from the beat. Knowledgeable, persuasive, and even poetic, Wynton became almost as famous for his diatribes as for his music, promoting a revisionist history that treated the signal events of the sixties and seventies as mere cul-de-sacs along jazz's main branch.)

The music made by Wynton did not just copy earlier styles, but rather attempted to master and adapt the work of past innovators. Wynton added some noteworthy tricks of his own. He and his followers broke up their compositions with sections in which the tempo became elastic, and in many of their pieces they included sudden shifts of rhythm or mood—a notably postmodern approach for musicians so resolutely conservative in other ways. More to the point, Wynton sought to include performance practices of his native New Orleans, even when the music had its roots in bebop: his band played post-bop riffs and harmonies, but the sense of interplay and camaraderie mirrored the polyphonic approach of traditional jazz. In his first recordings, Wynton featured his brother Branford, who would later prove the more adventurous of the two. You hear this not only in his long, serpentine solos that skirt free jazz, but also in his band Buckshot LaFonque, which incorporates jazz and rap—an idiom publicly excoriated by his brother.

The fact that the Marsalises first attracted widespread attention in Art Blakey's band is no accident. More than any other musician still alive in the eighties, Blakey with his Messengers had provided the hard-bop crucible from which the hot streams of neoclassic jazz now poured, three decades later. After Wynton's departure from the band, Blakey took advantage of the neoclassic movement—which his own early recordings had helped inspire—by welcoming a deluge of young saxists, trumpeters, trombonists, and pianists to the Messengers. All of them had studied the history of his bands, and all of them strove to leave their own mark where such heroes as Freddie Hubbard, Wayne Shorter, Lee Morgan, and Cedar Walton had trod before. (Among the more notable newer Messengers: pianists James Williams, Mulgrew Miller, and Benny Green; saxists Bobby Watson and Billy Pierce; trumpeters Wallace Roney and Brian Lynch.)

Plenty of other evidence exists for the fin-de-siècle quality of 1980s jazz. The organ—which had come to prominence in the soul-jazz craze of the 1950s and 1960s—experienced a rebirth in the hands of both talented young players and suddenly "rediscovered" greats from years past. Former avant-gardists began performing in more straight-ahead formats—either because they felt they had to, or because they felt they finally *could*. After many years in which the jazz orchestras (a symbol of bygone eras) had all but disappeared, several new ones took shape, occasionally affiliated with major cultural institutions such as Carnegie Hall. And after many years in which no young vocalists had arrived to take the torch from the Great Triumvirate— Billie Holiday, Ella Fitzgerald, and Sarah Vaughan—a large number of promising, tradition-minded singers began to emerge. (Think of Cassandra Wilson, Kevin Mahogany, Karrin Allyson, and Kurt Elling.)

In addition, the young musicians playing older music helped focus attention on the *old* musicians who still performed with energy and skill. The saxist Benny Carter and the trumpeter Doc Cheatham, both of whose experience extended to the earliest jazz of Armstrong and Hines, saw their playing careers revived, with albums, concerts, and honors. The remaining lions of bebop, such as Dizzy Gillespie and Stan Getz, had never really fallen from favor; now they seemed like living gods. Hardbop-era players—Sonny Rollins, Jackie McLean, Phil Woods,

James Moody—suddenly had new audiences of younger fans. Even the most rebellious and iconoclastic of these musicians now found themselves benefiting from a backward-looking reaction they might once have fought.

Nonetheless, iconoclasm hadn't disappeared; it just got lost in the shuffle of the neoclassic movement, as avant-gardists, world-music hybridizers, and even a few serious jazz-rockers continued plying their craft. Most important, various young veterans of the sixties and seventies had now reached the age where they could start reordering their priorities, sorting through their experiences, and creating a *new* music for the next decade. Such artists—including bassist Dave Holland, guitarist John Scofield, and a number of European players—aimed for a much broader "neoclassicism" than the Marsalis canon allowed. In it, such developments as free jazz and fusion would become ripe for re-examination and reinterpretation.

The Discs

Eric Alexander, *Full Range* (Criss Cross). Like many of his contemporaries, Eric Alexander set his sights early and stuck to his guns. After college he moved to Chicago for the express purpose of soaking up that city's noted tenor-sax tradition. After placing second in the prestigious Thelonious Monk Competition in 1991, he followed his plan to relocate to New York. Alexander's music shows an unmistakable fondness for Dexter Gordon's broad-backed tone, intrepid tempos, and inventive lyricism, and he plays with a similar propulsive drive. But Alexander *uses* this heritage rather than abusing it; he makes Gordon's pervasive influence one part of his stylistic portfolio, not the whole parcel. Recorded in 1994, this album shows Alexander to be a vivid storyteller (if still a bit callow); it also spotlights guitarist Peter Bernstein, who shares Alexander's straightforward sensibilities. No one should mistake Alexander for some young Turk intent on dismantling past idioms; he plays an updated brand of hard-bop jazz. But unlike so many of the wannabe-boppers who cloak their music in commentary about venerating past masters, Alexander lets his horn do the talking. He plays the hell out of complex chord sequences, goes for the deep heart of ballads, and uses the blues as a rugged cornerstone for elegant improvisational edifices.

Note: Despite its valuable catalog and wealth of excellent young American players, the Criss Cross label (from the Netherlands) can be hard to find or order. If that's the case, don't hesitate to grab Alexander's fine U.S. debut, *Straight Up* (Delmark), recorded sixteen months earlier.

Perhaps inevitably, many of the young musicians seeking to emulate the Marsalises' success starting by retracing their steps and thus sought out Art Blakey. Indeed, throughout the eighties, it seemed as if Blakey had installed a revolving door to his rehearsal room—one that brought a constant flow of talented young sidemen and sent them out as stars and leaders. Both Blakey's experience, and the almost foolproof Jazz Messengers concept, insured that each edition of the band would fit snugly into the continuum. Yet Blakey kept the music fresh by encouraging the arrivistes to contribute their own compositions. Even after these players moved on, some of their pieces became permanent additions to the Messengers' repertoire, right next to classics by Wayne Shorter, Bobby Timmons, and Benny Golson.

Album of the Year (Timeless). A great lineup headed up by Wynton Marsalis—not to mention the prophetic title (it really did win some "album of the year" honors in various polls)—make this 1981 recording a minor classic in the Blakey discography. Wynton had not yet released the first album under his own name, but he served as de facto leader of the Messengers; so this album provides an excellent introduction to his artistic concept (as well as crackerjack trumpet solos). But it also boasts some fire-breathing tenor from saxist Billy Pierce; an irresistible composition ("In Case You Missed It") and some especially well-balanced solos by altoist Bobby Watson, who became a respected leader later in the decade; and the dynamic, thoughtful pianist James Williams (who used this band as a stepping-stone to his own brilliant career). The new tunes share the program with a Charlie Parker classic, a Jazz Messengers evergreen ("Witch Hunt," from the sixties), and one more song dedicated to a former Messenger, pianist Bobby Timmons. You couldn't ask for a better snapshot of the Blakey "family tree" than this repertoire provides; and many of the solos come impressively close to the high-water mark established by Blakey's legendary sidemen of years past.

Even at the end of his life, and despite a serious loss of

hearing, Blakey continued to nurture the careers of younger musicians. On the 1990 CD *Chippin' In* (Timeless), recorded a few months before his death, Blakey led one of his best bands in years, and one of the biggest. For this recording, the front line swelled to four horns, with two tenor saxists as well as trombone and trumpet. The musicians ranged in experience from the rock-solid trumpeter Brian Lynch (who had already established his reputation on several recordings under his own name), to the saxist Javon Jackson (whose association with Blakey represented his national debut), to the teenaged wunderkind Geoff Keezer on piano. Lynch acted as assistant leader and brought along three swaggering tunes of his own, including the title track; and each of the quite varied soloists received ample opportunity to strut his stuff. Blakey sounds as enthusiastically fulminant as ever—as if he had just discovered the Messengers concept, instead of having safeguarded it during the previous four decades. His last recording, *Chippin' In* serves as a fitting epitaph, recapturing the power and precision of the greatest Messengers sextets. And in Lynch, Keezer, and bassist Essiet Essiet, it introduces the listener to musicians whose subsequent recordings have justified Blakey's faith in their abilities.

Terence Blanchard and Donald Harrison, *New York Second Line* (Concord). Try imagining a less enviable situation than the one facing trumpeter Terence Blanchard and alto saxist Donald Harrison when they joined Art Blakey in 1982. In replacing the Marsalis brothers, these childhood pals found themselves filling the shoes of the country's most famous young jazz musicians—under the spotlight trained on the world's longest-running jazz band. (But the transition proved relatively seamless: both young players had studied with the patriarch of the Marsalis clan, the pianist and teacher Ellis Marsalis, and Wynton himself had recommended them to Blakey.) Blanchard and Harrison stayed with the Messengers for two years before starting a well-seasoned quintet of their own. It starred Mulgrew Miller, a pianist of impressive fluency, and the Midwestern drummer Marvin "Smitty" Smith, whose complete comfort and command in virtually any setting quickly placed him in great demand. In their own soloing, the leaders struck different notes: Blanchard favored sophisticated puzzle-making, while Harrison concentrated on a cool soulfulness. But they maintained a sly compatibility, forged during their many years of friendship and honed in the Messengers. This album provides the best evidence of the tightly balled energy at the core of their music, and also of their ability to mix the spicy rhythms of their native New Orleans with the fast-paced glamour of New York—traits that further linked them to the music of Wynton Marsalis.

Carnegie Hall Jazz Band, *The Carnegie Hall Jazz Band* (Blue Note). At first, the Carnegie Hall Jazz Band seemed like a wanna-be competitor to the Lincoln Center Jazz Orchestra (see below) led by Wynton Marsalis. Both are repertory jazz bands affiliated with a major concert hall; both emphasize great compositions and arrangements of jazz history; and in Jon Faddis, the CHJB also hired as its musical director a precociously talented trumpet star (albeit from an earlier generation: Faddis had attained fame as a teenager in the early seventies, first with Charles Mingus and then with the Thad Jones–Mel Lewis Orchestra). But on the opening track of this distractingly good debut, it's clear that the CHJB has more on its agenda than just re-creating the past. "In the Mood" begins with a double-time re-creation of Glenn Miller's original hit recording. Then this surprisingly fast rhythm abruptly winds down to half-speed— at which point the harmony also shifts gears, abandoning the sweet, sunny chords of the original arrangement in favor of dark postmodern harmonic clusters. The song has now been transformed from an exercise in nostalgia into a musical experience relevant to listeners weaned on bebop, modal harmony, and the rhythmic tessellation of postwar jazz. On other tunes as well—notably Coltrane's "Giant Steps" and the Benny Goodman hit "Sing, Sing, Sing"—the CHJB stakes out the radical position that a repertory ensemble might actually *reinterpret* past glories from the repertoire, in addition to re-creating them.

Kenny Garrett, *African Exchange Student* (Atlantic). Kenny Garrett's alto sax has the dark, puckered timbre that Jackie McLean brought to the instrument, and the imagery of John Coltrane also plays a role in his style of improvisation. (In fact, in the mid-nineties Garrett recorded an entire album of Coltrane compositions.) With his sinuous, sometimes knotty phrases, he offers a neoclassicist's version of a jazz shaman, wielding music as both a boost for the body and a balm for the soul. Just a year older than Wynton Marsalis, Garrett made his first record in 1984; and as part of a neo-bop band called Out of the Blue, he emerged as a particularly forceful member of the new generation. But then he spent several years in Miles Davis's last groups, with their emphasis on electronics and funk and even hip-hop, and the experience changed him: it tightened his focus and loosened his strictures, and it certainly sharpened his reflexes. (In the eighties, the various saxists who played with Davis all ended up acting as the foil for the leader's staged antics and set pieces, which required them to remain alert to whatever the trumpeter might throw at them.) On this 1990 recording, made shortly after Garrett had left Davis's employ, his playing bristles with confidence; he tugs at the corners of older material, while his own tunes spin circles around the classic styles that inspired them. And the complexity of his solos points toward the increasing convolution that would mark them in years to come, while maintaining their emotional immediacy.

Benny Green, *Lineage* (Blue Note). Still in his twenties when he recorded this well-titled album (the first U.S. release under his name), Benny Green had already starred in the bands of Art Blakey and Freddie Hubbard. And if his résumé didn't provide enough of a clue, the music left no doubt about *which* lineage the young pianist had in mind. From his first appearance on disc, Green has shown a fluid and creative appreciation for the seminal hard-bop piano styles of the fifties—specifically, those of Wynton Kelly (who played with Miles Davis) and Tommy Flanagan (who played with just about everybody). At about the time he recorded *Lineage*, Green began to extend his homage to include the soulful piano funk that Bobby Timmons and Horace Silver popularized in the sixties. In fact, he opened this album with a dead-ringer version of Timmons's famous "Dat Dere," capturing the open voicings and crisp attack of its composer. Green's strengths include his marvelously lithe phrasing, his ability to craft complicated solos at crackerjack tempos, and his unself-conscious command of a storied idiom. They all make him a powerfully appealing player, though not always an adventurous one, as later albums would prove. But here—playing one of his best compositions (the sprightly "Phoebe's Samba") and digging into some unexpected buried treasures (such as

Bud Powell's disturbing "Glass Enclosure")—Green's earnest, energetic personality comes through loud and clear. And on an unaccompanied version of Thelonious Monk's "Ask Me Now," his choice of chords is at once spacious and intimate, like a well-designed cathedral.

Roy Hargrove, *The Vibe* (Novus). Of all the young musicians to follow directly in the wake of Wynton Marsalis, none has eclipsed Roy Hargrove, who received some famously public encouragement from Wynton—plus the gift of a trumpet— while still a high schooler. With an expansive command of the jazz tradition, Hargrove on his earliest solos displayed what would soon become his trademarks. These include a penchant for the lyrical improvisations of Lee Morgan and Freddie Hubbard; an artistic swagger more commonly associated with the saxophonists of his native Texas than with that region's trumpeters; and a pervasive, hip attachment to the blues. Hargrove's bands have traced a loose history of postwar jazz, starting with the group heard here—which partnered his trumpet with the alto sax of Antonio Hart to capture the classic bebop voicing— before moving on to the trumpet-and-tenor sound associated with postbop quintets. But in even his earliest work you'll also hear his love of Latin-jazz beats and a familiarity with contemporary pop. Both are in strong evidence on *The Vibe*, the third album under Hargrove's name. At his best, this still youthful trumpeter raises his style to the level of substance: his concise, gracefully structured solos make a statement about the beauty of form as well as the form of beauty. His economy of phrase thus transcends mere technique to become a philosophy of improvisation.

Tom Harrell, *Sail Away* (Contemporary). Like a scratch golfer, Tom Harrell improvises with concise, well-directed strokes and always seems to reach his destination with a minimum of extravagance. But even though the solo career of this versatile and highly respected trumpeter runs parallel to that of the other musicians in this chapter, he doesn't really belong here. By the time the eighties rolled around, he already had a decade of professional experience under his belt. (He was born in 1946, a generation before Wynton Marsalis.) Still, Harrell's music shares many of the neoclassicists' concerns; it also eschews most of their dogma in establishing a mature and open-minded artistic stance. Harrell's solos spark a cool excitement with their long-lined phrases, sustaining architecture, and crystalline chunks of melodic grace. They're pure, spacious, and so expertly chiseled that they often sound as if he'd written them in advance. (That's no small compliment, given his oft-noted abilities as a jazz composer.) Harrell learned much from Bill Evans's loping lyricism and muscular elegance, while his tone has a sort of backlit glow, like Chet Baker's. He swings just a bit behind the beat, with the relaxed attitude of a man early for a date. On this album, his best of the eighties, Harrell led a forceful band that included the new-cool-school guitarist John Abercrombie, former Jazz Messenger pianist James Williams, and the nuanced tenor saxist Joe Lovano. The song list includes his best-known composition, the Brazilian-flavored title track.

Dave Holland, *Seeds of Time* (ECM). As jazz in the nineties would eventually show, the Marsalis Movement's "back to basics" approach could offer something more than the chance to revisit past styles; it held the opportunity to *reassess* those styles, and to combine them with the progressive implications of fusion and free jazz. Some musicians realized this sooner than others; one of them, the enormously gifted bassist Dave Holland, put together a multigenerational quintet that might just have been the most exciting band of the 1980s. Holland had played electric music with Miles Davis, and he had also played in the bionic avant-garde quartet of Anthony Braxton. In this band, you won't hear those idioms, but you *will* hear their residual effects (like background radiation from a couple of big bangs). When *Seeds of Time* came out in 1985, Holland was almost forty; trombonist Julian Priester and trumpeter Kenny Wheeler, both of whom had substantial avant-garde experience, were in their fifties. But alto saxist Steve Coleman was not yet thirty (and still a few years from establishing his sensational fusion of jazz and hip-hop—see chapter 9), and the protean drummer Marvin "Smitty" Smith was about twenty-four, the same age as Wynton Marsalis. Holland unified their various spheres of influence with his impeccable bass work, and with the strength of his composer's vision: he brilliantly applied the lessons of free improvisation within recognizable song structures, and he orchestrated the three horns as if he were leading a miniature big band.

Keith Jarrett Trio, *The Cure* (ECM). During the eighties, even Keith Jarrett—the iconoclastic pianist (see chapters 5 and 6) and controversial composer, thanks to his large-scale symphonic works—proved vulnerable to the desire for recapitulation. (It's worth noting, though, that he undertook these efforts independently from the influence of Wynton Marsalis, with whom he would eventually engage in a published war of words on the subject of neoclassicism.) In 1985, Jarrett released the first album (*Standards, Vol. 1*) by a new trio that included bassist Gary Peacock and drummer Jack DeJohnette, both noted individualists on their respective instruments; soon known as the "Standards" trio, they concentrated on the existing repertoire of American popular music 1930–60, as opposed to Jarrett's own tunes. In the ensuing decade, this band became the principal vehicle for Jarrett's lustrous, invigorating piano explorations. Both the format and the material placed Jarrett's piano playing in a new light. The clean interaction of the trio supported his most extravagant forays without cluttering them. And by applying skills honed by years of solo concerts, Jarrett could reveal his improvisational gifts and mastery of form for a new audience—even as he was recasting these tried-and-true songs in a distinctly modern mold. The trio recorded *The Cure*, considered by many their best album, at a concert in 1991; by then, their programs had grown to include a larger percentage of *jazz* standards, such as the songs by Duke Ellington, Dizzy Gillespie, and Thelonious Monk that appear here. But all these songs provide only a jumping-off point for the trio's uncompromised originality.

Kevin Mahogany, *Songs and Moments* (Enja). As a young saxophonist in the Kansas City area, Kevin Mahogany eventually grew frustrated with his limitations as an improviser. He could hear some great solos inside his head, but he couldn't always get them down to his fingers and out through the horn. He could sing them, though, and that convinced him to try another avenue of musical expression. Mahogany has a deep burled baritone that fits his surname; that, along with the smooth delivery with which he can phrase a ballad, has earned him comparisons with such classic crooners as Billy Eckstine and Johnny Hartman. But crooners don't usually scat, and when they do, they rarely display either the fire or the authority that Mahogany can summon up. Those qualities made him the perfect choice from among his generation when it came to casting a rough-and-tumble blues singer for Robert Altman's period film *Kansas City* (set in the thirties). Like the great Count Basie vocalist Joe Williams, Mahogany can also fit himself comfortably into blues choruses or pop tunes, but he started to force this versatility on his later albums. On *Songs and Moments*, his second, Mahogany polishes several hard-bop gems, dances his way through the title tune (by the Brazilian songwriter Milton Nascimento), and catches a speeding "A-Train" with a harrowing scat solo. And the album swaddles Mahogany's large sound in big-band orchestrations that both support and challenge him.

Even though he came to jazz a little later than his younger brother Wynton, saxist Branford Marsalis quickly impressed jazz aficionados. His solo work showed a probing imagination and a slippery command of the tenor saxophone's jazz history—a fluency with the styles of such artists as Dexter Gordon, John Coltrane, Sonny Rollins, and Wayne Shorter, which allowed him to reference these giants while creating far-flung improvisations quite his own. And Branford had a loose, ready-for-anything attitude that distinguished his work from the carefully contained playing of his brother.

On *Scenes in the City* (Columbia), his 1984 debut as a leader, Branford tossed a number of balls in the air, foretelling a career that would come to include progressive quartets and open-sided trios, collaborations with blues musicians and hip-hoppers, and bit parts in movies. The scene-stealer on this album is the audacious title track, a remake of a poetry-and-music confabulation created and first recorded by Charles Mingus in the mid-fifties. Sound effects and narration intact, it offers another view of the theatricality that would increasingly characterize Wynton's music too. *Scenes in the City* also found Branford juggling his various stylistic models—some Trane here, some Wayne there—almost as if he wanted to use this first album to cite his sources before moving on. Nonetheless, he offers an especially strong tenor solo on the opening track, and his soprano sax flies like a banshee on "Waiting for Tain," the first announcement of what would become a long-running partnership with drummer Jeff "Tain" Watts (a former member of brother Wynton's first bands). On two tracks, the album also features Kenny Kirkland,

an excellent and well-rounded pianist who would subsequently join Branford's working quartet.

The conventional quartet format soon proved limiting to
Branford. So while he continued to employ pianist Kirkland in
his *Tonight Show* band, he began working with Watts and
bassist Robert Hurst in the pianoless trio heard on *Bloomington*
(Columbia), recorded in concert in 1991. This format, made
famous by Sonny Rollins in the fifties, encourages longer, less
constrained solos: it emphasizes the spontaneity of improvisation rather than the structure of composition. (It thus provided
a perfect context for Branford to further distance himself from
his brother Wynton.) This doesn't mean that Branford abandons compositional principles entirely, or that he indulges in
ill-conceived exercises to prove his freedom. Indeed, on the
twenty-minute-long "The Beautyful Ones Are Not Yet Born,"
he plays a floating, introspective, and lovingly organized solo
that remains a career highlight. On both tenor and soprano, his
solos brim with strong ideas and knuckle-busting splendor.
Like an intrepid but obsessive hunting dog, he heads straight
for the prey by paradoxically investigating every corner of the
terrain. Meanwhile, his translucent tone and springy, propulsive technique give the music an almost rococo quality—even
though the epic scope of his soloing veers toward the Wagner-
ian. Always the most adventurous and exciting improviser of
the Marsalis family, Branford here reveals the barely controlled
abandon that has always shaped the most exciting jazz.

Few musicians of any idiom have had either as immediate
or as enormous an impact on their contemporaries as Wynton
Marsalis. By his twenty-fifth birthday he had already won six
Grammy Awards, for both jazz and classical recordings. Within
a few years he had become a national celebrity: his name figured in a *New Yorker* cartoon, right around the time that Bill
Cosby said he'd like his daughter to marry "a young man like
Wynton." At age thirty, he took over the Lincoln Center jazz
program in New York, by which time he'd already initiated an
ongoing and controversial public dialogue about what constitutes "true" jazz. Not incidentally, he had also radically altered
the jazz landscape for the late twentieth century.

Wynton's albums have grown steadily more sophisticated
and ambitious; they include ballet suites, extended tone poems,

and a nearly three-hour "jazz oratorio" that won a Pulitzer Prize. But in retrospect, his debut CD—*Wynton Marsalis* (Columbia/Legacy), recorded when he was twenty—contains some of his most persuasive playing. It showcased both Wynton's and his brother Branford's (see above) well-schooled command of the jazz mainstream, as well as their slick and imaginative innovations within that idiom. Several tracks featured Miles Davis's famous rhythm team of the 1960s, Ron Carter (bass) and Tony Williams (drums), who served as not just sidemen but also character witnesses: their presence seemed to testify to the brothers' place in the main line of jazz tradition. On the tune "Hesitation," Wynton and Branford engage in a rapid-fire romp structured around "I Got Rhythm"—a favorite of the beboppers—but they use the pianoless-quartet format that Ornette Coleman had championed in the sixties. "Hesitation" turned out to be as close to either bebop *or* free jazz as Wynton would ever get. As his career has gone forward, the trumpeter himself has gone back in time, seeking out progressively older influences—first Miles Davis, then Duke Ellington, and eventually his fellow New Orleans native Louis Armstrong. As a result, *Wynton Marsalis* not only lit the path for the next two generations of young jazz musicians; it also offered the most "modern" music Marsalis has recorded.

The addition of pianist Marcus Roberts to Wynton's band represented two important and interrelated developments: the self-propagation of Wynton's music, and the unveiling of a "second generation" of neoclassic jazz. Although only twenty-two months younger than Wynton, Roberts arrived in the band (in 1985) as an eager apprentice, having learned by heart every song on the trumpeter's first records. Sliding into the piano chair with barely a rehearsal, he provided tangible and quite spectacular evidence of the impact Wynton had already begun to have on his contemporaries—as well as proof that this music might become a canon for younger musicians as the century closed. On *J Mood* (Columbia), Wynton's music benefited from Roberts's strong left-hand phrases, the shifting textures of his accompaniments, and his ease at manipulating the often complicated composition forms used by the trumpeter. As much as any album in Wynton's discography, and considerably more than most of them, this one bristles with an energy born of balances—between composition and performance, between purpose and effect, and among equally equipped artists as they inspire each other.

In the mid-eighties, Wynton assembled a new septet designed to echo the sultry harmonies, sunny rhythms, and polyphonic improvising of the earliest New Orleans jazz. Marcus Roberts remained, joined by new stars Wessel Anderson (saxes) and Wycliffe Gordon (trombone). The septet received its "official" debut on three simultaneously released CDs grouped together as *Soul Gestures in Southern Blue*. But the best and brightest moment for this band came on an album recorded a little later—even though it came out a year *before* the trilogy mentioned above (which led to a fair amount of confusion). On the often ignored *Crescent City Christmas Card* (Columbia), Wynton uses the interwoven textures of early New Orleans jazz to redeem such overworked holiday tunes as "Carol of the Bells," "We Three Kings," and "Sleigh Ride." As guest artists, Jon Hendricks and the New Orleans clarinet legend Alvin Batiste make invaluable contributions; and there's a delightful irony to hearing steamy New Orleans swing applied to songs about wintry snow. Many people automatically discount any album with a Christmas theme, but Wynton's latter-day exploration of the oldest jazz style has never sounded so convincing.

Mulgrew Miller, *Hand in Hand* (Novus). In the "alternate universe" of the neoclassicists—the one in which each musician has a direct correlative in the jazz of the fifties and sixties—Mulgrew Miller becomes the young alter ago of McCoy Tyner. Just listen to the percussive attack, and the piston-driven melody lines of his solos. Miller also shows the impact of Herbie Hancock's approach to the piano, in pastel arpeggios, free-floating trills, and the softened contours of his chords. But Tyner and Hancock are the two major influences on this entire generation of pianists, so no surprise here. Miller stands apart from most of his colleagues thanks to his across-the-board musical maturity. A little older than most of these players, he began playing professionally in the late seventies, and he organizes his solos along clear but not obvious principles. His compositions (which fill this album) track a similar path: they have purpose, but they also have fun. A veteran of groups led by Art Blakey, Betty Carter, and trumpeter Woody Shaw, Miller also knows a thing or two about leading a band. He directs the music even when he's *not* soloing, and that constitutes one of the most impressive virtues on *Hand in Hand*. The lineup allows him to mix and match from among several musicians he had worked with on past recordings: tenor sax great Joe Henderson, the exhilarating trumpeter Eddie Henderson (no relation), Kenny Garrett (playing both alto and soprano saxes), and the respected vibraphonist Steve Nelson.

Mingus Big Band, *Gunslinging Birds* (Dreyfus). As the name might suggest, the Mingus Big Band plays only music written by the late Charles Mingus (chapter 4). But the exclusivity of that concept proves anything but limiting, since Mingus's music employed such wide-ranging themes and ran such a vast emotional gamut. (Mingus created the most important body of jazz composition after that of Duke Ellington and maybe Thelonious Monk.) By tapping so specifically into a past era, this orchestra leaves no doubt as to its neoclassic inspiration, but by taking significant liberties in their interpretation (all under the watchful eye of Mingus's widow, who administers the band), the MBB's members refresh the music and dance themselves out of the fin-de-siècle corner. In some cases—as with this album's "Jump Monk"—Mingus himself wrote the arrangements, using them in the occasional orchestras he assembled. But most of the MBB repertoire was only recorded by Mingus in small-band format, usually five or six pieces; so these arrangements (many by saxist and de facto bandleader Steve Slagle) represent brand-new bottles of Mingus's compositional vintage. Soloists carry a great importance in this band, as they did in Mingus's own groups. And just as he employed a slew of quite diverse sidemen, the MBB also stars a variety of excellent players, from still-youthful veterans to history-minded Gen-Xers. This album includes trumpeter Randy Brecker, trombonist Ku-Umba Frank Lacy, and saxist Chris Potter.

Nicholas Payton, *Gumbo Nouveau* (Verve). The best and the brightest? Certainly the youngest—but of all the accomplished trumpet players crowding the neoclassicist jazz roster, Nicholas Payton (born 1973) shows the most potential to become a dominant force in mainstream jazz. This is based on more than just his technical ability, thanks to which Payton can summon the fire of Louis Armstrong as well as the mercurial flights of bebop;

more important, he has shown an impressive musicality in organizing his influences and applying modern musical principles to them. Payton's first appearances begged comparisons to Armstrong—Payton also hails from New Orleans, and his playing can attain the vulcanized tone and rawboned swagger that were Armstrong's trademarks—but they came in the context of the band led by Elvin Jones, the all-bets-off drummer who powered John Coltrane's avant-garde in the sixties. On this 1996 album, Payton plays New Orleans antiques—Armstrong's "Weather Bird" and even "When the Saints Go Marching In"— but splits his time between respectful re-creations of and versions updated by modernist rhythms and post-bop harmonies. These tunes lose their hoary stubble under Payton's razor-sharp interpretations; and when he brings his soulful simplicity of line to newer material (as he has done on two of his other recordings), he charts a course worth hearing both now and as it develops. *Gumbo Nouveau* also stars saxists Jesse Davis and Tim Warfield (see below), making it a terrific introduction to three highly talented youngsters.

Courtney Pine, *Destiny's Song + The Image of Pursuance* (Antilles). Although he plays saxophone instead of trumpet, Courtney Pine's first recordings positioned him as England's answer to Wynton Marsalis: a young, gifted, black jazz musician, committed to the music's tradition, and steadfast in defending the respect it deserved. (This proved especially novel in 1980s Britain, where jazz had become a basically white domain, and young black musicians tended to dive straight into ska, reggae, and funk.) But whereas Wynton homed in on Miles Davis and then Duke Ellington, Pine showed from the start that he had passionately absorbed John Coltrane's lessons. Especially comfortable on the midtempo lopes that Coltrane popularized, he unfurls a robust tone on both tenor and soprano saxes; and more than those of any of his contemporaries, his solos seek and sometimes find a spiritual focus. Later albums would find Pine working to incorporate his reggae roots and then hip-hop/rap music, but *Destiny's Song* revels in the pure musculature of postbop exploration. Pine comes up with mesmerizing, dervish tenor solos on several tunes—a power trio track called "Guardian of the Flame" and the fiery "A Ragamuffin's Tale"—and while he doesn't quite succeed with an unaccompanied deconstruction of the famous Thelonious Monk ballad " 'Round Midnight," he comes close enough.

Chris Potter, *Pure* (Concord). The best saxophonist of his generation? In the opinion of many musicians and a growing number of observers, Chris Potter deserves that label, and his music suggests he can handle the responsibility. Potter is one of the youngest musicians covered in this chapter (birthdate: Christmas week, 1970), but his maturity as an improvising saxophonist has been evident ever since he joined Red Rodney's quintet while still a teenager. His great facility on all the saxophones (tenor, alto, soprano) doesn't call attention to itself; instead, it conveys the logic of his improvisations with a cool confidence. And Potter, unlike several of his more famous contemporaries, has not allowed his music to stand still: with each album, he's expanded the range of both his material and his improvising. This questing has led him to occasionally make use of electronics; to work with giants of the previous generation, such as guitarist John Scofield and drummer Jack De-Johnette; and to write songs of increasing complexity and depth. Like Sonny Rollins, Potter keeps reinventing himself, sometimes subtly, and sometimes in big leaps. But his absolute authority as an improviser lets him maintain his identity in any situation— from leading his own quartet, to soloing with the Mingus Big Band, to touring with the clandestine rock "group" Steely Dan. *Pure* finds him working with frequent partner John Hart on guitar, in a quintet that features pianist and organist Larry Goldings (but virtually none of the traditional organ-jazz fare).

Marcus Roberts, *Deep in the Shed* (Columbia). As explained above (in the section on Wynton Marsalis), the blind pianist Marcus Roberts burst onto the scene as both acolyte and henchman to Wynton's ways. Before long, he had established his own career as a bandleader, a reinterpreter of past giants—George Gershwin and Thelonious Monk, to name the two most prominent examples—and as a deep-blues soloist. Roberts's booming left-hand chords plumb the piano's lower fathoms and anchor the music to his steady beat; with his right he plays spare, somewhat dark improvisations that burst into fireworks less often than you'd expect. Roberts leads a seven-piece band for most of this 1990 album—his second as a bandleader—but it still manages to display his unhurried approach to improvisation. It also presents several compositions that remain among Roberts's most attractive tunes (even though they mirror the music being written at this same time by Wynton). Roberts's music rests on a bedrock of spiritualism, and these songs—along with his heartfelt solos, and the isolation and meditation conveyed by the album title—evoke that inspiration. In fact, it seeps through with more impact than on his later albums, which attempt to convey the same message in more heavy-handed ways.

Neo and Improved

Art Blakey continued to make excellent recordings until his death, and enough remain in the catalog that you can buy one a year—for the rest of your life—and still not go wrong. Standouts among his 1980s discs include *Keystone 3* (Concord), with both Marsalis brothers on hand; *New Year's Eve at Sweet Basil* (Evidence) or *Blue Night* (Timeless), which feature the band starring Terence Blanchard and Donald Harrison; and *Feelin' Good* (Delos), documenting a short-lived edition in which Wallace Roney and Kenny Garrett shared the front line. *Art Collection* (Concord) samples various Messengers lineups from 1978 to 1985.

The Blanchard-Harrison tandem came up with several solid dates—*Discernment* (Columbia) being the best available—before parting company. After that, give a nod to *The Billie Holiday Songbook* or Blanchard's collaboration with Brazilian songwriter Ivan Lins, *The Heart Speaks* (both on Columbia)—two of the albums Blanchard has had time to record between scoring films directed by Spike Lee.

Kenny Garrett is well represented on the Coltrane tribute mentioned above—*Pursuance: The Music of John Coltrane*, on which guitarist Pat Metheny appears as a guest sideman—and *Songbook*, a 1997 release that concentrates on Garrett's own tunes (both albums on Warner Bros.).

In general, the eighties saw a renewed interest in the alto saxophone, after decades in which the tenor held sway. Jesse Davis goes directly to the source, affecting Charlie Parker's sound and much of his style, as best heard on *High Standards* (Concord). Antonio Hart, who arrived as the other horn in Roy Hargrove's band, makes his most compelling statements on *Don't You Know I Care* (Novus) and the 1997 *Here I Stand* (Impulse/GRP). Mike Smith kneels at the shrine of Cannonball Adderley but personalizes that influence on *The Traveler* (Delmark). And Vincent Herring makes more oblique use of Adderley's legacy on *Folklore: Live at the Village Vanguard* (MusicMasters).

Pianist Benny Green's very first album—*Prelude*, recorded for Holland's Criss Cross label—remains an especially good one. The 1997 *Kaleidoscope* (Blue Note) saw him starting to break out of the stylistic rut in which he seemed to have landed. He can also be heard as the main voice in the trio led by bassist Ray Brown during the nineties: try *Seven Steps to Heaven* (Telarc).

The neoclassicist generation abounds in fine pianists, however. Cyrus Chestnut's U.S. debut, *Revelation* (Atlantic), was anything but—at least, to those who'd heard him behind Wynton Marsalis and Betty Carter. His subsequent discs have only occasionally lived up to the expectations forged by this album, on which every aspect of his soft-spoken style, with its gospel-inflected voicings, fell into place. Geoff Keezer, the youngster mentioned in connection with Art Blakey (above), might well turn out to be the best of the bunch; *Curveball* (Sunnyside) shows you why.

Roy Hargrove followed up *The Vibe* with several fine albums and two superlative ones: the live album *Of Kindred Souls* (Novus) and the studio all-star album *Tenors of Our Time* (Verve), which features several top tenor men who play on a couple of tunes apiece. Hargrove changed direction completely in 1997 by forming a Cuban-jazz band called Crisol and recording the spirited *Habana* (Verve), which won a Grammy.

After Wynton Marsalis, Hargrove is certainly the best known (and arguably the most accomplished) of the kid trumpeters, but he has stiff competition.

The even younger Russell Gunn aims high on his second album, *Gunn Fu* (HighNote), which shows a talented, lyrical improviser still finding his voice. The youthful veteran Brian Lynch, who played in the last edition of the Jazz Messengers (see above), has spent the nineties shuttling between the postbop expressionism of Phil Woods's quintet and the sizzling rhythms of Eddie Palmieri's octet; in between them you'll find *At the Main Event* (Criss Cross) and *Spheres of Influence* (Sharp 9). The lesser-known Scott Wendholt could end up eclipsing them all: for his best work to date, look for *Through the Shadows* (Criss Cross).

Tom Harrell's music, which never exactly fit the neoclassic mold, has steadily grown more distinct from it. *Form* (Contemporary) and *Upswing* (Chesky) help trace this evolution, which reached fruition in his 1996 album *Labyrinth* (RCA), on which Harrell shares his spotlight with the up-and-coming tenor saxist Don Braden.

One of the most accomplished of eighties trumpeters is Wallace Roney, although his talent gets lost in the shadows of his fealty to Miles Davis. Roney sounds like Miles, phrases like Miles, and onstage he even frowns like Miles, but he used this similarity to advantage on *Misterios* (Warner Bros.), a 1994 album with orchestrations that followed the trail Miles left on the famous *Sketches of Spain*. The small-group recordings made by Roney in the eighties are career high points, but they're currently out of print; his 1997 album *Village* (Warner Bros.) features some of his best work.

Some of Roney's least-mannered playing comes on a 1997 album he did not lead: the Grammy-nominated *Remembering Bud Powell* (Stretch/Concord) by Chick Corea. The album eulogizes but does not imitate Powell's pioneering bebop with a multigenerational lineup; in addition to Roney and his contemporary Kenny Garrett, it features the younger Christian McBride on bass, the middle-aged Corea, and the senior citizen (and former Powell sideman) Roy Haynes on drums. Highly recommended.

Although he is too young to have established much of a discography, Nicholas Payton's two subsequent albums suggest his ability to peruse jazz history and make it his own. *Doc Cheatham & Nicholas Payton* pairs him with a trumpet great sixty-eight years his senior, a genuine contemporary of Louis Armstrong's. His next collaboration, *Fingerpainting*, couldn't have strayed much farther from that concept: it explores the compositions of Herbie Hancock with a pianoless trio of trumpet, guitar, and bass. In this format, Payton's up-tempo solos start to resemble Fats Navarro's in their careful sculpture and cheery tone. (Both albums on Verve; you'll find the latter under bassist Christian McBride's name.)

* * *

After you've taken *The Cure*, you'll probably want to hear the source of Keith Jarrett's "Standards" trio, the aforementioned *Standards, Vol. 1*; next, the double CD *Still Live*; and for the insatiable fan, the six-CD documentation of the trio's weekend visit to a venerable New York City nightclub in the summer of 1994, *Keith Jarrett at the Blue Note*. The trio's level of interaction has deepened over time, so you can hear the music evolve from the first to the last of these dates. (A distinct exception to the "Standards" rule is *Changeless*, on which the same trio plays four long Jarrett pieces and no standards whatsoever.) They're all on ECM.

Kevin Mahogany's 1997 album, *Another Time Another Place* (Warner Bros.), does almost as good a job as *Songs and Moments* at presenting the singer in the best light, and is probably more readily available. Another Midwestern vocalist, Vanessa Rubin (out of Cleveland), made waves with her early-nineties disc *Pastiche* (Novus), on which her voice shared the spotlight with a series of terrific arrangements, while her style paid homage to Carmen McRae. These singers all fall into the neoclassic mold; those staking out newer territory appear in chapter 9.

Branford Marsalis's straight-ahead jazz work hasn't changed much since his third or fourth album; only *Renaissance* and *The Beautyful Ones Are Not Yet Born* will take you anyplace new in this vein. However, Branford's attempt to fuse his jazz with the blues—not jazz blues, but the electric, urban, Sweet Home Chicago variety—succeeded far more than expected on *I Heard You Twice the First Time*, featuring B. B. King and John Lee Hooker. They're all on Columbia.

Five of the young-lion tenor players were assembled under the heading "Tough Young Tenors" for the album *Alone Together* (Antilles). Several of them (James Carter, Tim Warfield, and Todd Williams) had come under the tutelage of Wynton Marsalis before heading off in strikingly different directions.

The tenor and soprano player who caused the biggest stir of the nineties, Joshua Redman, quickly settled into a somewhat predictable pattern in his solos and in his albums. While he lacks any real depth, he still commands an attractive and lively style and has led some excellent bands. *Mood Swing* features the tremendous pianist Brad Mehldau at the helm of Redman's working quartet. On his first recording, *Wish*, Redman played with three old friends of his father (Dewey Redman)—bassist Charlie Haden, drummer Billy Higgins, and guitarist Pat Metheny—and perhaps not surprisingly, it remains his least mannered and most accomplished work. (Both on Warner Bros.)

The pianist James Williams, mentioned several times above, led an exceptional post-Messengers band in the eighties, as heard on *Alter Ego* (Sunnyside). In the nineties, he assembled a new group called ICU, which included two male vocalists and revealed the gospel music that influenced him as he was growing up in Memphis: *Truth, Justice & the Blues* (Evidence).

A good place to appreciate Williams's expansive piano concept is his solo album *At Maybeck* (Concord), number 42 in a long-running series of unaccompanied keyboard recitals recorded at the tiny and acoustically welcoming Maybeck Recital Hall in northern California. During the nineties, the sheer breadth of this series has helped refocus attention on the solo-piano idiom. The best of these albums—all of which carry the same title, *At Maybeck*—belong to JoAnne Brackeen, Steve Kuhn, Jim McNeely, Jessica Williams, Gene Harris, John Campbell, Sir Roland Hanna, and Kenny Drew, Jr.

And finally, we return to the source. Wynton Marsalis played gorgeous solos over string backgrounds (which only occasionally cloy) on *Hot House Flowers*, while the double CD *Live at Blues Alley* gives an excellent account of his mid-eighties quartet in concert. Also consider *Intimacy Calling (Standard Time Vol. 2)*. But in the nineties Wynton has concentrated on conducting the Lincoln Center Jazz Orchestra (*Portraits by Ellington* is the best introduction) and composing large-scale works for concert stage and ballet. Of these, the double CD *Citi Movement* and the single disc *Jump Start and Jazz* work best. All of Wynton's music appears on Columbia.

chapter nine

Open on All Sides*
1990–?

Throughout this book, I've offered a historical perspective on the music surveyed in each chapter (Useful Lies and all); taken as a whole, the short essays that introduce these chapters form a very basic, greatly compressed narrative about the creation and evolution of jazz. Each chapter has explained where jazz stood in a given decade, how it got there, and where it would next travel.

No such luck here.

To some extent, the problem is patently obvious. Anyone who tries to write history before it has actually *become* history courts disaster: you might as well chart a storm before it occurs. (And just think of how often you end up cursing your local TV meteorologist.) How can we examine the ways in which the jazz of the nineties became the jazz of the next decade when the "aughts" have yet to take place? Obviously, confusion reigns because we lack the perspective of hindsight.

You can consider this concept the last Useful Lie in this book. For while the lack of hindsight might make such analysis tricky in any situation, it poses only part of the difficulty here. After all, by the late twenties, social critics and cultural observers had little trouble defining the jazz of that decade: the hot swing and licentious gallop of the music coming out of Chicago cut a clear swath and left its impact everywhere. (It even gave the

---

*Pianist Geri Allen gave this title to a tune she recorded in 1986, half a decade before this chapter gets going. But "Open on All Sides" turned out to be a perfect and prophetic description for jazz at the very end of the twentieth century, when musicians revisited or expanded upon the whole gamut of jazz idioms—past and present—in their attempt to chart the music's future.

period its nickname: the Jazz Age.) Similarly, listeners and writers recognized the hegemony of bebop while still knee-deep in the decade that spawned it; the debate centered not on the existence or direction of bop but on its legitimacy and esthetics. And in the mid-seventies, only a few years after Miles Davis's *Bitches Brew*, people had a name and some fairly accurate criteria for fusion jazz.

So the matter of timing represents only some of the difficulty in nailing down the jazz of the nineties. We have to also look at the music itself: a glorious goulash of styles and idioms, innovative approaches and reconstructive surgery, all coexisting and occasionally influencing each other. No one idiom fully predominates, and only a fool would try to tack a single descriptive label on this period. Technology and philosophy—in the forms of the computer and individualism—have allowed jazz musicians to ignore the crowd; and more important, they can ignore the large record companies that benefit most from categorizing music into easily marketable niches. Today, a musician can produce his own music in his basement studio, then sell it on the Web via his own home page; he doesn't have to label it anything.

But while technology has permitted this proliferation of styles, technology did not create it. The existence of so many different jazz idioms in the nineties points to the slow fade of the neoclassic movement—and to the inability of any other contemporary idiom to clear the path. And that in turn hampers our ability to predict which style history will choose or where jazz might land in the near future.

As suggested at the end of chapter 8, the success of Wynton Marsalis's neoclassic movement soon spurred a number of quite other-minded musicians into action. Some chafed under Marsalis's frequent pronouncements about the true course of jazz—or just grew bored with the bulk of the music associated with his followers—and began to design jazz in conscious opposition to the wannabe-boppers. Still others—saxist Tim Berne, guitarist Bill Frisell, and drummer Joey Baron first come to mind—simply continued to explore their own unique musical paths, biding their time until the public might catch up to them. (Artists have followed this course throughout history and across disciplines.)

But a significant number of restless and innovative musicians unexpectedly took Wynton's words to heart; they just did so in ways he hadn't anticipated. They seemed to say: "Perhaps the problem isn't the reexamination of the past; perhaps the problem lies in what *parts* of the past we're reexamining." Jazz people began to systematically examine, reconstruct, and recombine their shared heritage, like so many strands of musical DNA.

This process abounds in the nineties, and it informs several identifiable trends.

- While the neoclassic players have hewed to a fairly narrow line of jazz development, others have resurrected the music of Sun Ra, Ornette Coleman, and even Miles Davis's electric bands of the seventies. None of these would appear on the wannabe-boppers' listening list, but all of them have inspired noteworthy projects in the nineties.

- Some jazz musicians have gone a step further to resurrect their *own* pasts: they have reunited long-dissolved combos and returned to long-gone formats. A case in point: the Brecker Brothers, who in the nineties made two albums that reprised their funked-up music of the seventies (see chapter 6). Into this category you can also place the well-received recordings by Quartet West, in which Charlie Haden—bassist and onetime firebrand (see chapter 5 and the transition section "From There 2 Here")—leads his band through a sentimental journey of his own formative years.

- The most surprising trend of all is the renewed popularity of seventies fusion jazz; after all, fusion appeared to have died even before Wynton arrived to denounce it. This trend led to the phenomenon of *acid jazz*—a phenomenon in part because it so often ignores *any* jazz and in part because nobody seems able to define it (even though record companies and younger listeners toss it around with absolute authority). Supposedly coined by a London dance-hall deejay, the term *acid jazz* quickly became a catchall for an impossible array of music, from dark vocal pop to heavily sequenced instrumental music; most frequently, it also includes the sampled sounds and soulless beat of hip-hop, and occasionally, the transplantation of world-music rhythms.

Some of the more intriguing projects labeled acid jazz borrow heavily from the electric-organ, soul-funk jazz

that arose in the early and middle 1970s. This has led a
few major jazz labels to reissue this music—which until
recently resided in the farthest corner of the vault—under
the rubric "Roots of Acid Jazz." But whatever validation
such attempts might provide, very little acid jazz is likely
to survive into the next decade, if only because so little
of it has lasted through *this* decade. A mere handful of
jazz artists—notably Steve Coleman, Courtney Pine, and
the trio Medeski, Martin & Wood—have managed to spin
musical gold from this combination of elements.

- A frequently recurring theme in this chapter, and one that
  cuts across stylistic boundaries, concerns the desire of many
  musicians to reorder the priorities of jazz. Sometimes this
  involves a new balance between composition and improvisation, between innovation and revivalism, or between vocal and instrumental music. In any case, this investigation
  of the fundamental structure of jazz might well emerge as
  the defining characteristic of the nineties.

While musicians of all stripes have explored these questions,
the greatest number of them form a loose-knit coterie at the
southern tip of Manhattan. Starting in the mid-1980s, this "Downtown New York" scene has centered to a large extent on the
Knitting Factory. Now a world-famous performance venue, the
Knitting Factory has proved improbably successful through
the savvy marketing of unabashed avant-garde music—both
jazz and rock, and plenty of music that incorporates both. This
would be remarkable in any era, since the avant-garde (literally,
"ahead of the pack") attracts a relatively small listenership; in
the Neoclassic Age, it counts as something of a miracle. Such
important figures as clarinetist Don Byron, trumpeter Dave
Douglas, pianist Myra Melford (all with recommended albums
below)—as well as bassist William Parker and the engagingly
eclectic band The Jazz Passengers—have all benefitted from
their association with the Knitting Factory, which in the late
eighties launched its own exceedingly varied record label.

No discussion of this scene should omit John Zorn, a performer and especially a composer of unusually wide-ranging
tastes (see below). Serving as the spirit and conscience of the
Downtown scene in the eighties, Zorn often seems to have designed his music to indulge his self-avowed short attention

260 / THE PLAYBOY GUIDE TO JAZZ

span. This concept reached its zenith with his creation of *Cobra*, a wildly inventive "composition" based on game theory: in it, all of the music is improvised, but the shape of the piece derives from a series of predetermined (though malleable) rules. Zorn constructed *Cobra* with the idea that different groups of musicians—or even nonmusicians—could use it as a template to create a unique piece of music with every performance. And indeed, that's just what happened. For some time, even after Zorn had taken up residence in Japan, the Knitting Factory held regular performances of the piece as performed by all manner of interested parties; once, it was even given over to a group of music critics and journalists.

(*Cobra* belongs to a group of pieces that illustrate the last bulleted item above, as do the *conductions*—or "conducted improvisations"—of Butch Morris. Morris uses gestures and signals to lead groups of improvisers in the creation of large-scale works, combining the functions of composer and conductor. A variety of other musicians have found other ways to bridge the gap between cutting-edge jazz and new classical music in the nineties, including the Japanese pianist Aki Takase and the Argentinian-born saxist Guillermo Gregorio, both of whose work is recommended for the more experienced listener. In addition, artists already covered in chapter 5—notably Muhal Richard Abrams, Anthony Braxton, Marilyn Crispell, Roscoe Mitchell, Henry Threadgill, and the members of the Rova Saxophone Quartet—have continued to explore this musical crossroads.)

Despite the activity radiating from the Knitting Factory, the jazz map of the 1990s includes locales far removed from the wilds of lower Manhattan. As if to mirror the stylistic breadth of the music, such cities as Chicago, New Orleans, Kansas City, Los Angeles, and Detroit have again earned recognition as homes to distinctive stylistic movements. Just as important (if not more), the nineties have witnessed an increase in intercontinental collaborations: vintage avant-gardists and younger free-jazz players from this side of the Atlantic have established musical relationships with like-minded artists in Europe, particularly Germany, the Netherlands, Sweden, and Britain. This process has opened audiences to refreshing "new" artists and stimulated musical hybrids—while at the same time showing how much these widely separated players often share in common.

They all contribute to the polyglot atmosphere of the fin de siècle. Perhaps the tenth or twelfth edition of this book can put the events of this period into clearer focus; open on all sides, the music might well go almost anywhere. And indeed, that just might be the way history views the 1990s: as a period known more for its blaring coexistence of various jazz styles than for the hegemony of any one of them.

But for now, the albums recommended below should give you a jump on gaining your own perspective on these heady modern times.

The Discs

Geri Allen, *The Nurturer* (Blue Note). The ease with which pianist Geri Allen traverses the modern jazz spectrum can take your breath away: she has an uncanny ability to inhabit many different idioms without abridging either her melodic impact or her airborne swing. (A 1997 album featured both Ornette Coleman and trumpeter Wallace Roney, Allen's husband; and while they didn't appear on the same tracks, it still required enormous range to fit them both into the same hour of music.) Allen brought a lithe spirit to the early hip-hop-inspired fusion of Steve Coleman, and even though she has concentrated on acoustic jazz in the nineties, shades of that experience still color her bouncy rhythms and multifaceted compositions. On this 1990 recording, Allen—who cut her teeth on the Detroit jazz scene—hired a former mentor, the unimpeachable trumpeter Marcus Belgrave; she also invited compositions from several members of her sextet, which helps account for the especially fulfilling program. More than on most of her other recordings, *The Nurturer* finds Allen fulfilling the title role, supporting and showcasing fine solos from saxist Kenny Garrett and using her striking keyboard colorations to shape and nourish the music. The opening track, "Night's Shadow" (written by her percussionist, Eli Fountain), swings hard and true, and sets the stage for similarly rousing tunes by Belgrave and bassist Robert Hurst. But Allen's commanding presence at the piano leaves no doubt to whom this music really belongs.

Tim Berne's Bloodcount, *Low Life: The Paris Concert* (JMT/Polygram). Well into the nineties, the neoclassic jazz movement continued to receive the hype and the headlines. But the future of jazz probably rests with bands like this, led by a saxophonist with more than twenty years' recording experience. Tim Berne created Bloodcount in 1993 in hopes of deconstructing the jazz combo: he wished to "de-emphasize the usual soloistic approach" in favor of "more of a chamber-music approach to improvisation"—a concept previously explored by Lennie Tristano (see chapter 3), Ornette Coleman (chapter 5), and Ronald Shannon Jackson (chapter 6). Berne meets the challenge as they did, allowing the "accompaniment" lines played by bass and drums to share the spotlight with the saxophone improvisations, but he infuses a new level of flexibility: in this densely layered music, the focus can shift at the speed of sound. In the process, Berne manages to reconstruct a balance between structure and freedom. In addition, as you'll hear on this 1994 recording, he explodes the walls of traditional composition: instead of the conventional theme and variations, he intersperses thematic material throughout an entire piece. As a result, ensemble melodies seem to arise from the improvisations, rather than the other way around. Berne plays a virile brand of alto saxophone—shaped by his former mentor, Julius Hemphill (chapter 5)—and an agile, voluptuous baritone; in both cases, Chris Speed's tenor serves as a garrulous peer and partner. Their concurrent solo lines tumble into each other with a dangerous intensity, playing off rhythms at once primal and multidimensional.

B Sharp Jazz Quartet, *Looking for the One* (MAMA Foundation). Inspired by their elders, schooled in the tradition, retaining the time-tested format of sax plus rhythm—based on that description, the B Sharp Jazz Quartet might pass muster as one of the neoclassic jazz units led by Wynton's Kids. But this Los Angeles band makes use of poetry and even rap, hip-hop rhythms and world music; and an awareness of the fusion and avantgarde movements also rears its head. Exhibiting a much broader perspective of modern musical development than the wannabeboppers, B Sharp proves there's more than one way to fit into the jazz continuum. (They once described their music as "alternative jazz.") On this, the band's third and breakthrough album, their tough-skinned brand of jazz modernism comes into full flower. Like their previous discs, it revolves around the axis of co-leaders Herb Graham, Jr. (drums), and Randall Willis (saxes); they share an aggressive stance that mixes flash and depth, while their startling keyboardist, Rodney Lee, makes the most of occasional forays on electric piano and organ. But unlike earlier recordings, this one concentrates entirely on their own compositions, which capture the pulse of the nineties and incorporate it into the jazz mainstream. On ballads and blues, they evoke a clean, dry-eyed passion. It recalls the history of California cool—from the stripped-down hip of Central Avenue (home of L.A.'s black jazz scene in the 1940s) to the sun-faded sentiment of movie jazz—and updates it into a strong argument for jazz regionalism.

Michael Brecker, *Tales from the Hudson* (Impulse/GRP). In the cyclonic solos of tenor saxist Michael Brecker, you hear the maturity of jazz fusion; his music bristles with electrifying energy and melodic complexity. But Brecker can't be relegated to such a self-limiting category as fusion. His background also includes plenty of non-electric, mainstream jazz, and he long ago adapted fusion's strengths into the larger context of post-bop jazz. Through his work with Horace Silver in the sixties, the Brecker Brothers Band in the seventies, scores of jazz albums (as a sideman), and literally hundreds of high-profile pop and rock record dates, Brecker's sound became the template for an entire school of modern tenor men. Like Brecker, these saxists (including Bob Berg and Bobby Mintzer, both recommended) use a hard-edged tone and unflagging technique to build upon John Coltrane's music of the early 1960s. But for all his impact, Brecker did not record his own albums until the nineties, at which point he quickly achieved a new—and newly personalized—level of acclaim. This 1996 album won Brecker two Grammy awards. It also stars guitarist Pat Metheny, whose distinctive, fluid lyricism proves surprisingly compatible with Brecker's own, and on two tracks, pianist McCoy Tyner joins the band, matching Brecker's superheated stylings note for note. And Brecker's blistering, take-no-prisoners solos on the album's bookends—the tunes "Slings and Arrows" and "Cabin Fever"—are alone worth the price of admission.

Don Byron, *Music for Six Musicians* (Elektra Nonesuch). Since its heyday in the Swing Era, the clarinet has not fared so well in jazz, usually overshadowed by its reed cousins, the saxophones. But Don Byron has given the instrument a new face for the nineties: a leading light of New York's Downtown scene, he applies his classically trained technique and spherical tone to a rainbow of musical idioms, from pre-jazz to free jazz. Much of Byron's success lies in his ability to bend his virtuosity to such an eclectic palette of styles and idioms—not only under the direction of others, but even within his own presentation. Many of the songs on this album refer to political figures and events, from L.A. beating victim Rodney King to presidential candidate Ross Perot, revealing Byron's strongly felt sociopolitical convictions. But while these concerns play an important part in his music, he eschews any attendant stereotypes or misconceptions. For instance, klezmer music and its descendant, Jewish nightclub music of the fifties—in both of which the clarinet plays a leading role—have also left a large impact on Byron's style; he's even recorded an album featuring the music of Borscht Belt bandleader Mickey Katz (the father of actor Joel Grey), which surely makes him the first dreadlocked African-American to count off a tune in Yiddish. Such experimentation has given Byron a well-earned reputation for bold iconoclasm and often wicked irony—both highly prized in the late twentieth century.

Steve Coleman, *Drop Kick* (Novus). Saxist Steve Coleman's music is audacious and controversial; it's also deeply immersed in the spirit of jazz, a point of dispute to his detractors. Throughout history, jazz has looked to the latest pop music as a means of adding fresh ideas to the tradition (at the same time imparting depth to the idioms from which it borrows). Coleman became the first musician to embrace hip-hop music—and still retain a jazz esthetic—when he assembled this band in the mid-eighties, right in the face of the neoclassic phenomenon. He also came up with the sesquipedalian, pseudoscientific moniker for his new music fusion: Macro-Basic Array of Structured Extemporization, or *M-Base* for short. Coleman joins many of those mentioned below in seeking to balance compositional frameworks and improvisational fireworks; in the case of M-Base, the phat funk beat and repetitive riffing form a springy skeleton for street-smart, sharply angled horn solos. Others have tried to make this hybrid work, but only a couple have enjoyed Coleman's success. He humanizes the mechanistic pop rhythms: in his music, they breathe and sway with the cool conviction of his unflappable alto. A later, in-concert disc contains playing more fiery and expansive—in a word *jazzier* (see the last section of this chapter)—but *Drop Kick* gives you a far better introduction to the M-Base philosophy. As on many of Coleman's discs, it includes guest artistry from bassist Dave Holland, his former boss, and vocalist Cassandra Wilson, an early collaborator.

Dave Douglas, *Five* (Soul Note). Every major "school" of jazz prays for a trumpeter like Dave Douglas: a player whose bright golden tone, impeccable articulation, and warm technique instantly place him in the mold of previous trumpet greats, even as he maps out new paths of improvisation. Douglas does more than contribute a sparkling, burnished vitality to progressive music in the nineties. The trumpet has been jazz's signature instrument since Louis Armstrong; the presence of such a high-caliber player, who can stand up to comparison with past giants, helps locate this music firmly within the sphere of jazz. Besides all that, Douglas swings with precision and authority, and he has lips of iron, lined in asbestos; few contemporary trumpeters playing in *any* style can compete with Douglas for power and stamina. As you'd expect from a trumpeter who came of age in the eighties, Douglas often echoes ideas associated with Miles Davis; but unlike most others bearing that mark, he uses these ideas to guide new explorations of his own. Douglas's presence in a half dozen bands and on a score of recordings points to his importance on New York's Downtown scene, and the CDs under his own name testify to a restless and provocative creativity. They include several discs by his oddly instrumented Tiny Bell Trio (trumpet, guitar, and drums), and a couple by the group that appears on this album—a sort of "string band" that comprises violin (played by the ear-opening Mark Feldman), cello, bass, and drums. *Five* mixes up a variety of Douglas's pithy, savvy compositions as it refracts the entire jazz-trumpet tradition.

Kurt Elling, *The Messenger* (Blue Note). With his authoritative baritone and charismatic delivery, Kurt Elling might almost pass for a traditional jazz crooner; but the more you listen, the more you realize that almost nothing else about him fits that mold. He sends his richly marbled voice down dark alleys, where it can growl as well as seduce, and his exuberant, blistering presentation owes as much to the Beat writers (Jack Kerouac and

Allen Ginsberg, in particular) as it does to Elling's personal pantheon of jazz instrumentalists. Elling combines equal parts poet and musician, fifties hipster and Generation-Xer, as he extends the vocalese tradition exemplified by such singers as Eddie Jefferson (chapter 3) and Mark Murphy (chapter 4). Within that lineage, he provides words for previously recorded horn solos: this album's "Tanya Jean," in which he tackles a long and complicated Dexter Gordon solo from 1965, is the most ambitious such project in more than thirty-five years. Elling reaches for the next level on his own solos as well, sometimes improvising both melodies and *lyrics*; he thus applies the principles of scat-singing to words as well as notes. (The best recorded example of this technique comes on "The Beauty of All Things," composed by Elling and his partner-in-time, the electrifying pianist Laurence Hobgood.) Elling has honed an adventurous edge more commonly found among instrumentalists than vocalists. This, combined with his abilities as a wordsmith, makes him one of the most intriguing figures in nineties jazz, both for what he has accomplished and where it promises to lead.

Bill Frisell, *Where in the World?* (Elektra Musician). In the world of electric guitarists—where cult heroes are born every other week—Bill Frisell has drawn attention and envy since his first recordings in the late seventies. But even though his brooding, raw-silk sound has filtered through a subsequent raft of jazz projects, not until the nineties did he earn across-the-board praise from mainstream critics and listeners outside of jazz. (*The New Yorker* magazine called him "the most distinctive stylist in contemporary jazz.") Frisell's patient phrasing and mournful, broad-band swaths of sound resemble nothing else in modern jazz, with the possible exception of the Norwegian guitarist Terje Rypdal (see chapter 6). His relentless reliance on this dark romanticism accounts for much of his artistry. But beyond that, in the nineties Frisell began exploring various aspects of American music—notably country and western and rural folk songs, but also brass-band music and vocal traditions of the early twentieth century—and his efforts along these lines have made him a commercial and critical success. In effect, Frisell's music telescopes Americana into a unique musical curio made up of past events and present eclecticism—a memento as heavily laden with nostalgia as it is postmodern.

While later albums (mentioned below) have garnered more attention, this recording documents the guitarist's inventive and accomplished quartet of the early nineties, in which cellist Hank Roberts provided pulsing counterpoint and a plaintive midrange voice. And the material hints at several of the directions Frisell would focus on in future recordings.

Joe Henderson, *So Near, So Far* (Verve). Several distinctive attributes make Joe Henderson a true original: his woody, grained tone; the fluttery expressionism of his upper register; his lithe swing, which alternately tugs and steamrolls the music; and his nomadic improvisations, which seem to wander but actually arrive like a smart bomb. The tenor of the times? Quite possibly. Henderson *did* receive early acclaim in the mid-sixties, as a valued sideman on Horace Silver and Lee Morgan dates, and even more exposure during his short stint with the jazz-pop band Blood, Sweat & Tears; still, he only achieved widespread success through a series of concept albums recorded in the nineties. The first, an album of compositions by Duke Ellington's alter ego, Billy Strayhorn, made Henderson an "overnight sensation" (three decades after he debuted); this one, subtitled *Musings for Miles*, was even better. Henderson worked for Miles Davis for only three months, back in 1967. But one year after the trumpeter's death, he gathered three of Miles's fusion-era sidemen, guitarist John Scofield, bassist Dave Holland, and drummer Al Foster, to play lesser-known tunes from Miles's repertoire—and delivered one of this period's great CDs. Most of these songs were known only through Miles's definitive versions of them, but some of these robust reinterpretations threaten to eclipse the originals. Scofield's thick, rugged guitar frames Henderson's saxophone in both contrasting and complementary ways; the repertoire fully engages his knotty lyricism, with its regular bursts of perfect song.

Joe Lovano, *From the Soul* (Blue Note). The discography of saxist Joe Lovano ranges wide enough to approach absurdity: from the twenty-four-karat soul of John Scofield's early-nineties band (see below) to his own experimental octet, as well as a bop-oriented two-tenor date with Joshua Redman (see chapter 8) and the jazz-classical melange of his mid-nineties triumph, *Rush Hour*. On all of them, you hear Lovano's intense humanity, which finds voice in his burry, organic tone—a welcome change

from the metallic gleam used by most of his contemporaries—
and in the rhythmic flexibility of his sidewinder solos, as they
slip and slide between cracks in the beat. *From the Soul* gets the
nod primarily for the presence of pianist Michel Petrucianni—a
romanticist in the mold of Keith Jarrett—and the former Ornette Coleman drummer Ed Blackwell, whose loping swagger
provides ballast and inspiration for the saxist. After years of
yeoman service in others' bands, the middle-aged Lovano
emerged as the saxist of the nineties: a portmanteau stylist who
represents a summation (as opposed to a hodgepodge) of his
instrument's recent history, and thus sets the stage for further
development. Lovano doesn't hide his debt to John Coltrane,
Wayne Shorter, and Joe Henderson; he doesn't need to because
his encapsulation of their work never overwhelms his own improvisatory skill. Besides, he has put all the pieces together
with too much integrity and originality; his gracefully gnarled
improvisations find intriguing routes between A and B and put
most other saxophonists in the backseat.

Myra Melford, *Alive in the House of Saints* (Hat Art) or *The
Same River, Twice* (Gramavision). Hard to choose between these
two albums by pianist and composer Myra Melford, whose
music has slowly emerged as one of the true joys in modern
jazz. If you like the open plane of piano trio, go for the first; if
you prefer a denser topography, the second album features a
quintet with trumpet, reeds, cello, and drums. In her trio,
Melford has developed a writerly concept in which carefully
structured compositions blossom into musical freedom. This
format encourages her powerful piano work, which segues
effortlessly among Chicago blues riffs, unabashed romance, rollicking themes reminiscent of the young Keith Jarrett, and busy
dissonances. (Like any pianist who employs rapidly darting
tone clusters, Melford has elicited comparisons to Cecil Taylor.
But she employs the vocabulary introduced by Taylor to quite
different ends, and in fact sounds nothing like him.) On *The
Same River, Twice* Melford shapes the sounds of her band (featuring trumpeter Dave Douglas) to mirror the variety of textures she achieves in her own piano work; this occasionally
creates the effect of a piano concerto, without diminishing the
impact of the other soloists. Melford's supportive compositions
give this music a remarkable cohesion and an almost tangible

stature, placing *River* among the more engrossing albums of the nineties. Both these discs embody Melford's interest in the work and philosophy of Frank Lloyd Wright. In his own words, Wright strove for architecture that "expresses [the] inner harmonies perfectly, outwardly, whatever shape they take"; through her free-form explorations and her cantilevered compositions, Melford seeks the same things.

Danilo Perez, *The Journey* (Novus). While still in his twenties, the Panamanian pianist Danilo Perez established himself among the sterling jazz musicians of his generation, starring in groups led by Dizzy Gillespie and Tom Harrell, and accepting the torch carried by Bill Evans and Keith Jarrett. On the other hand, Perez showed his equal mastery of Afro-Caribbean music—leaving no doubt that he could successfully abandon either idiom for the other. His real strength lies in the ability to seamlessly stitch these traditions into something almost without precedent: a jazz-and-Latin hybrid of such individuality, and with such a wide range of expression, that it can avoid the glib clichés that pepper most "Latin jazz." As much as anyone, Perez represents the likely course of jazz in the next century, as the boundaries between Americas continue to crumble. An album-length suite that traces the arrival and settlement of Africans in the New World, *The Journey* marked Perez as an accomplished and thoughtful jazz composer. It boasts both Joe Lovano (see above) and the Puerto Rican saxist David Sanchez, who has worked frequently with Perez and shares all of the cross-cultural qualities mentioned above; the first-rate percussion section cuts through the sometimes murky forest of sound to become another noteworthy "soloist." And the album also showcases Perez's subtly weighted attack, his Technicolor technique, and his ability to make any tempo seem to leap from the keyboard.

John Scofield, *Meant to Be* (Blue Note). With his rawboned sound, his gift for sharply chiseled improvisations, and his marriage of media—a trademark blend of hard-bop, fusion, electric blues, and the rock music he grew up on in the sixties—John Scofield has had more impact on modern jazz guitar than anyone except Pat Metheny. (Since Scofield rose to prominence in the 1970s and worked in the bands of fusion pioneers Miles Davis and Gary Burton, perhaps it's no surprise that he has pursued his own musical synthesis.) The best context for his music remains the quartet he led in the early nineties, in which reedman Joe Lovano shared the solo spotlight; Lovano's malleable tone and wily improvisations provide a splendid complement to Scofield's playing. And the best introduction to that band is this album, recorded at the height of their popularity. It contains eleven of Scofield's infectious compositions. They include up-tempo lines with chunky rhythms, like "Big Fan," and streamlined speedballs with titles like "Eisenhower" and "Lost in Space"; a New Orleans shuffle infects "Mr. Coleman to You" (which signals Scofield's enduring respect for Ornette) as well as the slower and eminently funky "Chariots." One key to this band's success is the young drummer Bill Stewart, who plays with a sparkling beat and lively interior rhythms, displaying enough imagination for two bands. Since much of Scofield's music has roots in the soul-jazz of the late sixties, he sometimes gets lumped in as an acid jazz player, but nothing could stray farther from the mark—as evidenced by his relentless and intrepid solos.

Matthew Shipp, *Zo* (Rise Records). Since the late 1980s—before he had turned thirty—pianist Matthew Shipp has attracted his fair share of critical bouquets and brickbats. Because he often creates thick textures from intersecting melody lines, and because he plays freely structured improvisation, he has inspired the inevitable comparisons to Cecil Taylor (chapter 5). But Shipp prefers the airy pointillism of rapid-fire single-note lines to the blunt and pummeling chords found in much of Taylor's music, and his improvisations have a quite distinct form and logic; he uses the musical language invented by Taylor to reach different conclusions altogether. *Zo*, a 1993 CD, pairs Shipp with bassist William Parker, a steadying accompanist and passionate soloist with whom he first played in the sonic maelstrom called the David S. Ware Quartet (see below); since then, Parker has also anchored most of the pianist's trio and quartet projects, using the blunt resonance of his sound to support Shipp like a buoyant sea. As the nineties have progressed, Shipp's popularity has grown among some unexpected audiences, such as punk-rock fans who had previously resisted jazz but who see *free* jazz as a beacon of rebellion; such listeners respond to Shipp's high-energy intensity and occasional passages of incantatory repetition. By decade's end he was issuing an increased number of albums boasting different contexts and collaborations, some of them listed below. But *Zo* gets my vote as the best representation of Shipp's craft, and a relatively accessible one at that. In addition to the three-part title piece, it includes a blustery, apocalyptic version of "Summertime," which opens the door on his music to less adventurous listeners.

8 Bold Souls featuring Edward Wilkerson, Jr., *Sideshow* (Arabesque). Although this pulsating, genre-spanning Chicago octet remains relatively obscure, few bands of the last two decades have inspired such lavish critical applause. This attention stems in large part from the expansive palette used by reedman Ed Wilkerson—the band's leader, arranger, and main composer—and from the refreshingly exuberant interplay of his musicians; nonetheless, it's his cunning artistic concept that ultimately steals the scene. Like many of his colleagues in the AACM (chapter 5), Wilkerson's work acts to telescope jazz history, connecting the music's African heritage to the techniques and creative issues found in free jazz and its offshoots. But by plugging into the sonic imagery of Duke Ellington's early bands, Wilkerson adds a new wrinkle; he also succeeds in framing the musical discussion in familiar (and delightful) terms. The Souls' unorthodox lineup—no piano, tuba and cello providing a hearty bottom to the ensemble, the two reedmen juggling eight instruments between them—simply feeds Wilkerson's fertile imagination. And using the colors at his disposal, he can frame and support even the most frantic avant-garde horn solo with warming chords or piercing accents. Wilkerson goes for the big score: this sixty-six-minute album contains just five works, three of them clocking in at thirteen minutes or more, including a masterful reworking of Ornette Coleman's famous "Lonely Woman."

Cassandra Wilson, *Blue Light 'Til Dawn* (Blue Note). The jazz diva of her generation, Cassandra Wilson has taken a circuitous route to her current stature. She worked within the structured avant-garde of Henry Threadgill (chapter 5), and she gave voice to the M-Base music of Steve Coleman, before arriving at this—a spare, mostly acoustic, and insinuating hit album that delves into African and blues roots. With her dusky timbre, her melismatic swoops, and her ability to maintain artistic control—even as she appears to lose herself in the music—Wilson leads the pack of noteworthy singers who have reenergized vocal jazz in the nineties. Her seductive, intoxicating style combines the voluptuous majesty of Sarah Vaughan and the rhythmic liberties introduced by Betty Carter; both musically and emotionally, she evokes a romantic complexity that avoids sentimentalism. It starts with the very first track, the hallowed torcher "You Don't Know What Love Is." This ballad usually features a standard piano trio and perhaps a horn; Wilson uses only the folk-music sound of acoustic steel-string guitar for accompaniment, and the song suddenly becomes utterly free of past associations. That last phrase applies to this entire album, since the program includes two tunes by acoustic blues legend Robert Johnson, one each by rockers Joni Mitchell and Van Morrison, and several uncategorizable tunes by Wilson herself. This has led some to question the music's credentials; but like several of her contemporaries, Wilson aims to redraw the jazz border, this album serving as her manifesto.

The Vandermark 5, *Single Piece Flow* (Atavistic). The Gen-X reedman Ken Vandermark looks like teen spirit in his crew cut, flannel shirt, and rolled-cuff jeans. Then he starts to play, and all hell breaks loose. Unlike most of their generation, both Vandermark and his frequent partner, saxist Mars Williams, have heard the siren call of John Coltrane, Albert Ayler, and Fred Anderson, as well as the witty interpolations of the Art Ensemble of Chicago. Their fervent, excited response echoes and extends the work of these avant-garde icons and includes plenty of the multiphonic blasts that you might expect; but Vandermark is far too shrewd to simply re-create these once-shocking sounds. So while his throaty tenor easily erupts with screams and shrieks, leaping from his quintet's sharp themes and rhythms, the surrounding music bathes his solos in unexpected colors: alto sax and bass clarinet combine with trombone or guitar, and the rhythms range from jaunty New Orleans march beats, to hard-core hard-bop, to blank verse. Vandermark exemplifies the bubbling, boisterous music of Chicago's post-AACM avant-garde, captured on a slew of CDs recorded for tiny labels. His immense technique, emphasis on strong compositions, and stunning control of his horns (primarily tenor sax and bass clarinet) have spread his reputation far beyond his hometown. This album, featuring Mars Williams and their constant bassist, Kent Kessler, stands among the best of its idiom. If the Jazz

Messengers had played free jazz, they'd likely have sounded like this.

Open House

Most of the artists listed above have come of age (musically speaking) in the nineties. But this decade has also witnessed a rebirth of popularity for a number of veteran musicians, many of whom (like the aforementioned Joe Henderson) had already made their impact on fellow musicians and a few cognoscenti. The following albums gave audiences of the nineties new insights—in some cases, *first* insights—into seasoned artists who continue to thrive as we head toward the millennium. The list covers only a half dozen of these important figures, but if you look around, you'll have no trouble finding many more.

Pianist Kenny Barron joined Dizzy Gillespie's group at age nineteen, worked in long-term collaborations with Freddie Hubbard and Stan Getz, and from the mid-1970s on began earning praise as a player who could "do it all," thanks to a fearsome technical command and a style that gathers up most of the previous quarter century's keyboard innovations. You'll find him on several albums mentioned in earlier chapters; in the nineties, go for either *Other Places*, a sensational Brazilian-flavored sextet date, or the trio recording *Wanton Spirit*, the best single exposition of his warm touch and encyclopedic piano knowledge. (Both albums are on Verve.)

Charlie Haden earns praise for his dry, beautiful tone and his harmonic freedom, both of which made him essential to the music of Ornette Coleman (chapter 5) and Keith Jarrett ("Jazz in Transition: Free 2 Roam"). Since then, Haden has occasionally reconvened his Liberation Music Orchestra, guested on more than two hundred CDs, and reached the greatest popular success with his band Quartet West. Formed in the mid-1980s, the group might be considered neoclassicist, except that in this case, all the players returned to their *own* pasts (the music of the forties and fifties) instead of trying to relive somebody's else's. The 1992 album *Haunted Heart* (Verve) remains the best played and best known of their discs.

The patient, ultrarelaxed voice of pianist and singer Shirley Horn caught the ear of Miles Davis in the early 1960s—no surprise, given both artists' concern with leaving space in their music—and he served briefly as her champion. Several live LPs in the eighties reintroduced her fragile magic to jazz listeners. But not until the nineties was there really plenty of Horn, thanks to a series of albums that inventively packaged her breathy, knowing style. You'll get more of her piano work on the small-group masterpiece *You Won't Forget Me* (1991), but most people reach first for *Here's to Life* (1992), which features string orchestra and pure romance; Wynton Marsalis provides solos on both albums (both on Verve).

After his tenure with Miles Davis in the 1970s, saxist and educator Dave Liebman packed away his tenor and concentrated wholly on the soprano sax, becoming one of that instrument's three leading proponents (along with Steve Lacy and Wayne Shorter). In the group Quest, which he co-leads with pianist Richie Beirach (with whom he first recorded in the early seventies), Liebman reflects his experience playing both fusion and avant-garde jazz while remaining in a structured, mainstream format. *Natural Selection* (Evidence), though recorded in 1988, was re-released in the nineties and is still the place to start.

Sonny Rollins, among the half dozen greatest tenor men in jazz history, continued to reap accolades throughout the 1980s and 1990s—despite a radical revision of his style in the preceding decade, during which his solos stopped resembling fully formed novellas and began sounding more like well-orchestrated sound bites. Widely acclaimed as the nineties' greatest living jazzman, Rollins's best album of this period is *Here's to the People* (Milestone); meanwhile, the double-disc anthology *Silver City* (Milestone) samples his music of the previous quarter century, and thus makes a perfect endpiece for the Rollins section of your library.

The band that alto saxist Phil Woods established in 1974 has continued till this day, with only a few personnel changes—three fourths of the original group remain to quietly become one of the longest-running acts in jazz history. Eschewing the peer pressure of contemporaneous events, they have built a huge repertoire and an admirable musical intimacy (which allows them to perform primarily in all-acoustic settings, nary a microphone in sight). As you'd expect, this venerable quintet plays with unusual consistency as well; nonetheless, *An Affair to Remember* (Evidence), with trumpeter Brian Lynch in the front line, makes the best starter.

* * *

Geri Allen proved her prescience with the 1986 album that lends this chapter its title; *Open on All Sides/In the Middle* (Verve) combines horns with her electric and acoustic keyboards to anticipate the direction that Steve Coleman (who plays here) would soon explore. It's still a gem. In the nineties, she has stuck mainly to acoustic music and made several trio albums, including the wholly satisfying *In the Year of the Dragon* (JMT), featuring bassist Charlie Haden and drummer Paul Motian. Meanwhile, Allen's own openness to many idioms places her in great demand, and she has done some of her finest playing as a sidewoman, enhancing most of the many albums on which you'll find her name; you can start with either volume of Ornette Coleman's 1996 *Sound Museum* (Verve).

Tim Berne's latest music appears on his own label, Screwgun; if you enjoyed *Low Life*, you may want to splurge on *Bloodcount Unwound*, a devastating, three-CD document of concerts recorded by the quartet edition of his band in the spring of 1996. To hear how he got to the music he plays now, you'll want *Diminutive Mysteries* (JMT), a knowing tribute to his mentor, Julius Hemphill.

Although Mike Brecker has recorded a couple of other albums under his own name, you'll find some of his strongest work elsewhere, most notably pianist McCoy Tyner's *Infinity* and pianist Horace Silver's *Hardbop Grandpop*, which reunites Brecker with his former (c. 1973) boss. (Both albums are on Impulse/GRP.)

The quintet assembled by Don Byron in the mid-nineties—employing several veterans of Steve Coleman's M-Base collective—shines on an album recorded at the Knitting Factory, *No-Vibe Zone*; for his historically accurate rendering of Catskills schmaltz and humor, *Don Byron Plays the Music of Mickey Katz* is the album referenced above. (Both on Elektra/Nonesuch.)

Byron's flexibility, and the paucity of new-music clarinetists, has made him a favorite of other musicians: he stands out on excellent albums by two modern drummers, each of whom will reward your attention. Byron's clarinet and bass clarinet lead the way on *Ornettology* by Ralph Peterson, featuring the quartet he calls the Fo'tet; a later album, *The Fo'tet Plays Monk*, does not feature Byron but does offer a marvelously lucid interpretation of the iconoclastic composer's work. (Both albums are on Blue Note.)

Another drummer, Bobby Previte, writes some of the most cohesive and original tunes in modern jazz, and his albums glisten with the virtuosity he assembles to play them. Byron appears on the scintillating *Weather Clear, Tract Fast* (Enja). An earlier masterpiece by Previte, *Pushing the Envelope* (Gramavision), was released in 1987, but it sounds as up-to-date as many of the albums in this chapter.

The Tao of Mad Phat—Fringe Zones (Novus) by Steve Coleman's Five Elements is the in-concert disc mentioned above: Coleman's full-blown solos spearhead the band, here augmented by special guests (including trumpeter Roy Hargrove). For another Five Elements album that incorporates a greater degree of mainstream jazz—without losing its M-Base foundation—try the captivating *Def Trance Beat (Modalities of Rhythm)* (Novus), arguably the best recording by this band.

Coleman's stature as a deeply committed improviser continues to grow, but the evidence was available years ago, as you can hear on several albums led by Dave Holland: *Seeds of Time* (see chapter 8); *Triplicate,* from 1988; and *Extensions,* from 1990 (all on ECM).

Meanwhile, the British saxist Courtney Pine infuses hip-hop into his solid jazz background on *Modern Day Jazz Stories* (Verve): John Coltrane meets LL Cool J. It poses a literate new-beat alternative to straight-ahead jazz, with rap beats, record-scratches, and rhythmically recurring samples, but mixes them *behind* his darkly vibrant tenor solos—thus recasting his jazz message for the nineties without drowning it out altogether.

As with Geri Allen and Don Byron, you'll find Dave Douglas performing on many other people's albums in the nineties. But he's still found time to record a significant array of his own music. *The Tiny Bell Trio* (Songlines), the debut album by his group of the same name, uses European folk music, movie themes, and Douglas's own compositions as fodder for concise and often witty improvisations; the excellent *Stargazer* (Arabesque) concentrates on the songs of Wayne Shorter. In each case, Douglas's sensational trumpetry transmogrifies the material.

* * *

At century's end, you can't place too high a premium on the clever reworking of past materials; the fact that the Either/ Orchestra also infuses a huge dose of its own inventiveness puts it over the top. With its irresistible musical humor, this ten-piece band in Boston both celebrates and subtly sabotages the big band tradition. Either *The Brunt* or *The Calculus of Pleasure* (both on Accurate) get my vote; in fact, they both do.

Another band high on irony is the Jazz Passengers, a wild and wooly septet that also employs plenty of flat-out satire; their combination of these qualities with colorful and impressive musicianship suggests that Frank Zappa lives after all. If you can find their terrific 1990 disc *Implement Yourself* (New World/Countercurrents), grab it. In addition, their 1997 disc *Individually Twisted* (32 Records) gains in irrealism from the presence of rock vocalists Elvis Costello and that old Blondie, Debbie Harry.

Bill Frisell's mid-eighties *Rambler* (ECM) combines elements of fusion, the new cool, and the country and western strains that would later dominate his music. His later albums have headed off in various and quirky directions; they include music inspired by the films of Buster Keaton; music meant to accompany the "Far Side" cartoons of Gary Larson; and the summation of his country and western intrigue (*Nashville*). Quite possibly the best of his late-nineties discs, the 1998 *Gone, Just Like a Train* unveils a striking new trio starring the well-traveled rock drummer Jim Keltner. These discs are on Nonesuch.

Frisell's peripatetic career has followed a number of different threads. His playing forms the distinctive link in several unusual bands led by drummer Paul Motian over the years: go for *Monk in Motian* (with saxist Dewey Redman) and *On Broadway, Vol. 1* or *Vol. 3* (featuring Joe Lovano), both on JMT. Frisell joins John Scofield as the front line in the two-guitar quartet Bass Desires, led by bassist Marc Johnson, best heard on *Bass Desires* (ECM). One of the most valued members of the downtown Manhattan scene, Frisell has appeared as sideman on numerous albums by a long list of leaders, his presence almost always signifying music of interest. But he has had an especially sympathetic and long-lasting relationship with drummer Joey Baron, as heard on *Down Home* (Intuition).

* * *

Baron, one of the most versatile and yet distinctive percussionists in modern music, also leads the oddly instrumented trio called Baron Down, with trombonist Steve Swell and the exciting and provocative saxist Ellery Eskelin; start with *Raised Pleasure Dot* (New World/Countercurrents).

Joe Henderson's best-selling, Grammy-winning breakthrough album, 1992's *Lush Life*, explored the repertoire of Billy Strayhorn in a variety of settings, from duo to quintet, and deserved every bit of the praise heaped upon it; on his 1995 *Double Rainbow*, he applied the same magic to the music of the recently departed Brazilian songwriter Antonio Carlos Jobim. Both on Verve, they spell out his popularity with cognoscenti and casual fans alike.

For more of Henderson's fellow tenor titan Joe Lovano, go to *Quartets: Live at The Village Vanguard*, a double disc documenting two separate Lovano-led foursomes; the first features a conventional rhythm section with Mulgrew Miller on piano, while the second pairs Lovano's saxes with the careful constructions of Tom Harrell's trumpet. His most straight-ahead playing comes on *Tenor Legacy*, co-starring Joshua Redman. Lovano has also undertaken several large-scale projects, with mixed results; the best is certainly *Rush Hour*, with compositions and arrangements by the esteemed conductor, music analyst, and writer Gunther Schuller. They're all on Blue Note.

Assembling various components of the largely undefined phenomenon called acid jazz, the trio of Medeski, Martin & Wood attained a remarkable following in the mid-nineties—some of it enhanced by their work as the opening act for the Grateful Dead! Proponents find mystery and depth in their subtle manipulations of repeated riffs and rhythms, à la the Dead's famous "space jams"; I'm not convinced, but you can make up your own mind with *It's a Jungle in Here* (Gramavision). They serve as guitarist John Scofield's rhythm section on his 1998 release *A Go Go* (Verve), and certainly benefit from the collaboration.

The still-young Danilo Perez has only a handful of albums under his own name; in addition to *The Journey* (above), go for the inventive *PanaMonk* (Novus), which sets several Monk compositions to inventive and understated Latin rhythms.

Meanwhile, David Sanchez—Perez's saxophone-playing alter-ego—has made two albums that tread much the same turf. Go for *Sketches of Dreams* (Columbia), which stars Perez, drummer Leon Parker, and trumpeter Roy Hargrove in a remarkably well blended mix of U.S. jazz with Caribbean rhythms and sensibilities.

John Scofield's distinctive guitar work has appeared in a variety of contexts this decade—most of them under his own name. He teams up in a two-guitar quartet with Bill Frisell on *Grace Under Pressure* and takes a similar tack with Pat Metheny on *I Can See Your House from Here*, highly recommended as a "summit meeting" between the era's primary guitar influences. *Groove Elation* places Sco's guitar in the context of horns, and the spunky arrangements bring out different facets of his playing. But if you're only buying one more album by Scofield, leap for *Hand Jive*. It teams him with the late saxist Eddie Harris (chapter 6)—who invented the shuffle-funk rhythm so expertly exploited by the guitarist—and will keep you smiling throughout the disc. (They're all on Blue Note.)

Metheny's own band remained one of the most popular groups in jazz, and its continued musical evolution made it also one of the more musically valid groups performing. *Quartet* (Geffen) uses a lean and relatively conventional format, while the follow-up *Imaginary Day* (Warner Bros.) builds on that platform by introducing hints of industrial-rock music in unexpected ways.

Besides Frisell, Metheny, and Scofield, the most striking guitarist of the nineties is Charlie Hunter. Hunter's bands do not have a bassist; they don't need one. Playing a unique eight-string electric guitar, Hunter uses the extra strings to play his own bass lines, even as he picks his improvised solos within the guitar's usual range. More than just a parlor trick, this technique allows Hunter to link his bass and melody lines the way an organist might; and in fact, some of his guitar effects recreate colors more commonly heard from the Hammond B-3. *Bing, Bing, Bing!* (Blue Note) offers by far the best introduction to his tough funk-filled music.

The organ in general staged a remarkable resurgence in the music of the nineties. This didn't only occur in the hands of no-nonsense newcomers like Larry Goldings (*Light Blue*, on Minor Music) and Dan Wall (who plays in guitarist John Abercrombie's trio on *Tactics*, on ECM). The organ renaissance also revived the fortunes of such earlier practitioners as Lonnie Smith, whose *Afro Blue* (MusicMasters) gives the organ treatment to songs by John Coltrane; and it turned the spotlight on the lesser-known veteran Jeff Palmer, whose *Ease On* (Audioquest) does anything but, in its high-powered reexamination of the jazz-organ formulas.

To hear more of Matthew Shipp and William Parker, you can head for the 1990 trio date *Circular Temple* (Infinite Zero)—which comprises the four-movement title track—or jump ahead to Shipp's 1998 release *The Multiplication Table* (Hat Art), which features three standards among its eight tracks. Other picks include Shipp's quartet date *Critical Mass* (213CD), which features violin, and his duo date *Thesis* (Hat Art) with guitarist Joe Morris, another musician who has attracted attention outside the usual jazz circles.

Morris returns the favor on *Elsewhere* (Homestead), which features Morris with Shipp's regular trio, with galvanizing results. Morris displays a clean, unburdened sound, making his occasional use of extended technique and unusual textural effects all the more effective—his 1993 trio date *Symbolic Gesture* (Soul Note) is your ticket here—and he can also achieve the sort of high-energy incantation found in Shipp's music, as on his 1997 trio album, *Antennae* (AUM Fidelity).

Meanwhile, Shipp appears at his wildest and wooliest in the no-holds-barred quartet led by saxist David S. Ware, whose relentless "energy playing" has captivated some fans of later punk and thrash rock. Not for everyone's tastes, Ware's group is heard to best advantage on *Flight of i* (DIW) and *Cryptology* (Homestead).

In Chicago, the energetic and resourceful Ken Vandermark performs in a variety of groupings, most of which record for tiny labels. Several appear on Okkadisc (try the World Wide Web), including albums by the DKV Trio, named for Vandermark and his bandmates, bassist Kent Kessler and the jazz and world-music percussion master Hamid Drake; *DKV Live* pulls no punches. Easier to find, and if anything even more rewarding, is Vandermark's work with the NRG Ensemble, which he joined as the second saxophonist after the death of the band's founder, Hal Russell (see chapter 5). This band also stars fellow saxist Mars Williams, who until 1998 was a regular member of Vandermark's own band (above); to best hear their surprisingly tuneful take on avant-garde intensity, go for *This Is My House* (Delmark) or *Bejazzo Gets a Facelift* (Atavistic).

While such saxophonists as Michael Brecker and his followers would seem to have cornered the market on Coltrane, it's worth seeking out Walt Weiskopf, a tenor man whose debt to Trane is matched by his depth of knowledge. Weiskopf long ago escaped Coltrane's shadow to place his own stamp on punishing rhythms and bustling improvisations, as you'll hear on the Dutch import albums *Simplicity* and *A World Away*, the latter of which takes a new view of the sixties organ/guitar/saxophone lineup. They're both on Criss Cross, and worth the search.

8 Bold Souls, the Chicago band led by saxist Ed Wilkerson, scores again on the album *Ant Farm* (Arabesque). Another musician known for his work with the AACM, Henry Threadgill (see chapter 5), has produced several albums of quite complicated music. Most of those currently available showcase his typically idiosyncratic view of jazz fusion, a band called Very Very Circus (which features two tubas), best heard on *Carry the Day*. In the late nineties Threadgill moved to India and began using his new surroundings to color his music in unexpected ways. Book passage with *Makin' a Move*. (Both Threadgill CDs are on Columbia.)

Cassandra Wilson's most mainstream-oriented album, *Blue Skies* (Verve), came out in 1988; nonetheless, this collection of standards remains one of Wilson's best, and in fact one of the most satisfying albums recorded by *any* singer in the last twenty years. Of her later albums, *After the Beginning Again* (JMT) recaps her experience with electric music. The follow-up to *Blue Light* (above) was *New Moon Daughter* (Blue Note), highly recommended for its expanded instrumental textures and several very memorable songs written by Wilson.

Other vocalists of note include the Chicago pianist Patricia Barber, who like Wilson offers up disturbing lyrics in deceptively fragile packages. Barber offsets her eerily cool singing with expansive, often explosive keyboard improvisations: both *Distortion of Love* (Antilles) and the innovative *Café Blue* (Premonition)—which includes moody masterpieces written by Barber and one piece that uses words by poet Maya Angelou—reach beyond jazz and score at will.

Another fine singer, though without the multilayered complexity that marks Wilson and Barber, is Karrin Allyson. In some ways, her first album, *I Didn't Know About You*, remains her best, but the later *Collage* has a smoother, more consistent flow. They're both on Concord.

And the Canadian-born pianist/vocalist Diana Krall became one of the biggest sensations of the late nineties thanks to *All for You*—an album on which she re-created both the repertoire and the instrumentation (piano, bass, guitar) of the famous Nat "King" Cole Trio (see chapter 2)—and a follow-up album devoted to love songs and Hollywood glamour, *Love Scenes* (both on Impulse/GRP).

The eclecticism of saxist and composer John Zorn runs rampant through his discography—and also through his individual albums, many of which cram twenty or more short compositions into a single CD, and all of which reflect his music-junkie's passion for far-flung idioms. Zorn samples musical styles and spits them back with the about-face velocity found in the cartoon soundtracks that he counts as a major influence. For the best example of this, try *Naked City* (Elektra/Musician), featuring his band of the same name; but jazz is only one of a dozen items on their menu. For music that employs more of a jazz perspective, Zorn's 1989 album *Spy vs. Spy* (Elektra/Nonesuch)—which remakes the compositions of Ornette Coleman using rapid-fire rock rhythms—features some of the musicians mentioned above and reflects Ornette's totemic impact on revolutionaries a generation younger than himself.

Zorn's favored project of the late nineties is Masada, which sounds like it should play at Ornette Coleman's bar mitzvah: the band mimics the instrumentation of Ornette's quartets of the sixties (with Zorn's piquant alto and Dave Douglas's trumpet in front of bass and drums) but uses themes derived from klezmer and Jewish music to catapult the solos. The band's consistency makes its albums almost interchangeable, but *Beit* and *Het* (both on DIW) will start you off.

Masada is not alone: Zorn and a few others have spear-headed one of the least expected fusions of jazz and world music, "radical Jewish music," operating under the rubric of JAM (Jewish Alternative Movement). A good introductory blast comes from The Klezmatics on their album *Jews with Horns* (Xenophile), while a couple of discs on Zorn's own Tzadik label have a stronger edge and confirm the avant-garde underpinnings of JAM: David Krakauer's *Klezmer Madness!* and the 1998 album *Search for the Golden Dreydl* by the group Naftule's Dream. You can get your feet wet with the compilation album *Guide for the Perplexed* (Knitting Factory Works), which features several of these artists.

To get a taste of the various hard-hitting bands that helped make the Knitting Factory internationally famous as a source of new New York music, try *Live at the Knitting Factory, Vol. 3* (Knitting Factory Works), which includes tracks by Don Byron, the band No Safety, pianist Marilyn Crispell (chapter 5), and guitarist Brandon Ross, best known for his work in Cassandra Wilson's band.

chapter ten

An Essential Jazz Collection

Drawn from the albums recommended throughout the *Playboy Guide*, here are the fifty CDs most essential to building an introductory jazz collection—the idea being that the purchase of one each week, well within the budget of most listeners, will give you a basic library within a year. Those readers who had even a passing interest in jazz before buying this book will probably own some of these already. In that case, I advise you to substitute a recording from the same chapter as the one owned, based on the descriptions found there and, of course, on your own taste.

I have tried to limit this list to single-CD releases, although you'll find a few multiple-disc sets included. But if you have slightly deeper pockets, you'd do well to refer back to earlier chapters and, whenever possible, pop for some of the recommended two- and three-disc sets, since they usually cover a broader range of these artists' work.

I have *not* tried to make this a list of my favorite albums of all time, although several of those do appear here. Nor have I aimed for a list of the fifty best albums in jazz history. Lists like that would almost certainly emphasize one style or period over another. The golden age of the 1950s and 1960s, for instance, yielded enough classics alone to dominate nearly half of such a list. But this chapter is designed to provide a balanced overview: a useful and informative survey of a century's worth of jazz.

Which, of course, is impossible—not to mention fraught with peril. It hardly needs saying that the number of important, edifying, and just plain delightful albums *not* included here would stagger a strong man. I guarantee that no one who considers himself a jazz fan will read through this list without exclaiming, "How could he leave *that* out?" But that sentiment, while valid, misses the point. These albums will give you a foundation for understanding the evolution of jazz—a place from which to build further. (And it's worth noting that many essential artists whom I have not named—such as Lester Young, Dizzy Gillespie, and McCoy Tyner—do in fact play prominent roles on albums listed below.)

You might choose to purchase them systematically and in roughly chronological order—the order in which I have listed them—in which case you will re-create jazz history even as you learn it. Or you might choose to grab albums from whatever turns out to be your favorite era or style or artist, which probably comes closer to the way most of us delve into any subject that interests us. Nonetheless, I hope you will refer back to earlier chapters and follow the links to other albums and other artists and explore accordingly.

If you do that, this last chapter of the *Playboy Guide* can serve as the ultimate, stripped-down guide—not only to jazz, but also to the body of the book. It points you in the right direction. But don't miss the side trips, because in jazz, *all* the fun is getting there.

1. Louis Armstrong, *Volume IV, Louis Armstrong and Earl Hines* (Columbia/Legacy)
2. Bix Beiderbecke, *Vol. 1: Singin' the Blues* (Columbia/Legacy)
3. Jelly Roll Morton, *Birth of the Hot* (Bluebird)
4. Fats Waller, *Piano Solos: Turn On the Heat* (Bluebird)
5. Coleman Hawkins, *A Retrospective 1929–1963* (Bluebird)
6. Benny Goodman, *Sing, Sing, Sing* (Bluebird)
7. Count Basie, *The Essential Count Basie, Volume 1* (Columbia/Legacy)
8. Billie Holiday *The Quintessential Holiday, Volume Five* (Columbia/Legacy)
9. Duke Ellington, *The Blanton-Webster Band* (Bluebird)
10. Woody Herman, *The Thundering Herds 1945–1947* (Columbia/Legacy)
11. Charlie Parker, *Yardbird Suite: The Ultimate Charlie Parker Collection* (Rhino)
12. Bud Powell, *The Best of Bud Powell on Verve* (Verve)
13. Thelonious Monk, *Genius of Modern Music, vol. 1* (Blue Note)

14. Ella Fitzgerald, *Ella at the Opera House* (Verve)
15. Miles Davis, *Birth of the Cool* (Capitol Jazz)
16. Chet Baker and Art Pepper, *The Route* (Blue Note)
17. Clifford Brown and Max Roach, *Alone Together* (Verve)
18. Sonny Rollins, *Saxophone Colossus* (Fantasy/OJC)
19. Art Blakey & the Jazz Messengers, *The Big Beat* (Blue Note)
20. Sarah Vaughan, *Swingin' Easy* (Verve)
21. Charles Mingus, *Thirteen Pictures* (Rhino)
22. Dave Brubeck, *Time Out* (Columbia/Legacy)
23. Miles Davis, *Kind of Blue* (Columbia/Legacy)
24. John Coltrane, *Giant Steps* (Atlantic)
25. Bill Evans, *Sunday at the Village Vanguard* (Fantasy/OJC)
26. Stan Getz, *Getz/Jobim* (Verve)
27. Ornette Coleman, *Free Jazz* (Atlantic)
28. Cecil Taylor, *Silent Tongues* (Freedom)
29. John Coltrane, *A Love Supreme* (Impulse)
30. Horace Silver, *The Best of Horace Silver Volume Two* (Blue Note)
31. Herbie Hancock, *Maiden Voyage* (Blue Note)
32. Betty Carter, *The Betty Carter Album* (Verve)
33. Art Ensemble of Chicago, *Full Force* (ECM)
34. Charles Lloyd, *Forest Flower/Soundtrack* (Rhino)
35. Miles Davis, *Bitches Brew* (Columbia/Legacy)
36. Mahavishnu Orchestra, *Inner Mounting Flame* (Columbia/Legacy)
37. Weather Report, *Mysterious Traveler* (Columbia/Legacy)
38. Gary Burton & Chick Corea, *Crystal Silence* (ECM)
39. Keith Jarrett, *Köln Concert* (ECM)
40. Wayne Shorter, *Native Dancer* (Columbia/Legacy)
41. Pat Metheny Group, *Still Life (Talking)* (Geffen)
42. Wynton Marsalis, *J Mood* (Columbia)
43. Branford Marsalis, *Bloomington* (Columbia)
44. Dave Holland, *Seeds of Time* (ECM)
45. Roy Hargrove, *The Vibe* (Novus)
46. John Scofield, *Meant to Be* (Blue Note)
47. Bill Frisell, *Where in the World?* (Elektra Musician)
48. Cassandra Wilson, *Blue Light 'Til Dawn* (Blue Note)
49. Danilo Perez, *The Journey* (Novus)
50. Myra Melford, *The Same River, Twice* (Gramavision)

Index

Abercrombie, John, 197, 242, 280

Abou-Khalil, Rabih, 223, 224–25

Abrams, Muhal Richard, 142–45, 159, 170

Acuna, Alex, 192

Adams, George, 105, 167, 186

Adderley, Julian "Cannonball," xi, 83, 86, 88–89, 96, 117, 121, 126, 206, 231, 252

Adderley, Nat, 88, 89

Aebi, Irene, 154

Akiyoshi, Toshiko, 227

Albany, Joe, 56

Alexander, Eric, 236–37

Ali, Rashied, 161, 162

Allen, Geri, 256n, 261, 275, 276

Allen, Henry "Red," 25

Allyson, Karrin, 235, 282

Ammons, Gene, 73, 76, 124

Anderson, Fred, 146, 153, 272

Anderson, Ray, 148

Anderson, Wessel, 247

Arlen, Harold, 129

Armstrong, Louis, xiii, xiv, 5–13, 16–18, 21–25, 28–29, 34, 37, 62, 65, 86–87, 107, 120, 139, 141n, 246, 249

Art Ensemble of Chicago, 143, 146–47, 148, 153, 159, 272

Association for the Advancement of Creative Musicians (AACM), 142–48, 153, 157, 159–60, 164–65, 169, 228, 271

Auld, Georgie, 53

Ayler, Albert, 139, 141, 147, 151, 154, 159, 167, 272

Bacharach, Burt, 172

Badrena, Manolo, 192

Bailey, Derek, 141

Baker, Chet, 82–83, 89–90, 108–10, 118, 242

Barber, Patricia, 281

Barbieri, Gato, 161, 207, 211–12

Barefield, Eddie, 25

Barker, Thurman, 148, 153

Barnet, Charlie, 45

Baron, Joey, 257, 278

Barron, Kenny, 273

Basie, Count, 24–25, 30–34, 43–45, 47, 50, 52, 55, 58, 59, 69, 79, 87, 103

Batiste, Alvin, 247

Bauza, Mario, 61, 225

Beatles, 177, 218

Bechet, Sidney, 4, 7, 10–11

Beiderbecke, Bix, 7, 11–12, 18, 84

Beirach, Richie, 274

Belgrave, Marcus, 261

Bellson, Louis, 49

Bennink, Han, 158

Benson, George, 128, 177

Berg, Bob, 263

Berlin, Irving, 129, 130

Berne, Tim, 257, 261–62, 275

Bernstein, Leonard, 124

Bernstein, Peter, 236

Berigan, Bunny, 34, 45

Bey, Andy, 183

Bigard, Barney, 48

Big Black, 229

Black Artists Group (BAG), 142, 157

Blackwell, Ed, 150, 268

Blake, Eubie, 19

Blake, Michael, 228

Blakey, Art, 57, 66, 77, 80, 90–91, 101, 104, 107, 113–15, 117, 119, 121, 232–35, 237–38, 240, 247, 251, 252

Blanchard, Terence, 233, 238–39, 251

Blanton, Jimmy, 35

Bley, Carla, 183, 197, 207

Bley, Paul, 160

Bloom, Jane Ira, 201

Bluiett, Hamiett, 157, 164

Blythe, Arthur, 164

Bobo, Willie, 205

Bolden, Buddy, 4

Bonfa, Luiz, 206

Bowie, Lester, 143, 159, 234

Brackeen, JoAnne, 255

Braden, Don, 253

Braxton, Anthony, 143, 147–49, 159–60, 169, 242

Brecker, Michael, 197, 199, 258, 263, 275, 281

Brecker, Randy, 197, 248, 258, 263

Breuker, Willem, 158

Bridgewater, Dee Dee, 183

Brimfield, Billy, 146, 153

Brookmeyer, Bob, 83, 100, 108, 126, 127

Brötzmann, Peter, 158

Brown, Ari, 165

Brown, Clifford, 91–92, 107, 119, 128, 226

Brown, Ray, 232, 252

Brubeck, Dave, 82, 85–87, 92–93, 119–20, 217

B Sharp Jazz Quartet, 262–63

Buarque de Hollander, Heloisa, 215
Bullock, Hiram, 186
Burns, Ralph, 54, 68
Burrell, Dave, 164
Burrell, Kenny, 66, 88, 115, 120, 121, 128
Burton, Gary, 122, 178–79, 181–84, 189, 192–93, 197, 228, 269
Byard, Jaki, 132
Byas, Don, 38, 52, 53, 55
Byrd, Charlie, 205, 206
Byrd, Donald, 88, 115, 119, 120
Byron, Don, 259, 263–64, 275–76, 283

Cachao (Israel Lopez), 225
Calloway, Cab, 45, 46, 58
Campbell, John, 255
Carnegie Hall Jazz Band, 235, 239
Carney, Harry, 47
Carter, Benny, 22, 25, 34, 46–47, 49, 235
Carter, Betty, 167–68, 247, 252, 272
Carter, James, 254
Carter, Ron, 168, 170, 223, 246
Catlett, Big Sid, 10
Chaloff, Serge, 54
Chambers, Paul, 93, 96
Cheatham, Doc, 235, 253
Cherry, Don, 138–39, 150–51, 161, 207, 225–26

Chestnut, Cyrus, 233, 252
Christensen, Jon, 194
Christian, Charlie, 52–53, 58
Christian, Jodie, 169
Christy, June, 94, 102
Clark, Charles, 153
Clark, Sonny, 84, 114
Clarke, Kenny, 57, 58, 62, 76, 117
Clarke, Stanley, 183–84
Clayton, Buck, 32
Cobham, Billy, 189
Cohn, Al, 53, 54, 109, 124
Cole, Nat "King," 33, 44, 55, 102, 282
Coleman, George, 170
Coleman, Ornette, 73, 127, 131–33, 137–42, 146–52, 155, 160–61, 164, 166, 170–71, 188, 196, 199, 207, 225, 230, 246, 258, 261–62, 268, 270, 273, 275, 282
Coleman Steve, 242, 259–61, 264–65, 271, 275–76
Coltrane, John, xi, xiii, 46, 66–70, 76–77, 82, 87, 93–94, 96, 100–1, 112, 116–17, 120–21, 123, 127–28, 131, 133, 141, 151–53, 154, 161–62, 166–67, 172–73, 174–75, 194, 204–05, 209, 218, 221, 228, 231, 239, 244, 249, 251, 254, 263, 268, 272, 276, 280, 281
Condon, Eddie, 18
Connor, Chris, 94–95, 102

Cooper, Bob, 84, 104
Corea, Chick, 175, 178,
    180–81, 183–85, 192–94,
    197–98, 202, 205, 210–11,
    226, 253
Coryell, Larry, 175, 179, 182,
    184
Costello, Elvis, 277
Crispell, Marilyn, 160, 283
Criss, Sonny, 79
Crosby, Bing, 17
Curson, Ted, 105
Cyrille, Andrew, 156

Dalto, Jorge, 221
Dameron, Tadd, 55, 71, 109
Danielsson, Palle, 194
Davis, Eddie "Lockjaw," 124
Davis, Jesse, 231, 249, 251
Davis, Miles, xi, xiii, 7, 8,
    56–58, 64, 73, 79–80, 82–83,
    85–87, 89, 93, 95–97, 101–2,
    108–10, 114–15, 117–18,
    120–21, 125, 133, 137, 141,
    166, 168–70, 174, 178–81,
    183, 185–87, 188–90, 198,
    201, 206, 210–11, 231, 234,
    240, 242, 246, 249, 253,
    257–58, 265, 267, 269, 274
Dawkins, Ernest, 165
DeFranco, Buddy, 49
DeJohnette, Jack, 173, 243, 250
Deppe, Lois, 13
Desmond, Paul, 86, 92–93,
    127, 148

DiMeola, Al, 184
Dixon, Bill, 156
DKV Trio, 280
Dodds, Baby, 4, 15
Dodds, Johnny, 4, 8, 15
Dolphy, Eric, 105, 115, 131–33,
    139, 150–51
Dørge, Pierre, 212–13, 226
Dorham, Kenny, 116
Dorsey, Tommy, 30, 31, 33–34,
    48
Douglas, Dave, 259, 265, 268,
    276, 282
Drake, Hamid, 280
Drew, Kenny, Jr., 255
D'Rivera, Paquito, 213–14,
    217, 222, 226
Duke, George, 225
Dyani, Johnny, 212, 226

Eager, Allen, 109
Eckstine, Billy, 74, 80, 130,
    243
Edison, Harry "Sweets," 32,
    44
Eicher, Manfred, 181
8 Bold Souls, 271, 281
Eldridge, Roy, 9, 19, 25, 34, 48,
    107
Elling, Kurt, 235, 265–66
Ellington, Duke, xi, 7, 12–14,
    18–20, 24, 28–29, 31, 34–37,
    45–48, 50, 59, 65, 69, 76, 87,
    104, 130, 135, 153, 155, 163,
    206–7, 213, 216, 219, 224,

233, 243, 246, 248–49, 255, 267, 271
El'Zabar, Kahil, 143, 164–65
Ervin, Booker, 105, 229
Eskelin, Ellery, 278
Essiet, Essiet, 238
Eubanks, Kevin, 164
Evans, Bill (piano), xiv, 82, 96–99, 115, 121–23, 125, 192–93, 242, 269
Evans, Bill (saxophone), 201
Evans, Gil, xiii, 56, 85–86, 95, 97, 121, 186, 198, 206
Evans, Herschel, 32
Ewart, Douglas, 143

Faddis, Jon, 223, 239
Farmer, Art, 103, 108, 114
Farrell, Joe, 184
Favors, Malachi, 143, 159, 165
Feldman, Mark, 265
Ferguson, Maynard, 102, 104
Few, Bobby, 154
Fitzgerald, Ella, xiii, 17, 31, 37, 38, 65, 74, 75, 79, 129–30, 168, 235
Flanagan, Tommy, 88, 240
Forrest, Helen, 41
Fortune, Sonny, 175, 224
Foster, Al, 185, 267
Foster, Frank, 33
Fountain, Eli, 261
Franzetti, Carlos, 214
Freeman, Bud, 6, 18

Freeman, Chico, 143
Freeman, Russ, 89, 118
Freeman, Von, 169
Frisell, Bill, 257, 266–67, 277–78
Fuller, Curtis, 90, 93, 174

Ganelin, Vyacheslav, 158
Garbarek, Jan, 181, 194, 214–15
Garland, Hank, 179
Garland, Red, 96
Garner, Erroll, 64, 87–88, 90, 99, 122, 204
Garrett, Kenny, 231, 239–40, 248, 251, 253, 261
Garrison, Jimmy, 151
Gaslini, Giorgio, 158
Gentry, Bobby, 99
Gershwin, George, 130, 250
Getz, Stan, xiii, 54, 66, 68, 75, 87, 99–100, 122–23, 179, 182–83, 193, 202, 205–6, 215, 222, 235, 273
Gilberto, Astrud, 206
Gilberto, Joao, 206, 215
Gillespie, Dizzy, 34, 51, 53, 55–58, 61–68, 71, 74–78, 80, 81, 84, 106–7, 110, 124, 168, 174, 203–5, 210, 212–13, 221–22, 224–26, 235, 243, 269, 273
Gilmore, John, 123
Gismonti, Egberto, 216, 226–27

Giuffre, Jimmy, 54
Goldings, Larry, 250, 280
Golson, Benny, 119
Gomez, Eddie, 98, 122
Gonsalves, Paul, 36
Gonzalez, Andy, 225
Gonzalez, Ray, 221
Goodman, Benny, 6, 7, 20, 22, 25–28, 30–32, 37–38, 40–41, 45, 47–48, 53, 65, 87, 239
Goodman, Jerry, 189
Gordon, Dexter, xii, 44, 67–68, 74, 76, 80, 85, 100–1, 115, 123, 183, 236, 244, 266
Gordon, Wycliffe, 247
Graham, Herb, Jr., 262
Granelli, Jerry, 201
Granz, Norman, 49, 64
Grappelli, Stephane, 41, 49, 65
Gray, Glen, 21, 23
Gray, Wardell, 67, 74
Green, Benny, 235, 240–41, 252
Green, Grant, 116, 123, 128
Griffin, Johnny, 69–70, 76, 77, 119, 123, 124
Grillo, Francisco (Machito), 203, 212
Guaraldi, Vince, 205
Gunn, Russell, 252
Gurtu, Trilok, 199
Gysin, Brion, 162

Haden, Charlie, 139, 150–51, 171, 199, 207, 255, 258, 273–75

Hall, Jim, 112, 122
Hammer, Jan, 189
Hampton, Lionel, 28, 38, 45, 47–48, 52, 69, 113
Hancock, Herbie, xi, 101, 114–15, 117, 126, 166, 168–70, 175, 180, 183, 187, 197–98, 205, 223, 247, 253
Hanna, (Sir) Roland, 49, 105, 255
Hargrove, Roy, 233, 241, 251–52, 276, 279
Harper, Billy, 223, 224, 229
Harper, Philip, 232
Harper, Winard, 232
Harrell, Tom, 241–42, 253, 278
Harris, Barry, 88
Harris, Benny, 52
Harris, Bill, 54
Harris, Eddie, 168–69, 176n, 187–88, 198–99, 229, 279
Harris, Gene, 255
Harrison, Donald, 238–39, 251
Harry, Debbie, 277
Hart, Antonio, 241, 251–52
Hart, John, 250
Hart, Lorenz, 129, 130
Hawkins, Coleman, 19, 22, 25, 34, 38–39, 43, 45, 47–48, 50–54, 59, 65, 67, 71, 79, 128, 152
Haynes, Roy, 161, 197, 253
Heath, Jimmy, 169
Hefti, Neal, 32, 54
Hemphill, Julius, 157, 163–64, 262, 275

Henderson, Eddie, 248
Henderson, Fletcher, 20–25, 29–30, 34, 38, 43
Henderson, Joe, 107, 116–17, 170, 225, 248, 267, 268, 273, 278
Hendricks, Jon, 57n, 103, 247
Hendrix, Jimi, 180, 186, 192
Herman, Woody, 54, 56, 68–69, 75, 99, 109, 124, 221
Herring, Vincent, 252
Higgins, Billy, 139, 150, 199, 255
Hill, Andrew, 170
Hill, Teddy, 58
Hines, Earl "Fatha," 8–10, 13–14, 16–21, 23, 25, 30, 33, 45, 65, 99
Ho, Fred, 218, 227
Hobgood, Laurence, 266
Hodes, Art, 28
Hodges, Johnny, 35, 47, 48
Holiday, Billie, 17, 31, 34, 39–41, 43, 48–49, 65, 79, 89, 118, 235, 251
Holland, Dave, 236, 242, 265, 267, 276
Hollyday, Chris, 231
Holman, Bill, 102
Holmes, Richard "Groove," 128
Hooker, John Lee, 254
Hopkins, Fred, 145
Horiuchi, Glenn, 228
Horn, Paul, 215–16, 226

Horn, Shirley, 273
Hubbard, Freddie, xii, 90, 100–1, 115, 117, 124, 133, 150–51, 170, 196–97, 235, 240–41, 273
Humes, Helen, 55
Hunter, Charlie, 279
Hurst, Robert, 245, 261
Hutcherson, Bobby, 117, 123, 126, 133, 170

Ibrahim, Abdullah, 216–17, 227
Irakere, 213, 217

Jackson, Javon, 238
Jackson, Milt, 66, 69, 76, 106, 121
Jackson, Ronald Shannon, 163, 188, 262
Jamal, Ahmad, 101–2
James, Harry, 47
Jang, Jon, 217–18, 227
Jarman, Joseph, 143, 153, 159, 169
Jarrett, Keith, 90, 171, 173, 175, 181, 194–95, 199, 243, 254, 268–69, 273
Jazz Messengers, 90–91, 107, 113, 119, 126, 174, 198, 220, 232–33, 235, 237–38, 242, 251–52
Jefferson, Eddie, 79–80, 266
Jeffries, Alan, 55

Jenkins, Leroy, 143, 144
Jewish Alternative Movement (JAM), 283
Jobim, Antonio Carlos, 206, 215, 278
Johnson, Budd, 223
Johnson, Bunk, 4
Johnson, James P., 14–15, 19
Johnson, Marc, 277
Jones, Elvin, 112, 151, 161, 249
Jones, Jo, 32, 58, 59
Jones, Philly Joe, 93, 96
Jones, Quincy, 198
Jones, Thad, 32, 124, 208, 239
Joplin, Scott, 19
Jordan, Clifford, 123
Jordan, Duke, 64

Kamuca, Richie, 110
Katche, Manu, 214
Katz, Mickey, 264
Keezer, Geoff, 238, 252
Kelly, Wynton, 240
Keltner, Jim, 277
Kenton, Stan, 37, 94, 102, 109, 124, 214
Keppard, Freddie, 4
Kessel, Barney, 64
Kessler, Kent, 272, 280
King, B.B., 254
Kirk, Andy, 30
Kirk, Rahsaan Roland, 171–72, 229
Kirkland, Kenny, 244–45
Klezmatics, 283

Knepper, Jimmy, 105
Konitz, Lee, 73, 83, 102, 109, 125, 148
Krakauer, David, 283
Krall, Diana, 282
Krupa, Gene, 18, 34, 38, 56, 79
Kuhn, Steve, 255

Lacy, Ku-Umba Frank, 248
Lacy, Steve, 154, 162, 274
LaFaro, Scott, 98, 151
Lake, Oliver, 157, 164
Lambert, Hendricks & Ross, 57n, 80, 103, 113
Land, Harold, 91
Lang, Eddie, 11, 16
Lateef, Yusef, 88, 204, 218
Laws, Hubert, 205
Lê, Nguyên, 228
Lee, Rodney, 263
Levey, Stan, 110
Levy, Howard, 224
Lewis, George, 141, 143, 160
Lewis, John, 64, 85, 106, 126, 135
Lewis, Mel, 124, 127, 208, 239
Liebman, Dave, 185, 274
Lighthouse All-Stars, 84, 103–4, 114
Lins, Ivan, 251
Liston, Melba, 223, 224
Little, Booker, 92, 132
Lloyd, Charles, 171–73
Lockwood, Didier, 201
Lovano, Joe, 242, 267–70, 278

Lunceford, Jimmie, 25, 29, 30, 46

Lynch, Brian, 235, 238, 252, 274

Lyons, Jimmy, 156

McBee, Cecil, 173

McBride, Christian, 232, 253

McCall, Steve, 145, 153

McCandless, Paul, 195

McCann, Les, 199

McConnell, Shorty, 56

McDuff, Jack, 128

McGhee, Howard, 53, 64, 71

McKenna, Dave, 20

McKinney, William, 23

McKinney's Cotton Pickers, 23

McLaughlin, John, 178, 180, 184–85, 188–89, 192, 210, 218–19

McLean, Jackie, 90, 111, 114, 117–19, 128, 133–34, 231, 235, 239

McNeely, Jim, 255

McPartland, Jimmy, 6, 18

McPherson, Charles, 88

McRae, Carmen, 39, 129, 254

McShann, Jay, 54–55

Machito (see Grillo, Francisco)

Mahavishnu Orchestra, 180, 182, 184, 188–89, 218

Mahogany, Kevin, 235, 243–44, 254

Mandel, Mike, 184

Mangelsdorff, Albert, 158

Manne, Shelly, 102, 104, 109

Marmarosa, Dodo, 64

Marsalis, Branford, 90, 233–35, 237, 244–46, 251, 254

Marsalis, Delfeayo, 233

Marsalis, Ellis, 233, 238

Marsalis, Jason, 233

Marsalis, Wynton, 90, 119, 174, 230n, 231, 233–36, 237–39, 241–47, 249–52, 254–55, 257–58, 274

Marsh, Warne, 73–74, 125

Masada, 282, 283

Maupin, Bennie, 185

Mays, Lyle, 189, 219

Medeski, Martin & Wood, 259, 278

Mehldau, Brad, 254

Melford, Myra, 259, 268–69

Mendes, Sergio, 206

Metheny, Pat, 97, 161, 182, 189–90, 197, 199, 208n, 210, 219, 251, 255, 263, 269, 279

Miley, Bubber, 12

Miller, Glenn, 31, 40–41, 44, 239

Miller, Mulgrew, 235, 238, 247–48, 278

Mingus, Charles, xiii, 46, 75, 104–6, 115, 125–26, 133, 136, 153, 167, 239, 244, 248

Mingus Big Band, 239

Mintzer, Bobby, 263
Mitchell, Blue, 128
Mitchell, Roscoe, 143, 159
Mobley, Hank, 91, 107,
    114–15, 119, 121, 123
Modern Jazz Quartet, 76, 106,
    126, 170
Moncur, Grachan, 133
Monk, Thelonious, 36, 51,
    53–55, 57–58, 62, 64, 69–71,
    74, 76–78, 96, 104, 111,
    120–21, 123, 127, 129, 133,
    135, 154, 160, 162, 170, 212,
    224, 241, 243, 248, 250, 278
Montgomery, Wes, 106–7, 126
Moody, James, 66, 77, 79, 80,
    236
Moore, Glen, 195, 224
Moore, Oscar, 33
Moreira, Airto, 184, 211, 223,
    225
Morell, Marty, 98, 122
Morgan, Lee, 90, 91, 93, 107,
    116, 119, 124, 126, 173, 241,
    267
Morris, Joe, 280
Morton, Jelly Roll, 1–3, 7,
    15–16, 19–20, 203
Moten, Bennie, 24–25, 30
Motian, Paul, 275, 277
Mouzon, Alphonse, 175, 184
Moye, Famoudou Don, 143,
    159
Mulligan, Gerry, 56, 83, 85, 89,
    95, 108–9, 120, 125–27, 139,
    206, 228

Murphy, Mark, 115, 130, 266
Murray, David, 157, 164, 227
Murray, Sunny, 147

Naftule's Dream, 283
Narell, Andy, 226
Nascimento, Milton, 210–11,
    222–23, 244
Navarro, Fats, 71, 78, 253
Nelson, Oliver, 101, 115, 133
Nelson, Steve, 248
New Jungle Orchestra,
    212–13, 226
Newman, Joe, 33
Newton, James, 227
Nock, Mike, 178
Noone, Jimmy, 4, 20
NRG Ensemble, 281

O'Day, Anita, 79, 94, 102
O'Farrill, Chico, 204, 212
Oliver, Joe "King," 1n, 5–6, 10,
    15–16, 139
Oliver, Sy, 29
Oregon, 195, 199–200, 202
Ory, Kid, 4, 8, 10, 15

Page, Hot Lips, 25
Page, Walter, 25, 32
Palmer, Jeff, 280
Palmieri, Eddie, 219–20, 252
Parker, Charlie, xiii, 32, 43,
    53–67, 71–75, 77–82, 84–86,

90, 110, 117, 121, 131–33,
137, 141, 149, 160, 164, 168,
203–4, 231, 234, 237, 251
Parker, Evan, 158, 160
Parker, Leon, 279
Parker, William, 259, 280
Pascoal, Hermeto, 211, 220–21
Pass, Joe, 127
Pastorius, Jaco, 191–92, 200
Payne, Cecil, 66
Payton, Nicholas, 248–49,
253
Peacock, Annette, 160
Peacock, Gary, 160, 243
Pedersen, Niels-Henning
Ørsted, 127
Pepper, Art, 83, 85–86, 102,
109–10, 124, 127
Perez, Danilo, 269, 279
Peterson, Hannibal Marvin,
186
Peterson, Oscar, 65, 76, 87–88,
110–11, 127–28
Peterson, Ralph, 275
Petrucianni, Michel, 268
Pettiford, Oscar, 58, 70
Phillips, Barre, 160
Phillips, Flip, 204
Piazzolla, Astor, 228
Pierce, Billy, 235, 237
Pine, Courtney, 231, 249–50,
259, 276
Ponty, Jean-Luc, 189, 201
Porter, Cole, 130, 135
Potter, Chris, 248, 250
Potts, Steve, 154

Powell, Bud, 62–63, 68, 70–72,
75, 78, 91, 111, 131, 141, 175,
241, 253
Powell, Richie, 91
Pozo, Chano, 61
Previte, Bobby, 276
Priester, Julian, 242
Puente, Tito, 221, 228
Pullen, Don, 105, 159, 167
Purim, Flora, 184, 211, 225

Raney, Jimmy, 75
Redman, Dewey, 171, 199,
224, 254–55, 277
Redman, Don, 20, 22–25,
29–30, 52, 55
Redman, Joshua, 254–55, 266,
278
Reinhardt, Django, 41, 49, 65,
107
Return to Forever, 180,
183–84, 197–98, 211, 226
Rhyne, Melvin, 126
Rich, Buddy, 34, 42, 44
Richards, Johnny, 102
Richmond, Dannie, 105,
167
Rivera, Mario, 221
Roach, Max, 46, 52–53, 57, 64,
70, 75, 91–92, 104, 111, 119,
137n, 140
Roberts, Hank, 267
Roberts, Luckey, 19
Roberts, Marcus, 233, 246–47,
250–51

Rodgers, Richard, 129, 130
Roditi, Claudio, 222
Rodney, Red, 250
Rogers, Shorty, 54, 104, 124
Rollins, Sonny, xiv, 39, 67,
    69–71, 82–83, 87, 111–13,
    119, 121, 128, 162, 235,
    244–45, 274
Roney, Wallace, 231, 235, 251,
    253, 261
Ross, Brandon, 283
Rouse, Charlie, 70, 77
ROVA Saxophone Quartet,
    163
Royal, Ernie, 223
Rubin, Vanessa, 254
Rudd, Roswell, 162
Rugolo, Pete, 102
Ruiz, Hilton, 229
Rumsey, Howard, 103–4
Rushing, Jimmy, 32
Russell, George, 136
Russell, Hal, 165, 281
Russell, Luis, 9
Russell, Pee Wee, 18
Rypdal, Terje, 181, 195–96,
    266

Samuels, Dave, 226
Sanborn, David, 197
Sanchez, David, 269, 279
Sanchez, Poncho, 228–29
Sanders, Pharoah, 161–62,
    173, 224
Sandoval, Arturo, 217, 226

Santamaria, Mongo, 204–5,
    228
Sauter, Eddie, 123
Schuller, Gunther, 135, 136,
    278
Scofield, John, 182, 236, 250,
    267, 269–70, 277, 279
Seifert, Zbigniew, 200
Shankar, Lakshminarayana,
    218
Shaw, Artie, 30, 31, 41–42, 45,
    47
Shaw, Woody, 123, 173–74
Shearing, George, 75, 78
Sheldon, Jack, 109
Shepp, Archie, 154–55, 162
Shipp, Matthew, 280
Shorter, Wayne, xi, 90–91,
    116–17, 126, 168, 174,
    178–80, 186, 190–92, 210,
    222–23, 244, 268, 274, 276
Silver, Horace, 82, 90, 103–4,
    109, 113, 116, 173, 240, 263,
    267, 275
Sims, Zoot, 20, 109, 124, 127
Sinatra, Frank, 31, 33–34, 39,
    48, 78–79
Singleton, Zutty, 10
Slagle, Steve, 248
Smith, Jimmy, 82, 113–14, 126,
    128
Smith, Leo, 143, 144
Smith, Lonnie, 128–29, 280
Smith, Marvin "Smitty," 238,
    242
Smith, Mike, 252

Smith, Willie "the Lion," 14, 19

South, Eddie, 49

Spanier, Muggsy, 18

Spaulding, James, 101

Speed, Chris, 262

Stenson, Bobo, 181

Stewart, Bill, 270

Stewart, Rex, 48, 49

Stitt, Sonny, 66, 72–73, 79, 124

Strayhorn, Billy, 35, 46, 206, 267, 278

Sun Ra, 134–35, 155–56, 162–63, 258

Swallow, Steve, 182, 191

Swell, Steve, 278

Tabackin, Lew, 227

Tatum, Art, 13, 30–31, 42, 49, 59, 99, 110, 170

Taylor, Art, 111

Taylor, Billy, 55

Taylor, Cecil, 131, 135, 141–42, 154, 156–57, 160, 163, 268

Teagarden, Jack, 9–10

Terry, Clark, 127

Teschemacher, Frank, 6

Thigpen, Ed, 127

Thomas, Leon, 173

Thornhill, Claude, 56

Thornton, Argonne, 56

Threadgill, Henry, 145, 271, 281

Timmons, Bobby, 88, 89, 91, 103, 237, 240

Tiso, Wagner, 223

Tjader, Cal, 205, 228

Towner, Ralph, 195, 199–200

Tristano, Lennie, 62–63, 73–74, 84, 125, 148, 262

Trumbauer, Frankie, 7, 11, 18, 92

Turrentine, Stanley, 92

Tyner, McCoy, 49, 116, 151–52, 174–75, 225, 247, 263, 275

United Nation Orchestra, 65, 213, 226

Urbaniak, Michal, 200

Valdes, Chucho, 217

Vandermark, Ken, 165, 272, 280–81

Van Gelder, Rudy, 116

Van't Hof, Jasper, 162

Vasconcelos, Nana, 225

Vaughan, Sarah, 39, 65, 74, 79, 129–30

Venuti, Joe, 16, 20

Vinnegar, Leroy, 110

Vitous, Miroslav, 190

Walcott, Colin, 195, 199, 225

Wall, Dan, 280

Waller, Fats, 16–17, 19–20, 30, 33, 42–43, 50, 130

Ware, David S., 280

Ware, Wilbur, 112
Warfield, Tim, 249, 254
Washington, Dinah, 130
Washington, Grover, Jr., 200
Watson, Bobby, 235, 237
Watters, Lu, 62
Watts, Jeff "Tain," 244
Weather Report, xiii–xiv,
    179–80, 184, 189–91, 200,
    202, 223
Webb, Chick, 37
Weber, Carl Maria von, 26n
Weber, Eberhard, 181, 200
Webster, Ben, 25, 35, 38, 48, 50,
    60, 127, 152
Weiskopf, Walt, 281
Wells, Dickie, 32
Wendholt, Scott, 253
Wess, Frank, 33, 69
Weston, Randy, 210, 223–24,
    229
Wheeler, Kenny, 181, 242
White, Lenny, 184
Whiteman, Paul, 16, 18
Wilkerson, Edward, 143, 165,
    271, 281
Williams, Cootie, 25, 56
Williams, James, 235, 237, 242,
    255
Williams, Jessica, 255

Williams, Joe, 45
Williams, Mars, 272, 281
Williams, Mary Lou, 60
Williams, Todd, 254
Williams, Tony, xi, 133, 168,
    170, 178, 180, 192, 246
Willis, Randall, 262
Wilson, Cassandra, 235, 264,
    271, 281, 283
Wilson, Dooley, 210
Wilson, Teddy, 28, 30, 38, 39
Wong, Francis, 218, 228
Woods, Phil, 86, 97, 117–18,
    235, 252, 273
World Saxophone Quartet
    (WSQ), 157–58, 163–64

Yamashita, Yosuke, 229
Young, Larry, 185, 192
Young, Lester, 7, 32, 38–39,
    43–44, 47, 50–51, 55–56, 59,
    65, 67, 75, 78–79, 84, 87, 92,
    105

Zappa, Frank, 178, 201, 275
Zawinul, Joe, 117, 178–80, 185,
    190–91
Zorn, John, 259–60, 282, 283